INTEGRATED PRODUCTION
CONTROL SYSTEMS

INTEGRATED PRODUCTION CONTROL SYSTEMS
Management, Analysis, Design

David D. Bedworth
James E. Bailey
Arizona State University

1807 1982

JOHN WILEY & SONS, INC.
New York   Chichester   Brisbane   Toronto   Singapore

for **GINNY** and **PETRA**,
and for our children:
ALEX, MARGARET, MICHAEL, and **HEIDI**

*The happiest moments of my life have been
the few I have passed at home in the bosom of my family*
Thomas Jefferson

Library of Congress Cataloging in Publication Data:

Bedworth, David D.
    Integrated production control systems.

    Includes bibliographical references and index.
    1. Production control—Data processing.
I. Bailey, James Edward, 1942–   . II. Title.
TS157.B43   658.5'0028'54   81-10506
ISBN 0-471-06223-5   AACR2

Printed in the United States of America
10 9 8 7 6 5 4 3

PREFACE

The manufacturing field presently is undergoing changes that would have been quite difficult to predict a decade ago. The need to reduce waste and increase efficiency in production is reported as one of the United States' most pressing problems. Widespread productivity improvement through mechanization and automation, utilizing microprocessors, numerical-control machining centers, robotics, real-time control, and other innovations, is creating a need for a more sophisticated approach to production control. Real-time computer systems utilizing integrated database concepts permit more timely and informed decisions relating to the production process. Quantitative approaches deemed esoteric even now by many practitioners will become a necessity if computer-aided manufacturing systems are to perform up to their potential. This book was written with these realities in mind. *Integrated Production Control Systems* provides a computer-oriented quantitative basis for the analysis and improvement of productivity in modern manufacturing. The topics covered include the functions of information processing and flow, production planning, inventory analysis, and scheduling.

The text is oriented toward the junior or senior levels in quantitative business or industrial-engineering programs. The material also has been utilized satisfactorily as preparatory material for students entering Masters' programs from disciplines other than business or industrial engineering. Prerequisite mathematical knowledge is limited for the most part to introductory probability and statistics, in addition to college algebra. Classical optimization using linear programming and the calculus is employed at a beginning level in a few sections, and with the introduction of minimal supplementary material, this book can be used without knowledge of operations research or calculus. Certain business programs might prefer the material to have a production operations course as a prerequisite.

The book is designed to fall into three major categories: production planning, inventory analysis, and scheduling. All 10 chapters can be covered in their entirety in a one-semester or two-quarter course, assuming the minimal prerequisites are satisfied. The planning material covers network planning and analysis, forecasting, and aggregate planning. Inventory analysis builds on the traditional economic-order or production quantity models to lead into the systems-oriented materials requirement planning approach. Scheduling is covered in far greater depth than in most production control texts. We feel that this is an area that has to be utilized more fully if the implementation of computer-aided manufacturing is to be truly effective. It is possible to cover Chapter 8, "Scheduling with Resource Constraints," immediately after Chapter 3, "Project Planning," with no loss of continuity. Even though there is a logical tie-in between Chapters 3 and 8, covering the material in this fashion will break the planning and scheduling separation.

Four computer programs are presented and discussed in the text: PRE-DICTS is used for growth and cyclic forecasting; BEDSEAS performs a seasonal and growth forecast through seasonal index development; RESALL assigns multiple scarce resources to a project but can also be used to determine critical paths in project analysis; BABALB gives optimum multiple-product-line balancing solutions. ASCII FORTRAN 77 listings, developed on an UNIVAC 1110 computer, are given in Appendices B through E. A FORTRAN IV listing, developed on an IBM-compatible computer, can be obtained from the authors through Arizona State University, as can information regarding obtaining magnetic tape versions of the programs. In addition, the use of computerized optimization and statistical modeling routines are introduced.

Acknowledgement has to be made to John Wiley & Sons for permission to utilize some material from *Industrial Systems* (1973), by David Bedworth. Such material is utilized in Chapters 3, 4, 6 and 8.

It is not possible to acknowledge appreciation to all who have contributed to this book. Several individuals have tested major components of the material and their collective suggestions and criticisms have been invaluable. In this regard, we should like to thank Vinod Sahney, Jay Miller, John Estes, John Field, and Glen Dunlap. The faculty of Industrial Engineering provided a group atmosphere conducive to developing a text of this nature, and we want to attest that it is a pleasure to have all of them as colleagues. Special thanks have to go to Elinor Lindenberger, our manuscript typist. Even though personal tragedy struck during the manuscript development, Elinor demonstrated a personal strength and character that lifted the authors through some of the discouraging moments that occur in an activity such as text writing. To Elinor, we would like to say

"Grace was in all her steps,
heaven in her eye, In every gesture dignity and love"
From **Paradise Lost** by Milton

David D. Bedworth and James E. Bailey
Tempe, Arizona

CONTENTS

INTEGRATED PRODUCTION CONTROL SYSTEMS

ONE: THE ROLE OF PRODUCTION CONTROL

The first step, my son, which one makes in the world, is the one on which depends the rest of our days.

Voltaire

Formalized production control, in its earliest applications, was directed primarily at the production of manufactured goods. The purpose for production control was, and still is, to effectively utilize limited resources in the production of goods so as to satisfy customer demands and create a profit for investors. Resources include the production facilities, labor, and materials. Constraints, on the other hand, include the availability of resources, delivery times for the products, and the policies of management.

Effectively utilizing constrained resources is the task of the production control activity in a manufacturing organization. It has become patently clear, primarily since World War II, that production control functions of planning, forecasting, scheduling, and inventory control concepts can also be applied to organizations other than manufacturing. Thus, an approach used satisfactorily in scheduling appliances through an assembly line might be equally valid in sequencing patients through a hospital X-ray facility. Inventory control procedures developed for manufacturing might be equally beneficial to a bank or department store. Prediction of sales to allow better planning of a manufacturing facility over future time periods might be used in determining the number of hospital beds to authorize in the expansion of health services. In this book, the illustrations deal with the manufacturing process, but the reader should be aware that there is a much broader spectrum for production control application.

The Gantt or bar chart, as it is commonly known, was developed in World War I by Henri L. Gantt as a simple approach to scheduling. The Gantt chart, as will be seen in Chapter 3, provides a simple way to study and communicate complex relationships; it graphically illustrates when related tasks can be started so that precedent constraints are maintained and limited resources are well utilized. The ability to simplify a complex problem is the ultimate virtue of good management science. Those who would add complexity in the process of solving real-world problems are destined for frustration. Those who would follow Gantt and present intuitively obvious solutions will see their efforts employed and their careers rewarded. It is hoped that the reader will concentrate on developing an intuitive understanding while learning to present obvious solutions.

In any organization, the utility of production control is to increase productivity. A proper definition of productivity is the ratio of the value of goods and services produced divided by the value of resources used in production. If machines or people are idle because there is no work or if parts remain in inventory because a machine is not available, then resources are being wasted. The role of production control is to reduce this waste by intelligently coordinating the availability of people, equipment, and materials. In endless lists of cases, organizations have lost vast sums of money and even failed because they had too much inventory or too much capacity. Productivity improvements can be made through improved designs or more efficient production methods. Productivity can and should also be improved in any manufacturing or service facility through intelligent production control.

1.1 PRODUCTION CONTROL AS AN ORGANIZATIONAL ACTIVITY

In the final analysis, the task of the production control activity is to interpret the conflicting objectives of production, sales, and finance, then to reconcile them into coherent production plans and inventory policies. The role of the shop-floor people is to meet the schedule. Obviously, they would like a schedule that is sufficiently loose so that it can be met even when equipment breaks down, people stay home, and scrap parts are discovered. The role of sales is to maximize shipments and minimize delivery delays. Obviously, sales people would like large inventories, especially of finished goods. The role of finance is to minimize the amount of capital tied up in facilities, people, and inventory. Obviously, those in finance would like a lean shop and low inventory levels. The role of the total organization is to find some balance among the conflicting needs of the organization's components.

The question then becomes, Where should the production control activity fit in the organization? Should it report to the production executive, the sales executive, or the comptroller? There are probably as many answers to this question as there are manufacturing or service organizations. This is as it should be. Since production control performs many functions, it ought to be housed organizationally where these functions can best be performed. Perhaps a company should have centralized production control, so that a consistent balance of the conflicting needs can be made. This centralized department would be responsible for creating demand forecasts and for seasonal planning of production levels. It might also monitor and control sales, shipping levels, and raw material purchases, and be responsible for setting employment and overtime levels. The issuing of specific production and purchase orders might be left to individual units, which can better make the short-term adjustments in the light of dynamically changing conditions. Further, the detailed shop schedules indicating what to run next and using what equipment are delegated to the lowest level of management having the closest tie to the hourly situation. The best advice relative to organizational location is to put the various production control activities reasonably close to the source of information needed to make good decisions while spreading them out so that no single function (i.e., production, sales, or finance) seriously biases the decisions.

In analyzing a production control activity, certain questions should be asked. The best production control structure is the one that can satisfactorily answer these following questions.

1. Are all the activities of planning, scheduling, and inventory management identified and housed somewhere?

2. Do the people responsible for making the necessary decisions clearly understand their roles, the objectives of their decisions, the information available to them, and the accepted procedure for making decisions?

3. Do the people responsible for making the decisions have an accurate and timely information system?

4. Is there a system to identify when nonroutine situations occur and fast, unusual decisions are needed?

5. Are all the interfacing organizational activities content with the production control function and are they unlikely to confuse or sabotage its decisions?

If all of these questions can be resolved satisfactorily, the production control function is well organized. The concern then becomes whether the people involved have the best available decision-making techniques. The development of these techniques is the topic of this text.

1.2 PRODUCTION CONTROL AS A SYSTEM

The relationship of production control to the entire manufacturing organization is presented in Chapter 2, primarily as a means for showing the necessary flow of information both into and out of the production control system. Just as production control interrelates with functions outside itself, so do the components within production control have a complex flow of interactions. A simplistic view of these interactions might be as diagrammed in Figure 1.1. It should be apparent that decisions in one component—say, scheduling—have a distinct effect on other components. For example, one way to ensure that production is never slowed by lack of materials is to inventory an excess of

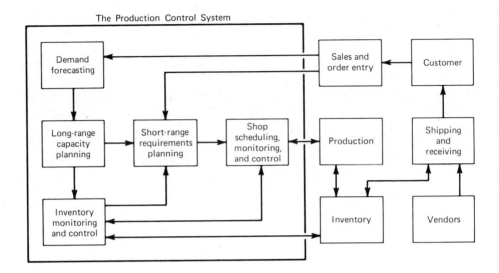

FIGURE 1.1　**Representative production control operating system.**

those materials. This might simplify the scheduling activity, but it does so at the expense of higher inventory expenses. For another example, one can ensure that production never misses a due date by increasing the delivery times and thus pushing customer demands off into the future. This might make the scheduling problem easier, but it does so at the expense of customer satisfaction. The production control activity is a system, and it must be viewed in its totality. It may not always be wise to require that production resources never be idle or that inventory costs be minimized or that due dates all be met. The objective of the production control system should be the objective of the total organization. Decisions that complement sales, production, and inventory are preferable to those that optimize only one function.

To illustrate the production control system, the reader should study Figure 1.1. The system is shown as a cyclic activity starting with the customer and moving counterclockwise through the figure. At this point we are concerned only with the activities located inside the larger box, titled "The Production Control System." A series of events represented in this box is introduced here and covered in detail in subsequent chapters of the text.

Demand forecasting is the starting point for the production control activity. For each class of product or service the future must be predicted. It is not unusual to have a lead time of many months between the time an order is placed to purchase raw materials and the time those materials are transformed and shipped out as finished goods, in which case the forecast must be for months into the future. This is called the forecasting horizon. In some cases, it is easy to predict sales for one to two years into the future. The delivery time between firm-order entries and deliveries may be a large fraction of the needed forecasting horizon. In other cases, accuracy beyond actual order entries may be very difficult. Without accurate forecasts it is impossible to accomplish the long-range capacity planning activity.

Capacity planning is the second step in the production control chain of events. The need is to know how many people to employ, how much overtime to schedule, and how much inventory to hold so that actual demand is economically met. If insufficient capacity or inventory is available, demand cannot be met and customers may be lost. If too much capacity and inventory exist, the company will be in a serious cash-flow bind. If the wrong products are in the pipeline, the company will be hurt at both ends, having unsatisfied customers and unsalable products. Without a reasonably accurate forecast of future demand, long-range capacity planning is not possible.

One concern of capacity planning is the amount of inventory to be held. An often-used plan in the face of cyclic demand is to build more than is needed during slow periods, thereby increasing inventory. Then, when demand is high, it can be met, in part from inventoried items. Therefore, inventory levels will vary from period to period. With these variations in inventory, the quantities made on each production order will also vary. The control of inventory is the act of comparing what is actually on hand with the desired quantity. Inventory control thus is affected by the decision made in capacity planning.

A second activity that feeds off of the capacity planning output is short-range requirements planning. This activity also responds to the decisions of inventory control. In the near term, the need for production from rough machining to final assembly must be determined. In effect, the activity is one of looking at near-term production capacity and goals, existing inventory levels, and discrepancies between those levels and desired inventory, then creating a master schedule of what to do in each production department during the next week or month. To some extent, inaccuracies in the forecasted demand and changes in the capacity plan can be overcome at this stage. Items that need faster or greater production can be "red-tagged" as urgent. Those items whose production levels can be reduced are easily handled with relatively minor impact on inventories. The amount of overtime and/or undercapacity can be adjusted. Thus there is a degree of flexibility within the broader limits of the capacity plan. The resulting output is the short-range requirements plan, or master schedule.

The master schedule is made without reference to the dynamic changes in the shop situation. If people fail to arrive for work or if a machine breaks down, the schedule must be changed. If scrap parts are found or tooling is temporarily unavailable, the schedule must be adjusted. The master schedule, then, identifies the weekly production goals for each department but does not determine how those goals are to be met. This is the role of the shop scheduling activity. At the beginning of each shift, the shop foreman must review where he is relative to the master schedule and what resources are available to him. He must then decide what to do during the shift, the sequence in which shop orders should be accomplished, and the resources to devote to those tasks. These production control decisions are then passed on to the production employee.

Thus, the production control activity is a chain of interrelated events that functions as a system. The decisions are made for different horizons in time and with different degrees of accuracy. Yet they must all occur if the ultimate objective is to be met: that is, to effectively utilize limited resources in the production of goods so as to satisfy customer demands and create a profit for investors.

1.3 SYSTEMS PLANNING AND ANALYSIS

Any complex system with interacting components, such as that described in Figure 1.1, requires a systematic approach for planning and analysis if the objective is to benefit the *overall* organization in some manner, and not just to benefit a select few of the interacting components.

One approach to the design of a production control system is to use the traditional systems approach (also referred to as the operations research approach). Steps involved in this approach include

1. Determining the objectives of the system.
2. Structuring the system (defining) and setting definable system boundaries.
3. Determining the significant components that make up the system.
4. Performing a detailed study on the components *in light of* the overall system.
5. Synthesizing the analyzed components into the system.
6. Testing the system according to some performance criterion.
7. Improving the performance by cycling through steps 2 through 6 as needed.

This approach to problems with interacting components is used in this text in many places. As would be true with experienced problem-solvers, the steps will not consciously be pointed out in the solution approaches, but the reader should readily see the approach in such areas as

1. Minimizing overall project costs in a network-oriented project (Chapter 3).
2. Determining that forecast model for which the model parameters minimize overall forecast errors (Chapter 4).
3. Balancing the costs of inventory, overtime, and stock-outs while satisfying fluctuating demand forecasts (Chapter 5).
4. Evaluating inventory policies that minimize overall costs inherent in ordering and holding inventory (Chapters 6, 7).
5. Determining an allocation of tasks to production stations that allows maximization of production flow (Chapter 8).

6. Scheduling sets of tasks and people so as to reduce idle time, in-process inventory, and tardy completions (Chapters 9, 10).

One philosophical comment should be made concerning item 7 in the steps that comprise the systems approach (see p. 6). The act of improving a systems performance may be far more expensive than the return obtained from actually making the improvement. As an example, consider the case of a company that engages a prominent consulting firm to improve the company's forecast procedures. If $250,000 is required to perform that study but the potential return from improved forecasts is $10,000 a year, should the improvement analysis be made? In many cases the answer is no. A thorough analysis of the potential benefits to accrue from an improvement effort should be made before embarking on the improvement project. As an example of the systems approach, a simple case example using the concepts presented in Figure 1.1, along with some hypothetical data and assumptions, is presented in Section 1.4.

1.4 SIMPLE CASE EXAMPLE—A SIMULATION†

Figure 1.1 introduced a simplistic feedback diagram as representative of how components in a production-control operating system might interact. A slightly modified system was simulated on a digital computer with hypothetical data and hypothetical internal policies in order to demonstrate the problems inherent in such a system when improvement is contemplated. This example also allows a few points to be made concerning the approach taken to studying the production control operating system with an eye to making improvements.

The operating system was simulated as shown in Figure 1.2.‡ Internal rules were as follows (note that these rules are for illustrative purposes only and are not to be interpreted as being in any way realistic).

1. The forecast is made by averaging N contiguous data points, with the latest data point occurring one time-period prior to the period for which prediction is being made. In other words, a moving average is the forecast technique and the forecast lead-time is one period. Values for N were 4, 6, and 8 in the simulation.

2. The Schedule Policy was to multiply the forecast by an error factor. Schedule error factors used were 0.8, 1.0, and 1.2. A factor of 1.0 assumed the forecast

---

† Certain concepts introduced in this section are amplified in later chapters. The purpose is not to cover fully forecasting, scheduling and inventory analysis, but rather to demonstrate their interaction.

‡ "Inventory" is assumed to be final product inventory in this example.

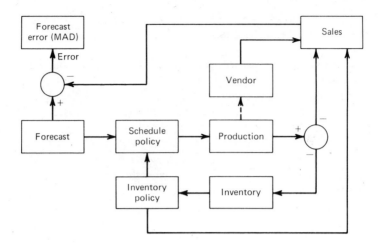

FIGURE 1.2   Simulated production control system.

to be exact, whereas the other two factors assumed either optimistic or pessimistic errors in the forecasts.

3. Inventory was used to satisfy demand any time inventory level was higher than a specified safety stock. Values used for safety stock were 0, 5, or 10 units. If production plus inventory did not meet sales requirements in any period, an outside vendor subcontracted the needed items. If sales were less than production in any period, then excess inventory accumulated.

Since there are three alternatives each for all three components (forecast, schedule policies, and inventory policies), there are 27 combinations of the parameters, any one of which might be optimum for a given set of data. Each combination was evaluated over 50 periods of forecast data to determine the

1. Parameter combination that optimized total system cost.
2. Parameter combination that optimized the production schedule policy cost.
3. Parameter combination that optimized the inventory policy cost.
4. Optimum forecast parameter that minimized total forecast errors.

Additional information used in the analysis:

1. Cost of holding an item of inventory in a time period or fraction of a period is $2 per item.
2. Cost of a vendor supplied item is $15 per item.
3. Cost of producing an item through production is $10 per item.

The results of running the simulation with the data given in Table 1.1,

TABLE 1.1 Data Sets for Case Example: set *A* Is Relatively Constant and set *B* Is set *A* with the Time Period Added to Form Growth

Time Period	Forecasted Demand Data Set A	Forecasted Demand Data Set B
1	10	11
2	12	14
3	13	16
4	7	11
5	9	14
6	15	21
7	9	16
8	5	13
9	11	20
10	13	23
11	16	27
12	12	24
13	9	22
14	12	26
15	7	22
16	9	25
17	9	26
18	15	33
19	5	23
20	8	28
21	3	24
22	10	32
23	12	35
24	13	37
25	15	40
26	12	38
27	8	35
28	6	34
29	9	38
30	9	39
31	10	41
32	12	44

Table 1.1. continued

Time Period	Forecasted Demand Data Set A	Forecasted Demand Data Set B
33	14	47
34	8	42
35	6	41
36	10	46
37	9	46
38	11	49
39	11	50
40	14	54
41	13	54
42	12	54
43	8	51
44	5	49
45	15	60
46	12	58
47	11	58
48	7	55
49	9	58
50	10	60

data set *A*, are shown in Table 1.2. The dollar values represent accumulated costs over the 50 time periods. Production schedule costs were assumed to be the sum of vendor and production costs. Inventory costs included charges in any period in which an item was stored in inventory as well as any period in which the item was used to supply a sales need.

Forecast MAD error is the *m*ean *a*bsolute *d*eviation of the forecast errors over prediction periods.

$$\text{MAD} = \sum_{i=1}^{M} \frac{|X_i - \hat{X}_{i-1}|}{M}$$

where

X_i is the true data value at period i

$\hat{X}_{i-1}$ is the forecast from the previous period, and

$$\hat{X}_{i-1} = \sum_{t=i-N}^{i-1} \frac{X_t}{N}$$

TABLE 1.2   Results from Running Production Control Model with Constant Data from Table 1.1, Data Set A

Schedule Factors Forecast (N)		0.8			1.0			1.2		
		4	6	8	4	6	8	4	6	8
Inventory Safety Stock	0									
	Production cost	$5375	$5020	$4910	$5185	$4900	$4700	$5020	$4820	$4565
	Inventory cost	$96	$92	$60	$260	$228	$180	$450	$410	$354
	Total cost	$5471	$5112	$4970	$5445	$5128	$4880	$5470	$5230	$4919
	Forecast MAD error	3.0%	2.8%	2.5%	3.0%	2.8%	2.5%	3.0%	2.8%	2.5%
	5									
	Production cost	$5375	$5020	$4910	$5185	$4900	$4700	$5020	$4820	$4565
	Inventory cost	$556	$532	$480	$720	$668	$600	$910	$850	$674
	Total cost	$5931	$5552	$5390	$5905	$5568	$5300	$5930	$5670	$5339
	Forecast MAD error	3.0%	2.8%	2.5%	3.0%	2.8%	2.5%	3.0%	2.8%	2.5%
	10									
	Production cost	$5375	$5020	$4910	$5185	$4900	$4700	$5020	$4820	$4565
	Inventory cost	$1016	$972	$910	$1180	$1108	$1020	$1370	$1290	$1194
	Total cost	$6391	$5992	$5810	$6365	$6008	$5720	$6390	$6110	$5759
	Forecast MAD error	3.0%	2.8%	2.5%	3.0%	2.8%	2.5%	3.0%	2.8%	2.5%

The results from Table 1.2 show the following:

1. The minimum *total cost* parameter combination results in a cost of $4880 with the schedule factor being 1.0, a safety stock of 0, and forecast N equal to 8. As Chapter 4 demonstrates, an average is a feasible way to forecast relatively constant data; therefore, a schedule factor of 1.0 makes sense. Chapter 4 will also show that the higher N value makes sense in this case.

2. Minimum production costs are $4565 and occur for a schedule factor of 1.2. This of course makes sense, as the higher production leads to minimum vendor costs that were 50% higher than production. Since the schedule factor is 1.2 and not 1.0, we see that minimizing production costs *does not* minimize overall costs.

3. Minimum inventory costs are $60 and occur for a schedule factor of 0.8. This also makes sense, as lower production minimizes inventory but of course increases vendor costs. Minimizing inventory costs *does not* minimize overall system costs.

4. Optimum forecasts (minimum MAD) occur for an N value of 8.

The data was next run with the growth data of Table 1.1, data set *B*. The results of this simulation are shown in Table 1.3. It should be mentioned that averaging is an incorrect way to handle ramp type data forecasting. The minimum total costs were $17,531. The minimum production costs occurred for the same set of optimizing parameters. Minimum inventory costs do not occur with the same set of parameters. Also, the optimum forecast parameters do not match those for total costs.

Conclusions should be self-evident.

Minimization of system components does not guarantee system optimization and usually will not result in system optimization.

Therefore, the usual approach of suboptimization through component optimization may not be the way to go with production control operating systems.

The text objective, then, is to approach analysis of the production control function in light of the overall system. In some cases, suboptimization is the only way to handle improvements. In many other cases, a good solution for the individual systems will have to be acceptable, so that the overall system objective is satisfied. Finally, the scheduling, inventory, and forecast policies in the case study were obviously oversimplified. A second objective for the text, tied to the first, is to develop approaches to finding realistic policies within the production control operating system that will work to the benefit of the overall system.

TABLE 1.3 Results from Running Production Control Model with Linear Data from Table 1.1, Data Set A

Inventory Safety Stock		Schedule Factors	0.8			1.0			1.2		
		Forecast (N)	4	6	8	4	6	8	4	6	8
0	Production costs		$19,515	$19,285	$19,125	$18,235	$17,930	$17,725	$17,710	$17,305	$17,055
	Inventory costs		$0	$0	$0	$96	$44	$12	$836	$662	$476
	Total costs		$19,515	$19,285	$19,125	$18,331	$17,974	$17,737	$18,546	$17,967	$17,531
	Forecast MAD error		3.7%	3.9%	4.7%	3.7%	3.9%	4.7%	3.7%	3.9%	4.7%
5	Production costs		$19,515	$19,285	$19,125	$18,235	$17,930	$17,725	$17,710	$17,305	$17,055
	Inventory costs		$460	$440	$420	$556	$484	$432	$1296	$1102	$896
	Total costs		$19,975	$19,725	$19,545	$18,791	$18,414	$18,157	$19,006	$18,407	$17,951
	Forecast MAD error		3.7%	3.9%	4.7%	3.7%	3.9%	4.7%	3.7%	3.9%	4.7%
10	Production costs		$19,515	$19,285	$19,125	$18,235	$17,930	$17,725	$17,710	$17,305	$17,055
	Inventory costs		$920	$880	$840	$1016	$924	$852	$1756	$1542	$1316
	Total costs		$20,435	$20,165	$19,965	$19,251	$18,854	$18,577	$19,466	$18,847	$18,371
	Forecast MAD error		3.7%	3.9%	4.7%	3.7%	3.9%	4.7%	3.7%	3.9%	4.7%

1.5 TEXT FLOW

The text is grouped into three major categories (though these categories are not formally distinguished one from each other): production control planning, inventory analysis, and scheduling. Chapters 2 through 5 are planning-oriented, Chapters 6 and 7 concern the inventory component of production control, and the last three chapters center on scheduling.

Chapter 2 is concerned with *information flow* in the production control environment. Valid and timely information is needed for effective management decisions regarding inventory, scheduling, personnel, materials, and so on. With recent computer advances, the ability to transmit production-related information on a real-time basis is now a reality. The advent of computer-aided manufacturing makes the timely flow of information not just desirable but mandatory.

Chapter 3 covers a topic considered by many production control purists to not fall in the production control spectrum. *Project planning*, with associated network philosophies, is an ideal tool for the production control specialist. In fact, the approach to project planning is an ideal approach to analyzing any complex interacting component system, such as a production control system.

Chapter 4 is concerned with *forecasting*, on which are based inventory and scheduling decisions. The forecast allows planning for the *future* time periods to be made. In fact, forecasting is probably the major key to effective production control.

Chapter 5 presents *aggregate planning*, which gives the analyst the ability to look at the *overall* production system in order to evaluate how variations in inventory policies and plant capacity might be treated in light of fluctuating demand over an extended period.

Chapter 6 presents *inventory control* from its traditional economic-order-quantity and economic-production-order-quantity approaches. *Materials requirements planning*, covered in *Chapter 7*, goes beyond the traditional approaches to develop inventory policies that consider the fluctuations and time factors of demand. Good forecasts and accurate inventory recordkeeping are mandatory for materials requirement planning. Thus, Chapter 7 ties in with Chapters 2, 4, and 6.

Chapters 8, 9, and 10 cover the field of scheduling from three perspectives: *limited-capacity scheduling, job-shop sequencing*, and *personnel scheduling*. The one facet that is often the most difficult to analyze and implement in production control is scheduling; rarely does the problem fit a known optimization technique. The scheduling material was developed with this difficulty in mind. The reader should develop a philosophy for approaching the problem that will allow an intuitively good solution to emerge. Chapter 8 could well be covered with no loss of continuity immediately following Chapter 3; the scheduling chapters are grouped apart from the early planning chapters for consistency only.

Four computer programs, with appropriate instructions for use, are given in the appendices. These programs will allow complex problems in production control to be solved. Specifically, they are geared to forecasting (growth and seasonal analysis), limited-resource scheduling (including the ability to compute critical paths in a network), and assembly-line balancing. Combining quantitative-solution procedures with computer assistance where beneficial should allow the reader to become comfortable with the production control cycle.

TWO: PRODUCTION CONTROL INFORMATION FLOW

Management is a complex information processing system, the purpose of which is to guide and control the performance of a business firm.

Ansoff

In order for information to be useful, it has to be accurate, valid, and timely. In the design activity, sophisticated computers and graphics equipment can greatly improve products through computer-aided design. If, however, the data supporting the equipment is not accurate, parts may not fit, holes not match, and the design not work. Similarly, in production control systems computerized forecasting, materials planning, and inventory management can greatly reduce costs and increase productivity. Nonetheless, if incorrect data is entered into the supporting database, the computer will give wrong answers and the production control function will fail.

The topics discussed in subsequent chapters, covering techniques for solving production control problems and how these techniques might be employed to enhance a manufacturing or service organization's productivity, have no value unless they can be implemented through the production control information system. This chapter explores how analytical techniques can be interfaced with an *existing* production control information system and what changes, if any, need to be considered. The actual design and analysis of an information system therefore will not be considered. It will be assumed, as just indicated, that an information system already exists. The information system may be a totally manual system, a collection of computerized components, or, at the present state of the art, an integrated database system with distributed input/output devices on the shop floor. Aspects of these information systems will be introduced in this chapter.

2.1 INTRODUCTION

Production management exists primarily to plan and control the efforts of the employees and the flow of materials within the organization. Materials in manufacturing are the parts (raw and in-process), the assemblies, and the finished products that are being created. As materials move from one operation to the next, the status of the parts changes and their progress needs to be monitored. Management must ensure that everything runs smoothly and efficiently. If parts are unavailable or if certain work centers become bottlenecks, the associated loss in productivity must be considered a production control problem.

The controlling activity of management is accomplished through the information system that monitors the production activity, assisting in identifying problems as they occur and communicating the corrective decisions to those who will implement them. Figure 2.1 shows in block format a representative manufacturing operation. The blocks in the figure are typical of the functions that occur in all manufacturing operations. Heavy double lines represent the flow of materials through the facility. The single lines suggest the flow of information needed to control the operations. The purpose of

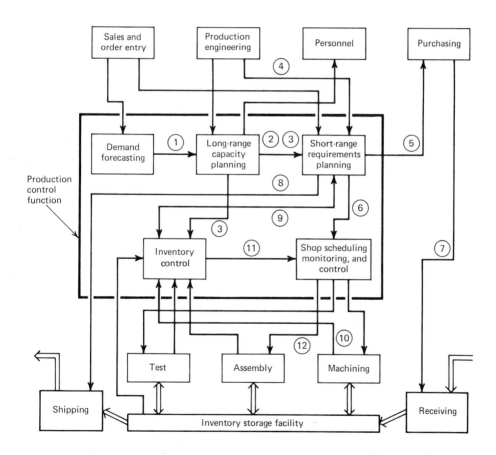

FIGURE 2.1   Flow of materials and information in a typical manufacturing facility.

Section 2.2 is to study the production functions and the production control information flow as a system; further, this section introduces simple forms and reports that make up the information flow in production control. These forms and reports are not intended to be implementable in any production control environment; rather, the intent is to show the type of information needed to allow effective production control decisions to be made. In Section 2.3, the concept of a computerized production-control information system is introduced. The function of such a computerized system is no different from that of the manual system. The inputs and outputs are also similar. The difference is that the data is collected and the reports may be returned via terminals spread throughout the plant. Section 2.4 presents a sample of the terminals that might be used. Taken as a whole, the chapter should assist the reader in understanding how production control interfaces with the rest of the organization and how it performs its function through a complex information system.

2.2 MANUAL PRODUCTION-CONTROL INFORMATION SYSTEM

Note in Figure 2.1 that several of the arrows are identified with circles containing numbers. These information flows will be discussed further in the subsequent material. The demand forecasting activities of production control play the role of balancing future demand, as seen by sales, with the capabilities of manufacturing and the concerns of financing. Typically, the company has a planning period of one month and a planning horizon of N months. How large N is, will be determined by the ability to see clearly into the future. For each period, a demand forecast for each product is made. Figure 2.2 is an example of a forecasting form for reporting future needs. Note that the forecast is final only for the next period and becomes increasingly vague as the periods move into the future. Note also that delivery-time estimates are made for each product. Finally, the forecast is signed off by several executives before release. The sales forecast information (Figure 2.2) is represented in Figure 2.1 by the arrow marked ①. From this point on, the goal of the planning processes is to meet the latest published forecast.

The next block of interest in Figure 2.1 is that of long-range capacity planning. Forecasted demand has to be translated into a forecast for production and inventory needs. A major input is of course the forecast report, Figure 2.2. Any changes in facility capabilities are input from production engineering. Other inputs from production engineering include process routings and production time standards. These inputs allow the determination of how much capacity is needed for each forecasted product in every planning area. A planning area is loosely defined as an independent production facility: for example, each assembly line might be considered as a planning area, as might a heat-treating department or a machining department devoted to a single class of products. In many facilities, the entire manufacturing plant forms a single planning area.

12-Month Sales Forecasts

Forecast Date _DEC. 4_   Product Group Name _MOD 53 Engines_   Product Group Number _53000_

Authorization Signatures								

Production Control _Hudwig_ , date _Dec 6_ . Marketing _H. Luura_ , date _12/6/80_

Manufacturing _Carl_ , date _6 Dec_ . Finance _L. L. Jones_ , date _12/12/80_

Month	1. Jan			2. Feb			3. Mar		4.	5.	6.	Delivery Estimates (weeks)		
Product Number	First	Latest Revision	Final	First	Latest Revision	Tent. Final	First	Latest Revision	First	First	First	Present	Month 1	Month 2
53400	70	75	78	75	80	80	75	80	80	80	90	4	4	5
53600	90	90	87	90	85	85	90	85	90	100	100	6	6	7
53800	30	30	36	30	35	40	30	40	30	30	30	3	3	2
53300	60	65	72	70	75	75	70	80	80	80	80	4	4	5

FIGURE 2.2   Illustrative forecasting report form.

The long-range planning group must convert the forecast for *products* into a forecast of *labor hours* required in each planning area. There are many ways in which the production plan might be presented. Figure 2.3 shows a simple summary of the production demand translated into planned production levels for two departments. This information is transferred to top management and to short-range planning as ② in Figure 2.1. During certain time periods, the production plan requires more labor capacity than indicated by demand; in other periods, the reverse is true. The variance in manufacturing effort will represent either an increase or a decline in inventory levels. Figure 2.4 illustrates a tabular report of production demand and month-end inventory for each product in the plan. This detailed information flow is depicted by ③ in Figure 2.1.

Short-range planning, the next block of interest in Figure 2.1, is perhaps the most complex and demanding activity in production control. Next month's *capacity* plan has to be translated into purchase authorizations and a master schedule for production. In order to do this, short-range planning needs a bill of materials to know what materials and components are required for each unit of product. Figure 2.5 exemplifies a bill of materials from which information flows through ④ in Figure 2.1. The short-range plan is frequently for a one-week period. However, the plan must coordinate the activities for many weeks at a time. If, for example, the plan is to assemble 50 units of product *ABC* five weeks hence, then it may have to place a purchase order for needed parts in the next week and build 50 subassemblies perhaps three weeks hence. Short-range planning is charged with creating orders for efforts in the next week to satisfy a variety of needs many weeks into the future.

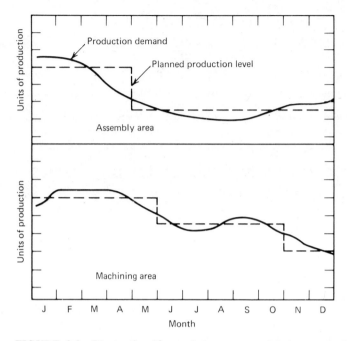

FIGURE 2.3   **Illustrative 12-month long-range plan for two facilities.**

Once the plan is formulated, purchase and shop authorizations are written. Figure 2.6 gives an example of an interdepartmental purchase authorization, which lists the parts that need to be purchased, the quantity needed, the date needed, and the planned date for receiving the shipment. Information flow represented by the purchase authorization form is depicted by ⑤ in Figure 2.1. The shop-order master schedule information flow is ⑥

	January			February			March		
Product	Inventory	Production	Demand	Inventory	Production	Demand	Inventory	Production	Demand
215062	505	210	427	288	210	315	183	420	348
312015	435	0	205	230	100	195	135	200	175
312050	856	100	653	303	250	403	150	250	308
473211	672	350	584	438	350	569	219	350	503

Production and Inventory Plan

FIGURE 2.4   **Detailed production and inventory plan tabulation for three months.**

Bill of Materials

Model Number ___6-53___   Drawing Number ___492-13214A___

Part Number	Part Description	Stock Location	Usage per Assembly	Expected Lead Time
536296	Bracket	21 Bin 72	4	4
536524	Gear box	21 Bin 5	1	8
536600	Bal. assy.	47 Rack B	1	10

Last Revision ___6/8___

Authorization ___EDB___

FIGURE 2.5 Illustrative bill-of-materials form.

Purchasing Authorization Order

Date of Issue ___FEB 4___

Part Number	Part Description	Quantity Needed	Latest Date Needed	Expected Receipt Date
7124321	Filters	800	3/10	3/1
536431	Castings	1200	5/31	5/15
624534	Block Castings	80	4/15	4/1

Authorization ___J. C. Chadwick___

Production Control ___H. Ludwig___

Purchasing ___W. C. Bickly___

FIGURE 2.6 Illustrative purchasing-order authorization form.

Shop Order Master Schedule

Date Issued __1/16/82__   For Week of __1/25__

Department __HEAT TREAT__   Shop Order Number __32104-82__

Part Number	Part Description	Operations	Quantity Needed	Latest Date Needed	Rough-Stock Location	Standard Time Required
632411	Rocker arms	80	1500	1/27	Dept. 108	37.50
536215	Push rods	40	800	1/26	21 Bin 6	22.00
264723	Injector	130	900	1/29	Rec'ng	18.50

Authorization __Brewton__

Production Control __H. Ludwig__

Manufacturing __Clark__

FIGURE 2.7 Illustrative shop-order authorization form.

Receiving Activity

Date of Issue __4/8/81__   Receipt Date __4/15__

Purchase Order Number	Part Number	Quantity Ordered	Item Disposition	Special Remarks
PO-6214-81	632145	80	to 21 Bin 90	Expedite
PO-6253-81	533451	1500	to 21 Bin 50	
	534621	100	to Dept. 40	
	621344	500	to 47 Rack E	

Authorization __RR__

FIGURE 2.8 Illustrative receiving-activity schedule form.

in Figure 2.1, and the form itself is illustrated in Figure 2.7. The form is designed to contain a list of all the requirements for one department during a given week: the parts to manufacture, the quantities needed, the due dates, the rough-stock locations, and the labor standard hours to produce the parts. The information on the form therefore gives the short-range planning target for all production departments.

Finalization of the shop and purchase plans allow the determination of expected receiving, shipping, and inventory-distribution activities. A receiving activity schedule is depicted in Figure 2.8, its associated information flow is ⑦ in the system flow of Figure 2.1. This report informs the receiving dock of what items to expect and what to do with these items as they arrive. Receipts are sorted by date so that items not received can be "red-lined" for action by purchasing, and also possibly by the shop.

A similar report is depicted in Figure 2.9 for shipment of finished goods. It, too, is sorted by date of shipment and it may have packing-slip documents attached. The intent of the report, once again, is to determine if the shipping plan is being met. If any item on the list is not available, exception action can be started. The information flow associated with this form is ⑧ on Figure 2.1.

The last report to emanate from the short-range plan is the materials-requirement plan, which is a complete plan for each item under inventory control. Figure 2.10 represents a materials-requirement plan for a four-week period. As will be seen in later chapters, inventory is an extremely costly part

Shipping Activity Schedule

Date of Issue ___8/13___   Shipping Date ___8/26___

Shipper Number	Invoice Number	Part Number	Quantity to Ship	Shipping Instructions
D 47121-81	A 13211	530000	4	REA
D 46995-81	A12984	710000	3	X-press

Authorization ___CBrown___

FIGURE 2.9 Illustrative shipping activity schedule.

Material Requirements Plan

Part Number ____534621____   Part Description ___IDLER GEAR___

	Week 1	Week 2	Week 3	Week 4
Gross	O	130	O	O
Scheduled Receipts	100	O	O	100
Expected Inventory	90	60	60	160
	O	O	O	O

Outstanding Purchasing or Shop
Order for Scheduled Receipts:

Order Number	Quantity	Due Date
S2456	100	12/8

Department Requiring Part __243__

Department Supplying Part __107__

Bin Location __21 BIN 19__

Economic Order Quantity __100__

Reorder Point __50__

FIGURE 2.10   Illustrative materials requirement plan.

of the manufacturing operation, and the materials-requirement plan is used to control these costs. The related information flow is represented in Figure 2.1 by ⑨. In summary, the flow of information into and out of the short-range requirements planning activity is the heart of the production control function. If the production control function is performed well, then all of the manufacturing activities will be coordinated and working together.

The next major block to be considered in the overall information flow depicted in Figure 2.1 is that encompassing inventory management. The inventory management role is to monitor the flow of materials throughout the plant, which means knowing where everything is at all times. It should be pointed out that inventory control is a subfunction of inventory management. The inputs to inventory management, as seen in Figure 2.1, are from long-range and short-range planning. Inventory management does not have scheduling control over the various manufacturing departments, but it must monitor the manufacturing activities to see if they will satisfy the inventory plan. Therefore, inventory management must receive inventory transactions from the inventory storage facility and all production departments when items are moved from one location to another. One simple, manual method for accomplishing this task is to have the material-handling operators (say, forklift drivers) process an inventory move ticket whenever they transport

Inventory Move Card

Shop Order Number	Part Number	Description	Last Operation Finished	Quantity
52143	532413	Bracket	20	53
52151	564311	Gear	50	60
52098	530010	Transmission	280	8

Moved from ___Q.C.___ To ___Assy.___

Remarks _____

Moved by ___Johnson___

Date ___6/9___

FIGURE 2.11 Illustrative inventory move ticket.

materials. Such a ticket is illustrated in Figure 2.11, its associated information flow is ⑩ in Figure 2.1. This information flow includes all information arrows to inventory management from machining, assembly, testing, and inventory storage. When items are moved from one location to another, they progress through the processing steps, and these moves constitute feedback as to how manufacturing is progressing. The information as to inventory transaction activity is then transmitted to the shop scheduling operation so that manufacturing progress can be monitored. Figure 2.12 represents an inventory activity report, which is ⑪ on Figure 2.1. Note that this report will list all available units of any part, what their manufacturing status is, and

Inventory Activity Report

Part Number	Part Description	Quantity Moved	Date Moved	Present Location	Last Operation Finished
531245	Jumper	100	11/7	120	60
712092	Blower	20	11/8	503	20

FIGURE 2.12 Illustrative inventory activity report.

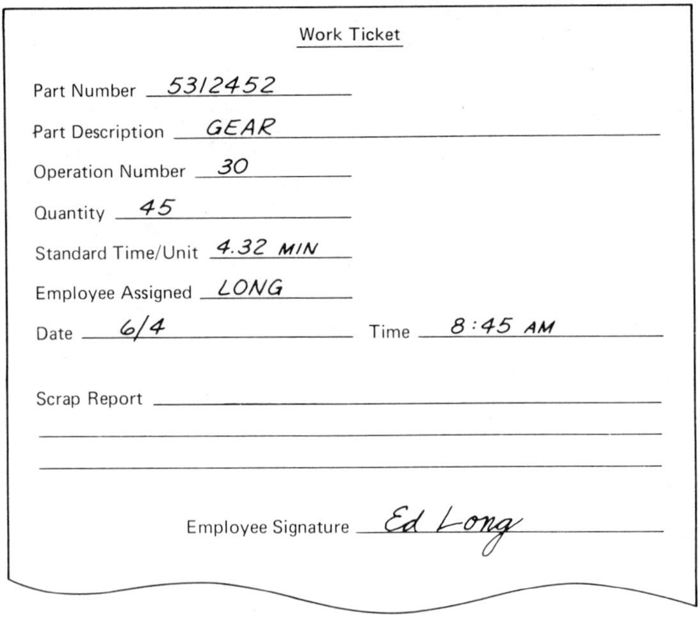

```
                          Work Ticket

    Part Number __5312452_____

    Part Description ___GEAR_____

    Operation Number __30_____

    Quantity __45_____

    Standard Time/Unit _4.32 MIN___

    Employee Assigned _LONG_____

    Date ___6/4_____  Time ___8:45 AM_____


    Scrap Report _____
                 _____
                 _____


               Employee Signature _Ed Long_____
```

FIGURE 2.13   Example of a work ticket.

where they can be located. Such information is very hard to maintain accurately but is very valuable.

The last block in Figure 2.1 to be discussed is that of shop scheduling, monitoring, and control. This is the final step in the production control chain of activities. The activity receives as input the weekly shop-order master schedule (Figure 2.7). It also receives the inventory activity report (Figure 2.12). Thus the shop scheduler knows every task that must be performed and the location of the raw materials for each task. The first role of the scheduler is to determine the sequence in which the tasks should be performed. The sequencing decision is typically made by the shop supervisor. This information is passed on to the employee who will perform the task in the form of a work ticket, illustrated in Figure 2.13. When the task is complete, the ticket is signed and the process of moving the material begins. The work ticket form is represented by ⑫ on Figure 2.1.

The flow of information and reports given in this section should not be viewed as being complete or the final word. They are *representative* of activities inherent in manufacturing production control. Procedures and forms already developed and being used by an organization will likely be better suited to that organization's specific situation. If problems do exist in production control, analyzing the information flow in a similar fashion to that presented in this section should help identify difficulties. The use of the computer in collecting and disseminating production control information should logically be of considerable benefit in all but the smallest of organizations, and this and related topics comprise the remainder of the chapter.

2.3 REAL-TIME COMPUTERIZED PRODUCTION CONTROL

Thus far we have discussed the extent of the information flows into, around, and from production control. The large volume of these information flows has made production control a prime candidate for computerization. In addition, the value of fast and accurate information flow suggests that the cost of extensive computerization is often justifiable. In this section, we shall briefly introduce the concept of an extensive, *real-time, integrated, database-oriented* computer system for production control.

We will start with a short review of digital computer terminology relevant to the topic at hand. First, what is meant by *real time*? In production control, this concept means that the production control programs are constantly active in the computer. The computer is always ready to receive inputs from the shop floor, and, as events occur in real time, those events are recorded in the computer. On the output side, certain programs can be accessed at any time. Indeed, some programs may be called automatically by the computer itself. Thus, if someone wanted to know in real time if a certain manufacturing job was being processed, a computer terminal could be used to ask the computer for the answer and the computer would have the information to allow a correct response. Therefore, the computer's data files are constantly being brought up-to-date and information in those files is constantly available.

The term *integrated* refers to the fact that many computers are interconnected. A large host computer, which works with the master files of *all* data, is connected with a variety of smaller computers that are limited to specific tasks. Perhaps one minicomputer monitors the machining shop area, another is used to manage inventory flow, and still another is used to enter sales orders. Each computer performs certain tasks independently and can be called by the host computer to perform tasks in conjunction with other computers in the system. Connected to the smaller computers are terminals and possibly even smaller computers. There might be automatic work-ticket readers at each shop foreman's desk as well as numerically controlled machine tools containing microprocessors whose controlling programs are stored in minicomputers. Figure 2.14 is a pictorial representation of an integrated computer system. In Section 2.4, typical input/output devices indicated in Figure 2.14 are discussed. Through such a system, any person or any equipment that needs to interact with the computer-based production control system can do so.

The last concept that needs to be introduced is that of *database orientation*. Just as hardware can be integrated, so also can the data files. In another concept of file-oriented systems, each program has its own data files: for example, an inventory management set of programs that have several data

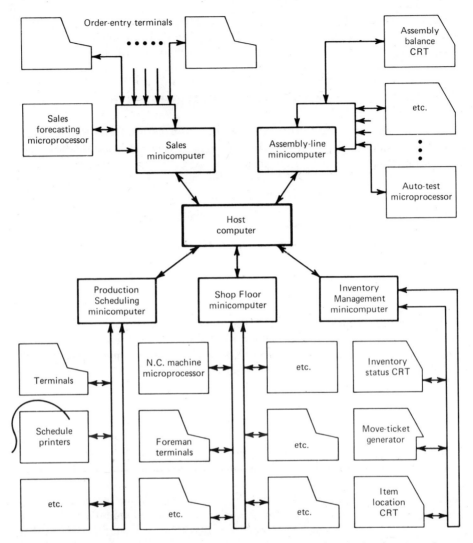

FIGURE 2.14 **Example of an integrated computer system for production control.**

files and a job scheduling system with other data files. Often, these separate files duplicate some of the same data. In many cases, *supposed* duplicated data do not agree. Consider the problem that might occur if the scheduling system called for Saturday overtime to assemble 100 of a given product, assuming that 100 of a needed component are available, but the inventory systems files show that 75 of those components were just removed and shipped out as spare parts. The problem is that the two data files now do not agree on the same data item. In a database-oriented system, there is only one place where key fields of data are stored, or, if several copies exist, *all* are

1. Sales order records.
2. Sales order status records.
3. Shipping order status records.
        4. Forecasted demand records.
        5. Sales history records.
6. Part number master file.
7. Bill of materials records.
8. Assembly process records.
9. Production routing records.
10. Time standards records.
11. Manufacturing cost records.
12. Inventory cost and control records.
        13. Raw materials inventory records.
        14. In-process inventory records.
        15. Finished-goods inventory records.
        16. Vendor-purchasing records.
        17. Purchasing order status records.
        18. Receiving order status records.
19. Shop loading-master schedule records.
20. Machine utilization history records.
21. Shop order status records.

FIGURE 2.15   Content of a typical production-control database.

updated simultaneously. Thus, all programs use portions of the same large database.

The database at the core of a computerized production-control system is likely to be very large. One might think of this database as a series of connected files containing all the data used in any production control information system. The host computer maintains the complete database. Each smaller computer contains only that part of the database that it is actively using. In Figure 2.15, the content of such a database is suggested. The records are divided into five groups to suggest which tend to be used together. One can imagine that the sizes of the files represented by these records are large and the variety of ways that the files would be related to each other are many. In other words, for realistic cases, the host computer will have to store and maintain a huge database. The cost of operating such a system is large indeed. However, consider the associated availability of data to the production control decision maker.

The flow of events in production control was suggested in Chapter 1. You first must forecast demand, then create a production capacity plan, and so forth. With the integrated data base system, these activities can be carried out almost simultaneously. As new knowledge about sales demand occurs, the sales history data can be updated. If a totally unexpected sale occurs, the sales-order status data can be updated. New capacity plans can be generated to see how the most recent input will affect the production capacity plan. If a purchased part arrives and is found unacceptable, the raw materials inventory and receiving-order status records can be updated immediately. Then a new master schedule can be determined to see the effect of rejecting the bad part. In short, the advantage of having all this data and keeping it up to date in real time is that the effect of unexpected events can be quickly employed to identify the best decisions in the face of these events. Management can thus control the production actively and with greater intelligence. The potential for savings is very tempting.

On the other hand, the cost of such a system is very high. A large computer can easily be absorbed. The cost of obtaining and implementing the database system and applications programs is obviously very high and the number of man-hours needed to operate and manage the system is large. Finally, the potential for disruption during the conversion to the system which requires that nearly every aspect of the business be changed to accommodate it, is great. There is no magic formula for measuring the costs and benefits.

2.4   SHOP FLOOR HARDWARE FOR INFORMATION PROCESSING

The day has not yet arrived—though it may be fast approaching—when information flowing into and out of the shop floor can be provided and received automatically with no operator assistance. Granted, computer-controlled machining centers, such as that shown in Figure 2.16, have the capability for providing machine-effectivity information utilizing a built-in microprocessor. The great percentage of industry's manufacturing equipment does not integrate computers within the equipment, and so operator intervention is needed to collect effectivity and productivity information. As an aside, the concepts inherent in Computer Numerically Controlled (CNC) machining centers are the concepts leading to the fully automatic factory. A fully automatic factory was but a dream just a few years ago but is certainly a feasible concept today. In fact, Japan has a refrigerator line that has the possibility for completely automatic assembly. Utilizing the CNC types of equipment in conjunction with automatic robots for transferring and positioning parts allows for completely automatic production. Such a manufacturing system is depicted in Figure 2.17. Automatic production, however, makes automatic information-processing mandatory. Since a large percentage of industry is not so completely automated, equipment designed for operator intervention has to be simple and relatively foolproof, and must allow for minimum worker interaction in order to minimize loss of both worker and machine productivity. The thrust of this section will be to introduce shop floor concepts that allow information to flow into and out of the manufacturing environment with as little disruption as feasible.

FIGURE 2.16 Typical CNC machining center. (Provided courtesy of the Kearney and Trecker Manufacturing Corporation.)

An advanced trend in manufacturing utilizes distributive computer systems in which local minicomputers communicate with efficient autonomous segments of the manufacturing facility. In turn, each minicomputer communicates with a large host computer that retains the manufacturing database for the entire system. *Local* data may be maintained by the local minicomputer, independent of the system database. Communication between hosted minicomputers is feasible through the large host computer. Minicomputers now have localized communication control of an autonomous segment of the plant, drawing on information from the host computer when needed. In this manner, high efficiency can be attained at both computer levels, host and hosted. A typical interactive computer system is shown in Figure 2.18.

The use of the distributed computer systems to allow information to be transmitted on a real-time basis for effective management decision making is called a Distributed Plant Management System (DPMS)†. A typical DPMS is

†Appreciation is tendered to the Digital Equipment Corporation for providing pictures of shop floor information-gathering equipment, as well as for allowing certain of the concepts to be used in this section.

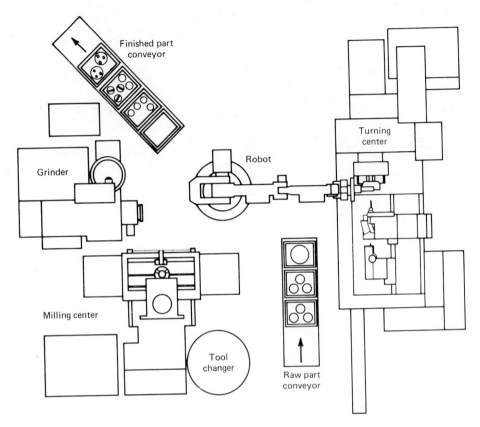

FIGURE 2.17   Flowline design manufacturing system. From "Integrating Robots into a Manufacturing System," by John G. Holmes. Reprinted with permission from 1979 AIIE Fall I.E. Conference Proceedings. Copyright © American Institute of Industrial Engineers, 25 Technology Park/Atlanta, Norcross, Ga. 30092.

as shown in Figure 2.19. Typical information flow and functions associated with the example system are as follows (numbers refer to the numbers by the figure blocks):

1. Raw Material Inventory receiving reports; material issue reports; raw material purchase orders.

2. Time and Attendance Recording; payroll information; standard costs; labor distribution reports.

3. Production Process test and measurement; instrument monitoring and process monitoring.

4. Factory Production work-in-progress reports; job-order status reports; maintenance monitoring.

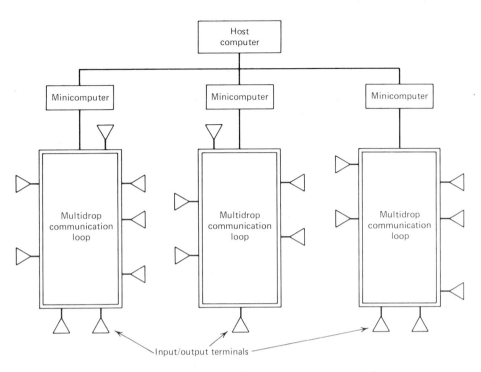

FIGURE 2.18 Typical interactive computer system.

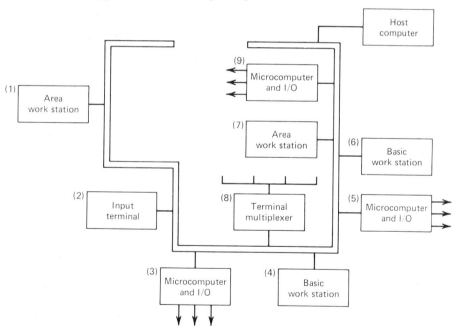

FIGURE 2.19 Typical Distributed Plant Management System. (Adapted with permission from Digital Equipment Corporation's *DPM Systems Brochure*. Copyright © 1979, Digital Equipment Corporation. All rights reserved.)

5.   Product Test; quality trend analysis; test result reporting.

6.   Order Processing; component/assembly issuing; job scheduling; shipping and packing documents.

7.   Finished Goods inventory reports; waybills; invoices; lot tracking.

8.   Supervisor Terminals for work orders, manpower and machine allocation, test and production results, productivity reports, attendance reports, inventory reports.

9.   Warehouse Conveyor Control; packaging control; order picking.

Major manufacturers of computer systems provide operating-system software to facilitate manufacturing-data collection from the shop floor so that information collected may be used in the development of procedures to facilitate production. A typical software operating system is the Digital Equipment Corporation's LOTS (Labor and Operations Tracking System), which

1.   Issues shop paper, such as process sheets, process routings, and job orders.

2.   Tracks work-in-progress by job or part and collects labor data according to work center, operation code, or employee.

3.   Generates status reports about loading profiles and job/part status.

4.   Provides real-time database maintenance, logging, and recovery.

5.   Interfaces with other systems such as other manufacturing management systems, costing systems, and production systems.

A typical LOTS system is depicted in Figure 2.20.

In order for the Distributed Plant Management System to be effective and for the operating system to be utilized to its potential, information has to be input from the shop floor. This information might be developed through CNC devices, as mentioned earlier, but in general it will have to be input by the worker on the shop floor. To give the reader a brief idea of the type of input devices available, three such devices are pictured and their features mentioned. Referring back to the *discussion* of Figure 2.19 will provide you with applications for some of these terminals.

Area Work-Station Terminal Figures 2.21 and 2.22   The area work-station terminal pictured allows industrial Type 3 or Type 5 badges to be read automatically in order to provide worker information to a central computer. Related data inputs can then be accepted for timekeeping, payroll, and other labor-oriented reporting. This particular terminal has eight transaction keys, 32-character alphanumeric display, keypad, and operator guidance lights, and allows for data input through an 80-column card. Additional shop-floor transactions thus are now feasible, including part tracking, work center supervision, material tracking, machine tracking, tool tracking, labor tracking, inventory control, and maintenance.

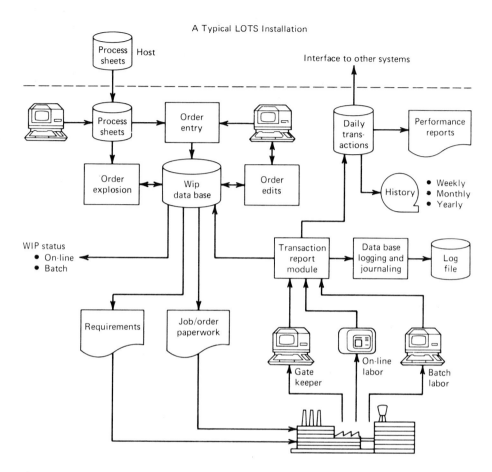

FIGURE 2.20   LOTS—a manufacturing software operating system. (Copyright © 1979, Digital Equipment Corporation. All rights reserved.)

Terminal with Wand Reader Figure 2.23   Machine operators and other plant workers are not being productive if large amounts of data are slowly input through a keypad device. Use of a wand that, when passed over the information strips, can read bar codes or magnetic strips not only cuts down on operator-nonproductive time, but also eliminates a great portion of error possibilities inherent in input typing. Adjacent to the wand input device in Figure 2.23 is a video terminal that can be hooked directly into a distributed plant-management system such as was shown in Figure 2.19. The video terminal could be placed at a foreman's station, for example, to allow interrogation of pertinent database information.

Increased application of sophisticated computer-aided-manufacturing concepts is seen as the path to improved productivity in manufacturing. Only

FIGURE 2.21　Badge reading at an area work station terminal. (Copyright ©1980, Digital Equipment Corporation. All rights reserved.)

FIGURE 2.22 Production reporting at an area work station terminal. (Copyright © 1980, Digital Equipment Corporation. All rights reserved.)

FIGURE 2.23   Terminal with wand input. (Copyright © 1980, Digital Equipment Corporation. All rights reserved.)

a brief introduction to the types of shop floor hardware available has been made in this section. The reader should be aware that considerable study and detailed economic evaluations have to be made prior to installing such equipment—assuming that the evaluations justify such a move. If systems and subsystems are installed, the concepts presented in subsequent chapters of this book will be especially helpful. However, these concepts will also be beneficial in those organizations that cannot justify automated processing, either of information or of product.

2.5 CAD/CAM

Computer-aided design (CAD) refers to a system in which a graphics display device, similar to that shown in Figure 2.23, allows product design and drafting to be accomplished in an interactive mode. Computer-aided manufacturing (CAM) has a broad range of definitions but always includes the use of a digital computer to enhance the shop-floor manufacturing process, including monitoring and control of machining equipment. Shop-floor information systems with automatic data gathering, as discussed in Section 2.4, will also constitute a CAM system.

Using CAD, a design can be generated rapidly using a light pen and terminal function buttons. Conventional drawing boards, calculators, and design manuals can be bypassed. Designs can be hard-copied using a copy device connected to the graphics terminal. As pointed out by Halevi†, the synergistic effort of achieving this close coupling between the designs and the computer has four important benefits.

1. Designers can immediately see and correct any gross errors in their drawings or input statements.
2. Designers can monitor the progress of a problem solution and terminate the run or modify the input data as required.
3. The designer can make subjective decisions at critical branch points which guide the computer in a continuation of the problem solution.
4. The graphic display may present data that cannot be readily understood or interpreted in a computer output listing or even in plotted output. Through clever programming, a computer-driven display can present multiple views, moving pictures, blinking lines, dashed lines, and lines of varying intensity.

The ultimate application of CAM occurs where the various operations and routings needed to allow production of the product are automatically directed by the computer, a process commonly referred to as computer-aided process planning (CAPP). Instructions can be generated by a program, called a post-processor, to allow tapes to be generated for numerical control machines that produce the product automatically. In some instances, direct numerical control (DNC) allows a controlling computer to send the controlling instructions to the machine tools directly, bypassing the tape step, once the machine-tool operator dials a predetermined code to the computer room signifying that setup for the part has been accomplished. (As of this writing, McDonnell Douglas has almost 200 DNC machines in its operation at St. Louis.) The automatic process-planning and computer-aided numerical-control functions are included in myriad functions encompassing computer-aided manufacturing. Of course, an integrated CAD/CAM system can be very expensive and may not be justifiable in many instances. Designing a product using CAD techniques, generating production planning through conventional manual techniques, using an independent minicomputer to generate NC tapes that then are used on NC machines also constitutes a CAD/CAM application. Any time CAD or CAM techniques are implemented, at whatever level, information response time has to be improved.

---

†Gideon Halevi, *The Role of Computers in Manufacturing Processes*, John Wiley, New York, 1980.

2.6   GROUP TECHNOLOGY

The manufacturing-shop-floor production control system, and the associated information system, can be improved using the concept of group technology. This is especially true when a job shop facility is driven by numerical-control equipment.

Basically, components being manufactured are *grouped* according to similarity of machining *functions* (not similarity of machines), so that a group of machines, commonly called a *cell*, can operate only on a subgroup of all the components being manufactured. For example, in an engine production facility, one cell might produce gears and another, shafts. Each component is assigned a complex digital code that defines types of machining needed, dimensional and quality-control characteristics, material, and so on. Cluster analysis, using the classification codes, realizes cell groupings. Load balancing of course plays a big part in the cell orientation, since going from a conventional machine shop to a cellular approach limits flexibility in assigning machines to products. In general, group technology requires more machines to manufacture for the same number of components.

What then are the benefits to be realized? Allison and Vapor† indicate significant improvements for the Naval Avionics Center in Indianapolis for the period 1/31/77 to 8/31/77.

1. The percentage of orders completed on schedule went from 37% to an average of 54%.

2. Average deviation from scheduled completion date went from 6.5 days to 1.1 days.

3. Average machine-shop cycle time decreased from 18.1 days to 12.5 days. From a shop-floor-information point of view, having a cell foreman responsible for timely completion of parts, the Naval Avionics facility found that part tracking and progress control was monitored better, with progress status being known immediately. Communications between shop foremen and other manufacturing groups improved, with a decidedly smoother day-to-day operation.

It should be apparent that reduced materials-handling and better overall control in a cell-oriented facility should be possible. But because of diminished flexibility in assigning machines to product, a precise scheduling and loading scheme is needed. Orientation to computerized scheduling with inherent quantified approaches becomes a necessity. Such approaches are discussed in Chapter 9.

One important final point should be made. Production control techniques for planning, forecasting, inventory management, and scheduling are limited

---

†J. W. Allison and J. C. Vapor, "GT Approach Proves Out," *American Machinist*, February 1979.

by the validity, timeliness, and accuracy of the information used by the techniques. Whereas most of this text's material is concerned with production control techniques, obtaining valid, timely, and accurate information may well be the most difficult task in operating an effective production-control system. Unfortunately, the best way to accomplish the development of the information system cannot be obtained through reading a textbook. Much of the process is common sense, and many of the procedures can be gleaned only through experience. The foundation has been offered in this chapter; the reader will have to build on that foundation using the experience of practicing production controllers.

2.7 REFERENCES

1. Allison, J. W., and Vapor, J. C., "GT Approach Proves Out," *American Machinist*, February 1979.

2. Halevi, Gideon, *The Role of Computers in Manufacturing Processes*, John Wiley, New York, 1980.

3. Holmes, John G., "Integrating Robots into a Machining System," *American Institute of Industrial Engineers Fall Industrial Engineering Conference Proceedings*, November 1979.

THREE: PROJECT PLANNING

"Brains first and then Hard Work. Look at it! That's the way to build a house," said Eeyore proudly.

A. A. Milne

The emergence of the digital computer as a "management tool" in the 1950s led to the development of certain techniques geared to facilitate large-project planning. Prior to the evolution of these systematic planning techniques, which we will classify generally as network techniques, the planning of large projects was hampered a great deal by the complexity of the projects themselves. This is not to say that the projects were not brought to a successful fruition; rather, there was no guarantee that the utilization of resources, such as time, manpower, money, and equipment, was accomplished in a fashion approaching optimality. Also, the combination of all the subcomponents, or jobs, of the project tended to be treated as separate entities in the planning stage, rather than as a total system. The combination of the computer and network techniques, along with some criterion of optimality, will certainly allow a most satisfactory plan to be devised to lead to the happy culmination of a project. Initial thought and planning is essential in major projects.

The goal of this chapter is to describe key project-planning network approaches and evaluate their benefits and fallacies. As an example, the Critical Path Method (CPM) will be found to give a range of project schedules that themselves will present a range of direct costs. Combining these direct costs with applicable indirect costs will indicate, from a planning point of view, those schedules that will accomplish project objectives with minimum total cost expenditures. A drawback to the Critical Path Method approach, however, is that it is strictly deterministic and so does not consider the fact that components, or jobs, within the project will not be accomplished as planned because of unforeseen, uncertain effects. In all probability, the only known large project that was accomplished in *exactly* the planned manner according to a developed schedule is that well-described in Genesis. The Project Evaluation and Review Technique (PERT) will be presented as an attempt to alleviate the deterministic restrictions of CPM. The fact that restrictive assumptions within the PERT probabilistic technique prohibit realistic application will be introduced and evaluated.

The CPM deterministic approach is by far the most widely used technique in industry for project planning. A case problem will evaluate costs in changing a hypothetical plant's production approach, and a computer solution to the problem will be integrated into the discussion. This same problem will be further evaluated in Chapter 8, in which certain CPM scheduling fallacies will be offset by limited resource analysis.

3.1 EVOLUTION OF NETWORK PLANNING TECHNIQUES

Historically, network analysis procedures had their inception with the traditional Gantt chart, or bar chart, developed by Henri L. Gantt during World War I. (One beneficial outcome of war has been the development of significant production procedures and techniques, but it is doubtful that anything else should be said about the benefits of war.) The Gantt chart is still widely used today and is quite useful in analyzing the feasibility of a CPM optimum-cost schedule, as will be seen later. A typical Gantt chart is shown in Figure 3.1. The historical interest lies in the Gantt chart's *graphical* representation of jobs to be accomplished, with length of a bar on the chart, such as *A*–1 in Figure 3.1, being an analog of the time required to accomplish activity, or job, *A*-1. Typical benefits of the Gantt chart are that

1. All jobs are graphically displayed in one easily understood chart.

2. By having the workers, or foreman, shade in the percentage of bar chart that corresponds to the percentage of job completed each basic work period, it is possible to check the overall progress of the system of jobs at any point in time. For example, Figure 3.2 shows the progress on June 7, with jobs *A*-1, *B*-1, *B*-2 completed and jobs *A*-2 and *C*-1 behind schedule. Unfortunately, the

Job (Activity)	Date Scheduled June											
	3	4	5	6	7	10	11	12	13	14	17	18
A-1												
A-2												
B-1												
B-2												
C-1												
C-2												
D-1												

FIGURE 3.1 Typical bar chart.

		Date Scheduled June										
		3	4	5	6	7	10	11	12	13	14	17	18
A-1													
A-2													
B-1													
B-2													
C-1													
C-2													
D-1													

FIGURE 3.2   **Bar chart with progress reporting.**

conventional Gantt chart does not indicate any possible cause of the problem existing with jobs A-2 and C-1. This will be corrected by the line-of-balance technique (see Section 3.6).

3. When resources required are limited, the Gantt chart allows an initial evaluation of the planned use of these resources (see Chapter 8).

The evolution from the Gantt chart to a network probably came with the advent in the late 1940s of the Navy's *milestone method,* a modified Gantt chart on which are indicated points in time, called milestones, occurring in the duration of jobs. Interrelationships between milestones are shown by connecting the affected milestones by solid lines. Obvious milestones for any job include the starting time of the job and the required completion point. Other milestones would be appropriate at significant points within a job, such as completion of a subbatch of parts that would then allow the start of another job. The milestone at the completion of the subbatch and the starting milestone of the second job comprise an example of an interrelationship between milestones, showing one job's *precedence* over another job. Figure 3.3 shows the Gantt chart example with milestones added. For this naive example it is now readily apparent that the culprit in activities A-2 and C-1 slippage is activity A-2, since a large portion of C-1 cannot be started until a milestone on A-2 has been achieved, which it has not. As with the Gantt chart, the milestone procedure is laudable as regards its aims but is only of somewhat passing interest except for its position in the evolutionary process leading to the planning network.

Now we come to the two techniques, developed concurrently but independently, that initially added some criteria of optimality to the project scheduling function. The Critical Path Method (CPM) evolved as a joint venture between Remington Rand and DuPont. The criterion of optimality inherent within CPM is the determination of a schedule that *minimizes* total

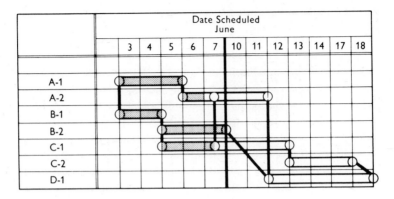

FIGURE 3.3   Bar chart with milestones showing precedence.

project cost. The Project Evaluation and Review Technique (PERT), in
addition to being developed concurrently with CPM, evolved a very similar
graphical or network philosophy. PERT first came to the public eye through
two brochures published by the Navy in 1958. Its criterion of optimality—if
optimality is the correct word—would be in determining a time schedule for a
particular project that would have a stipulated probability of successful
completion within the particular time constraint. For example, in a research-
and-development operation, management may wish to know for planning
purposes what schedule would have a 95% probability of being met. PERT
attempts to achieve this aim.

The attributes and deficiencies of CPM and PERT will be discussed in
separate sections of this chapter when each technique is more fully discussed
in its own right. Suffice it to say for the moment that CPM and PERT are both
computer-oriented techniques, that both define the concept of an *arrow*
network diagram, and that both define the concept of a *critical path.*

A network is depicted in Figure 3.4 for the same set of activities and
associated precedence relationships given for the milestone Gantt chart.
Arrows now represent the jobs or activities. Listed above each arrow is its

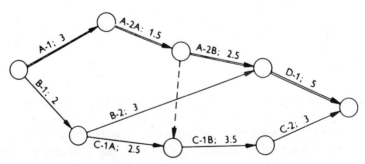

FIGURE 3.4   Typical arrow network.

coded designation followed by its duration time. The longest path through the network, called the critical path, is indicated by double-line activities. The dotted line is used to denote a nontime activity that denotes *precedence only* (pseudoactivity). Finally, activities *A*-2 and *C*-1 are each split into two activities to allow satisfaction of the milestone characteristics given earlier, in Figure 3.3.

CPM was designed strictly for the deterministic project problem. PERT attempted to allow evaluation of the stochastic research-and-development situation. However, PERT, while commendable, has many shortcomings and limitations stemming from computational simplification; these will be discussed more fully in Section 3.4. The Graphical Evaluation and Review Technique (GERT), built on developments by S. E. Elmaghraby and A. A. B. Pritsker, satisfactorily eliminates most of the PERT limitations but does pose some mathematical computation problems. It is, however, probably the most significant of the network scheduling approaches given in the evolutionary process. Unfortunately, coverage of GERT is beyond the scope of this text.

Before discussing the two major network approaches of CPM and PERT, a few key definitions will be presented, to establish a common foundation.

3.2 DEFINITIONS

Only those items pertinent to both techniques discussed in this chapter will be defined briefly at this time. Definitions limited to local applications will be given with the specific discussion of those applications. Obviously, some of these terms have been used under the assumption of general understanding. Now we will formalize their definitions for the common foundation.

Project	A large-scale system comprising several tasks that have to be coordinated and scheduled to allow successful attainment of a project objective. The design of a production process, for example, may be considered a *project*.
Job (activity)	One of several self-contained *tasks* that make up the project. It is these *jobs* that have to be coordinated and scheduled. In a student registration project, typical jobs might be payment of fees and the advisement process, to name just two out of many.
Arrow	A graphical representation of one job. There will be at least as many arrows as jobs in the graphical representation of a project.
Node (event)	Time points between which activities may be scheduled. Nodes will be displayed graphically as circles, and will be used for arrow connectors in the overall project graphical presentation.
Network (graph)	The graphical representation of the overall project, consisting of the arrow-node relationships. Figure 3.4 is, of course, typical of a network.

Resource	Anything required to aid in the successful attainment of the project. Typical resources are men, equipment, money, and time, among others. If available resources are unlimited, the satisfaction of the project is not affected by problems in resource scheduling. The interesting case, however, is one of *limited* resources, which then have to be taken into consideration in the scheduling and coordinating of the project.
Critical path	The longest path(s) through the arrow network, from the beginning of the project to the expected completion of the project. If there are no time breaks within the network, the sum of the expected job times on the critical path will equal the expected project duration.

3.3 CRITICAL PATH METHOD (CPM)

The fundamental objective of CPM is to evolve a project schedule that minimizes the total expected cost for the project, or to evolve a project schedule, or series of schedules, that fall into an allowable project-cost range. From a planning point of view, CPM has many desirable features, including the following.

1. The development of the necessary network allows a large-scale project to be seen as a complete system. Interaction of activities comprising the project can be seen at a glance and can be evaluated in light of their effect on other jobs. Without going through any optimization analysis, it is possible to foresee and eliminate potential bottlenecks before the project actually gets underway. Many users of network scheduling contend that this actual development of the network, allowing system interactions to be observed graphically, is the most beneficial aspect of CPM.

2. A *cost range* can be determined iteratively for a project that is dependent on a feasible range of schedule times. In turn, the cost range can be used to determine the economic feasibility of the particular project. A side benefit accrues from having to evolve *good* estimates of *time* and *cost* for each job so that the cost range and, ultimately, the *minimum* cost schedule can be determined.

3. Using a combination CPM network schedule and Gantt chart procedure, *resource* requirements for a particular schedule, or series of schedules, can be determined. Conversely, the effect of scarce resources as regards the cost range can be evaluated. This topic will be treated more fully in Chapter 8.

As indicated in Section 3.1, the CPM technique is *computer*-oriented, though small projects may be hand-evaluated. A *normal* time for a job is defined as that time required under so-called normal conditions. A *normal direct cost* for the project is determined by summing all the job *direct costs* evolved for each job *normal time*. The computer orientation comes through an iterative approach whereby the *project* schedule is now reduced from the normal schedule, probably by one time-unit such as days or weeks, in a fashion that *minimizes* the *increase* in project direct costs that arise from the increase in resource requirements required to accomplish the reduction in project time. Logically, only jobs on the *critical path(s)* are considered for reduction, or *crashing*, since crashing any other job would not reduce the overall project time. Iteration is continued until the shortest-duration, or *crashed* schedule is achieved. Adding the indirect costs, which decrease with a reduction of project duration time, to the direct costs, which increase with project duration time reduction, gives the schedule of project total costs.

Needless to say, this brief introduction does not give the assumptions inherent in the CPM technique, nor does it give the method for finding the *minimum* increase in direct costs as the project duration is reduced. These tasks will be accomplished by means of a small example. A larger case problem will be given at the end of the chapter.

Initially, the project has to be broken down into self-contained jobs. Cost and time estimates have to be made for each job. In both cases—cost and time—*normal* and *crash* estimates are required. The normal condition indicates values that would normally be expected if everything went as planned. Crash values are determined for the *minimum*, or crash times that it is estimated the particular jobs can take, assuming overtime or utilizing extra resources as available. Also, it is required that a network be constructed showing the interrelationships among jobs based on a knowledge and study of the precedence conditions existing between activities. For example, assume that the data in Table 3.1 have been evolved for a CPM study.

The first step is to construct the CPM network. (Though we have glibly

TABLE 3.1   Normal and Crash CPM Data for Example Problem

	Time (days)		Cost($)		Immediate Precedence Relationship[a]
Job (Activity)	Normal	Crash	Normal	Crash	
A	6	4	100	120	0
B	4	3	80	93	A
C	5	4	95	110	0
D	7	7	115	115	A and C
E	4	2	64	106	B and D
F	8	6	75	99	A and C
G	18	13	228	318	0

[a] Activities in this column have to immediately precede the activities in the same row, first column.

assumed certain precedence conditions with the data, it should be mentioned that correct network development is probably the most difficult step of the CPM procedure.) Since jobs A, C, and G have no immediate predecessors, they emanate from one starting node, as shown in Figure 3.5. Jobs A and C *immediately* precede jobs D and F, so it seems logical next to connect jobs D

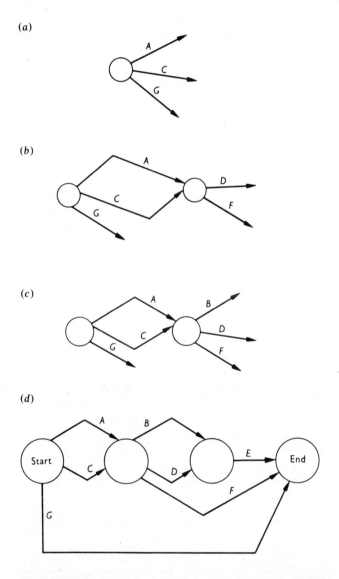

FIGURE 3.5 Development of *incorrect* network from Table 3.1 data.

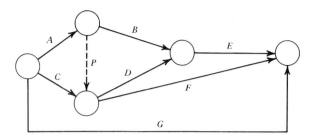

FIGURE 3.6   Correct network for Table 3.1 data.

and F. Only jobs B and E remain to be assigned. B is dependent on job A, so we will add this to our network, as shown in the third step in Figure 3.5. Finally, job E has as immediate predecessors jobs B and D. These are then fed to a common node, from which we evolve job E. To close the network, all jobs not now leading to a node are fed to an ending common node, culminating in the final network of Figure 3.5. Unfortunately, this network is incorrect from a precedence point of view! What went wrong? Job B, From the final network, has *both* jobs A and C as immediate predecessors. The relationship required in Table 3.1 is that *only* job A immediately precede job B. If a schedule were implemented with the erroneous network as a guide, slippage on job-C work would force a delay in the start of job B—a delay that is not justifiable. The way out of this dilemma would be to separate jobs A and C by having them enter different nodes. Job B would follow the job-A final node, and jobs D and F would be subsequent to the job-C final node. A pseudojob, P, is then drawn from the job-A node to the node where job C ends, denoting that job A *has to precede* jobs D and F. Obviously, activity P has no time or cost values. The correct network for this simple case is depicted in Figure 3.6.

Now we can attack the question of which schedule will minimize the project total costs. First we will look at the direct-cost picture. The values given in Table 3.1 are the job *direct costs*. The first CPM assumption—and this certainly could be waived in small hand-computations—is that a linear relationship exists for each job, between the normal and crash situations. For example, Table 3.1 shows that the range of allowable times for job A is two days and cost range is $20. The linear cost-change per day is then $10, which indicates an assumed cost for a five-day schedule would be the normal cost plus $10. This linear relationship, depicted in Figure 3.7, follows the equation

$$\text{Cost Change/Unit Time} = \frac{[\text{Crash cost} - \text{Normal cost}]}{[\text{Normal time} - \text{Crash time}]} \qquad (3.1)$$

The Cost Change/Unit Time (CCUT) for each job is given in Table 3.2; this will be the basis for cost-increase minimization, thus reducing schedule time by crashing.

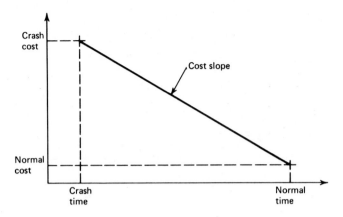

FIGURE 3.7   Relationship of normal and crash data to the cost slope.

The general procedure to follow in determining the minimum cost schedule is as follows.

a. Determine the *project normal schedule*: that is, the project schedule with normal times for all jobs.
b. Determine the *critical path(s)* for the normal schedule.
c. Determine the Cost Change/Unit Time (CCUT) for all jobs.

TABLE 3.2   Example Problem Cost Slopes

Job (Activity)	Cost Change/Unit Time[a]
A	$\dfrac{(120-100)}{(6-4)} = \$10$
B	$\dfrac{(93-80)}{(4-3)} = \$13$
C	$\dfrac{(110-95)}{(5-4)} = \$15$
D	no allowable change—cannot be crashed
E	$\dfrac{(106-64)}{(4-2)} = \$21$
F	$\dfrac{(99-75)}{(8-6)} = \$12$
G	$\dfrac{(318-228)}{(18-13)} = \$18$

[a]Based on Equation 3.1, with data from Table 3.1.

d. *Direct cost* for the normal schedule is the sum of the job normal costs.

e. Reduce (crash) the schedule by one time unit. Only those jobs on the critical path(s) are considered for crashing. Only *one* job on each critical path is crashed. (This should be obvious, as crashing two jobs on one path would crash the project by two time-units.) The job on each path that is crashed is the one that will achieve a *minimum* total CCUT for *all* paths to be crashed.

f. Direct cost for the new schedule is the previous schedule's direct cost plus the CCUT for each crashed job leading to the new schedule.

g. Perform steps *a* and *b* for the *reduced* time schedule.

h. Steps *e*, *f*, and *g* are continued until a critical path(s) is realized that has all its jobs at the crash, or minimum time. The minimum project time has now been realized, with the project minimum direct costs for each schedule falling between the normal and crash schedule.

i. The minimum total cost for each schedule is obtained by summing the schedule's minimum direct cost with that schedule's indirect cost. The *indirect* costs would be those costs charged *per* basic unit of time—say, a day—on an overhead basis, as contrasted to *direct* costs which are primarily the labor and materials that are directly chargeable to the project.

j. The overall minimum of the minimum total costs for all schedules realizes the "optimum" schedule.

It can be seen that steps *e, f, g,* and *h* are iterative in nature. Also, since projects may entail a thousand or more jobs, it should be apparent that the problem of determining the job(s) that realize the minimum CCUT for each project can get very complex, especially when several critical paths are involved. The problem, therefore, is highly adaptable to digital-computer solution, and most major computer manufacturers have a CPM routine available in their program libraries.

The CPM steps will now be clarified by a solution to the example problem. The network of Figure 3.6 and the data given, or calculated, in Tables 3.1 and 3.2 are utilized in this solution. The sequence of steps is subtitled to correspond to the sequence just presented.

Step a   The project *normal schedule* is found by determining the *minimum* time, T_M, that each node can occur, and still allow the project to be completed, assuming the project starting time is zero. Mathematically, this may be designated by

$$T_M = \max[(T_M)'_i + J_i] \qquad (3.2)$$

where $(T_M)'_i$ is the minimum occurrence time for the immediately preceding node numbered *i*. An *immediately preceding* node is one that has *one* job, with time J_i, leading from that node into the node under consideration.

If Figure 3.6 network's five nodes are numbered as shown in Figure 3.8, Equation 3.2 gives values for T_M as shown in Table 3.3. The project normal time is found to be 18 days.

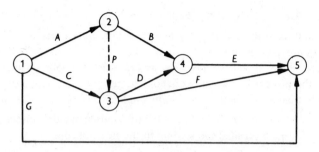

FIGURE 3.8   Example network with node numbers added.

Step b   The result above was formed by job *G* emanating from node 1, which was the only path leading to a total of 18 days. Therefore, the *initial critical path* is job *G*. Also, it can be seen from Table 3.3 that the next-longest path length in the project will be 17 days. This means that if a job on the critical path is crashed one day, and that job is *not* on the next longest path (*APDE*), then two critical paths will exist for a schedule of 17 days. These will be *G* and *APDE*.

A complex network requires a more formal procedure for determining the critical paths, one that is hopefully amenable to digital computer analysis.† The determination of T_M is frequently called the forward pass calculation. If

TABLE 3.3   Computation of Minimum Node Times

Node	i	$(T_M)'_i$	J_i	$(T_M)'_i + J_i$	T_M
1	—	—	—	—	0
2	1	0	A ; 6	6	6
3	1	0	C ; 5	5	6
3	2	6	P ; 0	6	
4	2	6	B ; 4	10	13
4	3	6	D ; 7	13	
5	1	0	G ; 18	18	18
5	3	6	F ; 8	14	
5	4	13	E ; 4	17	

---

†The computer program RESALL (see Appendix D) allows critical paths to be determined for a project even if resource allocation, the main purpose for the program, is not needed.

the latest time a node can be scheduled and still not slip the overall schedule is T_L, then the project T_L and T_M values can, in conjunction with the activity times, allow activities on the critical path to be determined.

T_L is found for all nodes in the same fashion as T_M in Equation 3.2 except that *subsequent* node times have intervening activity times subtracted and the *minimum* of all possible results give the node's T_L value. Mathematically, T_L can be formed by

$$T_L = {}_{\min}[(T_L)'_k - J_k]$$

where $(T_L)'_k$ is the latest occurrence time for the immediate succeeding node, with the time J_K being the activity time between the two nodes in question.

An activity is on the critical path if all three of the following conditions are met:

a. Starting node time T_L equals T_M.
b. Ending node time T_L equals T_M.
c. The difference in starting and ending node T_L values equals the activity time.

Since the T_L times require *subsequent* node times from a forward pass calculation, the determination of all T_L values is often called the backwards pass calculation.

Step c The Cost Change/Unit Time (CCUT) values were calculated in Table 3.2.

Step d The normal schedule *direct cost* is simply the sum of all the job direct costs for Table 3.1, and yields a value of $757.

Step e Crashing the network to 17 days can only be accomplished by crashing *activity G*, as that *is* the critical path; G goes to 17 days, as does the project.

Step f The 17-day direct cost is $757 + (CCUT for G), or $757 + $18 = $775.

The reduction to 17 days creates two critical paths, as mentioned earlier. These would be path G and path APDE. In order to reduce the project by another time period, it is necessary to ensure that *both* paths are reduced one day, with a *minimum total* increase in CCUT. The first approach would be to find a job that is on both paths to crash. None exists for G and APDE. To go to 16 days, then, G would have to be crashed with the job among A, D, or E that has the minimum CCUT. This would be A for path APDE. The increase in cost would be $10 for A added to $18 for G, which gives a total increase of $28. The iterative procedure continues for steps g and h until a project minimum is reached. These iterative steps are summarized in Table 3.4.

A few comments are in order concerning the results given in Table 3.4.

TABLE 3.4 Iterative Steps in Crashing Project

Iteration	Critical Path(s)	Job(s) Crashed and (New time)	Added Direct Cost(CCUT) ($)	Direct Cost ($)	Project Time (days)	Activities Now at Minimum Time
0	(G)	—	—	757	18	D
1	(G)	G(17)	18	775	17	D
2	(G)	G(16)	18	803	16	D
	(APDE)	A(5)	10			
3	(G)	G(15)	18	842	15	D
	(APDE)	E(3)	21			
4	(G)	G(14)	18	881	14	D, E
	(CDE)	E(2)	21			
5	(G)	G(13)	18	924	13	D, E, G, A, C[a]
	(APDE)	A(4)	10			
	(CDE)	C(4)	15			

[a]Paths G, APDE, and CDE are now all at their crashed minimum—the project is, therefore, at its minimum.

1. Iteration 3 has three critical paths. Since path G (job G) is not associated with the other two paths, it follows that G has to be crashed. In considering paths APDE and CDE, the following possibilities are available for crashing (D is already at its limit):

    A and C CCUT is $10 + $15 = $25

    A and E CCUT is $10 + $21 = $31

    C and E CCUT is $15 + $21 = $36

    E CCUT is $21

    Obviously, G and E are the jobs to crash.

2. Considering iteration 5, which has the same three critical paths, jobs D and E are at their limits. The next minimum CCUT from the above four possibilities would be to crash A and C. Since path G also has to be crashed, the minimum increase is obtained by crashing G, A, and C.

3. Upon reaching a schedule of 13 days, we are now constrained by jobs D, E, G, A, and C, all of which are at their minimum times. This means that paths G, APDE, and CDE are all at their minimum times, and so the project is restricted to 13 days. The allowable project time range is 18 days to 13 days, with a direct-cost range of $757 to $924.

Several computer programs are available for solving the CPM problem, and these would certainly be desirable for complex projects. Figure 3.9 gives sample UNIVAC 1110 computer printouts for the 16-day schedule, which *will be* found to be optimum in steps *i* and *j*. One printout (*a*) gives relative dating from time zero and another, (*b*) gives *calendar* dating. Calendar dating is a *must* for management reporting. Also, a computer summary of schedules (*c*) is given. One interesting point concerning the summary is that no cost is given for day 15. Recalling the iterative steps in Table 3.4, going from day 16 to day 15 and from day 15 to day 14 both required crashing jobs G and E. Obviously, the cost increase for day 16 to day 14 is linear and the direct cost for day 15 can be found by splitting the difference between days 14 and 16 direct cost—which gives us $842, the value determined in Table 3.4.

Steps *a* through *h* in the CPM procedure have now been completed. All that remains is to obtain, through steps *i* and *j*, the *minimum total cost schedule.*

Step *i* Logically, Project *indirect costs* have to be obtained through accounting procedures. We will assume for our example that indirect costs equal $500 plus ($30) multiplied by (schedule time). If this is the case, the schedule total costs are as calculated in Table 3.5.

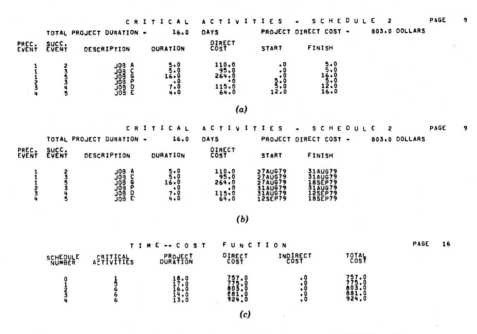

FIGURE 3.9   Sample output of computer solution for example CPM problem.

Step j   The minimum total cost schedule is found to be $1,783 for the 16-day schedule. If an allowable-total-cost feasibility was set by management at $1,790, for example, it can be seen from Table 3.5 that schedules of 16 and 17 days would be acceptable.

In summary, it can be said that CPM does indeed achieve an optimum minimum total cost schedule *assuming* the estimates are valid and assuming the basic times are *deterministic*. CPM has had its prime acceptance in the construction industry, where it might be said that relatively little stochastic

TABLE 3.5   Total Project Costs (Including Indirect Costs)

Time Schedule	Direct Cost($)	Indirect Cost($)	Total Cost($)
18	757	1040	1797
17	775	1010	1785
16	803	980	1783
15	842	950	1792
14	881	920	1801
13	924	890	1814

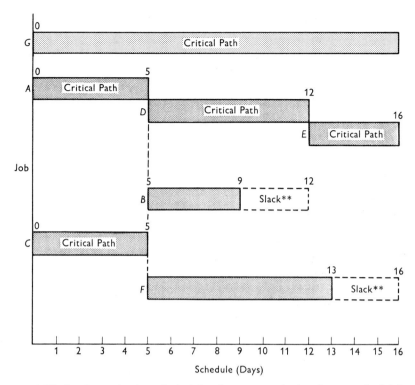

FIGURE 3.10   Optimum schedule for sample problem in Gantt chart format.

effect is present on most jobs. Also, construction estimates are among the best available. A fallacy of CPM that will be corrected in Chapter 8 is the fact that resources are assumed unlimited; if they are not, the schedule arrived at may not be feasible.

As an example, consider the optimum schedule of 16 days for the CPM problem just discussed, on a Gantt chart in Figure 3.10. It can be seen that jobs G, D, B, and F have to be worked on simultaneously at least for day 8. This is assuming jobs B and F are slipped to their latest possible schedule times. If each of these jobs required a forklift full-time during its schedule time, it is obvious that the minimum number of forklifts required is four, assuming no forklift requirement for the other jobs. If only three forklifts are available, the project cannot be met in 16 days. The easiest way out of this dilemma would be to start job F at time period 9. This would create a 17-day schedule.

A more detailed discussion of limited-resource assignment will be presented in Chapter 8. The next topic treated will be PERT, an attempt to introduce stochastic effects in research-and-development project evaluation.

3.4 PROJECT-EVALUATION AND REVIEW-TECHNIQUE (PERT)

One of the shortcomings of CPM has to be its deterministic character. PERT, designed for the research-and-development-type project, attempts to eliminate some of the possible objections to CPM by assuming that each job-time does come from some probability distribution, rather than having fixed time values. The objective of PERT is to obtain from mean and variance estimates for each job a probability distribution for the entire project. Actually, this overall distribution is obtained for the critical path, which is then assumed representative of the project completion characteristics. This latter assumption may or may not be valid, depending on the relative size and distributions of other paths through the network, as contrasted to the critical path. Once a project probability distribution is assumed, then the probability of attainment of certain schedules can be obtained. This then gives management planning information that can be used in evaluating the feasibility of the project.

The job probability distributions are assumed to follow a *beta distribution*, which has the characteristics of being unimodal with finite end points. Depending on the values of the parameters that describe the distribution, it may or may not be symmetrical. Possibly the main reason for adopting the beta distribution was the fact that the mean and variance can be *approximated* very simply by the equations given with typical beta distributions in Figure 3.11. Since the approximation of the mean is based on three parameters, it follows that these parameters (a, b, and m) have to be estimated. The PERT approach, therefore, utilizes *three* time estimates where CPM required two. One possible advantage for PERT is that it forces the planner to think a little more about the estimates for each job. The parameters of a, b, and m can be defined thus:

a The *minimum* time in which the job could reasonably be expected to be accomplished. This could be analogous to the *crash* time in CPM.

Beta Approximations:

$$\text{Mean} = \mu = \frac{a + 4m + b}{6}$$

$$\text{Standard Deviation} = \sigma = \frac{b - a}{6}$$

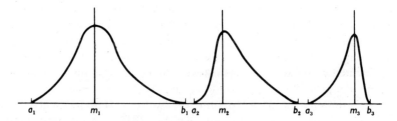

FIGURE 3.11   Typical beta distributions.

b   The *maximum* time in which the job would be expected to take, assuming "normal-type" problems crop up. In the *b* time estimate, those activities classified as "Acts of God" are excluded. Since *a* and *b* define the finite boundaries of the beta distribution, it follows that the estimates of *a* and *b* should take these expected boundaries into consideration.

m   That value of time that is expected to occur the most often. This might be analogous to the *normal* time in CPM.

Once the values of *a*, *m*, and *b* have been estimated for all jobs, their mean and standard deviations are computed, using the beta approximations. From the job means, the critical path(s) are determined in the fashion of CPM. The familiar *central limit theorem* from statistics is interpreted in the determination of the critical-path probability distribution. Basically, it is assumed that if one considers the sum of a group of *independent* variables, each with a mean μ_i and variance σ_i^2, then the sum of these variables will have a distribution that approaches normal, with mean μ equal to the sum of the $\mu_i's$, and a variance σ^2 equal to the sum of the σ_i^2. From the PERT point of view, the jobs on the critical path are assumed independent. The distribution of the critical path times, assuming the central limit theorem is applicable, is assumed normal, with the distribution mean equal to the sum of the means of those jobs on the critical path and the variance equal to the sum of the variances of these same jobs. Where multiple critical paths exist, the variance is assumed to be the larger of the path variances.

Once the project distribution parameters under the guise of the critical path distribution are obtained, the completion probabilities of certain schedules can be obtained using standard normal distribution tables, as given in Appendix A.

As a *PERT example*, consider the same network evolved for the CPM example, with PERT estimates as given in Figure 3.12. The first step in the PERT procedure is to determine the mean for each job, *i*, by:

$$\mu_i = \frac{a + 4m + b}{6}$$

Using these times, the critical path(s) are found in the normal CPM manner. The variance of those jobs on the critical paths are then determined by:

$$\sigma_i^2 = \left(\frac{b - a}{6}\right)^2$$

and the variance of the critical path(s) are determined by summing the individual job variances on the critical path(s). The maximum of these is then assumed to represent the project variance. The result of this initial analysis for the PERT data is summarized in Figure 3.13.

Since two critical paths accrue, the project variance is assumed to be the maximum of the two critical-path variances. For the path *APDE*, the variance

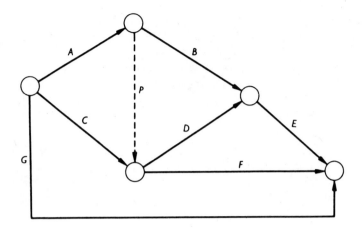

	PERT Time Estimates		
Activity	a	m	b
A	4	6	14
B	3	4	8
C	4	5	6
D	7	7	7
E	3	3	6
F	6	8	14
G	13	18	20

FIGURE 3.12   PERT example network and data.

would be

$$\sigma_A^2 + \sigma_P^2 + \sigma_D^2 + \sigma_E^2 = \frac{100 + 0 + 0 + 9}{36} = \frac{109}{36}$$

For the path G, the variance is

$$\sigma_G^2 = \frac{49}{36}$$

Path $APDE$ has the largest variance and so the project times are assumed to be normally distributed with mean, μ, equal to 17.50 and variance, σ^2, equal to 109/36.

Now, with the normal distribution data given in Appendix A, it is possible to determine the probabilities associated with certain schedules. Appendix A gives the cumulative normal distribution corresponding to the area shown shaded in Figure 3.14a. If the standard variable, Z, as given by the formula

$$Z = \frac{x - \mu}{\sigma} \tag{3.3}$$

I. Mean and Variance Calculations Give:————————

Activity	a	m	b	μ_i*	σ_i^2**
A	4	6	14	7.00	100/36
B	3	4	8	4.50	25/36
C	4	5	6	5.00	4/36
D	7	7	7	7.00	0
E	3	3	6	3.50	9/36
F	6	8	14	8.67	64/36
G	13	18	20	17.50	49/36

$$* \ \mu_i = \frac{a + 4m + b}{6} \qquad ** \ \sigma_i^2 = \left[\frac{b-a}{6}\right]^2$$

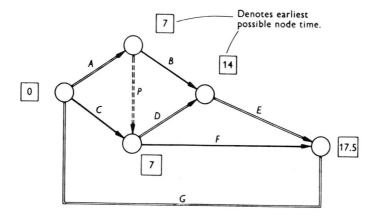

FIGURE 3.13　PERT network and computations.

A.　Definition of μ and x

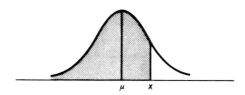

B.　Area with $x < \mu$

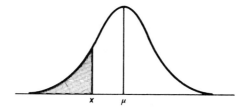

FIGURE 3.14　Areas under the normal curve.

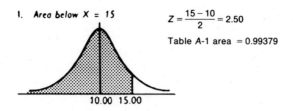

I. *Area below X = 15*

$$Z = \frac{15-10}{2} = 2.50$$

Table A-1 area $= 0.99379$

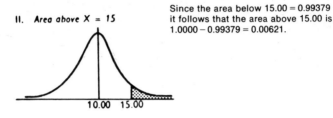

II. *Area above X = 15*

Since the area below 15.00 = 0.99379
it follows that the area above 15.00 is
$1.0000 - 0.99379 = 0.00621$.

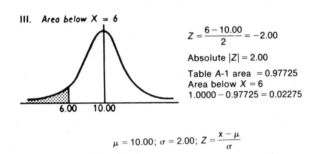

III. *Area below X = 6*

$$Z = \frac{6-10.00}{2} = -2.00$$

Absolute $|Z| = 2.00$

Table A-1 area $= 0.97725$
Area below $X = 6$
$1.0000 - 0.97725 = 0.02275$

$$\mu = 10.00; \ \sigma = 2.00; \ Z = \frac{x - \mu}{\sigma}$$

**FIGURE 3.15 Examples of normal distribution
probability determination.**

is negative, the table value for positive Z (from Appendix A) is subtracted from 1. The result is the shaded area shown in Figure 3.14b. Figure 3.15 gives a few example cases for clarification. For our PERT example, $\sigma^2 = \frac{109}{36}$ and $\mu = 17.50$. The probability for completing a schedule *within* 17.5 days would simply be the area of the normal curve lying *below* 17.50. This is, of course, 50%—which might not be very good from a planning point of view if 17.50 is a desired time constraint. A more logical approach is to determine that schedule which satisfies a particular *probability constraint*. For example, for our PERT problem, if management wants that schedule which has a 95% probability of being completed on time, how do we find it?

First of all we need to find the standard variable, Z, that corresponds to an area under the normal curve of 0.95.

Since Appendix A only gives the top 50% of the area, we need to find the Z value that gives an area of 0.95. This turns out to be about 1.64. Solving

Equation 3.3 in reverse, for the sample PERT data:

$$1.64 = \frac{x - 17.50}{\sqrt{\dfrac{109}{36}}}$$

and

$$x = \frac{(1.64)(10.45)}{6} + 17.50 = 20.35 \text{ days}$$

The interpretation would be that the probability of completing a 21-day schedule on time would be 95%.

PERT attempts to account for some of the stochastic effects prevalent in large-scale projects because of various uncertainties that exist. Specifically, the technique was originally designed for research-and-development projects, which certainly have a large degree of uncertainty, not only in completion times but also in the particular branches that are taken in the network. The end result of the PERT analysis is a probability statement concerning project completion that can be used in management decision-making. For example, if a 95% confidence level is set as satisfactory for completion, the schedule time that will meet that probability can be determined; then, a decision has to be made regarding the reasonability of such a schedule in a project go/no-go situation.

The PERT technique makes a definite contribution. However, it contains many assumptions that may prove somewhat untenable in certain situations. A few of these:

1. PERT requires that *all* jobs be traversed for project completion. This certainly is *not* the case in the research-and-development environment. For example, suppose your company is engaged in the development of machine-tool control by digital computer. A few of the initial jobs might be as shown in Figure 3.16. Once a decision has been made at node 3, only *one* of the two jobs emanating from node 3 will be performed. The same goes for nodes 6 and 7. The argument that the paths out of nodes 4 and 5 are the same holds no water either. The study, its approach and results, would be different for the single-machine versus multiple-machine control situation. One typical final path might be the double-arrow path, with all single-arrow jobs not even being tackled.

2. One consideration in determining a critical path is that the jobs on that path should receive priority treatment so as to ensure that the project will not slip. A fallacy of this argument can be seen in Figure 3.13. If G actually took 20 days and path *APDE* took 14 days—as they could with the given data—there would be no sense in pouring the main effort along path *APDE*, as our original analysis concluded.

3. The assumption of the data distribution for the jobs may not be valid. Even worse, the simple approximations used to calculate the mean and variance

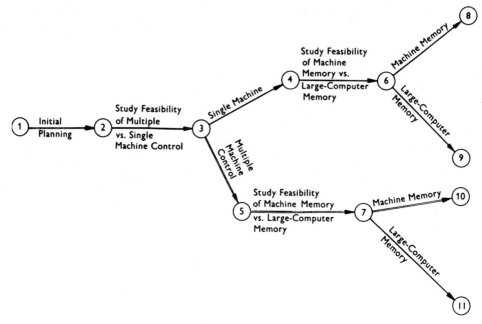

FIGURE 3.16 Research and development network.

may not be correct, especially if the time distribution does not follow the beta distribution.

4. The central limit theorem requires independence of jobs for the pure additive law to work for the mean and variance of the critical path. Conceptually, it is hard to conceive that the times for adjacent jobs would be independent.

5. In line with item 4, the normal distribution assumption for the project may be untenable.

Even though this short list of possible PERT errors may seem traumatic, PERT does present an approach to the stochastic project problem. Subsequent techniques have had one major obstacle—complexity. The next section will introduce some ways that have been suggested to combat the PERT problems.

3.5 NETWORK STOCHASTIC CONSIDERATIONS

Probably the most significant evaluation of PERT assumptions was accomplished by MacCrimmon and Ryavec.† One rather interesting concept

---

†K. R. MacCrimmon, and C. A. Ryavec, "An Analytical Study of the PERT Assumptions, "*Operations Research*, vol. 12, January–February 1964.

they introduced relates to the fact that the concept of a *critical activity* may be more valid than that of the *critical path* in PERT analyses. As they say,

> In a stochastic model, each path has a specific probability (in general, nonzero) of being the longest path at any particular time. However, if the network is large, the probability that any given path is the critical one may be very small. . . . Thus, the most probable critical path may occur only rarely, and an activity that has a high probability of being on a longest path may not be on this most probable critical path.

The objective of determining *critical activities* would be to determine those activities that you want to ensure have no schedule slippage. The usual PERT approach is to calculate a critical path, based on activity means, and then to assume that the activities on that path should be the ones to watch closely. It may be that some activities having the highest probabilities of being on a critical path will not fall on the critical path defined by activity means. Unfortunately, the critical-activity calculations can become extremely cumbersome, probably requiring a computer-simulation analysis in the realistic case. Be that as it may, the concept is certainly interesting.

As a critical activity example, consider the naive network given in Figure 3.17. Three times are given for each activity, with the exception of the two pseudoactivities. Each of the times given have the same probability of

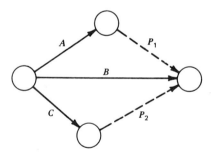

Activity	Times (t) Possible	Probability of Time (t), P(t)
A	1	1/3
	3	1/3
	6	1/3
B	2	1/3
	4	1/3
	5	1/3
C	1	1/3
	3	1/3
	7	1/3

FIGURE 3.17 Critical activity network example

TABLE 3.6   Activities Critical for All Possible Time Combinations

Activity A Possible Times	Activity B Possible Times	Activity C Possible Times		
		1	3	7
	2	B^a	C	C
1	4	B	B	C
	5	B	B	C
	2	A	A, C	C
3	4	B	B	C
	5	B	B	C
	2	A	A	C
6	4	A	A	C
	5	A	A	C

^{a} For combination of times $A = 1$, $C = 1$, $B = 2$; activity B is critical.

occurrence for simplicity of calculation, and these are the *only* times possible.

Since there are three parallel paths, each with three possible time-values, it follows there are 27 possible path combinations, each equally likely. Table 3.6 gives these possible time-values, along with the activities in each combination that are critical. Adding up all times that activities $A, B,$ and C are critical, we find

> **Activity A**   Critical 8 times.
> **Activity B**   Critical 9 times.
> **Activity C**   Critical 11 times.

Since there are 27 combinations, it follows that activity C has a probability of 11/27 of falling on a critical path. If the network were analyzed with activity arithmetic mean values, activities B and C would be most critical, with mean times of 11/3 versus 10/3 for activity A. By PERT, activity B would get the preferred attention since it would be on the critical path. If the three time-estimates for each activity were assumed to be the PERT beta estimates, then the resultant activity means for $A, B,$ and C would be 19/6, 23/6, and 20/6. Activity B would get the preferential treatment. If mathematically feasible, as far as computation is concerned, the *critical activity* approach still does assume that each activity will be traversed. It would be possible to

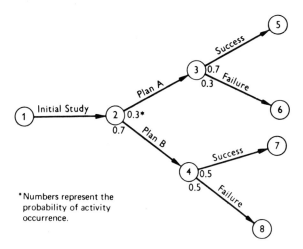

FIGURE 3.18   **Network with stochastic entry to activities.**

reevaluate the situation each time a node has been achieved in the actual project; however, this does not satisfy the desire to determine an *initial* expected duration of the project.

The problem of stochastic *entry* to activities was evaluated by Graham.† He considered that a known probability for entering each activity, once the activity's initial node had been attained, could be estimated. However, the activity *durations* were still assumed at some deterministic mean value. As an example, consider the network of Figure 3.18. Nodes 5 and 7 represent successful project attainment, whereas nodes 6 and 8 indicate the opposite result. The probability of attaining these nodes is as follows:

Node 5 $(0.3)(0.7) = 0.21$.
Node 6 $(0.3)(0.3) = 0.09$.
Node 7 $(0.7)(0.5) = 0.35$.
Node 8 $(0.7)(0.5) = 0.35$.

The probability of success, node 5 or node 7, would have a probability of 0.56. The expected duration of the project could be obtained by:

$$E(\text{Project Length}) = \sum_{\text{all paths}} (\text{Paths Lengths})(\text{Probability of Path}).$$

If the paths to nodes 5, 6, 7 and 8 have time values of 16, 15, 18 and 17,

---

†P. Graham, "Profit Probability Analysis of Research and Development Expenditures," *The Journal of Industrial Engineering*, vol. 16, no. 3, May–June 1965.

respectively, then the expected duration would be

$$(16)(0.21) + (15)(0.09) + (18)(0.35) + (17)(0.35) = 17 \text{ days}$$

Now, how about the combination of activity *length* stochastic effect and stochastic *entry* conditions? This can be handled by the Graphical Evaluation and Review Technique (GERT). In a general introduction to current network techniques, it is not fair to discuss GERT in just a few sentences. Unfortunately, the prerequisite technical knowledge required for GERT goes beyond that intended as a requirement for this text. Knowledge of flow-graph theory, probability moment generating functions, and transmittance calculations is required. The reader interested in further investigation of the application of GERT is advised to utilize those end-of-the-chapter references pertinent to flow-graph theory and to GERT itself in order to determine the validity of GERT for particular applications.[†]

3.6 PROJECT MONITORING: LINE-OF-BALANCE[‡]

The project planning techniques discussed so far have generally been oriented to *pre*project planning. An equally important planning problem is concerned with monitoring the project's adherence to the planned schedule and then planning action to correct deviations from the schedule. A simple but extremely effective approach for monitoring project progress and pinpointing some corrective action as needed is the line-of-balance (LOB) technique. LOB was developed during World War II, as were many innovative production techniques, for monitoring large military projects. From a production control point of view, LOB can be effective in maintaining production schedules where a large number of product units have to be produced according to an agreed-upon contract. Another area of utilization is the determination of in-process inventory levels needed to ensure completion of manufactured items on time (an exercise at the end of the chapter asks the reader to hypothesize how this might be accomplished).

LOB requires an objective chart, a progress chart, and a production lead-time chart. All three charts have to be developed in the preplanning phase of the production project, and their development will force sound planning at the project's inception.

Objective Chart   The objective chart shows the contract schedule contrasted to actual performance against that schedule. For example, suppose a microcomputer manufacturer agrees to subcontract microcomputers for a television game manufacturer according to the schedule given in Table 3.7.

[†]See references 9 and 10 (Whitehouse).
[‡]This technique is not truly applicable to PERT or CPM, because they are one-of-a-kind projects, not repetitive. Line-of-balance is widely applicable in many production projects.

TABLE 3.7   Contract Schedule for LOB

Number of Work Days after January 2	Cumulative Number of Microcomputers Produced by the Associated Work Days
0	0
20	10
40	25
60	45
80	70
100	105
120	150

Actual progress against the contract schedule is given in Table 3.8. The "actual progress" from the objective chart is not really used in the LOB approach, but it is always best to show as much valid and pertinent information as possible, so that effective decisions can be made. Figure 3.19 certainly shows that the 150 microcomputers contracted for will not be realized in 120 working days if the schedule is not expedited in some manner.

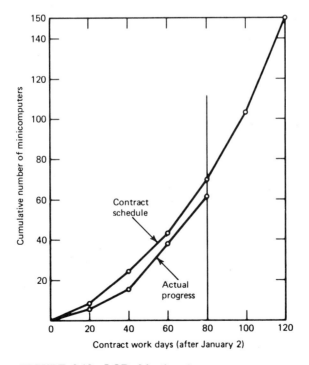

FIGURE 3.19   LOB objective chart.

TABLE 3.8   Actual Progress Data Through 80 Project Days

Number of Work Days after January 2	Cumulative Number of Microcomputers Produced by the Associated Work Days
0	0
20	8
40	18
60	35
80	62
100	
120	

Production Lead-Time Chart   The lead-time chart shows in network format the actual times required for producing one unit of the contracted product; in the current example, this unit is one microcomputer. In order to evaluate if and where problems are occurring, the lead-time diagram breaks the production of the unit into logical components, as shown in Figure 3.20.

The lead-time diagram tells us several things. First, the overall time to manufacture one microcomputer is a maximum of 12 working days. The nodes at the beginning and end of each activity represent unique points in time. In order for a particular unit to be completed by a particular date, the building of the control unit, for example, would have to commence at least eight working days prior to that date. This information, combined with the objective-chart information, can be used to show the required status of each node, in terms of the number of items required for the microcomputer that have to have passed through each node in order for the project to be completed by the final due date. Also, if the current status of each node is known, it is possible to determine where in the project problems are being caused. The third chart, the progress chart, allows this to be accomplished.

Progress Chart   The progress chart is a bar chart (one bar for each node given on the lead-time diagram) that shows the *actual* units that have progressed through each node as of the reporting date. In addition, using the lead-time diagram and the objective chart gives the *required* units through each node needed to guarantee just meeting the overall production schedule. And an analysis of the results can show not only *where* problems might exist, but also *why* they exist. The progress chart for the microcomputer example is given in Figure 3.21. Obviously, the information regarding actual units passing

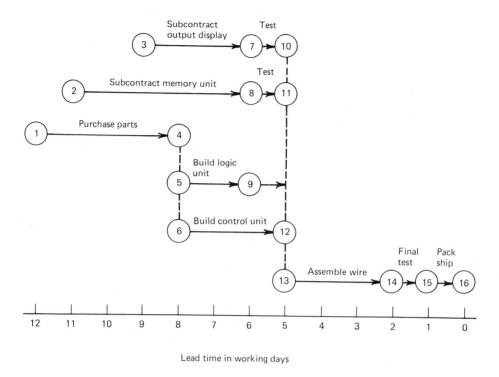

FIGURE 3.20 LOB lead-time diagram.

through each node has to be obtained from current records. For example, the progress chart shows that orders for 100 units have been released by purchasing (node 1) and that about 84 units have been delivered by the vendor (node 4).

The line-of-balance given on the chart shows the number of units that should have passed through each node in order to ensure that the overall schedule can be met. Comparing the line-of-balance with actual progress reveals the fact that nodes 5, 6, 8, 9, and 11–16 are behind schedule. As we shall soon see, a further investigation of the results will show where corrective action has to be taken in order to get the project back on schedule.

The line-of-balance is very simple to construct utilizing the *objective chart* and the *lead-time diagram*. The objective chart shows that to be on schedule, we should have completed at least 70 units through 80 days. The number of units passing through any node on the lead-time diagram would have to be 70 *plus* the number that would be *produced in the leadtime*. For example, node 1 has a leadtime of 12 working days. The number of items that would have to be released by purchasing is at least the number of units

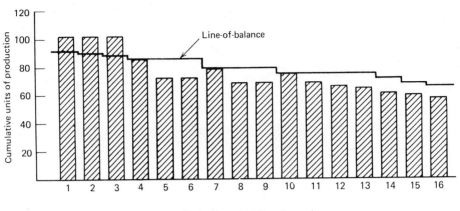

FIGURE 3.21   LOB progress chart.

required by contract workday 92 (80 days plus the 12-day lead time). This
would be about 91 units. In a similar fashion, nodes 4, 5, and 6 should have
had at least 84 units passing through, the number required at contract day 88
(80 days plus an eight-day lead time). The overall line-of-balance values are
given in Table 3.9.

Since nodes in the lead-time diagram were numbered in an ascending
sequence from left to right and top to bottom, it follows that scanning from
left to right those progress chart nodes not meeting the schedule will give an
indication of where major problems are occurring. The first two nodes to be
considered in this manner would be 5 and 6. The lead-time diagram shows that
even though sufficient parts are available for the logic and control units to be
on schedule, *starting* units into production is behind schedule. This of course
causes assembly and wiring, final testing, and pack and ship to be behind.
Similarly, node 8 being behind shows that the subcontractor building memory
units should be pressured to conform to the schedule, since he is causing
slippage in memory test, assembly and wire, final test, and pack and ship. The
amount of slippage in subsequent operations will show if the slippage is
caused entirely by preceding operations or whether part of the problem exists
in the specific operation itself. Since for Table 3.9, nodes 5 and 6 have the
most slippage of any node, it follows that the major problem regarding
slippage has to be the release of parts to the logic and control-unit production
functions.

The overall line-of-balance procedure would obviously be computerized
for large projects. Some organizations place the lead-time diagram on clear
plastic adjacent to the objective chart. If correct scaling is utilized, the
lead-time diagram can be folded over the objective chart in order to pinpoint
the units needed directly. Whatever the method used, there is no doubt that

TABLE 3.9 Line-of-Balance Values and Slippage

Node	Lead Time (Days)	Minimum Units Required (objective chart value at day (80 + lead time))	Actual Units Processed (Progress Chart)	Slippage (units)
1	12	91	100	0
2	11	90	100	0
3	9	86	100	0
4	8	84	84	0
5	8	84	70	14
6	8	84	70	14
7	6	81	81	0
8	6	81	70	11
9	6	81	70	11
10	5	79	78	1
11	5	79	70	9
12	5	79	68	11
13	5	79	66	13
14	2	74	64	10
15	1	72	63	9
16	0	70	62	8

the line-of-balance approach gives a simple yet effective method for project monitoring where the projects are repetitive in nature.

3.7 CASE PROBLEM—CPM

The conversion of a conventional numerical-control facility (N/C) to an integrated-computer-control operation (ICC) has been approved for the Automachine Company's specialized production facility. The ICC operation is expected to increase considerably production output and overall profits. During conversion, existing N/C equipment will be nonproductive for a considerable period of time. This period will be followed by a shorter partial-production (break-in) time. The Production Planning and Analysis group has been given the task of scheduling the conversion in the optimum manner possible.

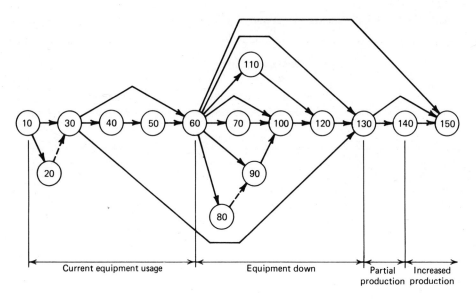

FIGURE 3.22   Case problem network diagram.

Many days were spent with the ICC contractor and plant maintenance people in order to identify which activities needed to be accomplished and to specify the interactions between those activities. The result of those meetings is the network diagram given in Figure 3.22, with activity descriptions as shown in Table 3.10. The discussions also evolved cost and time ranges for each activity, and the usual CPM assumption of a linear-cost slope for affected activities was made. The Production Planning and Analysis Group was told to only consider direct costs in their analysis, and these are given in Table 3.11. Finally, potential daily profits were estimated for the following four project conditions:

Current equipment status (N/C) $9500/day.

Equipment down $4500/day.

Partial production (break-in) $8500/day.

ICC operation $13,000/day.

These profit figures are independent of project costs. The unusual $4,500/day profit with equipment down results from selling excess inventory. Also, production workers' cost is given to the project's retraining activities during the down-time period.

The Production Planning and Analysis Group next ran the project data through a UNIVAC 1110 CPM program to determine feasible schedules and costs to the project. Five schedules resulted:

Schedule Number	Duration (days)	Direct Cost ($)
0	148	1,142,400
1	146	1,144,200
2	141	1,151,700
3	138	1,169,400
4	133	1,204,400

TABLE 3.10   Case-Problem Activity Descriptions

Activity	Description
10–20	Describe existing setup and conversion needs.
10–30	Develop specifications for new system.
20–30	Pseudoactivity.
30–40	Release bid material.
30–60	Work overtime to develop buffer inventory to cover down periods.
30–130	Rework inventory area to increase capacity.
40–50	Evaluate bids.
50–60	Let contract.
60–70	Instrument N/C equipment for ICC.
60–80	Construct computer room on production floor.
60–90	Modify standard minicomputer for Automachine's specifications.
60–100	Redo electrical supply.
60–110	Develop ICC Software.
60–130	Retrain retained workers for ICC.
60–150	Retrain released workers.
70–100	Test N/C instrumentation off-line.
80–90	Pseudoactivity.
90–100	Install computer.
100–120	Install wiring—computer to N/C.
110–120	Test ICC software off-line.
120–130	Test ICC software on-line.
130–140	Phase-in production.
130–150	Cleanup.
140–150	Final check and sign off.

TABLE 3.11   Case-Problem CPM Data

Activity	Direct Costs ($)		Duration (days)	
	Normal	Crash	Normal	Crash
10–20	5000	7000	10	7
10–30	30,000	37,500	30	25
20–30	—	—	—	—
30–40	1000	1000	3	3
30–60	200,000	200,000	20	20
30–130	87,500	105,000	75	50
40–50	1300	1300	10	10
50–60	600	600	4	4
60–70	160,500	160,500	35	35
60–80	185,000	240,000	30	28
60–90	19,000	19,000	20	20
60–100	14,000	19,000	42	38
60–110	35,000	35,000	43	43
60–130	90,000	90,000	60	60
60–150	120,000	120,000	80	80
70–100	8000	8000	10	10
80–90	—	—	—	—
90–100	7500	10,000	15	10
100–120	20,500	25,000	25	20
110–120	30,000	45,000	25	22
120–130	12,000	12,000	8	8
130–140	105,000	140,000	15	10
130–150	4500	4500	5	5
140–150	6000	6000	5	5

Figure 3.22 shows that three nodes are critical to the cost analysis. Node 60 gives the length of time during which current usage of the equipment is maintained. Node 130 shows when partial production with ICC can be started. Node 140 indicates when increased production with ICC is feasible. Table 3.12 gives the time data associated with the five schedules and the nodes under question. Exercises at the end of the chapter ask the interested reader to verify computer outputs given in this example.

Using the four profit values, overall costs during the project period can

TABLE 3.12 Time Data Associated with Case-Problem Feasible Schedules

Schedule Number	Current Equipment Usage (days) [Node 60]	Equipment Down (days) [Node 130–Node 60]	Partial Production (days) [Node 140–Node 130]	Increased Production (days)[a] [148 days–Node 140]
0	50	78	15	5
1	50	76	15	7
2	45	76	15	12
3	45	73	15	15
4	45	73	10	20

[a]In order to handle *all* schedules equitably in the cost analysis, increased production was evaluated for a 148-day schedule—the normal-time schedule

be found by:

$$\text{CPM Direct Cost}-(N60)\,(9500)-(N130-N60)\,(4500)$$
$$-(N140-N130)\,(8500)$$
$$-(148-N140)\,(13,000)$$

where N60, N130, etc., stands for the time to Node 60, Node 130, and so on. The net costs for the five schedules turn out to be as follows.

Schedule Number	Net Costs ($)
0	+123,900
1	+108,700
2	+98,700
3	+90,900
4	+103,400

The Production Planning and Analysis Group recommended schedule 3, in order to minimize overall losses. Figure 3.23 gives the *relative* dating schedule and Figure 3.24 gives the management *calendar*-dated schedule. The

```
                    ACTIVITY LIST - SCHEDULE 3                PAGE  10

            TOTAL PROJECT DURATION -    138.0  DAYS       PROJECT DIRECT COST - 116940.0 TENS OF $$

   PREC. SUCC.                          DIRECT     EARLIEST         LATEST              FLOAT
   EVENT EVENT  DESCRIPTION   DURATION    COST   START - FINISH  START - FINISH  TOTAL  FREE  INDEP.
```

PREC. EVENT	SUCC. EVENT	DESCRIPTION	DURATION	DIRECT COST	EARLIEST START	FINISH	LATEST START	FINISH	TOTAL	FLOAT FREE	INDEP.
	10	20	DESCR EXISTG	10.0	500.0	.0	10.0	15.0	25.0	15.0	.0	.0
**	10	30	SYSTEM SPECS	25.0	3750.0	.0	25.0	.0	25.0	.0	.0	.0
*	20	30	DUMMY	.0	.0	10.0	10.0	25.0	25.0	15.0	15.0	.0
*	30	40	RELEASE BIDS	3.0	100.0	25.0	28.0	28.0	31.0	3.0	.0	.0
**	30	60	BUFFER INVNT	20.0	20000.0	25.0	45.0	25.0	45.0	.0	.0	.0
	30	130	STORAGE CAPC	75.0	8750.0	25.0	100.0	43.0	118.0	18.0	18.0	18.0
*	40	50	BID EVALUATE	10.0	130.0	28.0	38.0	31.0	41.0	3.0	.0	.0
*	50	60	LET CONTRACT	4.0	60.0	38.0	42.0	41.0	45.0	3.0	3.0	.0
**	60	70	INSTR EXISTG	35.0	16050.0	45.0	80.0	45.0	80.0	.0	.0	.0
*	60	80	COMPUT ROOM	30.0	18500.0	45.0	75.0	45.0	75.0	.0	.0	.0
	60	90	COMPUT MODIF	20.0	1900.0	45.0	65.0	55.0	75.0	10.0	10.0	10.0
	60	100	REDO ELEC SP	42.0	1400.0	45.0	87.0	48.0	90.0	3.0	3.0	3.0
**	60	110	ICC SOFTWARE	43.0	3500.0	45.0	88.0	45.0	88.0	.0	.0	.0
*	60	130	TRN ICC PERS	60.0	9000.0	45.0	105.0	58.0	118.0	13.0	13.0	13.0
*	60	150	RETRAIN WKRS	80.0	12000.0	45.0	125.0	58.0	138.0	13.0	13.0	13.0
**	70	100	TST OFFLN MC	10.0	800.0	80.0	90.0	80.0	90.0	.0	.0	.0
**	80	90	DUMMY	.0	.0	75.0	75.0	75.0	75.0	.0	.0	.0
*	90	100	COMPUT INSTL	15.0	750.0	75.0	90.0	75.0	90.0	.0	.0	.0
**	100	120	WIRING-MC/CN	20.0	2500.0	90.0	110.0	90.0	110.0	.0	.0	.0
**	110	120	TST ICC OFFL	22.0	4500.0	88.0	110.0	88.0	110.0	.0	.0	.0
**	120	130	TST ICC ONLN	8.0	1200.0	110.0	118.0	110.0	118.0	.0	.0	.0
*	130	140	PHASE-IN PRD	15.0	10500.0	118.0	133.0	118.0	133.0	.0	.0	.0
*	130	150	CLEAN-UP	5.0	450.0	118.0	123.0	133.0	138.0	15.0	15.0	15.0
**	140	150	FINAL CHECK	5.0	600.0	133.0	138.0	133.0	138.0	.0	.0	.0

FIGURE 3.23   Relative-Dated schedule for case problem produced by computer.

```
                    A C T I V I T Y   L I S T   -   S C H E D U L E   3              PAGE  10

            TOTAL PROJECT DURATION -     138.0 DAYS        PROJECT DIRECT COST -  116940.0 TENS OF 10

PREC.  SUCC.                                DIRECT     EARLIEST          LATEST             FLOAT
EVENT  EVENT   DESCRIPTION      DURATION     COST    START - FINISH   START - FINISH   TOTAL  FREE  INDEP.

        10    20   DESCR EXISTS     10.0      500.0   22AUG80  26EP80   9SEP80 23SEP80   15.0    .0    .0
  **    10    30   SYSTEM SPECS     25.0     3750.0   22AUG80 23SEP80  22AUG80 23SEP80    .0     .0    .0
  *     20    30   DUMMY             .0        .0     26SEP80  26SEP80  23SEP80 23SEP80   15.0   15.0   .0
  *     30    40   RELEASE BIDS      3.0      100.0   23SEP80 26SEP80  28SEP80 30CT80    3.0     .0    .0
  **    30    60   BUFFER INVNT     20.0    20000.0   23SEP80 21OCT80  23SEP80 21OCT80    .0     .0    .0
        30   130   STORAGE CAPC     75.0     8750.0   23SEP80 12JAN81  19OCT80  7FEB81   18.0   18.0  18.0
  *     40    50   BID EVALUATE     10.0      130.0   28SEP80 12OCT80  30CT80 17OCT80    3.0     .0    .0
  *     50    60   LET CONTRACT      4.0       60.0   12OCT80 18OCT80  17OCT80 21OCT80    3.0    3.0    .0
  **    60    70   INSTR EXISTS     35.0    16050.0   21OCT80 13DEC80  21OCT80 13DEC80    .0     .0    .0
  *     60    80   COMPUT ROOM      30.0    18500.0   21OCT80  6DEC80  21OCT80  6DEC80    .0     .0    .0
  *     60    90   COMPUT MODIF     20.0     1900.0   21OCT80 21NOV80   7NOV80  6DEC80   10.0   10.0  10.0
        60   100   REDO ELEC SP     42.0     1400.0   21OCT80 22DEC80  26OCT80 28DEC80    3.0    3.0    3.0
  **    60   110   ICC SOFTWARE     43.0     3500.0   21OCT80 23DEC80  21OCT80 23DEC80    .0     .0    .0
  *     60   130   TRN ICC PERS     60.0     9000.0   21OCT80 19JAN81  10NOV80  7FEB81   13.0   13.0  13.0
  *     60   150   RETRAIN WKRS     80.0    12000.0   21OCT80 17FEB81  10NOV80  8MAR81   13.0   13.0  13.0
  **    70   100   TST OFFLN NC     10.0      800.0   13DEC80 28DEC80  13DEC80 28DEC80    .0     .0    .0
  **    80    90   DUMMY             .0        .0      6DEC80  6DEC80   6DEC80  6DEC80    .0     .0    .0
  *     90   100   COMPUT INSTL     15.0      750.0    6DEC80 28DEC80   6DEC80 28DEC80    .0     .0    .0
  **   100   120   WIRING-NC/CM     20.0     2500.0   28DEC80 26JAN81  28DEC80 26JAN81    .0     .0    .0
  **   110   120   TST ICC OFFL     22.0     4500.0   23DEC80 26JAN81  23DEC80 26JAN81    .0     .0    .0
  **   120   130   TST ICC ONLN      8.0     1200.0   26JAN81  7FEB81  26JAN81  7FEB81    .0     .0    .0
  *    130   140   PHASE-IN PRD     15.0    10500.0    7FEB81  1MAR81   7FEB81  1MAR81    .0     .0    .0
  *    130   150   CLEAN-UP          5.0      450.0    7FEB81 14FEB81   1MAR81  8MAR81   15.0   15.0  15.0
  **   140   150   FINAL CHECK       5.0      600.0    1MAR81  8MAR81   1MAR81  8MAR81    .0     .0    .0
```

FIGURE 3.24 Calendar-dated schedule for case problem produced by computer.

latter schedule assumed a five-day work week with holidays on December 25, 1980; January 1, 1981; February 16, 1981 (President's Day). The direct-cost figures in the computer output should be multiplied by 10, since the input data had to be coded because of restrictions on field size.

This case problem could obviously have been handled without a computer, as the reader can easily verify with certain exercises at the end of the chapter. The problem is intended to demonstrate that CPM-type algorithms can be applied to production-oriented systems and are not just restricted to construction projects. One very beneficial application in Phoenix, Ariz., involved the planning of moving hospital equipment and patients to a brand-new facility. Although cost optimization was not involved, as might well be the case in most applications, elimination of bottlenecks during the several-day move and optimization of the move *time* was accomplished.

To maintain the authors' philosophy that the initial chapters of this text be concerned with *planning*, the next chapter will cover forecasting, primarily as a planning tool. Readers who would like to continue further with the project scheduling material under limited resource constraints should go directly to Chapter 8 and then return to Chapter 4.

3.8 REFERENCES

1. Bedworth, David D., *Industrial Systems*; *Planning, Analysis, Control*, John Wiley, New York, 1973.

2. Bittel, Lester R. (ed.), "Network Planning Methods," in *Encyclopedia of Professional Management*, McGraw-Hill, New York, 1978.

3. M. Elmaghraby, S. E., "An Algebra for the Analysis of Generalized Activity Networks," *Management Science*, vol. 10, no. 3, 1964.

4. Fry, B. L., *Network-Type Management Control Systems Bibliography*, *Memorandum RM-3074-PR*, The Rand Corporation, Santa Monica, Cal., February 1963. (Lists most of the literature available prior to 1963.)

5. Graham, P., "Profit Probability Analysis of Research and Development Expenditures," *The Journal of Industrial Engineering*, vol. 16, no. 3, May–June 1965.

6. Kelley, James E., and Walker, M., "Critical-Path Planning and Scheduling," *Proceedings Eastern Joint Computer Conference*, 1959.

7. MacCrimmon, K. R., and Ryavec, C. A., "An Analytical Study of the PERT Assumptions," *Operations Research*, vol. 12, January–February 1964.

8. Moder, J. J., and Phillips, C. R., *Project Management with CPM and PERT*, 2nd ed., Reinhold, New York, 1970.

9. Whitehouse, G. E., "Extension, New Developments and Applications of GERT," Ph.D. dissertation, Arizona State University, August, 1965.

10. Whitehouse, G. E., *Systems Analysis and Design Using Network Techniques*, Prentice-Hall, Englewood Cliffs, N.J., 1973.

11. Wiest, J. D., and Levy, F. K., *A Management Guide to PERT/CPM*, 2nd ed., Prentice-Hall, Englewood Cliffs, N.J., 1977.

3.9 EXERCISES

1. Given below are a group of jobs along with their immediately preceding jobs. Develop a network for these jobs, minimizing as far as possible the number of pseudoactivities.

Job	Immediate Predecessor(s)	Job	Immediate Predecessor(s)
A	None	H	B, E
B	None	I	C, H
C	None	J	H
D	None	K	G, H
E	A	L	I, J
F	C, H	M	D, F
G	E		

2. Given below, are a group of jobs, along with their immediate preceding jobs. Develop a network for these jobs, minimizing as far as possible the number of pseudoactivities.

Job	Immediate Predecessor(s)
A	None
B	A
C	A
D	A
E	B
F	C, E
G	C
H	D
I	None

3. Normal activity times for the activities listed in Problem 1 are as given below. Determine the critical path(s).

Activity	Normal Time
A	3
B	5
C	4
D	3
E	6
F	7
G	4
H	5
I	6
J	4
K	4
L	2
M	5

4. Times and direct costs for the activities listed in Problem 2 are as given below. Determine the network's range of CPM schedule times and associated direct costs.

	Times (days)		Costs ($)	
Activity	Normal	Crash	Normal	Crash
A	5	5	2500	2500
B	6	4	4600	5200
C	10	8	3800	4800
D	7	6	2800	3200
E	3	2	4300	4650
F	3	2	1300	1600
G	2	1	5200	5900
H	6	5	4100	4600
I	10	7	6800	8450

5. Indirect costs for the project with data given in Problem 4 are $1,000 per day. Determine the schedule that has the minimum total cost. Also, sketch the indirect costs, direct costs, and total costs, all as a function of schedule time.

6. A CPM computer program could be of distinct help in solving this problem, though it can be accomplished manually. A pipeline project has the network given in Figure 3.25. Costs and times are as follows.

	Times (days)		Costs ($)	
Activity	Normal	Crash	Normal	Crash
10–20	10	10	200	200
20–30	20	20	2000	2000
20–40	40	40	1800	1800
20–70	28	20	3000	4000
30–50	8	8	900	900
50–60	30	12	3000	6240
60–80	24	14	4900	8200
70–90	10	10	400	400
80–90	12	8	2500	3200
90–110	10	5	3500	6900
90–120	6	6	400	400
100–110	6	5	500	750
110–120	4	4	600	600
120–130	4	2	1500	1500

Determine the feasible project time-range and direct cost for each.

Activity Descriptions

Activity	Description	Activity	Description
A	Lead time	K	Pseudo
B	Equipment to site	L	Test pipe
C	Get pipe	M	Cover pipe
D	Get valve	N	Clean up
E	Lay out line	O	Complete valve work
F	Excavate	P	Leave site
G	Pseudo		
H	Lay pipe		
I	Concrete work		
J	Install valve		

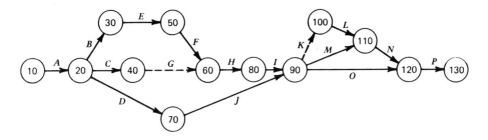

FIGURE 3.25 Problem 6 pipeline network.

7. Indirect costs for the project given in Problem 6 are $650 per day. Determine the schedule that minimizes overall costs.
8. Resources are required for the schedule determined in Problem 7 as follows:

Activity	Surveyors	Laborers	Welders	Trenchers	Crane	Trucks
10–20	0	1	0	0	0	0
20–30	0	4	0	0	0	2
20–40	0	2	0	0	0	1
20–70	0	2	0	0	0	1
30–50	1	2	0	0	0	0
50–60	0	2	0	1	0	0
60–80	0	4	1	0	1	0
70–90	0	1	0	0	1	0
80–90	0	5	0	0	0	1
90–110	0	2	0	0	0	0
90–120	0	2	0	0	0	1
100–110	0	2	1	0	0	0
110–120	0	3	0	0	1	1
120–130	0	4	0	0	0	2

Resources cannot be split between activities and are utilized during the entire duration of the project. If the maximum number of resource units available at any time to the project is as given below, is the minimum cost schedule feasible?

Resource	Maximum Available
Surveyors	1
Laborers	5
Welders	1
Trenchers	1
Crane	1
Trucks	2

9. Consider the following information for an extremely simple project, the network for which is given in Figure 3.26.

	Times (days)		Direct Costs ($)	
Activity	Normal	Crash	Normal	Crash
1–2	4	3	70	100
1–3	6	5	30	50
2–3	3	2	95	120
2–4	4	3	40	70
3–4	2	1	65	100

Determine the minimum direct costs for each feasible schedule.
NOTE: One difficulty in using the crashing algorithm that the computer can

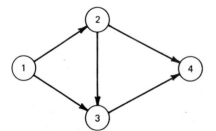

FIGURE 3.26   Problem 9 simple network.

easily resolve, is the fact that sometimes it is advantageous to *relax* an activity rather than crash it. This means that after an activity has been crashed at least one time-unit, it might be cheaper in a later iteration to *increase* the time of the activity.

10. Consider the network developed for Problem 1. PERT data is given for this network as follows:

Activity	a	m	b
A	1	2	3
B	2	4	6
C	3	3	3
D	3	5	7
E	1	1	1
F	1	4	7
G	2	3	4
H	1	3	5
I	3	3	3
J	4	5	6
K	2	3	10
L	5	5	5
M	8	9	16

a. What completion schedule has a 95% probability of being met?
b. What is the probability of completing activity H by six time-periods?
c. What is the probability of completing the project in 16 time-periods?

11. Consider the PERT network given in Figure 3.27 with the associated a, m, and b times given above each activity.

a. What is the probability of completing the project in 30 time-periods?
b. What project duration has a 65% probability of being met?
c. What is the probability of node 7 being completed within 20 time-periods?

12. The original PERT system had activities on nodes rather than on arrows. This meant that each node represented a job and arrows gave precedence relationships only. Even though the activity-on-arrow is now the more popular concept, why might activity-on-node networks be easier to develop?

13. Normally, CPM and PERT are techniques oriented to one-of-a-kind projects. Discuss the applicability of these techniques to repeating type projects, say in assembly-line development.

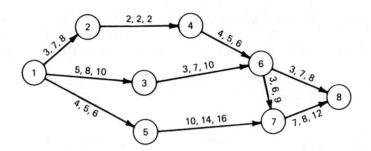

FIGURE 3.27   Problem 11 PERT network.

14. Consider the CPM problem with data in Problems 2, 4, and 5. Income is dependent on completion data and is estimated as follows:

    20 days—$85,000
    19 days—$90,000
    18 days—$92,000
    17 days—$93,000
    16 days—$94,000
    15 days—$96,000
    14 days—$98,000

    What schedule would you recommend that management follow? What does this say about the traditional CPM minimum total-cost schedule being optimum?

15. The case problem given in Section 3.7 was attacked by a computer that gave output for durations of 148, 146, 141, 138, and 133 days. The 138-day schedule was optimum. Evaluate the overall project profit and cost picture for durations of 137 days and 139 days, to determine if the intermediate values need to be considered.

16. The case problem in Section 3.7 considered only direct costs. Discuss under what circumstances it might be legitimate to attack a CPM-oriented problem without apparent regard to indirect costs.

17. Discuss how line-of-balance concepts might be applied to determining the amounts of buffer inventory required at various stages of a production line.

18. The RIPOFF Company has a contract to supply 900 quimlys over a 13-week period; 50 per week are required over the first six weeks, 75 per week over the next four weeks, and 100 per week over the last three weeks. The lead-time diagram for producing one quimly is given in Figure 3.28. So far, the number of quimlys that have progressed through each of the nodes in the lead time diagram are

Node	Units Processed
1	810
2	805
3	700
4	680
5	710
6	580
7	600
8	610
9	500
10	500
11	430

At the end of week 8, the contractor complains that RIPOFF is 20 units behind in deliveries. RIPOFF indicates that subcontractors, who control jobs 2–7 and 5–8, are to blame. Evaluate completely RIPOFF's claim.

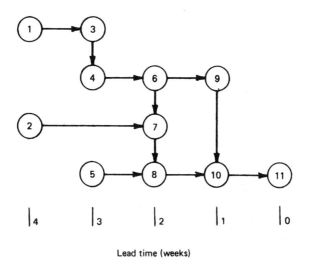

Lead time (weeks)

FIGURE 3.28   Problem 18 lead-time diagram.

FOUR: FORECASTING

If a man take no thought about what is distant, he will find sorrow near at hand.

Confucius

In planning a vacation, knowledge of future weather expectations, if feasible, would be desirable. Calling for a weatherbureau forecast might not be optimum, however, for example, in World War II Winston Churchill was quite caustic when he found that meteorological forecasts were accurate less than 50% of the time. His response supposedly was that "then they should forecast the opposite of what they scientifically determine and they would be accurate over 50% of the time." Of course, weather forecasting is not binary, and so Churchill's response was not really fair. It does show that *error analysis* might be used to good advantage, as will be seen later in this chapter.

Forecasting can be loosely classed into two types: qualitative and quantitative. A market research team asking user preference information in order to predict sales characteristics performs a *qualitative* forecast, though it might be rightly argued that analysis of the data accumulated is quantitative. This chapter will be oriented to forecasting in cases in which future values are assumed to follow historical data characteristics. Further, it will be assumed that the data is *correlated to time*, leading to the concept of *time-series analysis*. Sales trends, manufacturing-to-sales needs, and inventory characteristics are just three processes out of hundreds that usually can be analyzed and predicted through *time-series analysis* techniques.

4.1 GENERAL CONSIDERATIONS

Forecasting is a true "systems" tool. The underlying concepts of time-series analysis come from automatic control theory and statistical analysis. Certain techniques for determining predominant frequencies in information theory can be just as applicable to finding cyclic relationships in sales data. Mathematical procedures for determining polynomial relationships can certainly be applied to determining growth trends in sales data.

The most logical general consideration to be covered first is the *benefit* of forecasting. After this, the three forecasting criteria of accuracy, simplicity of calculation, and ability to adjust the rate of response will be discussed. The requirements for the forecast to a large degree will dictate the emphasis placed on the three criteria in each individual forecasting case. The last general consideration will be to discuss briefly the concept of *lead time* within the forecasting system. Obviously, a whole book could be written on the topic of forecasting. Such considerations as share of the market, correlation with federal indices, and so on, would be—and should be—discussed. However, those considerations deemed beneficial only for *sales* forecasting will not be discussed. Several excellent books and pamphlets† deal with this topic in detail. The following material, including the time-series information, is given as an *introduction* to the more general *systems* concept of forecasting.

The total cost of a forecast includes the cost of forecast-method development, the cost of actually making the forecast, and the cost of forecast errors. The cost of method development, while minimal, may result in high error costs. Minimizing error costs could result in a very complex forecasting procedure that would have high development costs and perhaps high application costs. Not realizing that forecasting costs are the sum of costs for interacting factors could easily result in a forecast procedure being more expensive overall than a nonforecast method. The most obvious *benefit* of using a forecast procedure is that a system employing a forecast is not operating in a vacuum as regards real-world conditions. The use of forecasting of course, assumes that conditions of *uncertainty* exist for the particular system. There are few sales-demand cases, in which the demand for the product exceeds the capacity to produce; demand is then limited to capacity. Long-term conditions may not be so predictable however. Therefore, in any system that has uncertain characteristics, such as customer whims, economic fluctuations, weather variations, or flight landing conditions, the ability to observe applicable conditions and make subsequent predictions allows a measure of knowledge to be inserted into the uncertainty categories. If nothing else, the need for forecasting to be based on something tangible necessitates *thinking* about what affects the forecast and to what degree. This, in itself, has to be a benefit of forecasting.

The two primary, and obvious, considerations to be made in determining a *forecasting approach* are What is the forecast to be used for? and Why is it to be used? The answers to these two questions will dictate, for the most part, the forecast approach. For example, suppose a large, multibuilding utility company wants a long-term forecast of office-space needs over a 20-year period. If this forecast is to be used to convince the board of directors that the office workers were going to be more efficient in the future, and if the

---

†One particularly excellent pamphlet is *Forecasting Sales—Studies in Business Policy, No.* 106, published by the National Industrial Conference Board, Inc.

reason behind this amazing conclusion is to bolster certain managers' positions in the eyes of the directors, then the tack taken by the forecast approach might be just to solicit opinions from managers. If, in the realistic case, the prediction is to be used to show additional space needs in five-year increments for *capital expenditure* planning in obtaining the necessary land, the forecast approach would be much more complex. Relating office-space needs to economic fluctuations, past trends, technology productivity improvements, population shifts, and other factors would be mandatory. A complex mathematical model would be needed, probably programmed for the digital computer.

Brown suggests that the criteria for forecasting fall into the three categories of *accuracy, simplicity of computation,* and *flexibility to adjust the rate of response.*† Even though these three criteria are primarily geared to time-series analysis, they are just as applicable to any type of forecast model.

The meaning of the term *accuracy* in forecasting is self-evident. It is a measure of how well a forecasted condition matches the actual condition when it occurs. In general, high accuracy requirements will not allow *simplicity of computation.* Therefore, a trade-off between the two is usually required. If time is of the essence—as in the prediction of when to adjust tension rolls in a steel-rolling process in order to maintain required steel thickness and yet avoid shear when the steel is moving at a speed of hundreds of feet a minute—a lot of time cannot be spent in actually calculating the forecast if data have to be computer-scanned every hundredth of a second. In the test of a rocket shot, on the other hand, a lot of time is available for weather prediction and so *simplicity of computation* is not a worrisome problem.

The *flexibility to adjust the rate of response* is a measure of the ability of a forecast to adapt to changing conditions. In the steel-rolling example, if the thickness of steel has been decreasing at a very gradual slope and suddenly steepens because of equipment malfunction, predicting when corrective action will take place based on the earlier gradual slope would be fallacious. The forecast technique has to be able to adjust model parameters, such as the slope in a ramp data change, with respect to time. If operational procedures for a rocket shot were so rigid that they *had* to be based on weather prediction—say, a week earlier—then such a shot would in all probability never be successful. In actual practice, real-time computers are utilized to constantly monitor weather conditions and accordingly adjust flight controllers until such time as the rocket is outside the Earth's atmosphere.

A further general consideration in forecasting is the *lead time,* defined here as the elapsed time between making the forecast and implementing the result of the forecast. For example, in predicting schedule requirements for a job shop, the lead time might be the elapsed time from making the forecast for a particular month—say, March—through the actual production time of,

---

†Robert G. Brown, *Smoothing, Forecasting and Prediction of Discrete Time Series,* Prentice-Hall, Englewood Cliffs, N.J., 1963.

say, May. One problem with a long lead time is that forecast errors grow as the length of lead time increases.

In automatic control situations, the forecasting lead times could range from less than a second in steel-rolling control to perhaps two or three minutes in cement kiln control. Such short lead-times require very short computational time while requiring high accuracy and flexibility of response. Special computational procedures are necessitated, oriented to digital computer application. Therefore, the exponential smoothing procedure will be developed as a curve-fitting technique that is beneficial for such critical problems. Techniques that satisfy the time-critical situation will also be valid for general forecasting problems, such as that found in the production control system.

How often to gather data is another problem. In sales forecasting, frequency is usually dictated by the requirements of the forecast. Forecasting for job-shop monthly scheduling would logically be based on monthly historical demand values. In process control, data may have to be filtered to remove process or instrumentation noise, and therefore, even though a prediction once a minute might be required by the process, data may be required at a much faster rate. However, the data cannot be brought in at a slower rate than the maximum allowable lead time. Even though sales forecasting may be thought of in some cases as ruler prediction—placing a ruler through a series of demand data and drawing a line through the points to give an estimate of demand at some future time period—it is apparent that several complicated interacting factors are involved in general systems forecasting, many of which are applicable to sales forecasting. Accuracy required, simplicity of computation, flexibility of response, lead time, and rate of data input all interact. Only on some cost criterion can all be optimized, possibly only through computer simulation.

4.2 DEFINITIONS

A few key definitions are given in this section to provide a common semantic foundation. Readers familiar with forecasting terminology should bypass this material.

Deseasonalization	Removal of seasonality from the data to facilitate growth analysis. (See **Trend—seasonal.**)
Error analysis	Evaluation of forecast errors to allow evaluation of forecast models (see **Model—forecast**) and model parameters.
Exponential smoothing	An iterative procedure for fitting polynomials to data for forecasting purposes.
Fitting coefficients	Coefficients in a forecast-model equation that are optimized according to some error criterion.
Forecast	Estimation of future value or characteristic.
Growth analysis	Procedure for determining growth (positive or negative) equation in a set of data for forecasting purposes.

Horizon		Number of future time-periods for which forecasting is required.
error =	**Lag**	Amount by which the forecast deviates from the true data value—synonymous with *error*.
	Lead time	Length of time in the future for which an individual forecast is made. A forecast made on Tuesday for the following Friday has a lead time of three days.
	Model—forecast	A mathematical expression that describes patterns in historical data. Extension of the mathematical model constitutes the forecast.
	Noise	Random variation about the underlying process that is not utilized in the forecast. One aspect of forecasting is separating the true underlying historical patterns from random deviations.
	Prediction	Synonymous with *Forecast.*
	Qualitative forecast	A forecast made without resort to a mathematical model. "Executive decision" might be one qualitative forecast.
	Quantitative forecast	A forecast that uses a mathematical model for prediction.
	Rate of response	Measure of the ability of a forecast model to react to true changes in data patterns.
	Regression analysis	A method for fitting mathematical models to historical data using the method of minimizing the sum of the fit errors squared.
	Time-Series analysis	The procedure for determining a mathematical model for a set of data that is correlated with time.
	Time-Series forecast	Prediction with a mathematical model that assumes the data is correlated with time.
	Trend	Underlying pattern (growth, seasonal, or cyclic) that exists within historical data and that forms the basis for mathematical modeling and prediction.
	Trend—cyclic	A regular repetitive trend within the data that conforms to the sum of one or more cycles. Frequently, this is a trigonometric relationship—say, one that follows a Fourier relationship.
	Trend–seasonal	A pattern within the data that occurs at multiples of certain time periods but that might not be so regular as cyclic trend. In monthly or weekly data within a year, the pattern might truly conform to seasonal time periods, such as fertilizer sales being heavy in the spring. In this text, cyclic relations will be used to approximate seasonal patterns in one specific technique.

4.3 TIME-SERIES PREDICTION

The remainder of the chapter will be concerned with the specific topic of *time-series analysis* as it applies to forecasting future events based on historical data-trend evaluations. This will only be an introduction to time-series analysis, a fascinating subject that could fill one or more books.† The one forecasting approach that is truly *systems*-oriented has to be that of *time-series* prediction. Process control, sales forecasting, population characteristics, flight control, quality control, and whole-blood transfusion to combat massive hemorrhage are just a few of many cases in which some facet of time-series prediction can be utilized beneficially.

Time-series analysis, with regard to prediction, can be classified as a curve-fitting technique. Assuming that characteristics of the curve fit will continue, the curve is extended into the future for predictive purposes. For example, if past data indicates that the linear equation $\hat{Y} = a + bt$ seems to be a reasonable fit, then a prediction of Y for $t = 9$ would be $\hat{Y} = a + 9b$.

Unfortunately, life is not usually linear. This is probably lucky, for otherwise forecasting would be a rather dull, nonchallenging task. According to the National Industrial Conference Board, company sales are usually affected by three basic factors: long-term growth trends, cyclical business fluctuations, and seasonal variations.‡ Random fluctuations about the composite of these factors clouds the pictorial trend. These random fluctuations will be referred to here as *noise* or *noisy conditions*. The problem in time-series prediction, then, is to determine all the additive trends that exist in a set of data, even though noise may be present.

The *objectives* for time-series forecasting are to (1) evaluate *significant trends* in historical data, (2) damp out noise in the data, (3) dynamically respond to *true* changes in demand as they occur, (4) project trends to the required future period for which forecasting is required, and (5) perform these objectives with optimum forecast parameters. The first two objectives define the curve-fitting function required in time-series forecasting. The simplest forecast procedure for time-series forecasting is the moving average, in which noise is damped by averaging several pieces of data. By updating the average sequentially with each new piece of data while dropping off the oldest value, it follows that true process-changes can gradually be tracked. The average is then used as the forecast for future values. Holding a value of one piece of data in each average means that the average will respond 100% to noise, as well as to true demand changes, with resultant wide fluctuations in forecast. Conversely, if 10 pieces of data are held in the average, only one-tenth of a noisy piece of data will be reflected in the forecast. Unfortunately, if a step change occurs in the data, then 100% response to the change will not be reflected for 10 periods.

---

†For example: E. Parzen, *Time-Series Analysis Papers*, Holden-Day, San Francisco, 1967.
‡*Forecasting Sales—Studies in Business Policy, No. 106.*

The response to true changes in the demand data is attained by dynamically representing the process as new data are obtained. The *moving average* accomplishes this by the addition of the newest piece of the data to the average while at the same time dropping off the oldest piece held in the previous average. The last two objectives—projecting trends and determining optimum forecast parameters—will be discussed in light of specific forecast techniques when these techniques are discussed.

A logical sequence of steps should be followed when forecasting through time-series analysis.

1. Plot the data and visually determine any obvious time-series characteristics.

2. If a growth factor such as a polynomial or an exponential is apparent, remove it from the data.

3. Determine if a significant cyclic trend is present. If a cyclic pattern is obtained and fitted, remove it from the original data.

4. Now evaluate the growth factor from the original data from which any cyclic effects have been removed. Initially run a rough check as to the type of growth, such as order of polynomial or exponential.

5. After a rough determination of the order of the growth equation, fit the data by some acceptable method: least-squares regression or exponential smoothing, for example. (These two topics will be discussed in Sections 4.4 and 4.5.)

6. A forecast for the future will consist of the addition of cyclic and growth trends—both extended to the future time-period.

7. Continually update the equation of fit as new data are added, on the basis that new data will constitute a better representation of current demand trends than older data. Updating also allows a dynamic tracking of process changes while damping out random fluctuations that exist around the underlying trends.

One paradoxical condition arises if cyclical and growth characteristics both are present in the data and a *dynamic* fit of the data is desired. In order to find the cyclic characteristics it is advisable first to remove growth effects. In order to solve accurately the growth equation, it is advantageous first to remove the cyclic effects. (Obviously, one has to be done before the other.) A rough estimation of a growth pattern can be made in step 1, and the results of this estimation then removed from the data. Next, any cyclic effects are then fitted, and these effects then are removed from the original or raw data. Also, if a cyclic trend is superimposed on a polynomial, the cycle will be treated like noise and the resultant fit will be a polynomial. Therefore, one way to find the growth trend in a mixed model is to attack all the data with a least-squares fit, assuming the growth trend is the only one present. Lastly, growth patterns are fitted as accurately as economically feasible. If a *static* or one-shot fit of the data is required, the least-squares approach could be used to fit a composite growth and trigonometric function. The problem with *fast* update is the time that would be taken in such a fit.

Section 4.4 looks at the nonoptimizing regression approach to *growth* analysis and prediction. Following, Section 4.5 introduces exponential smoothing as an *optimizing* growth analysis technique and Section 4.6 introduces the *seasonal index* method as an approach to seasonal analysis that includes *regression* growth considerations. A computer approach to optimizing growth analysis through exponential smoothing and seasonal analysis is presented in Section 4.7. This is an attempt to accomplish *automatically* the results recommended previously through the step-by-step approach. Error analysis to allow choice of a "best" forecasting technique is considered in Section 4.8.

4.4 GROWTH ANALYSIS BY REGRESSION

The most-general growth equation used in forecasting is the polynomial of the basic form

$$\hat{Y}(t) = a + bt + ct^2 + \ldots + gt^{n-1} + ht^n \qquad (4.1)$$

for an nth-order polynomial, where $\hat{Y}(t)$ is the *estimated* value of the true data value, $Y(t)$, at time period t, and $a, b, \ldots, h$ are fitted coefficients of the polynomial.

Truncating later terms allows several familiar curve-fitting equations to be evolved.

1. $\hat{Y}(t) = a$: *constant* model. $\qquad (4.2)$
2. $\hat{Y}(t) = a + bt$: linear model with slope b. $\qquad (4.3)$
3. $\hat{Y}(t) = a + bt + ct^2$: *quadratic* model with slope b and change of slope c.
$\qquad (4.4)$

The growth characteristics considered in this chapter will be limited to Equations 4.2 through 4.4. The same approach developed in here could be applied to any order of polynomial, but the quadratic is usually the highest-order fit needed in production control systems.

If it is not known which model is applicable to a set of data, applying a quadratic model is recommended. If the underlying trend is really linear, the coefficient c will approach zero. Similarly, a constant model will see the coefficients b and c tending to zero. For ease of explanation in this material, first a constant model will be fit, followed by a linear model. Lastly, equations for the quadratic model will be given and the interested reader will be asked in the exercise section to derive the quadratic fit using the same concepts given here for the linear and constant models.

Constant Model

When using the regression least-squares procedure in fitting data, the fitted values, $\hat{Y}(t)$, are compared with the true values, $Y(t)$. Errors are formed for each data value.

$$e(t) = Y(t) - \hat{Y}(t)$$

These errors are squared in order to remove sign problems in which large positive errors might offset large negative errors. The regression process then finds the coefficient(s) of fit that minimize the sum of the errors squared.

$$\text{minimize} \sum_{t=1}^{N}[Y(t) - \hat{Y}(t)]^2 \text{ for } N \text{ data values}$$

Equation 4.2 tells us that for the constant model,

$$\hat{Y}(t) = a$$

and so the single coefficient of fit is a.

Therefore, we need to minimize

$$\sum_{t=1}^{N} e^2(t) = \sum_{t=1}^{N}[Y(t) - a]^2 \qquad (4.5)$$

where a is a constant.

This is accomplished through classical optimization by taking the derivative of the sum of the errors squared with respect to a, setting the result to zero, and solving for a:

$$\frac{d\left[\sum_{t=1}^{N} e^2(t)\right]}{da} = -2\sum_{t=1}^{N}[Y(t) - a] = 0$$

The solution for a is now

$$a = \frac{\sum_{t=1}^{N} Y(t)}{N} = \bar{Y} \qquad (4.6)$$

The reader might note that the second derivative with respect to a is positive, thus ensuring a *minimum* error criterion.

Equation 4.6 shows that if a *constant* model is suspected, the *average* of the historical data values might be the best prediction of future values.

Linear Model

The error term to be minimized, using Equation 4.3, is now

$$\sum_{t=1}^{N} e^2(t) = \sum_{t=1}^{N}[Y(t) - a - bt]^2 \qquad (4.7)$$

Taking the partial derivative of Equation 4.7 with respect to a and setting the resultant equation to zero, followed by taking the partial derivative of

Equation 4.7 with respect to b and setting that resultant equation to zero, results in two simultaneous equations that if solved for a and b, give the a and b coefficients of fit that will allow minimization of the error criterion. This is accomplished as follows:

1.

$$\frac{d\left[\sum_{t=1}^{N} e^2(t)\right]}{da} = -2\sum_{t=1}^{N}[Y(t) - a - bt] = 0$$

and

$$a = \frac{\sum_{t=1}^{N} Y(t)}{N} - b\frac{\sum_{t=1}^{N} t}{N} \tag{4.8}$$

2.

$$\frac{d\left[\sum_{t=1}^{N} e^2(t)\right]}{db} = -2\sum_{t=1}^{N} t[Y(t) - a - bt] = 0$$

and

$$a\sum_{t=1}^{N} t + b\sum_{t=1}^{N} t^2 - \sum_{t=1}^{N} tY(t) = 0 \tag{4.9}$$

3. Substituting Equation 4.8 into Equation 4.9 gives

$$\frac{\sum_{t=1}^{N} Y(t)\sum_{t=1}^{N} t}{N} - \frac{b\left(\sum_{t=1}^{N} t\right)^2}{N} + b\sum_{t=1}^{N} t^2 - \sum_{t=1}^{N} tY(t) = 0$$

4. Solving for b gives

$$b = \frac{N\sum_{t=1}^{N} tY(t) - \sum_{t=1}^{N} Y(t)\sum_{t=1}^{N} t}{N\sum_{t=1}^{N} t^2 - \left(\sum_{t=1}^{N} t\right)^2} \tag{4.10}$$

The fitting procedure, using a linear model, would be to determine first the slope estimate, b, using Equation 4.10. This value for b would then be substituted in Equation 4.8 to allow the equation intercept a to be found.

Example of Linear Fit

Consider the set of data and associated intermediate calculations needed for determining a and b given in Table 4.1. The slope is found using Equation 4.10.

$$b = \frac{(7)(1575) - (315)(28)}{(7)(140) - (28)^2} = 11.25$$

This result is substituted in Equation 4.8 to allow the intercept a to be

TABLE 4.1 Data Set and Intermediate Computations Needed for Linear Fit

t	$Y(t)$	$tY(t)$	t^2
1	15	15	1
2	20	40	4
3	35	105	9
4	40	160	16
5	55	275	25
6	70	420	36
7	80	560	49
28	315	1575	140

found.

$$a = \frac{315}{7} - \frac{(11.25)(28)}{7} = \mathbf{0.0}$$

The reader should realize that getting an intercept value of 0.0 is of course by pure chance. If the linear model is assumed satisfactory for forecasting, also

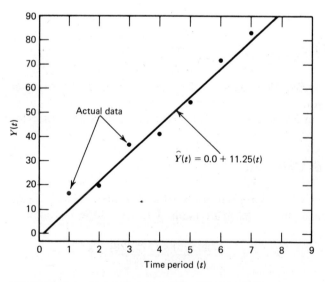

FIGURE 4.1 Fitted linear model related to data.

assuming the small data-set is reasonable, the short-term forecast would be by

$$\hat{Y}(t) = 0.0 + 11.25(t)$$

For example, $\hat{Y}(8) = 90.0$. The relation of the fitted model to the data can be seen in Figure 4.1.

Quadratic Model

The error criterion to be minimized for the quadratic fit would be

$$\sum_{t=1}^{N} e^2(t) = \sum_{t=1}^{N}[Y(t) - a - bt - ct^2]^2 \tag{4.11}$$

Simultaneous equations are evolved by taking partial derivatives of Equation 4.11 with respect to a, b, and c and then setting the three resulting equations to zero. The simultaneous equation solution is a little messy but results in

1. $b = \dfrac{\gamma\delta - \theta\alpha}{\gamma\beta - \alpha^2}$ \hfill (4.12)

where

$$\gamma = \left(\sum_{t=1}^{N} t^2\right)^2 - N\sum_{t=1}^{N} t^4$$

$$\delta = \sum_{t=1}^{N} t\sum_{t=1}^{N} Y(t) - N\sum_{t=1}^{N} tY(t)$$

$$\theta = \sum_{t=1}^{N} t^2\sum_{t=1}^{N} Y(t) - N\sum_{t=1}^{N} t^2 Y(t)$$

$$\alpha = \sum_{t=1}^{N} t\sum_{t=1}^{N} t^2 - N\sum_{t=1}^{N} t^3$$

$$\beta = \left(\sum_{t=1}^{N} t\right)^2 - N\sum_{t=1}^{N} t^2$$

2. Once b has been determined, c is found from

$$c = \frac{\theta - (b)(\alpha)}{\gamma} \tag{4.13}$$

3. The intercept a can be found using b and c, and results in

$$a = \frac{\sum_{t=1}^{N} Y(t)}{N} - b\frac{\sum_{t=1}^{N} t}{N} - c\frac{\sum_{t=1}^{N} t^2}{N} \tag{4.14}$$

Example of Quadratic Fit

Consider the data vector [16 24 34 46 60] for t values of 1 through 5. The tabular values needed for coefficient solution are given in Table 4.2. Solving

TABLE 4.2 Tabular Values for Quadratic Fit

t	t^2	t^3	t^4	$Y(t)$	$tY(t)$	$t^2Y(t)$
1	1	1	1	16	16	16
2	4	8	16	24	48	96
3	9	27	81	34	102	306
4	16	64	256	46	184	736
5	25	125	625	60	300	1500
15	55	225	979	180	650	2654

for α, β, γ, δ, and θ gives

$$\alpha = (15)(55) - (5)(225) = -300$$
$$\beta = (15)^2 - (5)(55) = -50$$
$$\gamma = (55)^2 - (5)(979) = -1{,}870$$
$$\delta = (15)(180) - (5)(650) = -550$$
$$\theta = (55)(180) - (5)(2654) = -3{,}370$$

And solving Equations 4.12 through 4.14 sequentially gives

$$b = \frac{(-1870)(-550) - (-3370)(-300)}{(-1870)(-50) - (-300)^2} = \frac{17500}{3500} = 5$$

$$c = \frac{(-1870)}{-1870} = 1$$

$$a = \frac{180}{5} - \frac{(5)(15)}{5} - \frac{55}{5} = 10$$

And the polynomial fit is

$$\hat{Y}(t) = 10 + 5t + t^2 \tag{4.15}$$

Time period 5 in the original data had $Y(5) = 60$. Checking Equation 4.15 for $t = 5$, we get $\hat{Y}(5) = 10 + (5)(5) + (5)^2 = 60$, which checks exactly. It should, since the given data were noise-free.

Suppose the data had been linear, rather than quadratic. Would the fit eliminate quadratic effects, as suggested at the beginning of this section? Take the quadratic data just analyzed and eliminate the t^2 term with the following residual vector: [15 20 25 30 35]. The tabular values for solution are given in Table 4.3.

TABLE 4.3 Tabular Data for Quadratic Fit of Linear Data

t	t^2	t^3	t^4	$Y(t)$	$tY(t)$	$t^2Y(t)$
1	1	1	1	15	15	15
2	4	8	16	20	40	80
3	9	27	81	25	75	225
4	16	64	256	30	120	480
5	25	125	625	35	175	875
15	55	225	979	125	425	1675

Solving for α, β, γ, δ, and θ:

1. Since α, β, and γ are not affected by $Y(t)$, they will be the same as for the quadratic fit.
2. $\delta = (15)(125) - (5)(425) = -250$.
3. $\theta = (55)(125) - (5)(1675) = -1500$.

Solving Equations 4.12 through 4.14 to get a, b, and c:

$$b = \frac{(-1870)(-250) - (-1500)(-300)}{(-1870)(-50) - (-300)^2} = 5$$

$$c = \frac{(-1500) - (5)(-300)}{-1870} = 0$$

$$a = \frac{125}{5} - \frac{(5)(15)}{5} - \frac{(0)(15)}{5} = 10$$

This gives a fit of $\hat{Y}(t) = 10 + 5t$, which is the linear fit of the given data. Similarly, if the data were constant, the coefficients b and c would be zero. Therefore, if a computer-automated system were being utilized, a logical approach would be to design the curve fit for the largest polynomial growth pattern feasible, and the solution will take care of itself when lower-order fits are really the solution.

One simplification that can be made for the linear fit that cannot be considered for the quadratic fit is coding the time data so that

$$\sum_{t=1}^{N}(t_c) = 0$$

where $t_c = [t - (N + 1)/2]$ if t runs from 1 to N. The intercept value will change, but since the interval t_c to $(t + 1)_c$ is held the same as t to $(t + 1)$,

TABLE 4.4   Tabular Values for Fitting Linear Data Using Coded Time Values

t	t_c	t_c^2	$Y(t)$	$t_c Y(t)$
1	-2	4	15	-30
2	-1	1	20	-20
3	0	0	25	0
4	1	1	30	30
5	2	4	35	70
	0	10	125	50

it follows that the slope will remain the same. This can be shown with the linear data just considered. The values of a_c and b_c with coded data from Equations 4.8 and 4.10 would be as follows:†

$$a_c = \frac{\sum Y(t)}{N} \qquad b_c - \frac{\sum t_c Y(t)}{\sum t_c^2}$$

The tabular values for fitting the data [**15 20 25 30 35**] would be as given in Table 4.4. Solving for a_c and b_c:

$$a_c = \frac{125}{5} = 25$$

$$b_c = \frac{50}{10} = 5$$

The values calculated earlier for a and b were 10 and 5, respectively. Therefore, $b_c = b$, but $a_c \neq a$. The intercept could be corrected to the original intercept by the formula

$$a = a_c - \left[\frac{N+1}{2}\right]b \qquad (4.16)$$

for the original data correlated to $t = 1$ through $t = N$. Therefore, a would be

$$a = a_c - \left[\frac{N+1}{2}\right]b = 25 - (3)(5) = 10$$

The general relationship between coded and noncoded time values is shown in

†*Note*: Σt in Equations 4.8 through 4.10 is zero when using the coded t approach.

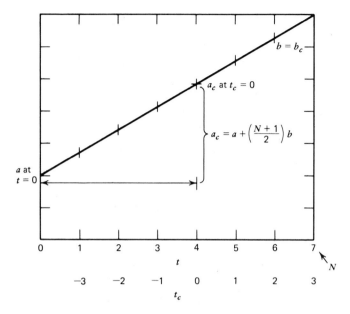

FIGURE 4.2 **Parameter relationships when true time versus coded time values are used.**

Figure 4.2. The only difference is a shifting of the time axis, which can easily be corrected by Equation 4.16.

Exponential Model

Regression is usually thought of as being applicable only to polynomial models. In actual fact, if it is possible with a model to take derivatives of the error criterion with respect to the parameters of fit, that model then is feasible for optimization through least-squares regression. An example of this procedure is mentioned in Section 4.7, in which trigonometric fits to a set of data are made for seasonal analysis. Suppose the following exponential model is considered.

$$\hat{Y}(t) = ae^{bt} \tag{4.17}$$

The reader will find that equations for a and b cannot be determined through the conventional approach. However, in many cases a transformation of the data might lead to a situation in which regression can be applied. A logarithmic transformation of Equation 4.17, for example, gives

$$\ln[\hat{Y}(t)] = \ln(a) + \ln(e^{bt}) = \ln(a) + bt \tag{4.18}$$

The result is a *linear* model with intercept equal to $\ln(a)$. Equations 4.8 and

TABLE 4.5 Tabular Values for Regression Exponential Fit

t	$Y(t)$	$\ln[Y(t)]$	$t\ln[Y(t)]$	t^2
0	2.50	0.92	0.00	0
1	4.12	1.42	1.42	1
2	6.80	1.92	3.84	4
3	11.20	2.42	7.26	9
4	18.47	2.92	11.68	16
10		9.60	24.20	30

Note: Regression examples up to this point assumed t goes from 1 to N. Regression fits will work for any range of t, with N being the number of t-values used. For example, $t = 58$ to 75 could be used in equations of fit, with N being 18.

4.10 for the conventional linear fit can be utilized *after* natural logarithms have been taken of the original data being fit. As an example, consider $\hat{Y}(t) = 2.5\,e^{0.5t}$. For t values of 0 through 4, this gives data values of 2.50, 4.12, 6.80, 11.20, and 18.47. Intermediate values needed for linear fit coefficients, a and b, are given in Table 4.5. Solving Equation 4.10 for the slope b:

$$b = \frac{(5)(24.20) - (9.60)(10)}{(5)(30) - 100} = \frac{25}{50} = 0.5$$

Equation 4.8 finds the intercept, which in this case is $\ln(a)$:

$$\ln(a) = \frac{9.60}{5} - \frac{(0.5)(10)}{5} = 0.92$$

The true value of a is of course the *anti-ln of* 0.92, or $e^{0.92} = 2.50 = a$. And so, as expected, we get

$$\hat{Y}(t) = ae^{bt} = 2.5\,e^{0.5t}$$

Several problems exist when using regression for forecasting, say, with a polynomial model.

1. A large amount of back data needs to be held.
2. All data are weighted equally.
3. We do not know how many values of back data to hold.
4. Updating coefficients of fit from time period to time period can be time-consuming and messy.

The exponential smoothing process, given in the next section, is an excellent way to offset these problems.

4.5 GROWTH ANALYSIS BY EXPONENTIAL SMOOTHING

Exponential smoothing is one of the more interesting mathematical techniques with direct applicability to systems forecasting. The procedure has all the attributes of a moving average and yet *no* back data have to be held. Undoubtedly, the most significant work with exponential smoothing was accomplished by R. G. Brown.[†] Exponential smoothing will be applied to the same polynomial models as were considered with regression in the previous section: namely, constant, linear, and quadratic.

The equation at the heart of exponential smoothing can be written:

$$\hat{Y}(t), 1 = \alpha Y(t) + (1 - \alpha)\hat{Y}(t - 1), 1 \qquad (4.19)$$

where $\hat{Y}(t)$, 1 denotes the tth value of first-order exponential smoothing or average, $Y(t)$ is the tth demand value, and α is a smoothing constant such that $0 \le \alpha \le 1$.

From Equation 4.19 it can be seen that if α is 1, then $\hat{Y}(t), 1 = Y(t)$. The average would be the most recent piece of data. Conversely, if α is 0, it follows that $\hat{Y}(t), 1 = \hat{Y}(t - 1), 1$. This means that the average would be the same as the previous average, with no response whatsoever to the most recent piece of data. An analogous situation exists in the conventional moving average, in which all N pieces of data held in the average are weighted by $1/N$. If N is 1, the new average would correspond exactly to the latest piece of data. If N is large, the effect of the most recent piece of data on the current average would be negligible. A moving average N of 1 then is relatable to an exponential smoothing α of 1, and one that is extremely large corresponds to an α of 0. If indeed exponential smoothing and the moving average are equivalent, it then follows that an α value between 0 and 1, tending toward 0 rather than 1, would be desirable to balance random effects and yet respond to demand changes.

An interesting aspect of $\hat{Y}(t)$, 1 is that it contains some portion of all data that has been smoothed even though no back data are specifically held. This can be seen by expanding the previous values of $\hat{Y}(t)$, 1 as follows, from Equation 4.19, using $\beta = (1 - \alpha)$:

$$\hat{Y}(t), 1 = \alpha Y(t) + \beta \hat{Y}(t - 1), 1$$

$$\alpha \beta Y(t - 1) + \beta^2 \hat{Y}(t - 2), 1$$

$$\alpha \beta^2 Y(t - 2) + \beta^3 \hat{Y}(t - 3), 1$$

[†]R. G. Brown, *Smoothing, Forecasting, and Prediction of Discrete Time Series*, Prentice-Hall, Englewood Cliffs, N.J., 1963.

which reduces to

$$\hat{Y}(t), 1 = \alpha Y(t) + \alpha\beta Y(t-1) + \alpha\beta^2 Y(t-2) + \ldots$$

and so

$$\hat{Y}(t), 1 = \alpha \sum_{i=0}^{t-1} \beta^i Y(t-i) + \beta^t \hat{Y}(0), 1 \qquad (4.20)$$

It can be seen that all past data are held in the average and that since α and β are both fractional values, the data are most heavily weighted for recent values, with weights decreasing monotonically as data get older. This has the advantage that the most recent data, which supposedly are the best data, contribute the most heavily to the average. Also, the contribution of the initial smoothing estimate, $\beta^t \hat{Y}(0), 1$, will approach zero as t gets large. This means that initial inaccuracies will eventually be damped out.

If the coefficients α, $\alpha\beta$, $\alpha\beta^2$, and so on of $Y(t)$ from Equation 4.20 are summed, it is found that

$$\alpha \sum_{i=0}^{t-1} \beta^i$$

reduces to

$$1 - \beta^t$$

which approaches 1 as t gets large. A fundamental criterion of a weighted average is that the weights sum to 1, and so $\hat{Y}(t), 1$ has this attribute.

Constant Model

Since regression analysis determined that the data *average* minimizes the sum of errors squared for a constant model, it follows that first-order exponential smoothing, $\hat{Y}(t), 1$ will be a feasible candidate for forecasting if a *constant* model is deemed applicable. For example, consider the data set given below:

t	1	2	3	4	5
$Y(t)$	8	6	10	8	7

The prediction of a value at any time point *beyond* 5 would be $\hat{Y}(5), 1$. Since

$$\hat{Y}(t), 1 = \alpha Y(t) + \beta \hat{Y}(t-1), 1$$

it follows that at time period 1 we would have

$$\hat{Y}(1), 1 = \alpha Y(1) + \beta \hat{Y}(0), 1$$

Since we do not know any value at time period 0, we have to estimate an initial value for $\hat{Y}(1), 1$ and use conventional exponential smoothing from then on. If the data are not very noisy, a logical value would be $Y(1)$ under the assumption of a constant model. If $Y(1)$ seems to be a noisy value, an

TABLE 4.6 Computation of $\hat{Y}(5), 1: \alpha = 0.2$

		A	B	A + B
t	$Y(t)$	$\alpha Y(t)$	$\beta \hat{Y}(t-1), 1$	$\hat{Y}(t), 1$
1	8	—	—	8.0
2	6	1.2	6.4	7.6
3	10	2.0	6.1	8.1
4	8	1.6	6.5	8.1
5	7	1.4	6.5	7.9

average of the first few data values would be reasonable for $\hat{Y}(1), 1$, and exponential smoothing results would be as given in Table 4.6. This also assumes an alpha value of 0.2, a made-up value for this example. $\hat{Y}(5), 1$ turns out to be 7.9, the value that would be predicted for the future under the constant-model assumption.

As an aside, the average of the five values is 7.8, quite close to $\hat{Y}(5), 1$. At no unique point in time would it be expected that the data average be the same as the exponential smoothing average, for α equivalent to N (a topic not addressed as yet). However, it has been proved that in the *long run*, the polynomial fit determined by using exponential smoothing will be the same as with a *regression* fit for the same model.† This would assume that α was equivalent to N. Developing the *linear* model will allow this relationship to be seen.

Linear Model

Let's define a *lag* as the difference between the true data value and fitted value. If the fit is a simple *average* but the data follows a linear growth (ramp), it is known that the lag at the most recent data value is $(N-1)/(2)$ times the (slope). For example, the data set [2, 5, 8, 11, 14] has a slope of 3 and an average equal to 8. The lag with the latest value of 14 is 6, which is equal to $(4/2)(3)$ using the given equation. Similarly, it can be shown that exponential smoothing will lag a ramp by

$$\left(\frac{\beta}{\alpha}\right)(\text{slope}) \tag{4.21}$$

---

†D. A. D'Esopo, "A Note on Forecasting by the Exponential Smoothing Operator," *Operations Research*, vol. 9, no. 5, 1961.

A logical relationship between α and N is therefore

$$\frac{(1-\alpha)}{\alpha} = \left(\frac{N-1}{2}\right)$$

or

$$N = \frac{(2-\alpha)}{\alpha} \tag{4.22}$$

Similarly,

$$\alpha = \frac{2}{(N+1)} \tag{4.23}$$

Therefore, if seven values were held in a regression fit, an equivalent exponential smoothing α would be 0.25.

Fitting a first-order polynomial can be accomplished with exponential smoothing almost as simply as for the constant model. Knowing that the expected value of $[Y(t) - \hat{Y}(t), 1]$ is $(\beta/\alpha)(b)$ from Equation 4.21, it follows that noise-free data will be paralleled by successive values of $\hat{Y}(t), 1$, in the fashion of Figure 4.3. If these values of $\hat{Y}(t), 1$ are averaged by exponential smoothing, it would be expected that the averages $\hat{Y}(t), 2$ will themselves parallel the $\hat{Y}(t), 1$ values, and also have a consistent lag of $(\beta/\alpha)(b)$, as in Figure 4.3. The following relationships can now be written

$$[Y(t) - \hat{Y}(t), 1] = [\hat{Y}(t), 1 - \hat{Y}(t), 2]$$

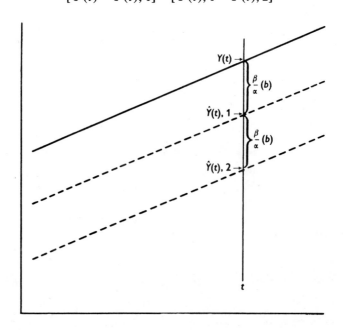

FIGURE 4.3 Relationship of $\hat{Y}(t), 1$ and $\hat{Y}(t), 2$ to noise-free data.

So, in terms of the smoothed statistics

$$Y(t) = 2\hat{Y}(t), 1 - \hat{Y}(t), 2 \tag{4.24}$$

Also,

$$[\hat{Y}(t), 1 - \hat{Y}(t), 2] = (b)\left(\frac{\beta}{\alpha}\right)$$

So,

$$b = \frac{\alpha}{\beta}[\hat{Y}(t), 1 - \hat{Y}(t), 2] \tag{4.25}$$

Equations 4.24 and 4.25 are predicated on the basis of perfect ramp data. With noisy data however, they will calculate *estimates* of a fitted line through the data. Therefore, these equations will be restated as

$$\hat{a}(t) = 2\hat{Y}(t), 1 - \hat{Y}(t), 2 \tag{4.26}$$

and

$$\hat{b}(t) = \left(\frac{\alpha}{\beta}\right)[\hat{Y}(t), 1 - \hat{Y}(t), 2] \tag{4.27}$$

The intercept, $\hat{a}(t)$, will occur at the *endpoint*, or more recent point, of the regression line.

Because the $\hat{Y}(t), 1$ and $\hat{Y}(t), 2$ values are expected to lag the data, it follows that initial conditions for the smoothed statistics should be calculated. From Figure 4.3, it can be seen that logical initial conditions would be

$$\hat{Y}(0), 1 = \hat{a}(0) - \hat{b}(0)\frac{(\beta)}{(\alpha)} \tag{4.28}$$

$$\hat{Y}(0), 2 = \hat{a}(0) - 2\hat{b}(0)\frac{(\beta)}{(\alpha)} \tag{4.29}$$

where $\hat{b}(0)$ is an initial estimate of the slope at $t = 0$ and $\hat{a}(0)$ is the estimate of $\hat{Y}(0)$.

Example

Consider the data originally given in Table 4.1 for a regression linear fit:

t	1	2	3	4	5	6	7
$Y(t)$	15	20	35	40	55	70	80

Initial conditions will be needed for $\hat{Y}(1), 1$ and $\hat{Y}(1), 2$. If the data seem to be linear and the endpoints are not too noisy, the estimates for $\hat{a}(1)$ and $\hat{b}(1)$, to be used in the smoothing initial conditions, may be found by

$$\hat{a}(1) = Y(1) = 15$$

$$\hat{b}(1) = \frac{Y(N) - Y(1)}{(N - 1)} = \frac{80 - 15}{6} = 10.9$$

TABLE 4.7 Calculation of $\hat{Y}(7), 1$ and $\hat{Y}(7), 2$ for Linear Model, $\alpha = .25$

t	$Y(t)$	$\alpha Y(t)$	$\beta\hat{Y}(t-1), 1$	$\hat{Y}(t), 1$	$\alpha\hat{Y}(t), 1$	$\beta\hat{Y}(t-1), 2$	$\hat{Y}(t), 2$
1	15	—	—	(−18.00)	—	—	(−51.00)
2	20	5.00	−13.50	−8.50	−2.13	−38.25	−40.38
3	35	8.75	−5.38	2.38	0.60	−30.29	−29.69
4	40	10.00	1.78	11.78	2.95	−22.26	−19.31
5	55	13.75	8.84	22.59	5.65	−14.49	−8.84
6	70	17.50	16.94	34.44	8.61	−6.63	1.98
7	80	20.00	25.83	45.83	11.46	1.49	12.95

Since these are only estimates, rounding $\hat{b}(1)$ to 11.0 will not cause problems. If the data had been very noisy, *regression* estimates for $\hat{a}$ and $\hat{b}$ would be needed. It should be recognized that we are developing exponential smoothing fits for rapid-update forecasts, say, through an on-line computer system. Starting the process with a small regression fit would be no problem in these circumstances.

The first- and second-order exponential smoothing calculations are given in Table 4.7. Smoothing initial conditions were found using Equations 4.28 and 4.29.† An α of 0.25 was used, since that value is equivalent to an N of 7.

$$\hat{Y}(1), 1 = 15 - (11)\left(\frac{0.75}{0.25}\right) = -18$$

$$\hat{Y}(1), 2 = 15 - (2)(11)\left(\frac{0.75}{0.25}\right) = -51$$

Estimates for $a(7)$ and $b(7)$ can now be found using Equations 4.26 and 4.27.

$$\hat{a}(7) = (2)(45.83) - 12.95 = 78.71$$

$$\hat{b}(7) = \left(\frac{1}{3}\right)(45.83 - 12.95) = 10.96$$

Realizing that the intercept occurs at the *end* of the line-of-fit, it follows that prediction from time period 7 would follow

$$\hat{Y}(7 + L) = \hat{a}(7) + \hat{b}(7)(L)$$

---

†Even though these equations specified initial conditions at time period 0, it should be evident that they may be computed at *any* time period; in this case, time period 1.

For example,

$$\hat{Y}(10) = 78.71 + (10.96)(3) = 111.59$$

Now, how does this linear fit compare with the earlier regression-fit accomplished in Section 4.4? The regression fit had a slope of 11.25 compared with the exponential smoothing slope of 10.96. These are close, but it must be remembered that exponential smoothing responds most heavily to *recent* data. The change in data (slope) from time period 6 to period 7 is 10, less than the *average* slope. Thus, exponential smoothing has adjusted to this reduction. The regression intercept, *a*, was 0.0—but this occurs at time period 0. The exponential smoothing intercept is 78.71, occurring at period 7. If we predict $\hat{Y}(0)$ with exponential smoothing, giving the equivalent of the intercept at time period 0, we would get

$$\hat{Y}(0) = 78.71 - (7)(10.96) = 1.99$$

Obviously, this is comparable to the regression value.

Quadratic Model

Any order of polynomial can be fit by exponential smoothing. The derivation of the fits can be mathematically complex, but the application is quite simple. The linear fit requires two orders of smoothing to be determined, and those are the only two back-values that need to be maintained. The quadratic model requires a third order of smoothing to be used with the other two orders.

$$\hat{Y}(t), 3 = \alpha \hat{Y}(t), 2 + (\beta)\hat{Y}(t-1), 3$$

It can be seen that the orders of smoothing can be computed iteratively in a very efficient manner using a calculator or digital computer.

The quadratic model to be fit is

$$\hat{Y}(t) = a + bt + ct^2$$

The coefficients are determined by

$$\hat{a}(t) = 3\hat{Y}(t), 1 - 3\hat{Y}(t), 2 + \hat{Y}(t), 3 \qquad (4.30)$$

$$\hat{b}(t) = \frac{\alpha}{2\beta^2}\{[1 + 5\beta][\hat{Y}(t), 1] - [2 + 8\beta][\hat{Y}(t), 2] + [1 + 3\beta][\hat{Y}(t), 3]\}$$

$$(4.31)$$

$$\hat{c}(t) = \frac{\alpha^2}{2\beta^2}\{[\hat{Y}(t), 1] - 2[\hat{Y}(t), 2] + [\hat{Y}(t), 3]\} \qquad (4.32)$$

with initial conditions

$$\hat{Y}(0), 1 = \hat{a}(0) - \frac{\beta}{\alpha}\,\hat{b}(0) + \frac{\beta(1+\beta)}{\alpha^2}\,\hat{c}(0) \qquad (4.33)$$

$$\hat{Y}(0), 2 = \hat{a}(0) - \frac{2\beta}{\alpha}\,\hat{b}(0) + \frac{2\beta(1+2\beta)}{\alpha^2}\,\hat{c}(0) \qquad (4.34)$$

$$\hat{Y}(0), 3 = \hat{a}(0) - \frac{3\beta}{\alpha}\,\hat{b}(0) + \frac{3\beta(1+3\beta)}{\alpha^2}\,\hat{c}(0) \qquad (4.35)$$

Example

Let's apply these computations to the quadratic data given in Section 4.4 for regression analysis, with t being 0 through 4 instead of 1 through 5.

t	0	1	2	3	4
$Y(t)$	10	16	24	34	46

The first step is to compute initial conditions for the three orders of smoothing using Equations 4.33 through 4.35. In turn, these need estimates for the coefficients a, b, and c at the initial time-period, which is zero in this example. The coefficients may be found by regression or by the following approximations if the data are not too noisy.[†]

$$\hat{c} = \frac{Y(T) - Y(T-1) - Y(1) + Y(0)}{2(T-1)}$$

$$\hat{b} = \frac{Y(T) - Y(0) - \hat{c}[T^2]}{(T)}$$

and

$$\hat{a} = \frac{\sum\limits_{t=0}^{T} Y(t) - \hat{b} \sum\limits_{t=0}^{T} t - \hat{c} \sum\limits_{t=0}^{T} t^2}{(T+1)}$$

where it is assumed that the time periods go from 0 to T. Since the intercept, $\hat{a}$, occurs at time period 0 and the initial data value occurs at time 0 also, no correction is needed. If we were getting initial conditions at time period 2, for example, $\hat{a}$ would have to be corrected by

$$\hat{a}(2) = \hat{a}(0) + 2\hat{b}(0) + 4\hat{c}(0)$$

[†] G. B. Schweid, "Simplified Formulas for Method of Differences Analysis," senior project in Design, Industrial Engineering Dept., Arizona State University, May 1971.

Since the given data are not noisy, the coefficient estimates are

$$\hat{c}(0) = \frac{46 - 34 - 16 + 10}{2(3)} = 1.0$$

$$\hat{b}(0) = \frac{46 - 10 - (1)(16)}{4} = 5.0$$

$$\hat{a}(0) = \frac{130 - (5.0)(10) - (1)(30)}{5} = 10.0$$

Initial conditions for the smoothing values are found with Equations 4.33 through 4.35 (assume $\alpha = 0.2$).

$$\hat{Y}(0), 1 = 10 - (4)(5) + \frac{(0.8)(1.8)(1)}{(0.04)} = 26.0$$

$$\hat{Y}(0), 2 = 10 - (8)(5) + \frac{(1.6)(2.6)(1)}{(0.04)} = 74.0$$

$$\hat{Y}(0), 3 = 10 - (12)(5) + \frac{(2.4)(3.4)(1)}{(0.04)} = 154.0$$

Table 4.8 develops the exponential smoothing values for time period 4. Equations 4.30 through 4.32 give the fitting coefficients needed for forecasting.

$$\hat{a}(4) = (3)(30) - (3)(46) + 94 = 46.0$$

$$\hat{b}(4) = \left[\frac{0.2}{(2)(0.64)}\right] [(5)(30) - (8.4)(46) + (3.4)(94)] = 13.0$$

$$\hat{c}(4) = \left[\frac{0.04}{(2)(0.64)}\right] [30 - 92 + 94] = 1.0$$

Prediction for future time period values would be by

$$\hat{Y}(4 + L) = \hat{a}(4) + [\hat{b}(4)][L] + [\hat{c}(4)][L]^2$$

If we wanted to predict for period 6, we would have

$$\hat{Y}(6) = 46 + (13)(2) + (1)(4) = 76.0$$

The regression quadratic fit for the same data gave, in Section 4.4, $\hat{Y}(t) = 10 + 5t + t^2$. For period 6, this would be 76.0, which is exactly the result achieved through exponential smoothing.

With small exponential-smoothing examples, it probably seems as though regression is the easiest way to forecast. It should be remembered that we are talking about forecasts with the following characteristics.

1. Responds to trend changes quickly.
2. Damps out noise.
3. Has a very short sampling interval for data.

TABLE 4.8   Calculation of Three Orders of Smoothing

t	$Y(t)$	$\alpha Y(t)$	$\beta \hat{Y}(t-1),1$	$\hat{Y}(t),1$	$\alpha \hat{Y}(t),1$	$\beta \hat{Y}(t-1),2$	$\hat{Y}(t),2$	$\alpha \hat{Y}(t),2$	$\beta \hat{Y}(t-1),3$	$\hat{Y}(t),3$
0	10	—	—	26.0	—	—	74.0	—	—	154.0
1	16	3.2	20.8	24.0	4.8	59.2	64.0	12.8	123.2	136.0
2	24	4.8	19.2	24.0	4.8	51.2	56.0	11.2	108.8	120.0
3	34	6.8	19.2	26.0	5.2	44.8	50.0	10.0	96.0	106.0
4	46	9.2	20.8	(30.0)	6.0	40.0	(46.0)	9.2	84.8	(94.0)
				$\hat{Y}(4),1$			$\hat{Y}(4),2$			$\hat{Y}(4),3$

Given:
$\qquad \alpha = 0.2$
$\qquad \beta = 0.8$
$\qquad \hat{Y}(t),k = \alpha \hat{Y}(t),k-1 + \beta \hat{Y}(t-1),k$
$\qquad$ where
$\qquad \hat{Y}(t),0 = Y(t)$

These characteristics require a digital computer, and exponential smoothing is very amenable to solution on a digital computer because of the iterative manner used in calculating the various orders of smoothing. The case study given at the end of the chapter will introduce a computer program to allow this.

Optimum α?

In regression analysis, it is not readily obvious how many values to hold in the fit. With a computer program handling exponential smoothing, it is possible to optimize on the smoothing coefficient, α. This, of course, would be the same as optimizing N in regression. Because the computations for exponential smoothing are so simple and iterative in fashion, it is possible to perform a search for the optimum α by performing forecasts with each eligible α and then picking that α which minimizes the error criterion. Error analysis, the heart of this optimization process, is discussed in Section 4.8. The digital computer program PREDICTS, presented in Section 4.7, uses this approach to optimize both α *and* the model of fit.

4.6   SEASONAL CONSIDERATIONS

Historical data is frequently biased because of *seasonal* characteristics. Monthly unemployment in the United States, for example, is high in summer months, when high school students look for work. Removing this bias is called *deseasonalization* of the data. A greeting-card company, as another example, might find that its November sales average 40% of annual sales, whereas April sales might average 30% of the yearly situation. Any prediction of future values has to take this seasonality into consideration, whereas *growth* analysis, because of the bias problem, should be accomplished on deseasonalized data.

The semantic term *seasonality* has its roots in monthly or quarterly data. In data analysis, a "season" is not a constraining factor. Mail handling in a post office might be done on a five-day-a-week basis, and Monday's and Friday's handling might account for 50% of the workload. Similarly, a bank teller might handle 40% of the daily workload between 11:30 A.M. and 1:00 P.M., although that time could comprise only 20% of the workday. Teller scheduling should consider seasonality across the workday, whereas mail handling exhibits seasonality across the workweek (as well as across the year).

Seasonal effects are frequently a specific *percentage* of a long-term trend, as exemplified by the previous examples. Seasonal *indices* provide one way to account for the seasonality with this type of data. For example, consider the

TABLE 4.9   Seasonal Data With Five Seasonals (Days) across the Period (Week)

Week	M	T	W	Th	F	Total	Daily Average
1	8	4	2	6	15	35	7.0
2	9	5	4	7	15	40	8.0
3	11	5	4	8	17	45	9.0
4	13	6	5	10	16	50	10.0

data in Table 4.9, which is seasonal across a five-day week. Three things are immediately apparent.

1. The data is *seasonal*. Mondays and Fridays are high, with lower values for the middle of the week.
2. The *totals* display no seasonality, but they do show a growth pattern.
3. The *daily averages* show the same relationships as shown by the totals.

One way to deseasonalize data, therefore, is to use totals across the period or average for the seasonal. A more common way is to determine *seasonal indices*, which indicate the fractional percent by which each seasonal falls above or below the *average* seasonal value. These indices can be used in deseasonalizing data and in predictions for the future, as will be shown with the example data.

First, indices are found for *all* the data, as shown in Table 4.10. This is

TABLE 4.10   Seasonal Index Computation

Week	M	T	W	Th	F	Total
1	1.14	0.57	0.29	0.86	2.14	5.00
2	1.13	0.63	0.50	0.88	1.88	5.02
3	1.22	0.56	0.44	0.89	1.89	5.00
4	1.30	0.60	0.50	1.00	1.60	5.00
Total:	4.79	2.36	1.73	3.63	7.51	
Average:	1.20	0.59	0.43	0.91	1.88	5.01

TABLE 4.11 Deseasonalized Data (unadjusted)

Week	M	T	W	Th	F
1	6.67	6.78	4.65	6.59	7.98
2	7.50	8.47	9.30	7.69	7.98
3	9.17	8.47	9.30	8.79	9.04
4	10.83	10.17	11.63	10.99	8.51

accomplished simply by dividing each data value by the daily average for the week in which that value is a member. The daily average for week 1 is 7, so the index for Monday is 8/7, or 1.14. The index for Monday in week 4 is 13/10, or 1.30. To smooth our random variations, the final index for Monday is the *average* of all the Monday indices—1.20 in our case. The sum of the five indices should be 5.0; if this is not the case, because of round-off errors, it should be normalized to 5.0. In Table 4.10, the total is 5.01. *Each* index should be corrected by multiplying by (5.00/5.01). It turns out that this does not change any of the initial values using only two fractional places.

Table 4.11 shows the data *deseasonalized* using the five indices. This is accomplished simply by *dividing* each original value by the average index. For example, Wednesday in the third week has a deseasonalized value of (4/0.43). To be *nonbiased*, the weekly deseasonalized data totals should equal the original totals. The total of the first week's values is 35, but the sum of the first week's deseasonalized values is 32.67—thus, the table is captioned "unadjusted". Adjustment would be achieved by multiplying each value by (35/32.67). A similar process would be followed for the other three weeks.

Now, to forecasting. Prediction is first accomplished through the *daily averages*, which, from Table 4.9, demonstrate a nonnoisy ramp increase of

TABLE 4.12 Forecast—Uncorrected

Week	M	T	W	Th	F	Daily Aggregate Forecast
5	13.20	6.49	4.73	10.01	20.68	11
6	14.40	7.08	5.16	10.92	22.56	12

TABLE 4.13 Forecast—Corrected

Week	M	T	W	Th	F	Total
5	13.17	6.48	4.72	9.99	20.64	55.00
6	14.37	7.07	5.15	10.90	22.51	60.00

one unit per week. The average value predictions for weeks 5 and 6 would therefore be 11 and 12. The individual daily predictions are found by multiplying the *average* forecast by the five indices, with the respective results as given in Table 4.12. The sum of the five forecasts in week 5 is 55.11, which is slightly higher than the prediction total of 55. To correct for this slight bias, all daily values are multiplied by (55/55.11) to obtain the results given in Table 4.13.

This overall procedure for handling growth and seasonality through indices is accomplished by the BEDSEAS computer program listed in Appendix B. The case problem given in Section 4.10 demonstrates the use of BEDSEAS.

4.7 PREDICTS—A DIGITAL COMPUTER PROGRAM FOR TIME-SERIES ANALYSIS†

PREDICTS is an acronym for *PRE*diction of *DI*s*C*rete *T*ime *S*eries. PREDICTS is designed to allow a user to analyze historical data series as to their benefit in predicting *future* values of the same series.

PREDICTS considers that data may be of two forms.

Growth pattern only.

Growth pattern plus cyclic effects.

Growth analysis is accomplished through exponential smoothing, whereas the cyclic analysis utilizes a form of Fourier Analysis.‡ The cyclic analysis is used to *approximate seasonal* characteristics.

---

†PREDICTS originally was developed by Chester Bradley and Peter Reese to partially satisfy the requirements of a graduate course in Forecasting in Industrial Engineering at Arizona State University. Permission to utilize PREDICTS as modified by David Bedworth was kindly granted by Mr. Bradley.

‡I. N. Sneddon, *Fourier Series*, The Free Press, Glencoe, Ill., 1961.

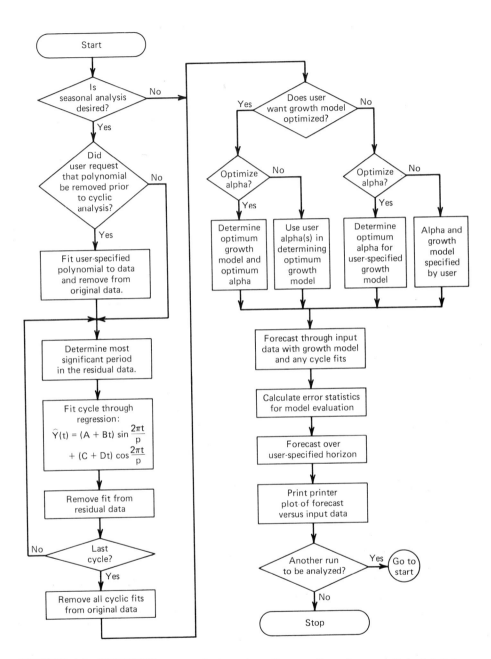

**FIGURE 4.4 PREDICTS approach to automatic growth and seasonal model deter-
mination.**

Cyclic Analysis

Cyclic analysis fits the equation

$$\hat{Y}(t) = (A + Bt)\sin\frac{2\pi t}{p} + (C + Dt)\cos\frac{2\pi t}{p}$$

The most significant period, p, is automatically determined through spectral analysis. The user may require up to five cyclic fits, although two is probably the maximum that should be utilized, or else the model might be fitting *noise*. If two cycles were requested, PREDICTS would first determine the most significant period in the data, say, p_1. The amplitude coefficients—A, B, C, and D—would then be found through regression. The fit

$$\hat{Y}(t) = (A + Bt)\sin\frac{2\pi t}{p_1} + (C + Dt)\cos\frac{2\pi t}{p_1}$$

would then be subtracted from the data. Next, the residual is analyzed to determine the next most significant period, say, p_2. The additional coefficients are found through regression analysis forming:

$$\hat{Y}(t) = (A_1 + B_1 t)\sin\frac{2\pi t}{p_1} + (C_1 + D_1 t)\cos\frac{2\pi t}{p_1} + (A_2 + B_2 t)\sin\frac{2\pi t}{p_2}$$
$$+ (C_2 + D_2 t)\cos\frac{2\pi t}{p_2}$$

Since the analysis to determine the significant periods requires that the data not have growth, an initial polynomial is fit to all the data and removed. Cyclic analysis is accomplished on the residual. The cycles are then pulled from the *original data* and exponential smoothing is applied for growth analysis. Upon conclusion, growth and cycle fits are added for forecasting purposes. For example, this may be

$$\hat{Y}(t) = a + bt + ct^2 + \sum_{i=1}^{k}\left[(A_i + B_i)\sin\frac{2\pi}{p_i} + (C_i + D_i)\cos\frac{2\pi}{p_i}\right]$$

PREDICTS will optimize on the growth model through error analysis (see Section 4.8) and will also determine, through a search routine, the optimum alpha. The user may override any of the search approaches to allow any growth model to be fit with any stipulated alpha value. An example of PREDICT's output is given in the case problem (Section 4.10) and a FORTRAN listing is given in Appendix C. Figure 4.4 gives a flow diagram for the overall process.

4.8 FORECAST ERROR ANALYSIS

When several forecast models are available for a particular situation, it follows that some unbiased procedure is needed to allow an evaluation of the models. In a similar vein, if only one model is available, some method is needed to allow a determination of the effectiveness of that model. The valid approach for both situations is the use of *forecast* errors.

The forecast error at time period t is the difference between the actual data value, $Y(t)$, and the forecast value for that period, $\hat{Y}(t)$:

$$e(t) = Y(t) - \hat{Y}(t)$$

The sum of the errors,

$$\sum_{t=1}^{N} e(t) = \sum_{t=1}^{N} [Y(t) - \hat{Y}(t)]$$

is not a valid measure of the effectiveness of a forecast technique but is a measure of bias or lack of bias. The sum of the errors should approach zero in the case of a model fit through regression analysis.

To eliminate the problem where large positive $e(t)$ values offset large negative $e(t)$ values, several alternatives are commonly used.

a. *Mean Absolute Deviation* (MAD):

$$\text{MAD} = \frac{\sum_{t=1}^{N} |Y(t) - \hat{Y}(t)|}{N}$$

b. *Mean Squared Error* (MSE):

$$\text{MSE} = \frac{\sum_{t=1}^{N} (Y(t) - \hat{Y}(t))^2}{N}$$

c. *Mean Absolute Percent Error* (MAP):

$$\text{MAP} = \frac{100}{N} \sum_{t=1}^{N} \left[\left| \frac{Y(t) - \hat{Y}(t)}{Y(t)} \right| \right]$$

The first two measures, MAD and MSE, give a means for evaluating forecast techniques or for different parameter conditions for one technique. The lower the value, the better the forecast through historical data. Unfortunately, the lowest value, unless zero, does not really give an indication of how "good" the forecast is, other than that it is better than those it is compared with. The final measure, MAP, allows an evaluation of the "goodness" of the forecast. A prediction MAD of 10.0 might sound terrific, but if the average size of the true datum is 1.0, the MAD is terrible. However, if the average true data size were 10,000, a MAD of 10.0 would require cries of jubilation.

The reader should realize that the *lead time* plays an important part in the determination of the error measure. If a lead time of 4 is being used, the error at time period 20 is formed by subtracting the prediction made at time period 16 from $Y(20)$. So, if 20 values of data are available with a lead time of 4, the error values can only be computed at times 5 through 20. MAD, for example, would be

$$\text{MAD} = \frac{\sum_{t=5}^{20} |Y(t) - \hat{Y}(t)|}{16}$$

Example

Consider the data

t	1	2	3	4	5	6	7	8	9	10
$Y(t)$	3	4	6	5	7	10	9	14	13	15

The PREDICTS program (see Section 4.8) was used to evaluate different exponential-smoothing alpha values and models for this data. Before running any test, though, the reader should be able to infer a few things about what model or parameters might be good. The data has a positive trend, so if a *constant* model were chosen it would be expected that a high alpha value would be optimum, since a high alpha puts a low dependence on the previous average. Similarly, it would be expected that a linear model would be a better model than a constant model, just because of the apparent trend. Results from the PREDICTS runs are given in Table 4.14.

The MSE and MAP values are only computed in PREDICTS for a particular model's optimum run, which is why only two values of each are given in Table 4.14. Also, the alpha value was constrained to be between 0.01 and 0.5. An optimum alpha value above 0.3 or so is indicative of an incorrect model; thus, the errors computed indicate that a constant model is invalid.

TABLE 4.14   Various Error Values for the Sample Data

Model	Alpha	MAD	MSE	MAP
Constant	0.1	3.3846	—	—
Constant	0.2	3.1797	—	—
Constant	0.3	2.9751	—	—
Constant	0.5	2.4492	8.5874	31.2223
Linear	0.01	0.9478	1.4382	11.9468
Linear	0.1	1.0190	—	—
Linear	0.2	1.0959	—	—
Linear	0.3	1.1785	—	—
Linear	0.5	1.4816	—	—

For the constant model, a MAD of 2.4492 superficially looks excellent. The MAP value shows that an average percent error of 31.2% is awful. Similarly, we might even have concern about the 11.95% error with the linear model. The very low alpha value of 0.01 is indicative that the linear model might be valid but that the data is quite noisy around the linear fit. With the models and alpha values evaluated, we would utilize a linear model with alpha equal to 0.01.

4.9 COMMENTS ON THE BOX–JENKINS APPROACH

It would not be fair to cover forecasting, even from an introductory point of view, without briefly mentioning the Box–Jenkins technique.[†] The general limitation of time-series analysis techniques used prior to Box–Jenkins has been, to a greater or lesser degree, that the analyst had to rely on his own experience and prior knowledge of the time series to assume the time-series model structure. The Box–Jenkins approach, however, lets the data speak for itself. It provides an objective and systematic approach to modeling and forecasting discrete time-series. The Box–Jenkins approach strives for the *best model* for forecasting purposes based upon time-series data. The concept of *best model* is not the usual one, found by a minimization of the fitting errors, but rather one that focuses on partitioning the data into predictable and random components. A model is considered adequate if all parameters are statistically significant and the errors from the model are independently distributed.

Theoretically, one has an infinite number of models from which to select the optimum for a given set of data. It is quite simple for different analysts to select different "best models" for a set of data—judgment and experience play important roles in the interactive procedure for determining a "best model."

The forecasting approach used in this chapter has been to present techniques amenable to rapid update, say, in an on-line process, with good response to process changes. Because of its user-interactive nature, Box–Jenkins does not fall in the class of techniques considered suitable for this purpose. A recent advance by Kang[‡] might cause this philosophy to change, but the mathematics involved is not suitable for introductory material. Suffice it to say that Box–Jenkins is a superb general forecasting tool. Its applicability to the automatic on-line forecasting case is still in question. One good *introductory* work on the subject is by Nelson.[§]

[†]G. E. P. Box and G. M. Jenkins, *Time-Series Analysis: Forecasting and Control*, Holden-Day, San Francisco, 1970.

[‡]A. Kang, "Identification of Autoregressive Integrated Moving Time Series," Ph.D. dissertation, Arizona State University, May 1980.

[§]C. Nelson, *Applied Time Series Analysis for Managerial Forecasting*, Holden-Day, San Francisco, 1973.

TABLE 4.15 Monthly Vehicular Injury
            Accident Data

	Year			
	1	2	3	4
Month				
1 (Jan.)	616	670	642	698
2 (Feb.)	617	690	696	669
3 (Mar.)	686	795	737	787
4 (Apr.)	594	664	694	749
5 (May)	596	625	732	777
6 (Jun.)	526	634	618	756
7 (Jul.)	540	610	653	642
8 (Aug.)	602	617	658	673
9 (Sep.)	665	708	682	840
10 (Oct.)	747	738	789	914
11 (Nov.)	756	674	703	935
12 (Dec.)	868	870	875	1020

4.10 CASE PROBLEM

To exemplify the use of computer programs for time-series prediction and analysis, consider the data given in Table 4.15 for monthly vehicular injury crashes in a major city. Prediction from such data is of course mandatory for effective emergency-medical-systems planning, law enforcement scheduling, and evaluation of experimental programs.

Before you even think about using a computer program, several things should be apparent from the data, especially if it is viewed as in Figure 4.5. First, there is an obvious growth pattern to the data. Second, data in the middle months of the year seem somewhat lower than at the end of the year, indicating probable seasonal aspects. Upon reflection, it is reasonable to expect seasonality within city vehicular injury accidents—if the city is a summer resort area, for example, it would be expected that accidents would rise in the summer, because of an influx of tourists. Also, holiday revelry at Christmas and New Year's might increase injury accidents.

The first computer program used to evaluate the data was BEDSEAS (see Section 4.6). Seasonal indexes for the twelve months in a year, determined by BEDSEAS, are given in Table 4.16, as is the deseasonalized data. It

TABLE 4.16 Seasonal Indexes and Deseasonal Data

Seasonal Indexes

1	2	3	4	5	6	7	8	9	10	11	12
0.9273	0.9449	1.0613	0.9513	0.9603	0.8897	0.8626	0.9005	1.0191	1.1227	1.0793	1.2810

Deseasonalized data is as follows:

Seasonal Segment

Period	1	2	3	4	5	6	7	8	9	10	11	12
1	666.2	654.9	648.3	626.2	622.4	592.9	627.8	670.4	654.4	667.3	702.5	679.6
2	721.1	728.8	747.6	696.6	649.6	711.2	705.8	683.8	693.4	656.0	623.3	677.8
3	690.3	734.5	692.4	727.4	760.0	692.6	754.8	728.5	667.3	700.7	649.4	681.1
4	754.2	709.5	743.1	788.9	810.9	851.5	745.8	748.8	825.9	815.7	868.1	797.9

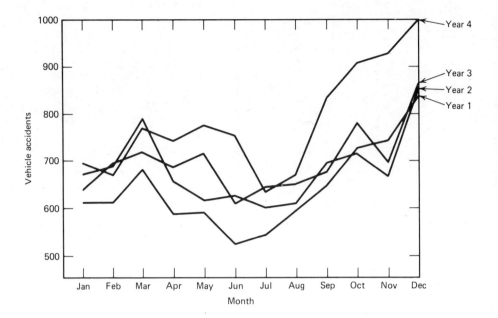

FIGURE 4.5 Injury accident data.

PREDICTION EQUATION THROUGH TOTALS IS:

(L)= 7854.250   -111.250(L)+   124.750(L)(L)

LEAD TIME   TOTAL
    5   10416.75

SEASONAL PREDICTIONS ARE AS FOLLOWS:

FORECAST PERIOD	1	2	3	SEASONAL SEGMENT 4	5	6	7	8	9	10	11	12
1	608.0	619.5	695.8	623.7	629.6	583.3	565.6	590.4	668.2	736.1	707.6	839.9
2	628.3	640.2	719.1	644.6	650.7	602.8	584.5	610.2	690.5	760.7	731.3	868.0
3	667.9	680.6	764.4	685.2	691.7	640.8	621.3	648.6	734.0	808.7	777.4	922.7
4	726.0	740.6	831.8	745.6	752.6	697.3	676.1	705.8	798.7	880.0	845.9	1004.0

• •

	FORECAST VALUES BEYOND GIVEN DATA ARE BELOW											
5	805.0	820.2	921.2	825.8	833.6	772.3	748.8	781.7	884.6	974.6	936.9	1112.0

MEAN ABSOLUTE ERROR DEVIATION THROUGH DATA IS   31.2213

MEAN PERCENT DEVIATION THROUGH DATA IS   4.4181

FIGURE 4.6 Forecast results from PREDICTS.

can be seen that December has an extremely high incidence of injury accidents (28% above the monthly average), whereas July is low (86% of the monthly average). The deseasonalized data shows that with obvious seasonality removed, the growth trend is more clear-cut. Forecasts through the historical data and extended beyond one year are given in Figure 4.6 with two measures of forecast error, MAD and MAP. The percentage error of 4.4181% has to be construed as being quite good. Finally, a printerplot of the data versus forecasts is given in Figure 4.7, with lines connecting the forecasts for clarity. Matching of the forecasts to data is readily seen to be quite good.

The same data was then analyzed by PREDICTS (see Section 4.7). It intuitively makes sense that on a monthly basis, vehicular injury accidents would reflect to some degree a constant multiple of the yearly value, with a different multiplier for each month. If this is the case, then the cyclic seasonal approach using PREDICTS undoubtedly will not be as good a forecast model as BEDSEAS. PREDICTS was run for comparative purposes only. Two cyclic analyses were requested, with the program optimizing both the growth model and the exponential-smoothing alpha value. The two cyclic fits had periods of 12 and 3. The most dominant period, 12, agreed with the intuitive feel that monthly accident data would be seasonal. The secondary period, 3, indicates a quarterly relationship, which also makes sense. The two cycles were automatically removed from the data by PREDICTS, and it was this residual that PREDICTS exponentially smoothed. A quadratic fit was found optimum with alpha equal to 0.01. The low alpha indicates that the data is probably quite noisy around the growth factor. The overall prediction equation, just as a matter of interest, is

$$\hat{Y}(t) = 834.75 + 8.04(t - 48) + 0.09(t - 48)^2$$

$$+ (-4.73 + .36t)\sin\frac{2\pi t}{12} + (63.06 + .36t)\cos\frac{2\pi t}{12}$$

$$+ (-10.35 + .49t)\sin\frac{2\pi t}{3} + (37.67 + .09t)\cos\frac{2\pi t}{3}$$

The average mean percent error, MAP, is 6.51%, compared with 4.4% using BEDSEAS. A printer plot of the results, developed by PREDICTS and given in Figure 4.8, demonstrates a wider fluctuation of the forecast from the true data than with BEDSEAS. With a different set of data, though, the reverse could be true. In determining the best approach, the user should use whatever is available. Comparing BEDSEAS and PREDICTS is one way to this solution. However, PREDICTS was developed for an on-line rapid-update forecasting program. Listings and user instructions for BEDSEAS and PREDICTS are given in Appendixes B and C.

Finally, the forecaster should take the environment into consideration. If gasoline were to be suddenly rationed, it should be expected that vehicular accidents would decrease. The same would be expected if the price of

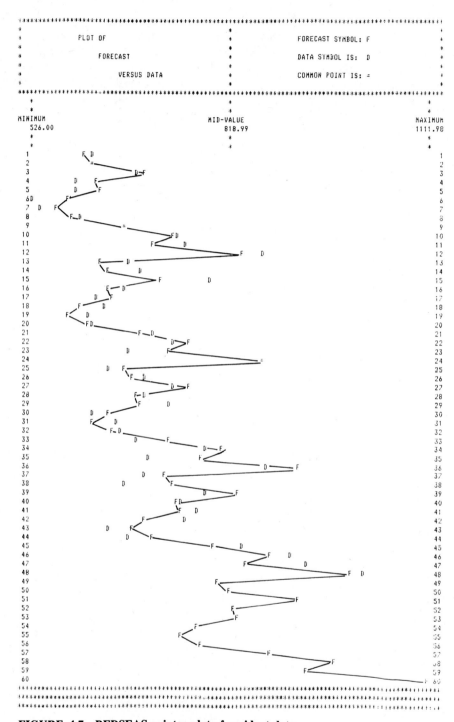

FIGURE 4.7   BEDSEAS printer plot of accident data.

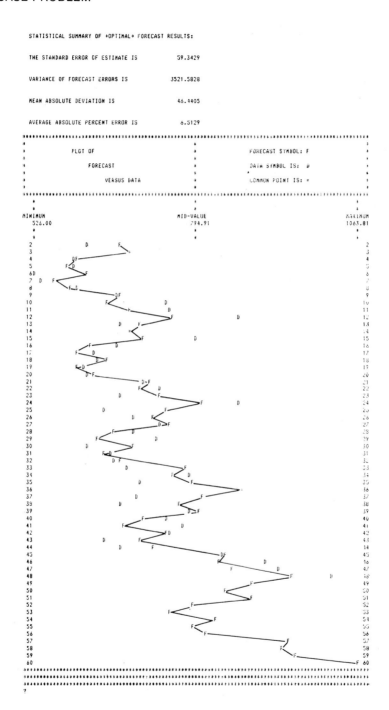

FIGURE 4.8   PREDICTS printer plot of accident data.

gasoline increased drastically. Also, if a large number of policemen were put on an anti-drunk-driving campaign, accidents should decrease. Historical data can only be a guide to, not a pure indicator of, the future.

4.11 REFERENCES

1. Box, G. E., and Jenkins, G. M., *Time-Series Analysis: Forecasting and Control*, Holden-Day, San Francisco, 1970.

2. Brown, R. G., *Smoothing, Forecasting, and Prediction of Discrete Time Series*, Prentice-Hall, Englewood Cliffs, N.J., 1963.

3. D'Esopo, D. A., "A Note on Forecasting by the Exponential Smoothing Operator," *Operations Research*, vol. 9, no. 5, 1961.

4. *Forecasting Sales—Studies in Business Policy No.* 106, National Industrial Conference Board, Inc., New York, 1964.

5. Kang, A., "Identification of Autoregressive Integrated Moving Average Time Series," Ph.D. dissertation, Arizona State University, May 1980.

6. Nelson, C., *Applied Time Series Analysis for Managerial Forecasting*, Holden-Day, San Francisco, 1973.

7. Parzen, E., *Time-Series Analysis Papers*, Holden-Day, San Francisco, 1967.

8. Shweid, G. B., "Simplified Formulas for Method of Differences Analysis," senior project in Design, Industrial Engineering Dept., State University, May 1971.

9. Sneddon, I. N., *Fourier Series*, The Free Press, Glencoe, Ill., 1961.

4.12 EXERCISES

1. The development of a radically new product does not seem to be amenable to time-series forecasting—Why? Suggest a procedure to allow prediction of sales of a three-dimensional-picture television set.

2. Derive the equations to allow a, b, and c to be determined in the model

$$\hat{Y}(t) = a + bt + ct^2$$

Use the regression approach developed for the constant and linear models.

3. Consider the following set of supposedly linear data.

t	1	2	3	4	5	6
$Y(t)$	4	7	9	13	16	18

Fit this data with both a quadratic and linear regression model to demonstrate that the quadratic model will "adapt" to a change in data trend.

4. Consider the following set of basically constant-model data.

t	1	2	3	4	5	6
$Y(t)$	5	3	6	7	4	5

Fit this data with both a linear and a constant regression model to demonstrate that the linear model can adapt to changes in the data trend. What if the data goes quadratic?

5. Consider the cyclic model

$$\hat{Y}(t) = \cos\frac{2\pi t}{p}$$

Show why regression analysis cannot be used in the determination of an optimum period, p, for a set of data.

6. Consider the cyclic model

$$\hat{Y}(t) = (A + Bt)\cos\frac{2\pi t}{4}$$

Use the regression approach in deriving equations to determine the coefficients, A and B, that optimize the model.

7. The data given below is supposed to conform to the trigonometric model given in Problem 6:

t	1	2	3	4	5	6	7	8
$Y(t)$	0.2	−3.0	0.3	3.7	−0.2	−4.5	0.1	5.4

Determine A and B in

$$\hat{Y}(t) = (A + Bt)\cos\frac{2\pi t}{4}$$

and forecast for time period 10.

8. Consider the model

$$\hat{Y}(t) = a(10)^{bt}$$

Using an appropriate linear transform, derive equations to allow the determination of a and b through linear regression.

9. Consider the following data.

t	1	2	3	4	5	6
$Y(t)$	8.0	12.0	20.0	32.0	48.0	80.0

Determine a and b in Problem 8's model and forecast period 8's value.

10. An exponential model was considered in this chapter for evaluation by regression analysis:

$$\hat{Y}(t) = ae^{bt}$$

Show why regression analysis will not allow equations for a and b to be determined unless a transform of the original data is made.

11. Consider the following data.

t	1	2	3	4	5	6	7
$Y(t)$	7	8	10	12	13	14	16

Fit a linear model by both regular regression analysis and with the coded-t approach where the time values sum to zero. Show that the solutions are equivalent in forecasting the value for time period 10.

12. Consider a noise-free constant-model set of data, $Y(t) = 10$ for $t = 1, 2, 3, \ldots 8$. First-order single smoothing is used, but with an initial condition at time period 1 of $\hat{Y}(1), 1 = 5$. Show that a high alpha value will damp out initial errors more quickly than a low alpha. Use alpha values of 0.1 and 0.6 to show this.

13. Consider a noise-free linear model set of data, $Y(t) = 3 + 2t$ for $t = 1, 2, 3, \ldots 8$. A linear-model exponential smoothing is used for forecasting, with initial conditions at $t = 1$ of

$$\hat{Y}(1), 1 = 3$$

$$\hat{Y}(1), 2 = 3$$

Show that initial errors are damped out at time period 8—use alpha equal to 0.5.

14. In the introduction to exponential smoothing material, it was stated that

$$\alpha \sum_{i=0}^{t-1} \beta^i \text{ reduces to } 1 - \beta^t$$

Prove that this is correct.

15. Consider the following data.

t	1	2	3	4	5	6
$Y(t)$	5	8	6	5	8	8

Use an appropriate exponential-smoothing model to predict $\hat{Y}(8)$ from time period 6. Use $\alpha = 0.2$ and justify your model.

16. Consider the following data.

t	1	2	3	4	5	6	7	8
$Y(t)$	4	7	9	10	13	15	18	22

Use an appropriate exponential smoothing model to predict $\hat{Y}(10)$ from time period 8. Use $\alpha = 0.1$ and justify your model.

17. The following data are thought to conform to the regression model $Y(t) = 2 + 3t + 0.5t^2$.

t	1	2	3	4	5	6	7	8
$Y(t)$	7	11	16	23	31	39	50	62

Use the quadratic exponential-smoothing model to predict $\hat{Y}(10)$ from $Y(8)$. Justify your initial conditions based on the regression model.

18. Consider the quarterly sales data:

	I	II	III	IV
1976	43	27	10	22
1977	49	35	14	27
1978	58	47	14	32
1979	71	53	18	35
1980	80	63	22	41

a. Determine appropriate seasonal indexes for each quarter.

b. Use the indexes in predicting quarter values for 1981.

19. Prove that if a set of data has a noise-free ramp with slope b, the moving average with N values will lag the true values by

$$\left(\frac{N-1}{2}\right)(b)$$

20. Prove that if a set of data has a noise-free ramp with slope b, first-order exponential smoothing will lag the true values by

$$\left(\frac{\beta}{\alpha}\right)(b)$$

21. Consider the data given in Problem 16. Initial conditions for exponential smoothing are

$$\textit{Constant Model} \quad \hat{Y}(1), 1 = 4$$
$$\textit{Linear Model} \quad \hat{Y}(1), 1 = -4$$
$$\hat{Y}(1), 2 = -12$$

a. Comment on the appropriateness of the initial conditions, given $\alpha = 0.2$.

b. Use error analysis with a lead time of 1 to show which is the most appropriate model to use.

22. Reconsider Problem 21: this time, a constant model is to be used but the α to use is not known. Use error analysis to determine which of α values 0.1, 0.5, 0.7 are the most appropriate. Intuitively, why would you expect the optimum α to be the one determined?

23. Consider Data Set A. Without doing any model fits, etc., suggest an appropriate forecasting model—plot the data, immerse yourself in the data, think about the environment in which the data exists (if known), and so on.

24. Based on the evaluation accomplished in Problem 23, use an appropriate computer program(s) to allow a forecast of the next two years' consumption. Assume a lead time of one year in your forecasts.

25. Consider Data Set *B*. Without doing any model fits, etc., suggest an appropriate forecasting model—plot the data, immerse yourself in the data, think about the environment in which the data exists (if known), and so on.
26. Based on the evaluation accomplished in Problem 25, use an appropriate computer program(s) to allow a forecast of sales over the next eight quarters. Assume a lead time of one quarter.
27. Consider Data Set *C*. Without doing any model fits, etc., suggest an appropriate forecasting model—plot the data, immerse yourself in the data, think about the environment in which the data exists (if known), and so on.
28. Based on the evaluation accomplished in Problem 27, use an appropriate computer program(s) to allow a forecast of the next 10 process values. Assume a lead time of 3 hours in your forecasts.
29. Consider Data Set *D*. Without doing any model fits, etc., suggest an appropriate forecasting model—plot the data, immerse yourself in the data, think about the environment in which the data exists (if known), and so on.
30. Based on the evaluation accomplished in Problem 29, use an appropriate computer program(s) to allow a forecast of the next six production values. Use a lead time of one in your solution.
31. Refer to the Phoenix Population and Area Chart, Figure 4.9 (taken from *The Phoenix Budget—January* 1, 1978). For each of the following questions, document your solution approach and give justification for the

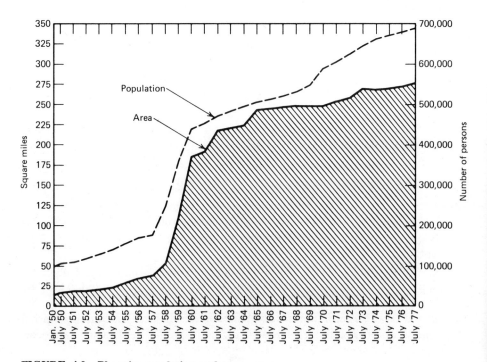

FIGURE 4.9 Phoenix population and area.

Year	Population (No. of Persons)	Area (Square Miles)
January 1, 1950	102,548	16.4
July 1, 1950	107,116	17.1
July 1, 1951	108,158	17.1
July 1, 1952	119,000	18.9
July 1, 1953	129,956	21.0
July 1, 1954	140,062	24.1
July 1, 1955	155,788	29.0
July 1, 1956	170,082	35.7
July 1, 1957	172,569	36.3
July 1, 1958	241,899	52.6
July 1, 1959	360,771	110.0
July 1, 1960	439,671	187.4
July 1, 1961	451,964	191.1
July 1, 1962	468,385	220.3
July 1, 1963	482,521	222.6
July 1, 1964	494,061	222.7
July 1, 1965	504,448	245.7
July 1, 1966	511,238	246.2
July 1, 1967	519,006	247.4
July 1, 1968	527,744	247.7
July 1, 1969	546,381	247.7
July 1, 1970	590,173	247.9
July 1, 1971	605,984	254.9
July 1, 1972	627,109	258.2
July 1, 1973	646,476	269.3
July 1, 1974	659,716	269.3
July 1, 1975	667,386	269.4
July 1, 1976	676,100	273.4
July 1, 1977	682,300	276.6

solution approach. Use any computer programs made available to you.

a. Predict Phoenix's population for 1980.

b. Predict Phoenix's area for 1980.

c. Determine the feasibility of predicting population from area.

d. Discuss the dangers in using time-series analysis to forecast city population and area values. Suggest factors that might affect Phoenix's population and how they might be taken into consideration when forecasting.

DATA SET *A*   **Annual Taxed Gallons of Motor Vehicle Fuel for Arizona (in 1000s)**

1948	190
1949	210
1950	225
1951	270
1952	290
1953	310
1954	315
1955	360
1956	390
1957	410
1958	465
1959	480
1960	525
1961	540
1962	585
1963	620
1964	640
1965	675
1966	720
1967	740
1968	810
1969	925
1970	985
1971	1060

DATA SET *B*   **Quarterly Sales Data**

	Quarter			
	I	II	III	IV
1974	425	980	1320	325
1975	515	1190	1410	330
1976	620	1450	1780	410
1977	725	1680	1900	480
1978	940	2310	2540	610
1979	1120	2775	3320	795
1980	1630	3850	4225	1210

DATA SET *C* **Process Data Taken at Three-Hour Intervals**
(read from left to right on first line, left to right second line, and so on)

54, 38, 100, 120, 48, 65, 135, 55, 39, 105, 119, 50, 64, 130, 60, 44, 108, 118, 53, 67, 135, 58,
41, 113, 125, 54, 71, 141, 61, 40, 111, 123, 54, 72, 140, 62, 46, 112, 120, 57, 74, 142, 65, 49,
114, 126, 55, 75, 53, 128, 130, 63, 76, 141, 73, 56, 130, 132, 62, 76, 150, 75, 56,133, 131,
65, 75, 138

DATA SET *D* **Production Data** (read from left to right on first line, left to right on
second line, and so on)

388, 419, 441, 450, 444, 427, 406, 390, 389, 409, 446, 499, 556, 604, 633, 635, 612, 571,
526, 493, 485, 510, 566, 643, 724, 790, 825, 821, 780, 715, 646, 595, 581, 612, 686, 787,
892, 976, 1017, 1006, 948, 859, 766, 698, 677, 715, 806, 931, 1060, 1161, 1209, 1192, 1116,
1003, 886, 800, 773, 817, 926, 1075

FIVE: AGGREGATE PLANNING AND MASTER SCHEDULING

Hear one side, and you will be in the dark; hear both sides, and all will be clear.

Halliburton

In the manufacturing environment, inventory, scheduling, capacity, and resources are just a few considerations requiring aggregate planning. As manufacturing facilities grow, the problems of planning and control become extremely complex. The production control department must schedule to meet fluctuating demands for increasing varieties of products. Master schedules must be found within the operating and customer-relations policies of the company. Clearly, a methodology is needed to assist the production control department in establishing these master schedules. The methods to do this are most often referred to as *aggregate planning* techniques.

5.1 OVERVIEW

The objective of aggregate planning is the productive utilization of both human and equipment resources. The word *aggregate* means that planning is conducted at a gross level intended to meet the total demand collected over all products, utilizing the total human and equipment resources over the entire facility. For example, the plan may call only for so many tons of steel, ignoring the breakdown of that demand into different products, such as coils, rolls, or bars. In addition, the plan may call for so many employees, ignoring differences in skill-type. To use aggregate planning, it is therefore necessary to find some surrogate product to represent the aggregation of all products and some number of employees needed to produce one unit of that product. In addition, it is necessary to find a plan to meet the fluctuating, period-by-period demand for the aggregated product-line. There are many options available to the aggregate planner. One simple option is to manufacture more than is needed during slow periods and hold the overage until a later date. This approach results in a more constant production rate at the expense of higher inventory costs. The opposite approach is to hire and lay off people while manufacturing exactly what is needed in each period. Entire shifts could be added or deleted as the need arises. Under this option, inventories are held to a minimum but the costs of hiring, training, and unemployment become extreme. Overtime is an option frequently used by aggregate planners, but there are definite limits to how much capacity can be varied by controlling overtime. Another option is to subcontract part of the work during peak periods and accept the associated increases in costs. A company simply may fail to meet all its demands during peak periods and hope that customers will gracefully accept the delays. Finally, companies often choose to maintain a fixed capacity of both people and equipment that will be fully utilized only when demand is high. Typically, production planners use some combination of these approaches when forming their aggregate plans.

In order to understand better what aggregate planning accomplishes, consider the following example. A small plant makes several models of commercial videotape players. The facility has the capacity to manufacture 38 units per day. Every unit, not shipped in the month it is made, incurs a $10 per month inventory-holding cost. Every unit back-ordered incurs costs of $25 for each month until it is shipped. The cost to manufacture a unit is $800 on regular time and $1000 on overtime.

Table 5.1 represents one possible aggregate plan to meet the forecasted demand for the company's products. The forecasted demand, shown in column 2 of the table, ranges from 400 units to 1500 units per month. In column 3, the cumulative monthly demand is given. The available days of regular-time and overtime production are given in columns 4 and 5. Production capacity varies from month to month, depending on the length of the month. In the case of August, capacity is low because of vacations. One possible aggregate production plan is given in columns 6 and 7 as regular-time and overtime production levels. For January, the regular-time production of 836 units equals 22 days times 38 units per day. In October, November, and December the plan calls for less production than could be accomplished on regular time, which implies layoffs in those months. The cumulative production of this plan is given in column 8. If the cumulative production in any month exceeds the cumulative demand, the excess shows up as inventory. If cumulative demand exceeds production, on the other hand, the unfilled demand must go into back-orders. Columns 9 and 10 list, respectively, the inventory and back-orders held in the various months. The remaining five columns provide the cost figures, in thousands of dollars, used to evaluate this potential plan. Column 11 gives the regular-time production costs. For Janu-

TABLE 5.1 Example Aggregate Plan

(1)	(2) Fore-casted Demand	(3) Cum. Demand	(4) Regu-lar time Days	(5) Over-time Days	(6) Regu-lar Time Prod.	(7) Over-time Prod.	(8) Cum. Prod.	(9) Inv.	(10) Back-orders	(11) R.T. Prod. Costs	(12) O.T. Prod. Costs	(13) Inv. Costs	(14) Back order Costs	(15) Total Costs
												× $1000		
Jan.	500	500	22	4	836	152	988	488	—	668.8	152.0	4.88	—	825.68
Feb.	750	1250	18	4	684	152	1824	574	—	547.2	152.0	5.74	—	704.94
Mar.	850	2100	22	4	836	152	2812	712	—	668.8	152.0	7.12	—	827.92
Apr.	1000	3100	21	4	798	152	3762	662	—	638.4	152.0	6.62	—	797.02
May.	1400	4500	22	5	836	190	4788	288	—	668.8	190.0	2.88	—	861.68
June	1500	6000	21	4	798	152	5738	—	262	638.4	152.0	—	6.55	796.95
July	850	6850	21	4	798	152	6688	—	162	638.4	152.0	—	4.05	794.45
Aug.	750	7600	13	3	494	114	7296	—	304	395.2	114.0	—	7.60	516.80
Sept.	600	8200	20	4	760	—	8056	—	144	608.0	—	—	3.60	611.6
Oct.	400	8600	23	4	483	—	8539	—	61	386.4	—	—	1.53	387.93
Nov.	400	9000	21	5	441	—	8980	—	20	352.8	—	—	0.50	353.3
Dec.	400	9400	20	4	420	—	9400	—	—	336.0	—	—	—	336.0
										6547.20	1216.00	27.24	23.83	7814.27

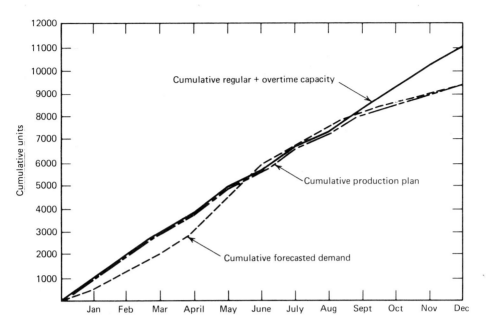

FIGURE 5.1   Graphical representation of aggregate plan shown in Table 5.1.

ary, regular-time costs of $668,800 equal 836 units times $800 per unit. Column 12 gives the overtime costs. Column 13 gives the inventory-holding costs, which equal $10 times the units held. Column 14 gives the back-order costs, which equal $25 times the units back-ordered. The last column gives the total production cost for each month. The grand total for this plan is $7,814,270.

The plan represented by Table 5.1 was created by plotting the cumulative demand as indicated by the dashed line on Figure 5.1. The regular-time plus overtime cumulative capacity was then plotted by the dark line. Obviously, any plan that plots below this capacity line is feasible. One of the many feasible schedules is the dash-dot-dash line in the figure, which represents a plan to manufacture to maximum capacity through August and then fall back to regular-time capacity and below through December.

Questions arise: Is there some other plan that would cost less? Is there a model that, if applied, will yield the minimum cost solution? Is there a simple heuristic approach that is easy to use and will result in a close-to-minimum-cost solution? These questions will be addressed in this chapter. The first (and oldest) approach explored will be the use of empirical analysis to model how management planned in the past. Such an approach is relatively simple. There is, however, no guarantee that the way management planned in the past was correct then or that it will be correct in the future. To overcome these deficiencies we will present a second approach, which builds a simplified model that can be solved using some known technique (linear programming, for example). The solution obtained would only be optimal for the simplified problem and not necessarily for the real world. If, however, the simplifying assumptions seemed reasonable, we could confidently implement the approach in the real world. Finally, a third approach will call for a rigorous and highly realistic model that could be exercised with a computer to evaluate a large sample of alternative solutions. There is no guarantee that the best of the sample is optimal. If, however, it was close to optimal in a test environment (where the optimal solution was known), we could have confidence that the approach would work well in the real world. After these aggregate planning approaches are presented, an approach to disaggregating the plan into a master schedule for each individual product will be discussed.

A master schedule is the output of aggregate planning and the starting point for most manufacturing control systems. The master schedule establishes finished-goods inventory levels, thereby affecting inventory management. It determines the production quantities that are inputs to the materials-requirement plan and results in labor-demand figures that must be met by personnel planning. It also establishes the quantities of finished goods available that marketing can promise for delivery. Finally, the master schedule informs Purchasing of the need to obtain subcontractor services. Without an accurately established master schedule, all of these activities would be largely guesswork. In a competitive environment, good aggregate planning is fundamental to success in manufacturing.

5.2 DEFINITIONS

In order to understand and subsequently apply the aggregate planning techniques presented below, the reader must become familiar with the vocabulary used in aggregate planning. In this section, a number of definitions are presented. The reader is cautioned to understand these terms thoroughly. One can read subsequent sections and grasp the mechanics of the approaches and yet not be totally conversant in the subject. True understanding requires more than mechanics. One must be able intuitively to grasp and interpret the application of the mechanics. This grasp centers on an understanding of the aggregate planning process and its vocabulary.

Production planning period   The segment of time that the organization wants its production plans to cover. This might be a month, or a week, or some other time segment. The length of the segment is governed by the ability to forecast the market accurately and the speed with which the organization can be adjusted to meet those market changes. If demand is difficult to forecast accurately in short periods, longer production periods are called for. In addition, as typical production runs get longer, the production period should be longer. Typically, an organization considering aggregate planning is likely to have accounting or other internal activities that already establish the planning period.

Production planning horizon

The number of periods into the future that are to be considered when making the plan. Governed by the market environment, the horizon can be no longer than the number of periods for which reasonable forecasts for demand can be found. In cases in which forecasts can be easily and accurately made far into the future, the horizon should consider how much of the future is most economic to consider.

Aggregate production unit

The unit of production recommended by the plan for the next planning period. It might be in gallons or board-feet or tons or numbers of widgets. Most organizations produce many different models of the same basic product. A shoe manufacturer, for example, might make a wide variety of shoes. The forecasted demand is made by shoe style or groups of shoes with similar market areas. These different products and their forecasted demands must be aggregated into one surrogate product. In addition, conversions are made relating individual production-time standards to the aggregate production-time standard for the surrogate product.

Aggregate production facility

The manufacturing facility to be covered by one plan. Many plants have more than one independent production activity at one location. Each of these independent activities can be considered separately. In addition, each facility employs people of different, and often non-interchangeable, talents who must be aggregated together as a total labor force.

Aggregate plan

The resulting plan for work-force size and production level in a given aggregate planning facility. The plan is generally made once each period for the following period. The planning decisions are made to minimize the total cost of meeting the forecasted demand for goods and services. The plan considers various cost items, as will be discussed below.

Disaggregation

The activity of converting the planned production level into quantities of each of the product models manufactured in the planning facility. If, for example, the aggregate plan calls for 500 of the aggregate production unit, disaggregation might result in a plan for 100 units of product *A*, 250 of product *B*, and 150 of product *E*.

Master schedule

The result of the disaggregation of the production plan. It lists those models to be produced in the next period and the quantities to be produced.

Work-force cost

The average cost to employ a production worker for one period of regular-time production. This cost must include all wages, benefits, and other support items that vary directly with the number of production workers. Production workers are those people whose employment varies with the normal ups and downs of production levels. Thus, if production support employees such as pipe fitters or electricians do not vary significantly with production levels, then they should not be considered in the work-force cost figure.

Production cost

The non-labor variable component associated with each aggregate production unit. It includes the cost of materials, in-process inventory, spoilage, and scrap. It is the expected change in total cost that would occur if output were changed by one unit of production with all else held constant. In some aggregate-planning models, the cost of labor is lumped in with these costs so that the regular-time production cost and the cost to produce on overtime can be more easily compared.

Inventory-holding cost

The lost opportunity resulting from tying up money in finished-goods inventory plus the cost of space to store the finished goods. Insurance, obsolescence, and other costs are sometimes included as part of this cost.

Hiring cost

The expected cost to increase the work force by one person. This would include items such as Personnel Department cost, training costs, inefficiencies, and the cost during early learning periods.

Layoff cost

The cost associated with reducing the work force by one person. Personnel costs, unemployment costs, and even lost goodwill should be included.

Stock-out costs

The expected losses resulting from failure to meet the demand for the product. If the customer merely waits for delivery, this cost may be small. If the customer goes elsewhere, the cost may be large. Loss in good customer-relations and the effect on future sales should also be considered.

Overtime cost   The cost of producing a unit on overtime. The cost of labor is different but the cost of materials is the same. As with production cost, this figure sometimes includes both labor and materials (or, more frequently, only labor).

Undertime cost   The cost associated with paying labor and utilities while the facility is functioning at less than 100% of its staffed capacity.

Subcontracting cost   The total per-unit cost if the production is subcontracted to an outside source. This cost must include the cost of differences in quality and reliability as well as the cost to consummate and control a subcontract.

5.3 EMPIRICAL APPROACH TO AGGREGATE PLANNING

Among the terms defined in the previous section were several cost factors that should be considered when aggregate-planning. The nature of these factors makes the modeling of the problem complex. Nonetheless, many published approaches to aggregate planning utilize a model.

This section outlines the empirical development of an intuitively appealing model based on management's historical decisions. This approach, first suggested by Bowman,† is called the "management coefficients approach." The underlying assumption is that experienced managers react correctly to the factors involved in aggregate planning. As demand forecasts increase, managers plan for more people and greater production. If inventory levels get high, they cut back on production. In the long run, managers tend toward "good" solutions. The problem is that they also tend to be inconsistent, favoring one factor or another depending on the mood of the day. Bowman concluded that it is better to add consistency to the managerial decisions than to use a simplified model designed to give optimal solutions.

To establish consistency, one first determines the factors that management considers when planning production. The factors of interest must be quantitative, and a history of their values must be available. To satisfy the

---

†E. H. Bowman, "Consistency and Optimality in Managerial Decision Making," *Management Science*, vol. 9, no. 1, January 1963. Reprinted by permission of E. H. Bowman. Copyright © 1963 The Institute of Management Sciences.

regression analysis assumptions, the factors should also be independent normally distributed random variables. Limiting oneself to quantitative factors is a problem. Managers often consider factors that cannot easily be measured. A company in a labor-tight community may not want to lay off this scarce resource. A company that must contend with strict supplier limitations may have to manufacture when it can get the materials. It is hard to include these types of factors in a model.

Knowing the factors, the analyst formulates one or more intuitively appealing models of the planning decisions. Using the historical data and regression analysis, the values of the coefficients and the multiple correlation coefficient are calculated for each model. Those models with the highest correlation coefficients are said to account more closely for the variation in the manager's historical decisions. If the correlation coefficient is very high, the model and managers agree very closely, which suggests that the managers are consistent and don't need a model. If the correlation is too low, one should be concerned that other factors are involved and the model will do poorly because it fails to consider them. It is hoped that the model will closely predict future decisions. To test this prediction question, the model is used independently to plan production in parallel with management's existing procedure. This should be done for six months to a year. An analysis of the costs of production are then made. Using these cost figures, the analyst calculates the cost associated with the six months of the present planning approach and the costs that would have occurred had the model's plan been used. If the model significantly outperforms the present approach, management likely will be eager to implement the new approach.

In order to understand this procedure better, consider the following example problem. An analysis of management's present approach indicates that two decisions are made each month. One decision establishes the work-force size and the other establishes the quantity to be produced. The factors of interest are the size of the previous month's work force, the need to bring inventory levels in line with a pre-established buffer level, and the forecasted demand for the next three periods. This analysis suggests the need for two models: a work-force model and a production model.

First, consider the work-force model, which is a function of the forecasted demand, inventory imbalance, and the previous month's work force: that is,

$$W_t = f(F_t, I^*, I_{t-1}, W_{t-1}) \tag{5.1}$$

where

W_t = work-force size in period t
F_t = forecasted demand in period t
I^* = desired inventory level
I_{t-1} = actual inventory at end of period $t-1$
f = the function relationship

One possible function, from Bowman, would be

$$W_t = \alpha_0 + \alpha_1 W_{t-1} + \alpha_2[I^* - I_{t-1}] + \alpha_3 F_t \qquad (5.2)$$

where α's are management coefficients to be determined.

The coefficient α_1 indicates how much of the variation in the historical work-force decisions can be explained by the previous period's work force. Therefore, α_1 tends to explain how much the managers considered this factor when planning. Similarly, α_2 tends to explain how much they considered the difference between actual and desired inventory. Finally, α_3 tends to explain the effect of forecasted demand. The α_0 coefficient is primarily an intercept required by regression analysis.

Moving on, consider the production-level decision that is a function of the work-force level, inventory imbalance, and the forecasted demand. In this case, suppose the concern for demand included the next three-period forecasts with emphasis on the near future: that is,

$$P_t = g[W_t, I^*, I_{t-1}, F_t, F_{t+1}, F_{t+2}] \qquad (5.3)$$

where

$$P_t = \text{production level in period } t$$

$$g = \text{the function relationship}$$

One possible function, also from Bowman, is

$$P_t = \beta_0 + \beta_1 W_t + \beta_2(I^* - I_{t-1}) + \beta_3 \sum_{i=0}^{2} \left(\frac{1}{i+1} F_{t+i} \right) \qquad (5.4)$$

where β's are management coefficients similar to the α's in Equation 5.2 and are similarly determined.

A wise question is, where did these two models come from? They were merely fabricated because of their intuitive appeal. For alternative forms, see Bowman or Gordon,[†] or create one yourself.

Table 5.2 provides a set of hypothetical values that fit the model given in Equations 5.2 and 5.4. For convenience, columns for $I^* - I_{t-1}$ and $\sum_{i=0}^{2} (1/(i+1))$ F_{t+i} are included in the table. For this test, I^* was assumed to be 50. Regression analysis was used with this data to determine the α and β coefficients of the models. It was also assumed that each unit of production required five hours of labor. Therefore, one worker would translate into eight units in the 40 hours of regular production time. For convenience, the regular-time $P_{R,t}$ and overtime $P_{0,t}$ production quantities are also given in Table 5.2.

The resulting regression equations and correlation coefficients, $r_{\hat{W}_t}$ and

---

†J. R. M. Gordon, "A Multi-Model Analysis of an Aggregate Scheduling Decision," Ph.D. dissertation, Sloan School of Management, Massachusetts Institute of Technology 1966.

TABLE 5.2   Sample Data for Management Coefficients Approach Example

t	F_t	I_{t-1}	W_t	P_t	$P_{R,t}$	$P_{\bullet,t}$	$I^* - I_{t-1}$	$\sum_{i=0}^{2}\left(\frac{1}{i+1}F_{t+i}\right)$
1	200	30	25	209	200	9	20	385
2	210	48	25	230	200	30	2	430
3	240	60	28	250	224	26	−10	473
4	300	27	28	270	224	46	23	492
5	250	50	28	270	224	46	0	403
6	200	49	25	200	200	0	1	330
7	160	65	22	175	175	0	−15	268
8	150	72	20	160	160	0	−22	240
9	100	95	18	120	120	0	−45	213
10	120	97	18	120	120	0	−47	267
11	160	55	18	120	120	0	−5	333
12	200	31	20	180	160	20	19	387
13	220	47	22	200	176	24	3	422
14	230	68	28	250	224	26	−18	477
15	260	77	30	270	240	30	−27	525
16	350	27	33	300	266	34	23	562
17	270	55	33	300	266	34	−5	452
18	230	65	30	240	240	0	−15	390
19	200	102	30	240	240	0	−52	340
20	180	100	22	176	176	0	−50	312
21	150	129	22	176	176	0	−79	302
22	170	134	22	176	176	0	−84	353
23	200	108	22	176	176	0	−58	412
24	250	70	22	176	176	0	−20	473

$r_{\hat{P}_t}$, as obtained from a computer program, are

$$\hat{W}_t = 1.49 + .503 W_{t-1} - .02(I^* - I_{t-1}) + .049 F_t \tag{5.5}$$
$$r_{\hat{W}_t} = 0.9322$$

$$\hat{P}_t = -63.2 + 9.62 W_t + 1.32(I^* - I_{t-1}) + .095\left(\sum_{i=0}^{2}\frac{1}{i+1}F_{t+i}\right) \tag{5.6}$$

$$r_{\hat{P}_t} = .9757$$

These correlation coefficients are very high. The question is, how will the models fare when compared to future management decisions? Table 5.3 shows a comparative set of data for six weeks. Included in the table are the actual management decisions, denoted W_t, $P_{R,t}$, and $P_{0,t}$. Also, the model's decisions, denoted $\hat{W}_t$, $\hat{P}_{R,t}$, and $\hat{P}_{0,t}$, are given. The production quantity values are given by the following equations, in which W_t represents work-force size, $P_{R,t}$ stands for regular-time production level and $P_{0,t}$ represents overtime production level.

$$\hat{P}_{R,t} = 8\hat{W}_t, \qquad \text{if } 8\hat{W}_t \le \hat{P}_t$$
$$= \hat{P}_t, \qquad \text{otherwise}$$
$$\hat{P}_{0,t} = \hat{P}_t - \hat{P}_{R,t}, \quad \text{if } \hat{P}_t - \hat{P}_{R,t} \ge 0$$
$$= 0, \qquad \text{otherwise}$$

Finally, Table 5.3 contains the inventory figure for both management's approach and the model, denoted I_{t-1} and $\hat{I}_{t-1}$, respectively.

Suppose the cost analysis of the manufacturing process established the following relationships.

1. The labor cost of regular-time production is a linear function of $153 per unit.

2. The labor cost of overtime production is $198 per unit for the first 20% increase over regular-time capacity (Saturdays) and $243 per unit for the next 20% increase (Sundays).

3. The unit cost of materials and overhead, excluding labor, obeys the equation Cost = 5000 + 150 (production quantity).

4. Monthly cost to carry inventory obeys the equation Cost = 1000 − 12 (inventory level) + 0.12 (inventory level)^2.

5. Cost to lay off obeys the equation Cost = 710 (no. of people) + 37 (no. of people)^2.

TABLE 5.3   Test Data for Management Coefficients Approach

Period t	F_t	W_t	$P_{R,t}$	$P_{0,t}$	I_{t-1}	$\hat{W}_t$	$\hat{P}_{R,t}$	$\hat{P}_{0,t}$	$\hat{I}_{t-1}$
1	260	28	224	30	49	25	200	26	49
2	270	30	240	35	54	27	216	64	26
3	305	35	280	40	69	30	240	47	46
4	370	40	320	40	49	35	280[a]	112[a]	−7
5	310	40	320	0	49	35	280	76	25
6	270	34	270	0	49	32	256	18	61
7	230								
8	230								

[a] For period 4, Equation 5.6 called for 407 units, but 392 was the max possible with 35 employees.

TABLE 5.4 Cost Comparison between Management's Actual Performance and Equations 5.5 and 5.6

Period t	Management Actual Costs (C)					Management coefficient Costs ($\hat{C}$)				
	C_{labor}	C_{matls}	C_{Inv}	$C_{hire\ layoff}$	Total Cost	$\hat{C}_{labor}$	$\hat{C}_{matls}$	$\hat{C}_{Inv}$	$\hat{C}_{hire\ layoff}$	Total Cost
1	40,212	43,100	700	8400	92,412	36,144	39,200	700	2400	78,444
2	43,650	46,250	702	1200	91,802	40,374	42,950	769	1200	85,293
3	50,760	53,000	743	6000	101,503	45,828	47,900	702	2400	96,830
4	56,880	59,000	700	6000	122,580	53,730	55,250	0	6000	114,980
5	48,960	53,000	700	0	102,660	52,938	54,650	775	0	108,363
6	41,310	45,500	700	5592	93,102	42,336	45,800	714	2463	91,313
Totals					613,059					575,223

6. Cost to hire obeys the equation Cost = 200 (no. of people) + 200 (no. of people)^2.

Using these cost equations, a comparison was made between management's decisions and the model's recommendations as given in Table 5.3. The resulting costs are shown in Table 5.4. Note that the model's decision resulted in a cost of \$575,223 for the six-month period. This was a savings of \$37,836, or 6.2 percent of the actual management decision. Therefore, the consistency offered by the model resulted in a significant savings

Several of the limitations of the management coefficients approach have already been brought out. One additional concern is added here. The methodology tends to consider those factors that were thought to be important during the period for which data was collected. What happens if the situation changes? Suppose economic conditions change and the limited availability of labor must be considered? Suppose a new contract changes the relative cost of labor to inventory? The model can no longer be changed to reflect these new conditions, because the managers are using the model and have stopped making their decisions intuitively. Therefore, there is no data with which to determine the new coefficients.

In light of this very significant limitation, the management coefficients approach must not be implemented blindly. Perhaps its safest use is as another input to management's continued intuitive-decision process. In this situation, the model will argue for consistency while management continues to consider the broader picture when formulating its aggregate plans.

5.4 OPTIMIZATION APPROACHES TO AGGREGATE PLANNING

One of the primary objections to the management coefficients approach is that there is no way of knowing how good the solution is. If the decisions used to generate the coefficients fail to consider the factors properly, the results will be biased away from the optimum solution. Could further savings be attained by developing a model that could be optimized mathematically?

Linear-programming optimization approaches to aggregate planning will be discussed in this section. Assumptions about the structure of the cost relationships are made for convenience in obtaining a solution. Since these assumptions are restrictive and cause a loss of reality, the approach results in an optimal solution to a simplified problem. Before using such an approach, the analyst must be satisfied that the loss of fidelity in making the assumptions is acceptable relative to the gain resulting from guaranteed optimality.

Considerable effort has been made in formulating the aggregate-planning problem as a linear-programming (LP) model. Bowman (1956)† suggested a

---

†E. H. Bowman, "Production Scheduling by the Transportation Method of Linear Programming," *Operations Research*, vol. 4, no. 1, February 1956.

transportation model in which the monthly production capacities are sources and the monthly demands are sinks. Buffa and Miller (1979)† present a generalized linear-programming formulation that considers the production level, work-force size, overtime schedule inventory, stock-out, hiring, and layoff decision variables. The primary assumptions of such models is that the cost of these variables is linear and that the variables can take on any real numbered value. For example, the assumption is made that the cost of stock-out is linear with respect to the quantity short. This is intuitively unappealing. If stock-out shortages are very low, customers will likely wait with few complaints; thus, the cost is essentially zero. If, however, the shortages become large, the customer will seek another supplier and the cost will become unacceptable. As a second example, assume that the quantity produced can take on any real value. It is more likely that production level will be an integer value. Figure 5.2 represents typical linear approximations of the cost of several factors involved in the generalized LP formulation. For some situations the errors caused by the linearity assumption may be insignificant, whereas for other situations the error may make the approach unacceptable.

The objective of the linear-programming formulation is to minimize total cost as given by Equation 5.7, subject to the constraints given by Equations 5.8 through 5.11.

$$\text{Min } Z = \sum_{t=1}^{T} A_{p,t}P_t + A_{r,t}R_t + A_{o,t}O_t + A_{i,t}I_t + A_{s,t}S_t + A_{h,t}H_t + A_{l,t}L_t \qquad (5.7)$$

Subject to

$$I_t - S_t = I_{t-1} - S_{t-1} + P_t - F_t \qquad \text{for } t = 1, 2, \ldots T \qquad (5.8)$$

$$R_t = R_{t-1} + H_t - L_t \qquad \text{for } t = 1, 2, \ldots T \qquad (5.9)$$

$$O_t - U_t = kP_t - R_t \qquad \text{for } t = 1, 2, \ldots T \qquad (5.10)$$

$$P_t, R_t, O_t, I_t, S_t, H_t, L_t, U_t, \geq 0 \qquad \text{for } t = 1, 2, \ldots T \qquad (5.11)$$

where

P_t = Production units scheduled in period t
$A_{p,t}$ = Cost per unit of production excluding labor
R_t = Hours of labor available for regular-time production in period t
$A_{r,t}$ = Hourly cost of labor on regular time
O_t = Hours of overtime schedule in period t
$A_{o,t}$ = Hourly cost of labor on overtime
I_t = Inventory in stock at end of period t
$A_{i,t}$ = Carrying cost per unit of inventory

†E. S. Buffa and J. G. Miller, *Production Inventory Systems: Planning and Control*, 3rd. ed., Richard D. Irwin, Homewood, Ill., 1979, pp. 258–60. Copyright © 1979 by Richard D. Irwin, Inc.

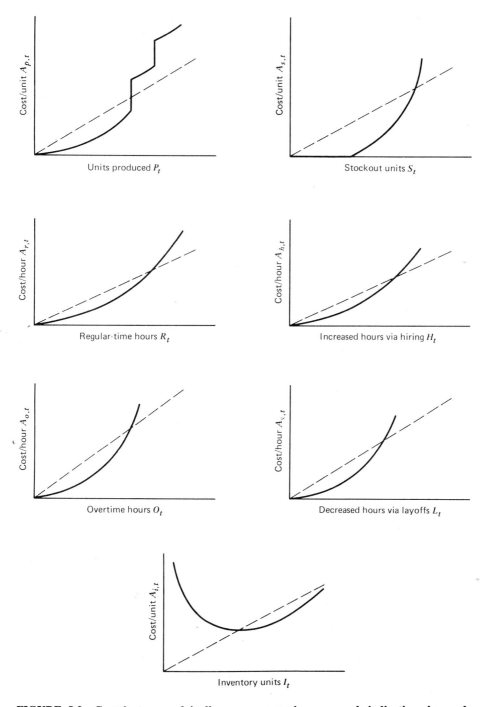

FIGURE 5.2 Cost factors used in linear programming approach indicating shape of realistic curve and linear approximation.

S_t = Stock-out quantity at end of period t

$A_{s,t}$ = Cost per unit of stock-out

H_t = New hires in hours for period t

$A_{h,t}$ = Cost to increase work for one hour

L_t = Layoffs in hours of period t

$A_{l,t}$ = Cost to reduce work force for one hour

U_t = Undertime in period t if production levels are less than work-force capacity

F_t = Forecast demand for period t

k = Conversion factor in hours of labor per unit of production

T = Planning horizon or number of periods to be considered

It is instructive to understand the intent of the several sets of constraints. Equation 5.8 requires a solution in which the period-by-period inventory levels remain consistent: that is, that the inventory level I_t or shortage level S_t in period t be equal to what it was in period $t-1$ plus the quantity produced (P_t) and less the quantity forecasted (F_t). This constraint assumes that all shortages will be carried forward for future delivery and that stock-outs never result in lost sales. If one removed the S_t and S_{t-1} variables from Equations 5.7, 5.8, and 5.11, the solution would be constrained to alternatives for which stock-out never occurs. Similarly, if one wanted to maintain a buffer inventory of I_B units, one could remove S_t and S_{t-1} and add another set of constraints of the form

$$I_t \geq I_B \quad t = 1, 2, \ldots T \tag{5.12}$$

An upper limit for inventory of I_{max} units could be included by adding a set of constraints of the form

$$I_t \leq I_{max} \quad t = 1, 2, \ldots T \tag{5.13}$$

Equation 5.9 represents a set of constraints that requires that the period-by-period work-force level be consistent: that is, that the work force in period t be equal to the work force in period $t-1$ plus the new hires (H_t) less the layoffs (L_t). As before, one can limit the solution to a no-layoff or a no-hire situation by eliminating either variable from Equations 5.7, 5.9, and 5.11. In addition, one can limit the size of the work force to some range—for example, greater than R_{min} and less than R_{max}, by adding constraints of the form

$$R_t \geq R_{min} \quad t = 1, 2, \ldots T \tag{5.14}$$

$$R_t \leq R_{max} \quad t = 1, 2, \ldots T \tag{5.15}$$

Equation 5.10 represents a set of constraints that define the extent of overtime (O_t) or undertime (U_t) needed to produce P_t units. Because O_t and U_t are expressed in hours, the units of production (P_t) is converted by the time standard k hours per unit. Subtracting the available hours of regular time (R_t) from the required hours (kP_t), one establishes the residual overtime or undertime hours. One can constrain the solution to alternatives where undertime is prohibited by eliminating U_t from Equations 5.10 and 5.11.

Other options can be considered with this formulation. If subcontracting were considered, for example, a new variable, C_t, could be invented. One would then add $A_{c,t}C_t$ to Equation 5.7, add C_t to Equation 5.8, subtract kC_t from Equation 5.10, and add C_t to Equation 5.11. Obviously, this linear-programming formulation is quite flexible.

To further understand this approach, consider the following linear-programming solution to the problem presented in Section 5.3. Recall that the cost analysis suggested that regular-time labor costs were \$153 per unit. In Equation 5.7 this figure is $A_{r,t}$ and must be expressed as dollars per hour. Dividing 153 by the five hours/unit time standard, we get $A_{r,t} = 30.60$ per hour. Similarly, the cost analysis had overtime costs as \$198 and \$243/unit for Saturday and Sunday work, respectively. A linear approximation of these costs could be \$210/unit, which when divided by the standard gives a \$42. value to $A_{o,t}$. The materials-and-overhead cost was given earlier as $5000 + 150P_t$. This, too, had to be approximated by a linear coefficient. The value chosen was \$175/unit for $A_{p,t}$. The cost to carry inventory was given by the polynomial $1000 - 12I_t + 0.12I_t^2$. This, too, had to be approximated, and a value of \$12. was chosen for $A_{i,t}$. The cost to lay off was earlier estimated as fitting the polynomial $710L_t + 37L_t^2$ and is now approximated by \$800 per man laid off. Because $A_{l,t}$ is expressed in units of dollars per hour of time lost because of lay off, we divide the 800 by 40 and set $A_{l,t} = 20$. Finally the cost to hire and train was assumed to fit the model $200H_t + 200H_t^2$ and is here approximated by \$600 per man or $A_{h,t} = 15$ per hour.

For this example problem, stock-outs were to be prohibited and thus the variable S_t and coefficient $A_{s,t}$ were removed from Equations 5.7 and 5.8. The resulting linear-programming model for the six-week test period is as follows:

$$\text{Min } Z = \sum_{t=1}^{6} 175.0\,P_t + 30.6\,R_t + 42.0\,O_t + 12.0\,I_t + 20.0\,L_t + 15.0H_t \quad (5.16)$$

subject to

$$I_t = I_{t-1} + P_t - F_t \qquad \text{for } t = 1, 2, 3, 4, 5, 6 \qquad (5.17)$$

$$R_t = R_{t-1} + H_t - L_t \qquad \text{for } t = 1, 2, 3, 4, 5, 6 \qquad (5.18)$$

$$O_t - U_t = 5.0\,P_t - R_t \qquad \text{for } t = 1, 2, 3, 4, 5, 6 \qquad (5.19)$$

$$P_t, R_t, O_t, I_t, H_t, L_t, U_t \geq 0 \qquad \text{for } t = 1, 2, 3, 4, 5, 6 \qquad (5.20)$$

and

$$R_0 = 22 \times 40 = 880.0$$

$$I_0 = 70.0$$

$$F_1 = 260, F_2 = 270, F_3 = 305, F_4 = 370, F_5 = 310, \text{ and } F_6 = 270.$$

A computerized linear-programming package was able to solve this problem in 28 iterations and established the following results.

$Z = 576{,}922.50$	dollars
$P_1 = 283.75$	units produced
$P_2 = 283.75$	units
$P_3 = 283.75$	units
$P_4 = 283.75$	units
$P_5 = 310.00$	units
$P_6 = 270.0$	units
$R_1 = 1418.75$	hours of regular-time production
$R_2 = 1418.75$	hours
$R_3 = 1418.75$	hours
$R_4 = 1418.75$	hours
$R_5 = 1418.75$	hours
$R_6 = 1350.00$	hours
$O_5 = 131.25$	hours of overtime production
$I_1 = 93.75$	units held in inventory
$I_2 = 107.50$	units
$I_3 = 86.25$	units
$H_1 = 538.75$	hours of capacity hired
$L_6 = 68.75$	hours of capacity laid off

The $576,923 cost figure is slightly greater than that found using the management coefficients approach. This does not say that management out-performed the optimal solution; rather, it says that the linear approximation lost so much reality that the management coefficients did better with the real-world problem than was possible with the simplified problem. If one were to evaluate the plans given in Table 5.3 using the objective function given by Equation 5.16, management's decisions would cost $620,471 and the management coefficients approach would cost $586,029. If one were to put the LP solution values through the more exact cost-analysis equations, the linear-programming solution would result in a total cost of $759,255, which is worse than even management's present decisions. This suggests that in this case, the linear simplification does cause too much error.

Nonetheless, the linear-programming approach overcomes the most significant limitations of the seat-of-the-pants and management-coefficients approaches. It does offer the consistency lacking in management's unmodeled efforts. It also can be changed as the cost environment changes. If labor becomes scarce, one can increase the cost to hire accordingly and the model will avoid changes in work-force size. Or, if other factors change, the model can be adjusted by conducting another cost analysis. The question is, Are the increases in cost stemming from simplification of the problem worth the gain in consistency and flexibility?

Another optimization approach to aggregate planning is referred to as the "linear decision rule" as presented in Holt, Modigliani, Muth, and Simon.† The cost restriction in this approach is less restrictive than the linear requirements used here. The approach is also harder to implement. The more serious student should also study the linear-decision-rule approach.

5.5 PARAMETRIC APPROACH TO PRODUCTION PLANNING

Clearly, one must find an approach to aggregate planning that does not require linear or even quadratic limitations on the cost equation. Jones developed such an approach calling it "Parametric Production Planning."‡ In order to get around the cost limitations, Jones relaxed the need to guarantee optimization and utilized a computerized-search technique to create rules that yield low-cost decisions. Two such rules are developed in terms of four parameters. The first rule gives the size of the work force, and the second rule yields the production quantity.

Each of the four parameters can take on values from 0.0 to 1.0. The idea is to examine many combinations of values for the parameters and record the decisions that would be made should those values be selected. A highly realistic cost equation is then used to establish the total cost resulting from those decisions. Those parametric values that result in the minimum cost are said to be the best values of those tested. Unfortunately, one can't evaluate all possible values of the parameters and there is no way of knowing if some untested set would offer an even lower cost situation. In other words, the Jones approach offers a good but not guaranteed minimum-cost solution.

The counter-argument of this "nonguaranteed" question is that the resulting solutions in controlled test situations have been shown to yield very close to minimal solutions. Since there is no solution approach that guarantees an optimal solution without first simplifying the problem, a near-optimal solution to a more realistic problem might be a good engineering decision. Further, if the cost equation is unimodal and fairly flat near its minimum, an analyst can get as close to the absolute minimum as is realistic and feel confident of the result.

As indicated before, this approach requires three models: the work-force decision rule, the production-level decision rule, and a realistic cost equation. Consider first the work-force rule. Fundamentally, the work force for period t is set equal to what it was in period $t - 1$ plus some fraction of the difference

†C. C. Holt, F. Modigliani, J. F. Muth, and H. A. Simon, *Planning Production, Inventories, and Work Force*, Prentice-Hall, Englewood Cliffs, N.J., 1960.
‡C. H. Jones, "Parametric Production Planning," *Management Science*, vol. 13, no. 11, July 1967. Reprinted by permission of C. H. Jones. Copyright © 1967 The Institute of Management Sciences.

between what it was in $t - 1$ and the ideal work-force size: that is,

$$W_t = W_{t-1} + A(W^* - W_{t-1})\dagger \tag{5.21}$$

where

W_t = work-force size in period t
W^* = the ideal work-force size
A = a parameter whose value is to be determined, $0 \le A \le 1$

The question now is, What should the ideal work force level be? If the forecast for the next period is F_t and the labor standard is K regular-time employees per unit of production, then the work force needed to exactly meet this forecast is KF_t. A more appealing idea is to consider the demand for the next N periods using a weighted sum. That is, the ideal work force is given by

$$W^* = \sum_{n=1}^{N} b_n KF_{t+n-1} \tag{5.22}$$

where

b_n = the weighting factor in period n
K = work standard in people per unit of production
F_t = forecasted units of production in period t
N = planning horizon; periods into the future

Jones tested two models to generate values for the weighting factors as a function of a single parameter. He settled on the following form:

$$b_n = \frac{B^n}{\sum\limits_{n=1}^{N} B^n} \tag{5.23}$$

where

B = the weighting parameter for future forecasts and is to be determined, $0 \le B \le 1$

In addition, Jones added an adjustment to account for any deviation between the ideal inventory level I^* and the present inventory level I_{t-1}. He weighs this inventory adjustment term by the weighting factor associated with the next period. This is,

$$I_{adj} = b_1 K(I^* - I_{t-1}) \tag{5.24}$$

where

I^* = desired inventory level

I_{t-1} = ac al inventory at end of period $t - 1$

---

†The reader will note that this is simply exponential smoothing for a constant model, as first presented in the previous chapter.

Therefore, the final work-force rule becomes

$$W_t = W_{t-1} + A\left[\sum_{n=1}^{N}\left(\frac{B^n K F_{t+n-1}}{\sum\limits_{n=1}^{N} B^n}\right) - W_{t-1} + \frac{BK(I^* - I_{t-1})}{\sum\limits_{n=1}^{N} B^n}\right] \qquad (5.25)$$

The production-level decision rule is very similar to the work-force rule. Fundamentally, the rule is to produce in period t the maximum possible (on regular time) with the work force W_t plus some fraction of the difference between that quantity and the desired quantity. That is,

$$P_t = \frac{W_t}{K} + C\left(P_t^* - \frac{W_t}{K}\right) \qquad (5.26)$$

where

P_t = production quantity for period t
W_t = the work force determined by Equation 5.21
P_t^* = the desired production to meet future demand
K = labor standard
C = weighting parameter to be determined, $0 \le C \le 1$

As before, the desired production level is the weighted sum of the next N forecasted demands with the weight being given by d_n where

$$d_n = \frac{D^n}{\sum\limits_{n=1}^{N} D^n} \qquad (5.27)$$

In addition, the production rule includes an adjustment for inventory imbalance. Therefore, the production rule is given by

$$P_t = \frac{W_t}{K} + C\left[\sum_{n=1}^{N}\left(\frac{D^n F_{t+n-1}}{\sum\limits_{n=1}^{N} D^n}\right) - \frac{W_t}{K} + \frac{D(I^* - I_{t-1})}{\sum\limits_{n=1}^{N} D^n}\right] \qquad (5.28)$$

Note that Equation 5.25 must be solved for period t before Equation 5.28 can be solved. Thus, given a set of forecasted demands $F_1, F_2, \ldots F_N$ and values for $A, B, C,$ and D, a computer can calculate first W_1 and then P_1. Knowing P_1, I_o and the actual demand in period 1, the computer can then calculate I_1. Now, the computer drops F_1 and adds in F_{n+1} and calculates $W_2, P_2,$ and I_2. After some number of cycles, the rules have developed a plan given by the values $W_1, P_1, W_2, P_2, \ldots$

The cost of this plan can be evaluated using the most realistic cost-model available. There is no need to consider only continuous linear or quadratic cost equations. The idea is to evaluate systematically the total cost for a wide variety of values for $A, B, C,$ and D.

To better understand the approach and compare its value to alternative methods, the problem developed earlier was solved using parametric produc-

TABLE 5.5   Test Data for the Parametric Production Planning Example

t	F_t	F_{t+1}	F_{t+2}	I_{t-1}	W_t	P_t	$P_{R,t}$	$P_{0,t}$
1	260	270	305	49	25	250	200	50
2	270	305	370	50	28	271	224	47
3	305	370	310	61	30	294	240	54
4	370	310	270	15	33	349	264	85
5	310	270	230	4	36	322	288	34
6	270	230	230	6	36	293	288	5

tion-planning rules. The cost model was given in Section 5.3 as a set of six equations. The computer was programmed to yield the minimum-cost set of parameters for the 24 weeks of data represented in Table 5.2. To be consistent with the earlier models, the planning horizon N was set at 3, K was set at 1/8 units per worker period, I_0 was set at 70, and W_0 was set at 22 workers. Each of the parameters was allowed to take on the values from 0 to 1.0 in steps of 0.125. The minimum-cost set of parameters for the 24-week data set was $A = 0.25$, $B = 1.00$, $C = 0.75$, and $D = 0.375$. The total cost for this parameter set was $1,688, 489$. This result gave the following work-force and production-level rules.

$$W_t = W_{t-1} + 0.25[0.04(F_t + F_{t+1} + F_{t+2}) - W_{t-1} + 0.04(50 - I_{t-1})] \qquad (5.29)$$

$$P_t = 8W_t + 0.75[0.66\, F_t + 0.25\, F_{t+1} + 0.09\, F_{t+2} + 8W_t + 0.66(50 - I_{t-1})] \qquad (5.30)$$

As mentioned before, the cost model was that presented in Section 5.3.

The rules were applied to the six-week test period shown in Table 5.5, which also indicates the aggregate plan that was developed. The cost of this plan was $596,955, which was better than management's actual solution ($613,058) and the linear programming solution ($759,225) but not so good as the Bowman coefficient solution ($575,223). It is interesting to note that the parametric planning solution outperformed the LP solution by producing less on regular time and more on overtime and that the management coefficients method outperformed parametric planning by producing still less on regular time and more on overtime. The LP solution went to 35 employees immediately and remained at that staffing level until the last period. Both the management-coefficients and the parametric-planning approaches put on employees more slowly, which would likely be a more acceptable real-world situation. Finally, the LP solution carried large inventories for the first three periods and none thereafter, whereas the other two approaches carried less inventory but did so consistently. Even with all these differences in solution, the total costs were quite close.

5.6 DISAGGREGATION TO A MASTER SCHEDULE

Recall that the aggregate plan does not deal with the specific products manufactured in the plant; rather, it is a plan for some representation of the collection of products. The aggregate plan suggests the work-force size and production quantities for the plant as a whole. To be useful, the aggregate plan must be disaggregated into production quantities for each of the individual products. This disaggregation becomes the master schedule for the period at hand.

There have been a number of attempts to solve the disaggregation problem. Attempts to include multiple products in the aggregate planning models have not been accepted because of the rate at which problem complexity grows as realism is added. Hax and Meal[†] have suggested a four-part hierarchial approach to the total problem. The four parts of the approach are represented by the rectangles in the flowchart depicted in Figure 5.3. The third part of their approach is to apply inventory control models to disaggregate the plan: that is, the problem is a multiproduct inventory-control situation with constrained production capacity. This section shall present a procedure for the third part of their hierarchy. For another approach, the reader is referred to the Hax and Meal paper.

Before going into the procedure, the reader should understand the nature of the product mix situation. Most manufacturing facilities produce several families of product lines. A family might be defined as a group of products so similar that it is economically or technologically wise to produce them together. In other words, since the cost of changeover between families is large relative to the cost of changeover between products within a family, it is better to satisfy the needs of all products within the family before switching to another family. In certain plants, portions of facilities may be devoted solely to one family of products. In this case, the facility can be treated as independent of the rest of the plant and the entire aggregate-planning problem can be solved separately. Therefore, the disaggregation problem is one of setting quantities for each product within the family. In other situations a facility may be used to produce items that fall into two or more family groups. In this case, the disaggregation problem first must determine which families are to be included in the next period and then how many of each product to produce. A procedure to solve this problem follows.

The first step in the procedure is to select which families to include in the master schedule. This is done by examining the quantities on hand and forecasted demands for each product in each family. If any product in the family is likely to attain its safety-stock level before the end of the period, the

---

[†]A. Hax, and H. Meal, "Hierarchical Integration of Production Planning and Scheduling," in M. A. Geisler, *Studies in the Management Sciences*, vol. 1, *Logistics*, North-Holland, New York, 1975.

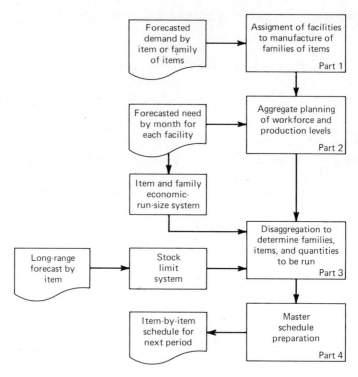

FIGURE 5.3 **Sequence of events in the creation of a master schedule. (Adapted from A. Hax and H. Meal, "Hierarchical Integration of Production Planning and Scheduling," in M. A. Geisler, *Studies in the Management Sciences*, vol. 1-*Logistics*, 1975. Permission granted by North-Holland Publishing Company.)**

entire family of products is included in the production schedule.† Ideally, all the products in a family should run low at the same time. More formally stated: for each item j in each family i, if the expected quantity $q_{ij,t}$ at the end of period t is less than its safety stock levels s_{ij}, all products in the family are candidates for production in that period. If $I_{ij,t-1}$ is the inventory level of item j at the end of period $t-1$ and the demand is $D_{ij,t}$, then

$$q_{ij,t} = I_{ij,t-1} - D_{ij,t} \tag{5.31}$$

And if

$$\min_{\text{all } j \text{ in } i} \{q_{ij,t} - s_{ij}\} \leq 0 \tag{5.32}$$

then all items j in family i are considered for production in period t.

---

†The reader not familiar with inventory control semantics might like to review the definitions section in Chapter 6.

TABLE 5.6   Example for the Disaggregation Problem

Family	Item	Inventory	Demand	Safety Stock	Expected Quant.
i	j	$I_{ij,t-1}$	$D_{ij,t}$	s_{ij}	$I_{ij,t-1} - D_{ij,t}$
A	1	240	170	50	70
A	2	285	200	75	85
A	3	122	100	40	22^a
B	4	223	130	50	93
B	5	290	170	50	120
B	6	193	110	40	83
B	7	420	210	60	210
C	8	235	150	40	85
C	9	135	100	50	35^a
C	10	180	140	50	40^a

[a]Items whose available quantities will be less than safety-stock values if not produced.

Consider the example given in Table 5.6, which includes 10 items divided into three families. Comparing the last two columns of the table, one can see that items 3, 9, and 10 will run below the safety-stock level if we don't schedule them for production. Therefore all items in the family A and C (i.e., items 1, 2, 3, 8, 9, and 10) are to be considered for production. Call this set of items Z. The remainder of the disaggregation procedure holds for both the one family and the multifamily cases.

The second step is to determine how many of each item in each family should be produced. For each item j in i, call this quantity Q_{ij}. Because we want each item to run out at the same time and to be produced together, the number of times per year that each item is run, N_i, will be the same for the entire family. The question now becomes, what is the most economic value for N_i? To find this value, the total cost of setup and of holding inventory is expressed in terms of N_i. Then, by differentiating and setting the result to zero, the optimal value can be found. Consider the unit cost for each item to be C_{ij}. If the total annual demand is T_{ij}, the quantity produced in each run is T_{ij}/N_i. Over time, the average inventory on hand will be $1/2(s_{ij} + T_{ij}/N_i)$ where s_{ij} was defined as the safety-stock level. If the cost of tying up money in inventory is I, then the annual cost of holding inventory is given by

$$\text{Cost to hold} = 1/2\, C_{ij} I (s_{ij} + T_{ij}/N_i) \qquad (5.33)$$

The cost of setup from any other family to family i is given as S_i. We will ignore the cost of setup between items in the family, since it is small relative to the interfamily setup cost. Thus, the annual cost of setup is given by

$$\text{Cost of setup} = S_i N_i \qquad (5.34)$$

The total annual cost of a decision to produce family i items N_i times a year is given by

$$\text{Total cost} = \left[\sum_{\substack{\text{all } j \\ \text{in } i}} 1/2\, C_{ij} I \left(s_{ij} + \frac{T_{ij}}{N_i} \right) \right] + S_i N_i \qquad (5.35)$$

If the total-cost equation is differentiated with respect to N_i and set to zero, the following is obtained

$$\left(-\frac{I}{2N_i^2} \sum_{\substack{\text{all } j \\ \text{in } i}} C_{ij} T_{ij} \right) + S_i = 0. \qquad (5.36)$$

Solving for N_i and calling it N_i^*, one gets

$$N_i^* = \sqrt{\frac{I}{2S_i} \sum_{\substack{\text{all } j \\ \text{in } i}} C_{ij} T_{ij}}. \qquad (5.37)$$

Finally, using the fact that N_i^*, the optimal number of runs, equals T_{ij}/Q_{ij}^*, one can solve for Q_{ij}^*, the optimal quantity of item j to run each time.

$$Q_{ij}^* = \frac{T_{ij}}{N_i^*} = \sqrt{\frac{2T_{ij}^2 S_i}{I \sum_{\substack{\text{all } j \\ \text{in } i}} C_{ij} T_{ij}}}, \qquad (5.38)$$

where

$$T_{ij} = \text{annual demand for item } j \text{ in family } i$$
$$S_i = \text{set up cost associated with family } i$$
$$C_{ij} = \text{unit cost for item } j \text{ in family } i$$
$$I = \text{value of money used to hold inventory}$$
$$Q_{ij}^* = \text{economic order for item } j \text{ in family } i \text{ if it is}$$
$$\text{to be produced } N_i^* \text{ times a year}$$

Thus, for every item in set Z, a value of its most-economic order quantity can be calculated.

Suppose we converted these economic order quantities into the same units as were asked for the aggregate plan and then we summed over all items in Z. This would give us the production quantity in terms comparable to the aggregate plan

$$Q_{\text{total}}^* = \sum_{\substack{\text{all } j \\ \text{in } Z}} Q_{ij}^* K_{ij} \qquad (5.39)$$

where

$$K_{ij} = \text{conversion factor for item } j \text{ in family } i \text{ to attain}$$
$$\text{equivalent aggregate-planning units}$$

TABLE 5.7 Example of Adjustment for the Disaggregate Problem

(1) family	(2) item	(3) Q_{ij}^*	(4) K_{ij}	(5) $Q_{ij}^* K_{ij}$	(6) $Q_{ij}^*(\text{adj})$	(7) $Q_{ij}^*(\text{adj})K_{ij}$
A	1	120	0.85	102	76	64.6
A	2	180	1.10	198	114	125.4
A	3	100	0.90	90	63	56.7
C	8	120	0.75	90	76	57.0
C	9	140	0.85	119	89	75.65
C	10	140	0.80	112	89	71.2
				$Q_{\text{total}}^* = 711$		$Q_{\text{total}}^*(\text{adj}) = 450.55$

Comparing Q_{total}^* to the aggregate plan P_t for period t, we note the likely difference. The need is to adjust each value Q_{ij}^* so that the sum equals P_t. This could easily be accomplished by a simple ratio where the desired adjustment factor is P_t/Q_{total}^*. That is,

$$Q_{ij}^*(\text{adj}) = Q_{ij}^*(P_t/Q_{\text{total}}^*) \tag{5.40}$$

To examine this further, consider again the example given in Table 5.6. Table 5.7 gives further details for the items in the A and C families. Note that $Q_{\text{total}}^* = 711$. Suppose that the aggregate plan called for 450 units of production in period t. The adjustment factor then would be 0.633. The adjusted production quantities are given in the column headed $Q_{ij}^*(\text{adj})$. Note that when converted to the aggregate plan units, the total production becomes 450.55, which is as expected with slight round-off error.

An alternative to the simple ratio approach would be to examine the expected quantities at the end of the next period. In Table 5.6, these values for the six example items are 70, 85, 22, 85, 35, and 40 units. Ideally, we would like to have all of these numbers reach their safety-stock levels simultaneously at the end of the next period. To encourage this, we would first adjust the order quantities by the difference between the expected quantities and the safety-stock levels. This adjustment could bring the Q_{total}^* into closer agreement with P_t. Table 5.8 represents this idea. Note that the column 3 values generated via Equation 5.31, were first adjusted by subtracting the values in column 4. These values were then converted to their aggregate planning equivalent in column 6 and adjusted to meet the 450-unit plan as shown in column 7. The difference between column 7 in Table 5.8 and column 6 in Table 5.7 thus represents different master-schedule solutions.

Using this procedure, the aggregate-planning production rate can be converted into a disaggregated master schedule. Those families of items that must be run in the next period are identified and the economic order quantity

TABLE 5.8   Example of Alternate Adjustment for the Disaggregate Problem

(1) family i	(2) item	(3) Q_{ij}^*	(4) $(I_{ij,t-1} - D_{ij,t} - s_{ij})$	(5) = (3)–(4) Q_{ij}^*	(6) $Q_{ij}^* K_{ij}$	(7) Q_{ij}^*(adj)
A	1	120	20	100	85	64
A	2	180	10	170	187	110
A	3	100	−18	118	106	76
C	8	120	45	75	56	48
C	9	140	−15	155	132	100
C	10	140	−10	150	120	97
					686	

for each item is adjusted to satisfy the planned production level. These production quantities are still not ready for release to manufacturing. The question of the availability of raw materials and the proper production sequence have not been addressed. The issues of material requirements and job sequencing will be discussed in Chapters 7, 8, and 9.

5.7   CONCLUSIONS

In the production-control flow of events, aggregate planning plays a critical role. The demand forecasts for various products in many environments tend to fluctuate significantly on a period-by-period basis. By accumulating the forecasted demands for each product into an aggregated total, production planning can envision the period-by-period demand.

The role of aggregate planning is to smooth out the production level so that the aggregated demand can be met in a minimum-cost fashion. Companies that do not do aggregate planning operate so as to satisfy only short-term requirements. If demand fluctuates significantly over time, such companies find themselves faced with too much or too little inventory, or with too much or too little labor capacity. In many industries, improper levels of inventory and labor are very costly. In such situations, good forecasting and aggregate planning should be considered seriously.

5.8   REFERENCES

1. Bowman, E. H., "Production Scheduling by the Transportation Method of Linear Programming," *Operations Research*, vol. 4, no. 1, February 1956.

2. Bowman, E. H., "Consistency and Optimality in Managerial Decision Making," *Management Science*, vol. 9, no. 1, January 1963.
3. Buffa, E. S., and Miller, J. G., *Production Inventory Systems: Planning and Control*, 3rd. ed., Richard D. Irwin, Homewood, Ill. 1979.
4. Gordon, J. R. M., "A Multi-Model Analysis of an Aggregate Scheduling Decision," Ph.D. dissertation, Sloan School of Management, Massachusetts Institute of Technology, 1966.
5. Hax, A., and Meal, H., "Hierarchical Integration of Production Planning and Scheduling," in M. A. Geisler, *Studies in the Management Sciences* vol. 1, *Logistics*, North-Holland, New York, 1975.
6. Holt, C. C.; Modigliani, F.; Muth, J. F.; and Simon, H. A., *Planning Production, Inventories, and Work Force*, Prentice-Hall Inc. Englewood Cliffs, N.J., 1960.
7. Jones, C. H., "Parametric Production Planning," *Management Science*, vol. 13, no. 11, July 1967.

5.9 EXERCISES

1. List the factors that can be altered by an aggregate plan to meet the objectives of management.
2. Discuss the relative strengths and weaknesses of the empirical, optimization, and parametric approaches to aggregate planning.
3. Suppose you were asked to develop an aggregate planning system and you wanted to choose among the approaches suggested in this text. Discuss the analysis you would conduct in order to select an approach.
4. The procedure for disaggregation presented in section 5.6 was fairly simplistic. Using the Science Citation Index in your library, look up Hax and Meal as well as Zollar to find newer approaches to disaggregation.
5. Use a graphical approach to find an aggregate plan using data set *A*. Attempt to find a very low cost plan. Assume the following.

initial inventory	50 units
cost to carry inventory	$25/unit/month
cost to manufacture (regular time)	$300/unit
cost to manufacture (overtime)	$400/unit
cost of stock-out (assume no lost sales)	$50/unit
present capacity	5 units/day
cost to increase capacity	$500/unit *hiring cost/unit*
cost to decrease capacity	$400/unit *firing cost/unit*

6. Do Problem 5 for data set *B*.
7. Do Problem 5 for data set *C*.

8. Using the graphical approach, solve Problem 5 with the following changes in assumptions.
   Cost to carry *inventory* $50/unit/month
   What effect will an increase in inventory cost have on the solution?

The following table of data is given in conjunction with several problems.

| | Forecasted Demand | | | Available Days | |
Period	Set A	Set B	Set C	Reg. Time	Overtime
				X	X
1	50	50	120	22	3
2	60	60	155	18	3
3	55	70	165	23	3
4	55	65	200	21	3
5	50	55	65	22	4
6	45	80	50	21	3
7	40	250	40	20	3
8	70	250	40	20	3
9	95	110	45	22	4
10	260	100	60	22	4
11	240	80	140	21	3
12	210	60	150	20	2

9. Do Problem 8 for data set *B*.
10. Do Problem 8 for data set *C*.
11. Using the graphical approach, solve Problem 5 with the following changes in assumptions.

   Cost of stock-out (*assume lost* $200/unit
   sales are not passed forward
   and met in a future period)

   What effect will an increase in stock out cost have on the solution?
12. Do Problem 11 for data set *B*.
13. Do Problem 11 for data set *C*.
14. Using the graphical approach, solve Problem 5 with the following changes in assumptions.

   Cost to increase capacity $300/unit
   Cost to decrease capacity $1000/unit

15. Do Problem 14 for data set *B*.
16. Do Problem 14 for data set *C*.

17. Equation 5.2 modeled the work-force decision as a function of the previous decision, inventory imbalance, and a one-period forecast. Develop another regression model that incorporates the desired work-force size suggested in Equation 5.22. Use a three-period planning horizon.

18. If a computerized regression program is available, evaluate the model developed in Problem 17. Compare the total cost of this model for the data given in Figure 5.3.

19. Set up the objective function and constraints for a linear programming solution to the aggregate planning problems represented by the first three months of data set *A* as assigned by your instructor and given above. Use the assumptions given in Problem 5 supplemented as follows

Regular-time labor cost	$200/unit
Overtime labor cost	$300/unit
Hours of labor available	80 hours

20. Do Problem 19 for data set *B*.

✕21. Do Problem 19 for data set *C*.

22. If a computerized LP package is available, use it to solve Problem 19.

23. Using the following set of data and the cost equation given in Section 5.3, use a computer search program to find the optimal set of parametric planning parameters.

Period	Forecast	Actual Demand
1	120	110
2	140	156
3	180	184
4	175	168
5	190	185
6	210	198
7	180	190
8	180	180
9	160	165
10	175	163
11	150	157
12	130	122

✕ 24. Using the following data, calculate the quantity $Q_{ij}^*(adj)$ from Equation 5.40 if each item is to be manufactured.

Family i	Item j	Total Sales T_{ij}	Unit Cost C_{ij}	Conversion K_{ij}
A	1	5200	11	0.90
A	2	3400	18	1.20
B	3	2500	21	0.85
B	4	4300	16	1.05
B	5	4900	28	0.85

Aggregate plan production level   = 2500
Cost of money I   = 0.25
Cost to set up family A   = $50
Cost to set up family B   = $60

25. Research the Holt, Modigliani, Muth, and Simon approach to aggregate planning and write a four- or five-page review.

26. Research W. H. Tauberts "Search Decision Rule" approach to aggregate planning and write a four- or five-page review.

SIX: INVENTORY ANALYSIS AND CONTROL

Constantly choose rather to want less, than to have more.

Thomas A. Kempis

If materials and supplies in industry are not available when needed, survival of the industry might be in question. Paradoxically, if an overabundance of materials and supplies is maintained, the industry might be in just as much trouble, because of the capital tied up in those materials and supplies. The way out of this dilemma is to develop a *cost model* that considers both sides of the question and then optimizes in some manner, such as by minimizing the cost.

6.1 INTRODUCTORY COMMENTS

From the *production* point of view, the prime functions of inventory control are

1. To ensure that the production function is not hampered by lack of required items or, for that matter, a surplus of items. The production function is assumed to be developed in such a fashion that prior objectives will be satisfied with conditions optimized according to some specified criterion.

2. To ensure that the procedures developed for obtaining and storing required inventory items will be such that a minimum cost is expended on the inventory function, commensurate again with satisfying system objectives.

The American Production and Inventory Control Society† has defined

---

†*APICS Dictionary of Production and Inventory Control Terms*, American Production and Inventory Control Society, Chicago, 1966.

inventory control as

> *The technique of maintaining stock-keeping items at desired levels, whether they be raw materials, work-in-process, or finished products.*

The determination of desired levels and maintaining inventory at these levels is the heart of the inventory control problem. The definition is clearly aimed at the control of production inventory. Equally applicable is the determination of desired levels and maintaining these levels for a purely department store–type of activity. This is implied in the definition, though, with either the raw-materials or finished-product category of stock item.

The scope of inventory control takes in all facets of the production or business operation. Not only is it applicable to department stores and production facilities, but it is equally germane to such operations as supermarkets, warehousing, service station operations, and myriad others. From this point of view it is *systems*-oriented, in that the solution approaches are certainly applicable to a large variety of different operations.

Probably inventory control should cover primarily

    a. Raw-stock inventory levels.

    b. Batch production of component items.

    c. In-process inventory analysis.

    d. Final product inventory.

Items *a*, *b*, and *d* reflect topics oriented to the material covered in this chapter. Item *a* can be treated as an *economic-order-quantity* problem, in which some quantity is ordered for each inventory item at an appropriate time such that inventory-holding costs and ordering costs are minimized. Item *b* presents a very similar problem, except that instead of instantaneous receipt of an entire order, as with the economic-order-quantity problem, items are produced at a finite rate in batches for consumption in the same facility. In the latter case, consumption is at a much *lower* rate than production.

Item *c*, which will not be covered in any detail here, refers to the specialized *production* problem in which connecting production operations are *buffered* by in-process inventory banks. The overall product has to be produced through a sequence of these operations—as in the manufacture of an automobile, for example. If a panel-stamping machine is one operation in the sequence, it is obvious that the multimillion dollar line should not be shut down if just the panel-stamping operation fails. So an inventory level of panels is maintained within the process sequence for such a contingency. The size of the inventory level would be dependent on both the production rate and the *probability* of operation failure.

The value of in-process (or buffer) inventory can be shown by a simple example. Figure 6.1 represents three production stations in a production facility with possible in-process inventory storage provided *between* stations.

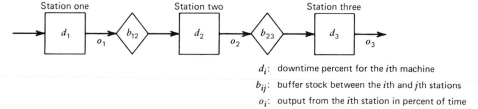

d_i: downtime percent for the ith machine

b_{ij}: buffer stock between the ith and jth stations

o_i: output from the ith station in percent of time

FIGURE 6.1 Three-station line with buffered inventory.

If all b_{ij} in-process inventory levels are zero, indicating no space for storage, the output percentages (of time) are as follows.

$$O_1 = 1 - d_1$$

$$O_2 = 1 - d_1 - d_2 + d_1 d_2 \quad \text{(assuming independence of machine downtimes)}$$

$$O_3 = 1 - d_1 - d_2 - d_3 + d_1 d_2 + d_2 d_3 + d_1 d_3 - d_1 d_2 d_3$$

If d_1, d_2, and d_3 are 5%, 10%, and 2%, respectively, we find that O_1, O_2, and O_3 are 95%, 85.5%, and 83.81%. Of course, O_1 and O_2 would be constrained to 83.81% since no buffer stock is allowed.

If unlimited inventory is allowed between stations—say, all b_{ij} are infinite—and this inventory is initially available, then the outputs are

$$O_1 = 1 - d_1$$

$$O_2 = 1 - d_2$$

$$O_3 = 1 - d_3$$

This assumes buffer inventory will flow to the subsequent machine when the previous machine is idle. The system output, O_3, will be 98%, a considerable improvement over the no–buffer-inventory condition. In reality, we have a limit on in-process inventory storage and a limited initial buildup for all b_{ij}. Analysis includes queuing studies that can become quite complex. The interested reader might like to refer to Buchan.†

The fourth category of inventory control, that of final product inventory required for customer satisfaction, is based on *forecasting analysis*. Item d then dictates production rates required that will have a significant bearing on items a through c.

Inventory is a *cost* to the operation. It requires capital that is not working for the operation, except that it does allow the operation to work efficiently and allows customer satisfaction, without which the operation would not exist.

---

†J. Buchan and E. Koenigsberg, *Scientific Inventory Management*, Prentice-Hall, Inc., Englewood Cliffs, N.J., 1963.

An idealistic yet ideal situation would be to have on hand at all times sufficient inventory just to match the demand at any given instant in time, with only one order charge for all time—an obvious impossibility. Forecasts of demand are subject to error because of the inherent uncertainty of customer whims and economic conditions. Inventory systems are *dynamic*, not static, thus requiring dynamic and not static policies.

Because of the dollar aspects of inventory, inventory planning can assist in *effective budgeting*. This point is well made by Stockton.†

> Inventories are an asset in the firm and, as such, appear in dollar form on the balance sheet. From a financial standpoint, inventories represent a capital investment and must, therefore, compete with other asset forms for the firm's limited capital funds.

In some plants as much as 75% of the sales dollar is spent for inventory, so it is important that material costs be closely controlled.

The investment in inventories is usually one of the largest items on the balance sheet (after plant and equipment). Having good knowledge of these costs through inventory analysis and control goes a long way toward developing an effective budget. In this regard, *inventory management* rather than inventory control may be the tough problem. The percentage of cost to invest in inventory is one of the more difficult management decisions.

Most of the following material is concerned with determining order quantities or batch production levels. However, there are many reasons for holding inventories higher than dictated by some optimized model, including, typically,

a. Buying in larger quantities may sometimes result in overall inventory cost reduction because of *quantity discounts*. One large airplane manufacturer uses a small computer to evaluate the benefit of price breaks in relationship to the entire inventory-cost picture.

b. Predicted price increases or labor increases, necessitating later price increases, can suggest benefits in buying inventory now at a reduced price. Again, the overall inventory-cost picture should be evaluated.

c. Projected strikes indicating difficulty in inventory procurement would certainly dictate that inventory stockpiling is desirable. The automobile manufacturers' relationship with the steel industry is a frequent case in point.

Most of the disadvantages in having too-large inventory levels accrue

---

†R. S. Stockton, *Basic Inventory Systems: Concepts and Analysis*, Allyn and Bacon, Boston, Mass., 1965.

from the increased costs that result. A few would include

a. Interest on investment in inventory. (This represents lost potential capital profit.)

b. Storage or space charges.

c. Taxes and insurance.

d. Physical deterioration and its prevention.

e. Obsolescence.

Many more could be mentioned. Close control must be exercised over inventory so that procurement and holding costs are the lowest possible consistent with availability of material, space, and capital. As Magee and Boodman† point out,

> .... *costs, and the balancing of opposing costs, lie at the heart of all production and inventory control problems. The cost elements essential to a production or inventory problem are characteristically not those reported in summary accounting records.*

The main purpose of this chapter is to define, determine, and balance these opposing costs. This latter purpose will be accomplished through the development of graphical and mathematical models of the inventory system, which will then be optimized by unit inventory-cost minimization.

Very basically, there are two categories of unit inventory cost.

a. Unit costs that tend to decrease as the size of the order increases. Primarily these would be the unit cost of physically ordering the inventory or the unit cost of setting up for a batch of items.

b. Costs that tend to increase as the size of the order increases. These include physical *storage costs* or warehouse depreciation charges and storage operating costs. Also included would be *carrying charges*—including *interest* or inventory investment, which is interpreted as a lost potential profit.

Inventory storage costs such as rent, heat, light, and janitor service may be computed by allocating all the costs of renting and operating storerooms to the items in *proportion* to the space occupied. The storage costs increase with respect to the time inventory is held in storage, and so dimensions for unit storage costs are usually dollars/unit of inventory per unit of time. If several

---

†J. Magee, and D. M. Boodman, *Production Planning and Inventory Control*, McGraw-Hill, New York, 1967.

different products are stored in the same basic storage space, charges are usually calculated on the basis of the average amount of inventory held over an order or batch consumption time. If only one product is stored in a facility, all charges associated with that facility will be assigned as storage costs for the item. Unit costs are then based on the *maximum* quantity of inventory expected in the facility.

Carrying charges are usually based on the *average inventory* during a batch-use cycle. Such items as taxes, insurance, and interest charges on capital investment in inventory are typical of these carrying charges. Usually, the interest charge would be based on the *return* achieved on the firm's assets. This may well be in the range of 15% to 25%.

The total cost of carrying inventory is a function of the number of times the items are purchased as an order or produced as a batch, and the actual quantities purchased. For example, suppose an item is purchased for stock and the usage is $2000 per year. One order might be placed for $2000, or 12 orders for $167 each, the latter scattered at equal intervals through the year. The *average* inventory in the first case, assuming uniform depletion, is $1000, but only $83.50 in the second. The order costs for the second case would be considerably higher than for the first. It is the *sum* of these costs that has to be minimized. Far from being trivial, the cost of purchasing is frequently in the range of $50 to $100 per order; hence the futility of ordering just one box of paper clips at a time.

Several methods are available for costing inventory on the balance sheet. Ideally, if items in inventory were used immediately upon receipt of the item, each item could be priced at its input value. However, the realistic case has inventory in storage for varying lengths of time, with input prices of inventory relative to the time certain lots were received. Two familiar methods for pricing inventory, knowing that individual prices are not constant, are the FIFO and LIFO techniques.

FIFO ("first-in, first-out") prices items on the basis of the *oldest lot* currently in storage, until that particular lot is exhausted. A lot is defined as one order-quantity. Items withdrawn after exhaustion of this lot are then priced on the basis of the next oldest lot, and so on. LIFO ("last-in, first-out") is the inverse of FIFO. With LIFO, outgoing items are priced according to the cost of the *latest lots* received until an amount of inventory corresponding to that lot is released. Subsequent items then are priced according to the next-most-recent lot until that is completely released.

The justification for FIFO and LIFO is mentioned by MacNiece.†

    a. FIFO is applicable when manufacturing costs must reflect actual sequences of

---

†E. H. MacNiece, *Production Forecasting, Planning and Control*, John Wiley, New York, 1961.

price fluctuations for raw materials. It certainly is applicable for perishable items that physically have to be routed first-in, first-out to prevent spoilage.

b. LIFO permits stock to be carried on the books at old prices, so that inventory values do not change greatly from one accounting period to the next. Current fluctuations in the price of raw materials are more realistically reflected in the current cost of sales.

From a tax point of view, either method is valid as long as it is used consistently.

Finally, prior to examining some approaches to quantitative inventory control, comment should be made regarding *inventory information.* Large quantities of inventory items require a complex information structure to keep track of the inventory. Input/output records, for example, can get horrendous. Physically tagging items for control can become a headache. Chapter 2 gave an overview of the entire system information picture, with approaches to handling the information problem automatically.

6.2 DEFINITIONS

Before getting into specific inventory policy and model discussions, it will be well to unify a few key definitions, even though a few of these terms already have been presented in the introductory material. The reader with a semantic knowledge of inventory control terms could well pass over this section.

ABC system	A ranking of inventory items according to the *annual* capital cost for each item. The items that contribute to some large percentage of the total capital cost—say, 70% or so—are classified as *A* items, those that contribute to the lowest 5% or 10% are *C* items, and the remainder are *B* items. Inventory policy differs for each category.
Batch	A number of units of a particular inventory item *produced* in a manufacturing facility for use in products produced in that facility. After a *batch* of one inventory item is produced on a machine or set of machines, a *different* item then is batched.
Costs—(interest)	The cost of investing in an inventory item held over time that can be construed as a lost investment because of money tie-up. Interest rates can easily be in the 15%-to-25% range.

Costs—(order)

The cost of ordering inventory items from a vendor (seller). A single purchase order might easily cost a company $50 to $100. Delivery (shipment) costs are included in the purchase order charge.

Costs—(setup)

When inventory is *produced* in the facility rather than purchased, the cost of getting ready (paperwork and machine setup) constitutes setup costs.

Costs—(storage)

The costs actually incurred in storing an inventory item over time. The actual cost of the storage facility has to be apportioned to the inventory items.

Costs—(unit)

All inventory costs apportioned to one item of inventory—as contrasted, for example, to total costs for a *batch* of items.

Economic Order Quantity (EOQ)

The *number* of inventory items that, when ordered, *minimizes* the unit costs of inventory.

Economic Manufacturing Quantity (EMQ)

Equivalent to EOQ, except for manufactured items.

Lot

A number of units of a particular inventory item *purchased* from a vendor (seller). This is analogous to the *batch* for manufactured inventory items.

Model—graphical

A geometric representation of inventory usage over time for a particular inventory item.

Model—mathematical

A mathematical equation that describes the graphical model. Minimizing the mathematical *cost* model realizes the EOQ or EMQ.

Order policy

Procedure defining when an inventory item needs to be replenished and by how many items.

Reorder level

If an inventory item is reordered when the number of units of that item dip below a *specified* level, that level is called the reorder level. Policies that utilize reorder levels frequently are classified as *continuous review* policies to reflect the need to "continuously" monitor the item to determine its level.

Reorder time

If the inventory policy calls for an inventory item to be reordered *periodically* rather than according to inventory *level*, the day on which the inventory is next to be reordered is called the *reorder time*. Policies utilizing reorder times are classified as *periodic review* policies.

Safety stock

A number of units of an inventory item, additional to the economic order or batch quantity, maintained to protect against an unusually high demand or long lead-time in lot delivery or batch preparation.

6.3 *ABC* INVENTORY SYSTEM

Our concern now is with modeling inventory systems so that the costs of the system will be optimized commensurate with maintaining inventory objectives. The result of this optimization will be the development of inventory policies. A typical policy might tell us how much of ˮ particular item to order at a specified time. "Time" could mean either traditional calendar time or the current inventory level of the particular item. With multi-item inventory systems, such as in department stores, the United States Air Force, mail-order catalog systems, and so on, it might be that when several different policies occur, the actual cost of *policy implementation* makes the overall inventory system far from optimum. This is yet another case of subsystem optimization not necessarily forming an optimized aggregate system. One way to cut down on the implementation costs of inventory control is with the so-called *ABC* method.

There are many situations in which a large percentage of cost is contributed by a small percentage of items. In the manufacture of an automobile, for example, even though there are hundreds of components, one of which would be cotter pins, some 70% or 80% of the total component-cost comes from probably 15% or 20% of the actual number of items. The same relationship holds for family budget expenditures—as one look at the automobile and house-mortgage payments will attest. A large proportion of the world's wealth will be found to be in the hands of a small proportion of its population. These types of relationships were widely publicized by *Vilfredo Pareto* (1848–1923), an Italian economist and sociologist, whose empirically derived *Pareto's law* covered the distribution of incomes.

The same relationship frequently exists with items held in inventory. A relatively small percentage of the items will contribute to a disproportionate percentage of the cost. Controlling closely the inventory-holding costs of these high-cost items will clearly lead to effective control of a large percentage of the overall inventory costs. Clerical costs will at the same time be reduced.

The common inventory-control method for handling this is the *ABC* method, according to which inventory is classified into high-value (*A* class), medium-value (*B* class), and low-value (*C* class) items. The classification does not have to follow the three-class approach, but it is by far the most common. The actual percentage of total items held in each class is quite arbitrary, but typical is a breakdown by Magee and Boodman:†

Class A   The top 5% to 10% of the items, which accounts for the *highest* dollar
inventory investment.

---

†Magee and Boodman, *Production Planning and Inventory Control.*

Class B The middle 20% to 30% of items, which accounts for a *moderate* share of the inventory.

Class C The large remaining group of stock-keeping items, which accounts for a *small fraction* of total cost.

The major difference in policy for these items is that investment should be held down for class *A* items; therefore, an optimized policy that minimizes costs should be held quite stringently. Class *C* items should be overstocked to insure non-runout, with little control required. The middle group is a little hazy as far as policy is concerned. One possible approach for class *B* items is to manipulate policies a little to allow blanket policies to cover several items. However, this approach also may be feasible for class *A* items, and this could be a reason for using an *AB* method rather than *ABC*.

The technique should be quite clear, but a little example might clarify it further. Consider the list of inventory items given in Table 6.1, with their estimated annual usage and unit investment cost (purchase cost). Obviously, this is a very limited number of inventory items and except for academic reasons would not warrant *ABC* analysis.

TABLE 6.1   **List of Inventory Items and Annual Investment Costs**

Item Identification	(1) Annual Usage	(2) Item Investment Cost($)	(1) × (2) Annual Investment($)
A-15	50	3.00	150.00
A-34	1000	1.05	1050.00
A-21	475	2.00	950.00
B-7	10	10.00	100.00
B-15	2600	0.50	1300.00
B-28	600	5.00	3000.00
B-81	1000	0.25	250.00
CD-84	2000	11.00	22,000.00
CD-91	3000	0.10	300.00
G-4	100	0.40	40.00
G-15	600	0.10	60.00
G-25	440	2.50	1100.00
H-10	2000	0.25	500.00
			30,800.00

TABLE 6.2   Cumulative Inventory Annual Investment

Item Identification	Annual Investment($)	Cumulative Annual Investment($)
G-4	40.00	40.00
G-15	60.00	100.00
B-7	100.00	200.00
A-15	150.00	350.00
B-81	250.00	600.00
CD-91	300.00	900.00
H-10	500.00	1400.00
A-21	950.00	2350.00
A-34	1050.00	3400.00
G-25	1100.00	4500.00
B-15	1300.00	5800.00
B-28	3000.00	8800.00
CD-84	22,000.00	30,800.00

If the annual investments are ranked in an increasing sequence with accumulated annual investment also calculated, we get the data in Table 6.2, which now will dictate *ABC* classification. Clearly, unit CD-84 stands by itself and should constitute class *A*. It's a little hard to define class *B*, but items A-21, A-34, G-25, B-15, and B-28 are quite high in value compared with the remaining items. The resultant class items and dollar percentages are given in Table 6.3. Performing tight control procedures on item CD-84 would control 71.4% of the total inventory investment while physically controlling only 7.7% of the inventory items. If a two-class system is used, close control is made for the more expensive items and loose control is made for the rest of the items.

The overall *ABC* philosophy is rather important. It shows how a large, complex problem of multi-product policies can be simplified, while at the same time favoring the *overall* objective of minimizing costs—both operational and inventory costs. The same philosophy can be extended into many fields.

6.4   EOQ MODELS FOR PURCHASED PARTS

When determining optimum order quantities, order points, or order times, it is helpful to portray *graphically* the patterns of inventory fluctuation before developing the mathematical inventory models that will themselves lead to the optimized policy. Logically, the graphical representations will be a plot of

TABLE 6.3 Inventory Item Classification by the *ABC* Method

	Items	Class Annual Investment($)	Percentage of Total Items (13)	Percentage of Total Investment ($30,800)
Class A	CD-84	22,000.00	7.7	71.4
Class B	B-28; B-15; G-25; A-34; A-21	7400.00	38.5	24.0
Class C	H-10; CD-91; B-81; A-15; B-7; G-15; G-4	1400.00	53.8	4.6

inventory levels versus time, showing the depletion and accretion characteristics that are inherent in a dynamic inventory situation. First, only *deterministic* inventory cases will be considered. Later we will present cases in
which it is realized that uncertainty will occur.

The basic and most simple inventory model is one in which items are
ordered from an external vendor at some constant order quantity, Q. It is
assumed that each order will arrive where needed at exactly that time when
the previous order completely depletes. Also, it is assumed that depletion of
stock is at some constant linear rate. This model, commonly called the
economic-order-quantity model, has as its real-world application such cases
as department-store ordering or factory raw-material acquisition. The major
problem, of course, is that delivery and/or consumption of an order rarely

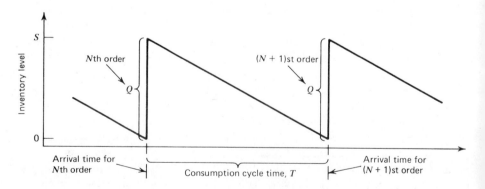

FIGURE 6.2 Graphical inventory model with no safety stock.

conforms to the deterministic assumptions. On the average, however, the stochastic variations may balance such that early delivery effects, for example, counteract late delivery variation, so that the deterministic case may be a reasonably good approximation.

The graphical representation of the EOQ model is given in Figure 6.2. The figure should be self-explanatory, but some definition of terms is in order.

Order Quantity, Q The number of units of one particular stock item ordered at one time. The *optimum* order quantity determined through later mathematical modeling will be symbolized by Q_o. The optimization of Q will be based on the criterion of minimum total-inventory costs per consumption cycle, T.

Consumption Cycle, T The time elapsing between receipt of adjacent orders. It can be defined as the expected time for depletion of one order of size Q units.

Depletion Rate, D The rate, in terms of units per unit time, at which the particular item of inventory is depleted. The unit time may be in terms of hours, days, years, etc. The mathematical definition of depletion rate from Figure 6.2. is

$$D = \frac{Q}{T} \qquad (6.1)$$

An objective of inventory control can now be stated as follows: Knowing the expected depletion rate from prior forecasting and analysis, and knowing the various component costs of inventory, what order quantity Q_o will minimize the total inventory cost during the cycle time T?

Many ramifications of the basic EOQ model can now be made, to evolve a more realistic picture. For example, knowing that it is quite possible for order $(N\text{-}1)$ to be exhausted some time prior to order (N) arriving would lead to the conclusion that it should be advantageous to have a number of extra units on hand to act as a safety buffer. Occasionally, order $(N\text{+}1)$ might arrive *before* order (N) is depleted. In the long run, the number of extra safety items, now to be called *safety stock*, will average to some constant value, *ss*. A common inventory control policy will be found to be the (s, S) policy. When inventory depletes to a reorder level s, an amount is ordered to bring inventory up to a desired level, S. If we plan on a safety stock of ss items and the amount ordered is Q, then S is equal to $Q + ss$. In Figure 6.2 there is no safety stock, so S would be equal to Q.

Reorder Time The time period at which an order has to be processed in order for receipt of the order to be as desired. The relationship of reorder time (T_R) to vendor lead time (T_V) and order arrival time (T_A) is given in Figure 6.3. Mathematically, it can be seen that

$$T_R = T_A - T_V \qquad (6.2)$$

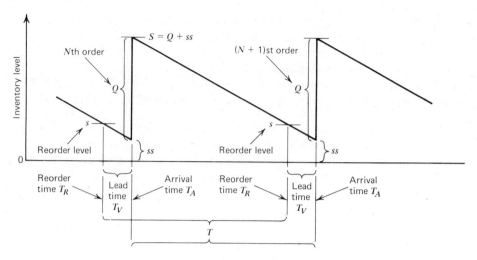

FIGURE 6.3   Graphical inventory model with inventory safety stock.

The average time between adjacent T_R times will be the cycle time, T.

Reorder Level   With a constant depletion rate of inventory, D, and with an assumed constant vendor lead-time, T_V, it follows that an order should be placed when inventory reaches a level equal to

$$s = ss + (D)(T_V) \tag{6.3}$$

This, of course, assumes that the Nth order has a desired arrival time that corresponds to that time when inventory recedes to a level equal to that of the safety stock, ss.

Now that the introductory concepts of *graphical* modeling have been presented, we need to develop a mathematical cost model that can be minimized. The objective of the mathematical analysis will be to find that order quantity Q_o that minimizes inventory unit costs for some inventory pattern defined graphically, as in Figure 6.2 or 6.3. Since the model is cost-oriented, the cost components must first be defined.

P   *Cost* of *purchasing* or *producing* one lot or batch of parts. Dimensionally, P will have units of dollars per order or batch.

I   *Interest charges* per unit of inventory per unit of time. Interest costs are a function of how many units are held in inventory and for how long. Thus, the dimensions for I will be dollars per product-unit/time unit. Since interest is a function of how much capital is invested in the product that is not realizing any profit, it follows that

$$I = (i)(C)$$

where i is the fractional interest rate per unit of time and C is the investment cost in dollars per item of inventory.

π **W** *Charge* for *storing* an inventory item, typically a *warehousing* cost. As with I, W has dimensions of dollars per product unit/time unit.

H *Overall inventory holding cost* factor, which includes both interest and storage component of the total cost.

TC Total *unit* cost to be minimized. This will be the appropriate sum of order costs, interest charges, and storage costs added to purchase cost.

Typically, interest charges are based on the *average* number of units on hand during the time in which inventory is being evaluated. This time would be the cycle time, T. The average quantity should make intuitive sense. If the quantity is constant over T, interest charges should certainly be based on that quantity. But if the quantity decreases uniformly from Q to zero, interest charges initially would be based on Q, but at the end of the evaluation period would be based on zero units. A happy medium is to base overall interest charges on the average inventory.

Two standard ploys are used for charging storage or holding costs. If only one product is being stored in a particular section of the facility, storage charges should always be based on the *maximum* quantity expected in storage. When several products are stored in the same area, charges would usually be based on *average* inventory expected for the product, on the theory that the other products would be charged for the remainder of the storage time. If it is known that a particular product will tie up a specified storage space for a certain percentage of time, storage charges would be based on that particular percentage, rather than average inventory.

The total unit cost, TC, is formed from the sum of the individual unit costs. For example, if Q units are ordered at an order cost equal to P, the unit order cost is P/Q. If interest and storage charges are both based on average inventory, the interest and storage cost per unit during the cycle time, T, would be

$$\frac{(I + W)(T)(\text{Average Inventory})}{Q}$$

The division by Q is to give a cost per unit based on an evaluation period that is the order or batch time. Therefore, the cost model when storage charges are based on average inventory (several products in the same storage area) is

$$TC = C + \frac{P}{Q} + \frac{(I + W)(T)(\text{Average Inventory})}{Q}† \qquad (6.4)$$

---

†The capital investment cost, C, is included in the total cost equation but the reader should realize that C is not included in the inventory costs to be optimized.

For the model depicted in Figure 6.2, inventory consumption period T is

$$T = \frac{Q}{D}$$

where D is the depletion rate of inventory. So now Equation 6.4 can be rewritten

$$TC = C + \frac{P}{Q} + \frac{(I + W)(Q)(\text{Average Inventory})}{QD}$$

and

$$TC = C + \frac{P}{Q} + \frac{(I + W)(\text{Average Inventory})}{D} \qquad (6.5)$$

If only one product is being considered for the storage area, with unused storage area lying empty when inventory is depleted, storage charges are based on *maximum*, not average, inventory. This would result in the following equation.

$$TC = C + \frac{P}{Q} + \frac{(I)(\text{Average Inventory})}{D} + \frac{(W)(\text{Maximum Inventory})}{D} \qquad (6.6)$$

Remember, these two equations only hold if $T = (Q/D)$, which itself holds only if inventory has a *continuous* linear consumption rate. Now we will consider two optimum economic-order-quantity calculations.

The initial model was given pictorially in Figure 6.2. The main reason for the pictorial presentation of the dynamic inventory patterns is to enable the determination of the average inventory for insertion into the mathematical models. For the EOQ model this average inventory is simply $Q/2$, since it has a maximum of Q, a minimum of zero, and is linear in between. Equation 6.5 is applicable if it is assumed that multiple products are held in the storage facility. Inserting $Q/2$ for average inventory, we get

$$TC = C + \frac{P}{Q} + \frac{(I + W)(Q)}{2D} \qquad (6.7)$$

To find that Q which minimizes TC, we need to take the first derivative of TC with respect to Q, set the result to zero, and solve for Q.

$$\frac{d(TC)}{dQ} = -\frac{P}{Q^2} + \frac{(I + W)}{2D} = 0 \qquad (6.8)$$

Solving for Q_o realizes

$$Q_o = \sqrt{\frac{2DP}{I + W}} \qquad (6.9)$$

where Q_o is the order quantity that minimizes unit inventory costs. The reader can verify that the second derivative of TC with respect to Q is positive, indicating that Q_o does in fact minimize TC.

One point of interest arises if we multiply Equation 6.8 by Q:

$$\frac{P}{Q} = \frac{(I+W)Q}{2D} \tag{6.10}$$

We now can see that in the total unit-cost equation, Equation 6.7, the order quantity that minimizes unit costs occurs at the point in the model where the ordering-cost component, P/Q, equals the holding-cost component, $(I+W)Q/2D$. This indicates that the basic EOQ problem could be solved graphically, as shown in Figure 6.4.

Now, let's consider the EOQ model for the case in which only one product is stored in the facility. This situation is modeled by Equation 6.6. The possibility of safety stock is not being considered, so the average inventory during a consumption cycle, T, is still $Q/2$. Maximum inventory is Q. Equation 6.6 can now be written as

$$TC = C + \frac{P}{Q} + \frac{(I)(Q)}{2D} + \frac{(W)(Q)}{D}$$

or

$$TC = C + \frac{P}{Q} + \frac{(I+2W)(Q)}{2D} \tag{6.11}$$

Taking the derivative of TC with respect to Q results in

$$\frac{d(TC)}{dQ} = -\frac{P}{Q^2} + \frac{(I+2W)}{2D} = 0 \tag{6.12}$$

Solving for Q_o results in

$$Q_o = \sqrt{\frac{2DP}{I+2W}} \tag{6.13}$$

Since the holding cost factor, H, is a function of *both* interest and storage

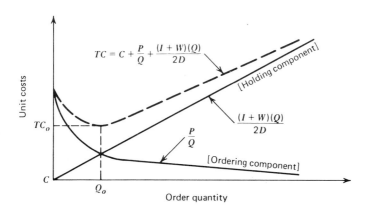

FIGURE 6.4 Breakpoint analysis for inventory cost components.

components, it follows that both Equations 6.9 and 6.13 can reduce to

$$Q_o = \sqrt{\frac{P}{H}} \tag{6.14}$$

with H for the multiple-product situation being

$$\frac{I + W}{2D} \tag{6.15}$$

and for the single-product storage, H is equal to

$$\frac{I + 2W}{2D} \tag{6.16}$$

The total-cost equation can of course be written as

$$TC = C + \frac{P}{Q} + HQ \tag{6.17}$$

with the minimum value of TC being

$$TC_o = C + \frac{P}{Q_o} + HQ_o \tag{6.18}$$

Example

The following data on a particular product might have been obtained from the Accounting and Industrial Engineering departments.

$$D = 800 \text{ units per year}$$

$$P = \$70 \text{ per order}$$

$$i = 20\% \text{ per year}$$

$$C = \$120 \text{ per unit}$$

$$W = \$1.80 \text{ per unit-month}$$

All time units have to be dimensionally consistent, so it would be logical to put W on a yearly basis.

$$W = (1.80)(12) = \$21.60 \text{ per unit-year}$$

Also, interest *charges* per unit-year are needed.

$$I = (120)(0.2) = \$24 \text{ per unit-year}$$

Assuming storage charges are for this one product only, the holding-cost factor can be found from Equation 6.16.

$$H = \frac{24 + (2)(21.6)}{(2)(800)} = 0.042$$

The economic order quantity, Q_o, is found using Equation 6.14.

$$Q_o = \sqrt{\frac{70}{0.042}} = 41 \text{ units}$$

Minimum total costs per unit can be found through Equation 6.18.

$$TC = 120 + \frac{70}{41} + (0.042)(41)$$

which gives

$$TC = 120 + 1.71 + 1.71 = \$123.42$$

This is a good place to point out that of the $123.42, only $3.42 is variable; the $120 capital cost is fixed. The actual *investment* in inventory of course includes the purchase charges. In determining the optimum order quantity, Q_o, we could have left C out of the total cost equation and realized the same result. Also, the reader should not be surprised that in the solution, $1.71 occurred twice. This is because, as shown in Figure 6.4, Q_o occurs when the *purchase order* costs equal the *storage* charges.

Finally, we could now find the consumption cycle time, T, knowing that $T = Q/D$.

$$T_o = Q_o/D = 41/800 = 0.05 \text{ years}$$

If we have 300 working days per year, this would dictate that we order every 15th working day. In actual fact, whether or not we ordered every 15th day would be dependent on the inventory *policy* being used.

6.5 INVENTORY ORDER POLICIES

Looking back at Figure 6.3, we can formulate three realistic order policies. One possible policy is to reorder a particular item when the inventory dips to level s, the previously defined reorder level. The order quantity would be Q_o such that the expected inventory level upon receipt of the order is $Q_o + ss$. This, in Figure 6.3, is called an amount S. This policy is generally called the (s, S) policy. The reorder level is determined by adding the expected demand in the reorder lead-time to the desired safety stock.

The (s, S) policy is typical of what was possibly the original inventory control policy, the two-bin system, in which units of inventory in the storeroom or factory floor are actually stored in two bins. One holds s units and the *sum* of the two holds S units. Items are drawn from the bin *not* holding the s units. When this bin is empty, an order is made to replenish both bins. While waiting for receipt of the order, units are drawn from the bin originally holding s items. This situation is frequently seen in book and record departments. A red tag near the bottom of the stack indicates reorder. The remaining items constitute s, which provides a supply until the new order arrives.

If the (s, S) policy is observed, it should be apparent that ordering may not be accomplished on a strictly cyclic basis, T time units apart, because of *uncertainty* in demand—a topic discussed later. Frequently, cyclic ordering is desired. When this is utilized, the orders are made at reorder times T_R. However, usually only sufficient items to bring the expected level of inventory at time T_A to $Q_o + ss$ are ordered. Now the reorder quantity, Q, is considered a variable, and $[Q_o + ss + (D)(T_V) - Q_{current}]$ units are ordered at T_R. This will be classified as a (t, S) policy. A variant of the (t, S) policy is that replenishment is made only if the inventory level at time T_R is equal to or less than some specified s value. If current inventory, $Q_{current}$, is greater than s, then no action is considered at that time. This policy will be classified as a (t, s, S) policy.

A comment should be made concerning the economic order quantity *if* a safety stock is utilized. Since safety stock is a *constant*, *average* inventory and *maximum* inventory over cycle time, T, will change from the earlier EOQ models by an amount equal to adding the safety stock. When the derivative of total cost is taken with respect to Q, the safety stock drops out. As a result, Q_o is unchanged from the models considered *without* safety stock. The change comes about in the actual value of total cost, TC. Equation 6.18, for example, will change to

$$TC_o = C + \frac{P}{Q_o} + H(Q_o) + \frac{ss(I + W)}{D} \qquad (6.19)$$

The reader is asked to verify that this is so.

6.6 EMQ MODELS FOR MANUFACTURED PARTS

The EOQ model assumed that all units in a particular order arrive simultaneously and instantaneously at time T_A. The arrival *rate* then may be considered to be infinite. If items are *produced* in a facility for use or sale, this arrival rate would probably not be infinite, though if sufficient items for a year's use are produced in a single day, the arrival rate might well be approximated as with the EOQ model. If that time for producing the order is significant, graphical portrayal will change. Now we have to consider the arrival picture and the depletion situation and sum the two, as is depicted in Figure 6.5.

The batch quantity that minimizes total unit-inventory costs, equivalent to the order size in the EOQ situation, is called the Economic Manufacturing Quantity, EMQ.

Some things that should be obvious from Figure 6.5 will be mentioned while discussing the graphical result of the batching model.

a. $A \geq D$: The arrival rate (A) has to be equal to or greater than the depletion rate (D) or we cannot have continuous depletion. Of course, if the model were

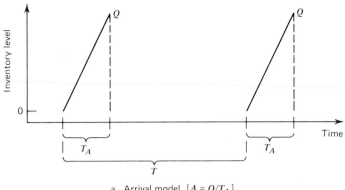

a. Arrival model, $[A = Q/T_A]$.

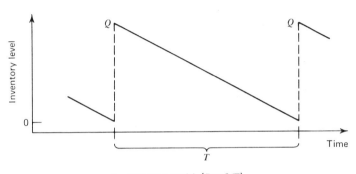

b. Depletion model, $[D = Q/T]$.

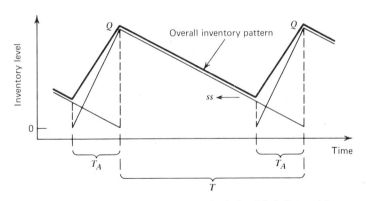

c. Overall batch inventory — combination of arrival and depletion models.

FIGURE 6.5 Graphical model for a batching situation.

such that the depletion was not continuous, this would not be mandatory. Further, if A equals D, there is no fluctuation of inventory and so no inventory control problem exists as such. Usually, in a production system batched items, such as a specific printed circuit card, can be produced at a much greater rate than they are consumed in the production facility.

b. $T_A = 0$: $A = \infty$: If the time for producing a *batch* of units is zero, or approaches zero, the arrival rate is infinite. When this occurs, the batch model reverts to the EOQ model. The *batch* model is really a *general* inventory model, with the EOQ model being a special case.

c. ss = safety stock: Because $A > D$, it follows that a safety stock is needed. However, this is only a realistic, usable safety stock if the items are usable in consumption as soon as they are produced. The physical storage space for at least ss units all the time is of course correct, unless the produced items are stored on something like an overhead conveyor in a process such as drying or curing. For the batch model, ss is really a start-up level rather than safety stock. The term *safety stock* will be used to show consistency with purchasing EOQ models.

d. $ss = f(Q)$: It follows that the batching safety stock is dependent on the size of Q required. This can be shown as follows, using trigonometric relationships from Figure 6.5.

  1. $D = \dfrac{Q}{T}$

  2. $A = \dfrac{Q}{T_A}$

  3. So, $Q = DT = AT_A$

  4. $ss = DT_A$

But the arrival rate, A, and depletion rate, D, are constants, so T_A/T is a constant.

$$D = \frac{Q}{T} = \frac{ss}{T_A}$$

and

$$ss = Q\left(\frac{T_A}{T}\right) = Q\left(\frac{D}{A}\right) \tag{6.20}$$

So, ss is a direct function of Q when A and D are fixed.

Variants of the batching model can be made by adjusting the time at which items are produced with relationship to the consumption (depletion) pattern. In Figure 6.5, the position for the arrival model in the combined model was predicted on minimizing overall inventory while ensuring that batch $(N + 1)$ would *all* be available when batch (N) was depleted. If no

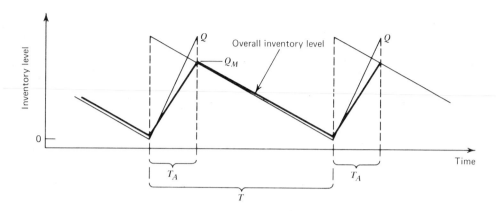

FIGURE 6.6 Modified batching model.

safety stock were desired and if an item produced is immediately usable, then the batching model could be as shown in Figure 6.6. The addition of safety stock, ss, would allow for uncertainty in the levels of either consumption or production.

The maximum value of inventory for which to provide storage, Q_M, is seen to be less than the quantity produced each cycle. It can be shown that Q_M is a function of Q, using trigonometric relationships from Figure 6.6.

1.
$$D = \frac{Q_M}{T - T_A}$$

2.
$$D = \frac{Q}{T}$$

So,

$$Q_M = Q \cdot \left[\frac{T - T_A}{T}\right] = Q \cdot \left[1 - \frac{T_A}{T}\right] \tag{6.21}$$

But earlier, T_A/T was shown to be a constant, as used in Equation 6.20, so $[1 - (T_A/T)]$ has to be a constant, and $Q_M = f(Q)$. As T_A becomes small with respect to T, Q_M approaches Q and we again get the original EOQ model. Many other changes in the pictorial models, for both the EOQ and EMQ models, could be suggested. Only the basic ones have been presented. The reader should be able to model graphically any realistic situation if the rudimentary concepts presented so far are utilized.

If multiple products use the same batch inventory storage area, the mathematical model given by Equation 6.5 is still applicable.

$$TC = C + \frac{P}{Q} + \frac{(I + W)(\text{Average Inventory})}{D} \tag{6.22}$$

P is now the batch setup charges instead of the purchase order cost. Average inventory is a function of the graphical model. For Figure 6.5 this would be $[(Q - ss)/2] + ss$, or $(Q + ss)/2$ during both period $(T - T_A)$ and period T_A. This then has to be true over the entire consumption period, T. Equation 6.22 now becomes, knowing $ss = Q(D/A)$ from Equation 6.20

$$TC = C + \frac{P}{Q} + \frac{(I + W)(Q)[1 + (D/A)]}{2D}$$

Taking the derivative of TC with respect to Q and setting this equal to zero results in

$$Q_o = \sqrt{\frac{2PD}{(I + W)[1 + (D/A)]}} \qquad (6.23)$$

A different graphical batching model is given in Figure 6.6. In this case, the $(N + 1)$st batch is started in production as soon as the Nth batch is depleted. This assumes that when one item is produced in the batch, it is immediatley usable for consumption, even though the entire batch has not been completely produced. The total-cost equation from Equation 6.5 is still applicable.

$$TC = C + \frac{P}{Q} + \frac{(I + W)(\text{Average Inventory})}{D}$$

The average inventory over T is $Q_M/2$. But from Equation 6.21, we saw that $Q_M = Q[1 - (T_A/T)]$. Therefore, average inventory is $(Q/2)[1 - (T_A/T)]$. We saw earlier that

$$T_A/T = D/A$$

The equation for total unit cost to be minimized is now

$$TC = C + \frac{P}{Q} + \frac{(I + W)(Q)[1 - (D/A)]}{2D}$$

and

$$Q_o = \sqrt{\frac{2DP}{(I + W)[1 - (D/A)]}} \qquad (6.24)$$

The relationship between this EMQ value, Q_o, and the EOQ value should be apparent to the reader. In the *purchasing* situation, the arrival rate for the lot (A) is assumed infinite. Therefore, D/A approaches zero and Equation 6.24 reduces to the EOQ equation. To repeat a point made earlier, the batching situation is the *general* inventory situation, with the purchasing model being a special case. This is evident again with Equation 6.24 reducing to the EOQ value.

6.7 FALLACIES AND REALITIES

Even though the order and batching procedures discussed so far are widely accepted and implemented, there is no doubt that the overall inventory *system* is not optimum, even though the policies for individual items may well be optimum, at least under the assumptions made. Seven possible fallacies will be presented in this section, along with possible ways to alleviate the fallacies. The reader undoubtedly can broaden both the fallacy list and the alleviation methods.

I. *Scheduling Not Feasible*   If an inventory model realizes a certain order quantity (EOQ), there is certainly no reason to believe that this is necessarily a valid number. An EOQ may be 975 units, but it might only be possible to order in groups of 50. It is not automatically apparent that 950 or 1000 units should be ordered. *Both feasible* values should be substituted into the item's *total-cost* (*TC*) equation to determine which is smaller. Similarly, a batched item's EMQ value might not allow for realistic scheduling with other products or components that have to be produced. Also, production for an integer number of shifts might well allow for an orderly setup change. A solution to these problems might be achieved through the *Lot Range* or *Batch Range*, depending on whether the purchase or batch situation is prevalent.

For example, consider Figure 6.7, which shows an allowable total-cost value (TC^*) higher than the optimum (TC_o). The resulting *order quantity range*, Q_l to Q_u, usually has a percent deviation from Q_o much larger than that of the cost, TC, from TC_o.

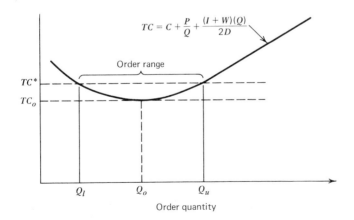

$$TC = C + \frac{P}{Q} + \frac{(I + W)(Q)}{2D}$$

Order range

TC^*

TC_o

Q_l Q_o Q_u

Order quantity

FIGURE 6.7   Graphical description of the order range.

Consider the general-cost model

$$TC = C + \frac{P}{Q} + \frac{(I + W)(Q)}{(2)(D)} \qquad (6.25)$$

We will allow TC to deviate by a certain percent above TC_o. However, it is doubtful that the item's fixed cost, C, would be allowed to deviate. Since C is *not* a function of Q, we can drop it and call the total cost TC'.

$$TC' = \frac{P}{Q} + \frac{(I + W)Q}{(2)(D)} \qquad (6.26)$$

Multiplying both sides of Equation 6.26 by Q and rearranging terms, we get

$$\frac{(I + W)(Q)^2}{(2)(D)} - (TC')(Q) + P = 0$$

The two solutions for Q can be found by the quadratic formula

$$Q_{u,l} = \frac{TC' \pm \sqrt{(TC')^2 - \dfrac{4P(I + W)}{2D}}}{\dfrac{(I + W)}{D}}. \qquad (6.27)$$

Thus, if we specify a specific total-cost value (less C), TC', we can determine the range of order quantities that result.

As an example, consider the following data for a multiproduct facility.

$C = \$100$ per unit

$I = \$20$ per unit-year

$W = \$25$ per unit-year

$D = 1500$ units per year

$P = \$50$ per order

TC_o' is found for Equation 6.26:

$$TC_o' = \frac{50}{Q_o} + \frac{(45)Q_o}{(2)(1500)}$$

Q_o is the EOQ value found using equation 6.9:

$$Q_o = \sqrt{\frac{2DP}{I + W}} = \sqrt{\frac{(2)(1500)(50)}{45}} = 57.74 \text{ units}$$

TC_o' is now found to be

$$TC_o' = \frac{50}{57.74} + \frac{(45)(57.74)}{3000} = \$1.73/\text{unit}$$

Suppose we allow a value of TC' that deviates 5% from TC_o', say, $\$1.82$.

The range on the order quantity, found from Equation 6.27, is

$$Q_{u,l} = \frac{1.82 \pm \sqrt{(1.82)^2 - \frac{(4)(50)(45)}{(2)(1,500)}}}{\left[\frac{45}{1,500}\right]}$$

which results in

$$Q_u = 79.3, \text{ or } 79.0$$

and

$$Q_l = 42.0$$

The lower end of the order range is 27% below Q_o and the upper end is 37% above Q_o. Both percentages are considerably higher than the 5% deviation allowed above TC_o'.

To extend the example, assume 300 working days a year. For the EOQ value of 57.7, this dictates ordering every 11.5 days. The range on this cycle time, assuming Q_l and Q_u, would be 15.9 days to 8.4 days. Ordering every 10 days—say, two weeks—might be very convenient. Similarly, an order quantity of 50 might be more realistic than 57.7 (57 or 58). It should also be obvious that the percent increase from TC_o to TC (rather than TC_o' to TC') is less than 5%. TC_o is $TC_o' + \$100$, or 101.73, whereas TC is $TC' + \$100$, or 101.82. The percent increase is only 0.09% per item with capital cost, C, included.

The idea of a purchase range can be useful in setting up policy B in an ABC inventory system. This will be demonstrated in a case problem in Section 6.9.

II. Vendor Agreements   The EOQ model assumes that a purchase order cost is mandatory each time an order is delivered. Much of the paperwork costs inherent in the *order cost* can be eliminated through specific vendor agreements. For example, to simplify deliveries, a vendor might agree to ship monthly on one annual purchase order. For convenience, the vendor might reduce shipping costs in order to offset added buyer-holding charges. The solution approach is to develop and evaluate a model for *both* cases.

For example, in the previous example, Q_o was 57.74 units and TC_o had a value of $101.73. The net annual cost for the annual demand of 1500 units would be $152,595.

Suppose the vendor could ship on a cyclic basis along with deliveries of other items. The vendor suggests deliveries every 10 working days (50 items per delivery). The agreement would allow the order cost to be $20 per order, in contrast to the original $50 per order. However, a fixed annual charge of $85 is assessed to handle the initial paperwork. The cost per unit would be

$$TC = 100 + \frac{85}{1,500} + \frac{20}{50} + \frac{(45)(50)}{(2)(1,500)}$$

or \$101.21. The net annual cost would be \$151,815, a savings of \$780 over the EOQ situation. Granted, the example is contrived. But it does represent the approach that should be taken, given alternative policies.

III. *Implementation Costs* The one major cost not considered in the usual inventory models is the cost to *implement* the so-called optimized system. The cost of reviewing inventory levels, the need for automating review, and so on should be considered if a change in the inventory system is contemplated. The inability of EOQ models to optimize the larger system has caused many companies to switch to an alternative approach, materials requirement planning (MRP). This possible solution to fallacies is so important that the topic is assigned an entire chapter in this text.

IV. *Cost Determination* Whereas it is assumed that interest charges, purchase order costs, storage costs, and fixed costs are known with certainty, in reality these costs are updated rarely and could be incorrect. Love† spends an entire chapter of his inventory text on this topic and the reader involved with setting such costs is well advised to review that material.

V. *Limited Storage Space* It has been assumed that storage space is available for the inventory quantities needed to be stored. Frequently, this is not a realistic assumption. A cost model could be developed considering the bound on storage space, or one could be evolved that takes rental space into consideration.

VI. *Budget Limits for Multiple-Product Case* Budget limits obviously create a significant problem if multiple products are considered. The analyst has to determine how the available budget can be spread over the different inventory items.

VII. *Probabilistic Inventory Systems* It has been assumed that vendor lead-times and demand patterns have been deterministic. The mathematics of determining optimum inventory systems subject to probabilistic conditions can be very complex. The reader should be aware that analysis of inventory systems under such conditions has been considered. One possible reference is Naddor.‡ The next section will present one approach to handling uncertainty in inventory analysis.

---

†Stephen F. Love, *Inventory Control*, McGraw-Hill, New York, 1979.
‡E. Naddor, *Inventory Systems*, John Wiley, New York, 1966.

6.8   INVENTORY MODELS UNDER UNCERTAINTY

The assumption has been made in the previous material that deterministic conditions prevail in inventory situations. Usually this assumption is not valid, though deterministic solutions frequently yield reasonable approximations to the stochastic case. Basically, the probabilistic characteristics inherent in the EOQ model are caused by

a. The vendor of a particular item not always delivering the items at exactly the required date, because of uncertainty in his own operation.

b. Runout of the particular item not being exactly on a specified date, therefore creating the possibility of running out of the item for a certain length of time. Conversely, the creation of inventory levels higher than desired is also a possibility if delivery is consistently made prior to a desired due date.

Needless to say, an analysis of stochastic conditions requires historical data regarding delivery dates as contrasted to order dates for particular vendors. The traditional problem in performing analyses in industry is lack of applicable data. It is quite a simple matter to record delivery dates in relation to order dates on order cards for each item. These are updated each time an item is ordered and each time an order is delivered.

Initially, we will consider only *vendor lead-time* uncertainty, as depicted in Figure 6.8. The lead time will be defined as the time from order initiation to order delivery. The lead-time histogram, plotted from 50 values obtained from historical files, is given in Table 6.4. The dotted line, of course, approximates the shape of the underlying probability distribution, which will be assumed to be normal. The cumulative area, working from the left of the distribution to a

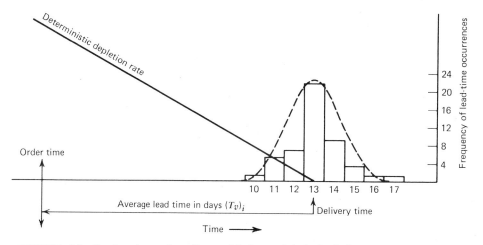

FIGURE 6.8   Stochastic vendor effects with deterministic depletion.

TABLE 6.4 Historical Vendor Lead-Time Data

Lead Time $(T_V)_i$ in Days	Frequency (f_i) of Occurrence of Lead Time $(T_V)_i$
10	1
11	6
12	7
13	22
14	9
15	3
16	1
17	1
	50

particular lead-time, represents the probability of delivery being within that lead-time value.

Normally, a lead time would be set so that the receipt of the order would be within the lead time at some specified probability, say, 98%. Assuming a normal distribution of the data of Table 6.4, the standard deviation of lead time, σ_{T_V}, is found by

$$\sigma_{T_V} = \frac{\sum_{i=1}^{N} [(T_V)_i - \bar{T}_V]^2 f_i}{\sum_{i=1}^{N} f_i}$$

where $\bar{T}_V$ is the lead-time average equal to

$$\frac{\sum_{i=1}^{N} f_i (T_V)_i}{\sum_{i=1}^{N} f_i}$$

and N is the number of histogram classes.

The required calculations, given in Table 6.5, evolve

$$\bar{T}_V = 13$$

$$\sigma_{T_V} = 1.3$$

If a probability of 98% were stipulated for receipt of an order within a lead time, this lead time would be computed as follows.

TABLE 6.5 Calculation of $\bar{T}_V$ and σ_{T_V} for Vendor Lead-Times

$(T_V)_i$	f_i	$(T_V)_i(f_i)$	$[(T_V)_i - \bar{T}_V]^2$	$[(T_V)_i - \bar{T}_V]^2(f_i)$
10	1	10	9	9
11	6	66	4	24
12	7	84	1	7
13	22	286	0	0
14	9	126	1	9
15	3	45	4	12
16	1	16	9	9
17	1	17	16	16
	50	650		86

$$\bar{T}_V = 650/50 = 13$$

$$\sigma_{T_V} = \sqrt{\frac{86}{50}} = 1.3$$

Number of standard deviations above $\bar{T}_V$ for 98%:

$$Z = 2.05$$

from Appendix A. Since

$$Z = \frac{[(T_V)_i - \bar{T}_V]}{\sigma_{T_V}}$$

$$2.05 = \frac{(T_V)_i - 13}{1.3}$$

and

$$(T_V)_i = 16 \text{ days (rounded up)}$$

So if the demand curve is purely deterministic, the next order should be made 16 days *prior* to the expected runout of the current inventory to ensure receipt before runout with a probability of 98%.

This problem becomes more complex when demand characteristics, as well as the delivery lead-time conditions, are stochastic. With the problem just considered—that with a known and fixed demand but with a variable lead-time, once the lead time has been determined, a quantity would be ordered equal to some economic order quantity calculated as discussed in our deterministic analysis. With a varying demand pattern and varying lead time, this might not be true.

A typical situation is as depicted in Figure 6.9. The three points A, B, and

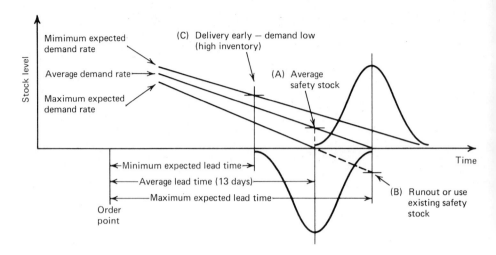

FIGURE 6.9 **Effect of both uncertainty of supply and demand.**

C denote average and worst-case stock conditions. If demand is average and if the lead time is average, a safety stock around point A would be realized. But if conditions continue "average," this safety stock will grow in size, since it would comprise the amount each cycle left from the *previous order* when the new order arrives. Note that "previous order" is mentioned, not "previous inventory level." If lead times and demand tend to maximum, runout conditions will occur and get worse and worse.

A solution might be to have an order/demand relationship as given in Figure 6.10. The expected average safety-stock, or remainder of the previous order, is zero. So if a true safety stock were initially set and if demand and lead-times were both normally distributed, then it would be expected that the true average safety-stock would hover around the initial value in inventory. A safety stock is desired in order to protect against high demand/maximum lead time combinations.

Three possible ordering policies were introduced in Section 6.5 and will be reconsidered here, since they are most applicable to the situation that is uncertain.

Policy (s, S)   Here, a reorder quantity is predetermined—say, s. A Q_o value is determined, possibly by using conventional EOQ formulas and based on an average demand rate. A desired safety stock, ss, is considered to protect against emergency conditions. When current inventory depletes to a level s, an order of (Q_o) is made on the assumption that current inventory will deplete to ss by the time the new order arrives. Thus, expected inventory on arrival of the order is ($Q_o + ss$), or S. What should this s value be? Logically, it should be a function of lead time and demand rate, possibly average demand rate multiplied

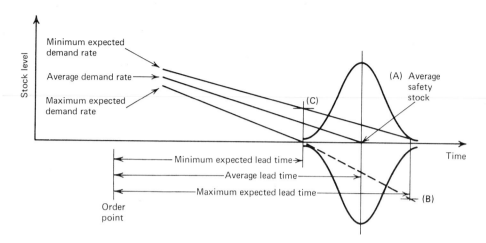

FIGURE 6.10 **Effect of shifting demand depletion/lead-time relationship.**

by average lead time. Some authors suggest maximum demand rate multiplied by maximum lead time for s to protect against drastic conditions, and then lowering s if inventories start to build.

Policy (t, S) An obvious disadvantage for (s, S) is that a continuous monitoring of inventory is required in order to catch the inventory level at s. The reorder is not cyclic from a time viewpoint. The (t, S) policy evaluates the inventory level after each time cycle, T. For protection, T might be based on

$$T = \frac{Q_o}{\text{Maximum Expected Demand Rate}}$$

where Q_o is that order quantity which minimizes unit inventory costs.

At each review period, sufficient units are ordered so that upon delivery, an expected $(Q_o + ss)$ units total will be on hand. The order quantity is not necessarily Q_o now; it will vary. Using the concept of s from the policy (s, S), if Q units are on hand, the quantity ordered is $[Q_o - (Q - ss)]$. One problem now is that if Q is close to Q_o, when demand is low, small quantities will be ordered. Also, if demand is high, possible runout could be realized if Q is very low.

Policy (t, s, S) This policy guards against the first problem. Inventory is checked every cycle, but an order is made only if the quantity on hand is equal to or less than s. The same interpretation is made for $(Q_o + ss)$ as was made with the two previous policies.

6.9 CASE PROBLEM

The Playee Toy Company has decided to incorporate an *ABC* inventory system. Only 45 items are to be included, so it is a very small inventory problem. Annual item usage and unit costs are given in Table 6.6. Playee's management has asked that the following tasks be accomplished.

1. Define the *ABC* system.
2. Determine annual inventory costs under specified *ABC* policies.
3. Evaluate the increase in annual costs for the *ABC* system over having EOQs specified for *all* items.

The policies specified by management are

Policy A Hold tight control on EOQ levels.

Policy B Group items so that *cyclic* ordering and *monitoring* of the *group* is feasible. Management will allow item inventory cost (*not* including the purchase cost, *C*) to increase up to 10% above EOQ costs.

Policy C Order quarterly and hold a safety stock equal to one-twentieth of annual demand.

Accounting determines needed information as

$i = 20\%$ per year interest charges on investment.

$W = \$1.50$ per unit-year storage charges.

$P = \$80$ purchase order costs.

The first step is to determine which items fall into which classes *A*, *B*, or *C*. Table 6.7 gives the total annual costs for each of the 45 items, with items

TABLE 6.6 Annual Data for Inventory

Item	Units/Year Demand	Unit Cost
AA-04	865	0.05
AA-81	2000	0.001
AB-24	128	1.37
AE-05	186	125.50
AH-15	4800	0.88
AN-54	500	0.36
AY-03	100	0.50

TABLE 6.6 (*Continued*)

Item	Units/Year Demand	Unit Cost
AY-16	2000	0.01
BK-17	750	0.30
BX-12	9050	3.20
CC-12	850	64.53
CD-04	54	125.00
DA-12	85,000	0.0003
DB-81	50,000	0.0001
DF-10	2569	1.59
EY-60	15,000	0.002
FG-15	3500	6.50
GK-10	650	1.80
GX-90	85	0.86
LE-45	375	4.50
LM-60	48	1080.00
LP-05	10,000	0.002
LY-04	3500	0.0015
MB-10	15	3.85
MN-01	14,800	0.001
MX-15	350	2.60
PO-01	760	0.15
UR-10	19,000	0.016
XB-50	2850	2.20
XE-40	25	38.40
XE-41	500	0.15
XH-10	7500	2.95
XH-14	96	15.20
XX-09	150	6.42
XY-01	680	0.21
XY-10	28,000	0.002
XY-77	960	0.10
YA-16	25,000	0.006
ZD-15	3550	0.38
ZF-05	280	0.18
ZM-12	10,000	0.20
ZN-05	1400	0.15
ZP-40	45	5.20
ZP-45	567	3.20
ZR-50	2500	0.75

TABLE 6.7   Items Ranked According to Annual Investment

Item	Total Annual Cost (Item)	Cumulative Annual Cost (Inventory)
CC-12	$54,850.50	$54,850.50
LM-60	51,840.00	106,690.50
BX-12	28,960.00	135,650.50
AE-05	23,343.00	158,993.50
FG-15	22,750.00	181,743.50
XH-10	22,125.00	203,868.50
CD-04	6750.00	210,618.50
XB-50	6270.00	216,888.50
AH-15	4224.00	221,112.50
DF-10	4084.71	225,197.21
ZM-12	2000.00	227,197.21
ZR-50	1875.00	229,072.21
ZP-45	1814.40	230,886.61
LE-45	1687.50	232,574.11
XH-14	1459.20	234,033.31
ZD-15	1349.00	235,382.31
GK-10	1170.00	236,552.31
XX-09	963.00	237,515.31
XE-40	960.00	238,475.31
MX-15	910.00	239,385.31
UR-10	304.00	239,689.31
ZP-40	234.00	239,923.31
BK-17	225.00	240,148.31
ZN-05	210.00	240,358.31
AN-54	180.00	240,538.31
AB-24	175.36	240,713.67
YA-16	150.00	240,863.67
XY-01	142.80	241,006.47
PO-01	114.00	241,120.47
XY-77	96.00	241,216.47
XE-41	75.00	241,291.47
GX-90	73.10	241,364.53
MB-10	57.75	241,422.32
XY-10	56.00	241,478.32
ZF-05	50.40	241,528.72
AY-03	50.00	241,578.72
AA-04	43.25	241,621.97
EY-60	30.00	241,651.97
DA-12	25.00	241,676.97

TABLE 6.7 (*Continued*)

Item	Total Annual Cost (Item)	Cumulative Annual Cost (Inventory)
AY-16	20.00	241,696.97
LP-05	20.00	241,716.97
MN-01	14.80	241,731.77
LY-04	5.25	241,737.02
DB-81	5.00	241,742.02
AA-81	2.00	241,744.02

ranked from maximum to minimum cost. Cumulative annual costs also are given. There is an obvious item-cost break between items XH-10 and CD-04. The first six items will be classed as A items. Another natural break occurs between MX-15 and UR-10. Items for UR-10 and below will be classed as C items. Other breaks would be feasible, but the ones chosen are very clear-cut. A summary of the ABC breakdown is given in Table 6.8, which shows that the ABC expectancy, as far as item and cost percentages are concerned, are met.

A computer program was written to determine EOQ values and associated costs for the class A items. The calculations performed for each item were

    I. *Economic Order Quantity:*

$$Q_o = \sqrt{\frac{2PD}{(I+W)}} \qquad \text{(Assumes random storage; } I = iC)$$

    II. *Optimum Unit Inventory Costs:*

$$TC_o = \frac{P}{Q_o} + \frac{(I+W)(Q_o)}{2D} \qquad \text{(not including } C)$$

    III. *Total Annual Unit Costs:*

$$TAC_o = (TC_o)(D)$$

Results of the computations are given in Table 6.9.

For class B items, the program computed the following.

    I. *Economic Order Quantity* (See class A).

    II. *Optimum Unit Inventory Costs* (See class A).

    III. *Allowable Unit Inventory Costs:*

$$TC' = (1.1)TC_o$$

TABLE 6.8 *ABC* **Breakdown**

	Items	Percent of Total Items	Class Cost	Percent of Total Cost
Class A	CC-12; LM-60; BX-12; AE-05; FG-15; XH-10	13.3	$203,868.50	84.3
Class B	CD-04; XB-50; AH-15; DF-10; ZM-12; ZR-50; ZP-45; LE-45; XH-14; ZD-15; GK-10; XX-09; XE-40; MX-15	31.1	$35,516.81	14.7
Class C	UR-10; ZP-40; BK-17; ZN-05; AN-54; AB-24; YA-16; XY-01; PO-01; XY-77; XE-41; GX-90; MB-10; XY-10; ZF-05; AY-03; AA-04; EY-60; DA-12; AY-16; LP-05; MN-01; LY-04; DB-81; AA-81	55.6	2358.71	1.0

IV. *Allowable Range on Order Quantity:*

$$Q'_{u,l} = \frac{TC' \pm \sqrt{(TC')^2 - \dfrac{4P(I+W)}{2D}}}{\left(\dfrac{I+W}{D}\right)}$$

V. *Allowable Range on Time between Orders* (*T'*)

$$T'_{u,l} = \left[\frac{Q'_{u,l}}{D}\right](52) \qquad \text{(assumes 52 working weeks/year)}$$

TABLE 6.9 Class *A* Inventory Costs

Item	Q_o	TC_o	TAC_o
CC-12	97.2	$1.65	$1403
LM-60	5.9	26.92	1292
BX-12	822.6	0.19	1720
AE-05	33.5	4.78	889
FG-15	447.2	0.36	1260
XH-10	757.8	0.21	1575
	Class *A* inventory costs:		$8,139

A summary of these computations is given in Table 6.10. The objective now is to find a cyclic schedule whereby each of the items in class *B* can be ordered and monitored according to that cycle. Since we have 52 working weeks per year, 13 weeks, 26 weeks, and so on might be logical ordering points. Of course, each item's cycle time value has to fall within its T'_u and T'_l, or the bound on annual inventory costs being restricted to 10% above minimum costs will be violated. One possible cyclic sequence, from Table 6.10, is shown on the top of page 210.

TABLE 6.10 Range Computations for Class *B* Items

Item	Q'_u	Q'_l	T'_u	T'_l
CD-04	28.1	11.6	27.1	11.2
XB-50	755.3	311.2	13.8	5.7
AH-15	1054.7	434.5	11.4	4.7
DF-10	740.8	305.2	15.0	6.2
ZM-12	1588.1	654.2	8.3	3.4
ZR-50	767.1	316.0	16.0	6.6
ZP-45	320.8	132.2	29.4	12.1
LE-45	246.3	101.5	34.2	14.1
XH-14	90.6	37.3	49.1	20.2
ZD-15	935.3	385.3	13.7	5.6
GK-10	368.4	151.8	29.5	12.1
XX-09	144.7	59.6	50.1	20.7
XE-40	32.5	13.4	67.6	27.9
MX-15	259.4	106.9	38.5	15.9

Order Every	*Item*
26 weeks (semiannual)	CD-04; ZP-45; LE-45; XH-14; GK-10; XX-09; XE-40; MX-15 (XE-40 violates the time range slightly, but *overall* system costs will be within the 10% increase over TC_o)
13 weeks (quarterly)	XB-50; DF-10; ZR-50; ZD-15
6.5 weeks (semiquarterly)	AH-15; ZM-12

Now, order quantities and associated costs have to be determined for class *B* items.

    I. *Order Quantity (Q_B):*

        $Q_B = D/2$ for semiannual ordering

        $Q_B = D/4$ for quarterly ordering

        $Q_B = D/8$ for semiquarterly ordering

    II. *Unit Costs (TC_B):*

$$TC_B = \frac{P}{Q_B} + \frac{(I + W)(Q_B)}{2D}$$

   III. *Annual Item Costs (TAC_B):*

$$TAC_B = (TC_B)(D)$$

Results are given in Table 6.11. When compared with EOQ costs, it is found that grouping causes a 3.37% increase in annual costs, far below the allowable 10%. Of course, if item purchase costs (C), are included, the percent increase is negligible. Hidden savings are the big advantage for grouping—the savings involved in cyclic review, possibly requiring less-complex inventory monitoring and reduced personnel.

    Class *C* items are ordered quarterly with a safety stock equal to D/20. Computations involved are

    I. *Order Quantity (Q_c):*

$$Q_c = D/4$$

    II. *Unit Cost (TC_c):*

$$TC_c = \frac{P}{Q_c} + \frac{(I + W)Q_c}{2D} + \frac{(D/20)(I + W)}{D}$$

$$= \frac{320}{D} + \frac{7(I + W)}{40}$$

TABLE 6.11   Item *B* Costs after Grouping

Item	Q_B	TC_B	TAC_B
CD-04	27	$9.59	$518
XB-50	713	0.35	998
AH-15	600	0.24	1152
DF-10	642	0.35	898
ZM-12	1250	0.16	1600
ZR-50	625	0.33	825
ZP-45	284	0.82	466
LE-45	188	1.03	387
XH-14	48	2.80	269
ZD-15	888	0.29	1030
GK-10	325	0.71	462
XX-09	75	1.76	264
XE-40	13	8.54	222
MX-15	175	0.96	336
			$9427

Optimum costs for class *B* items: $9120.67

III.   *Total Annual Cost* (TAC_c):

$$TAC_c = (TC_c)(D)$$

Results for class *C* are given in Table 6.12. It can be seen that the annual costs have a dramatic increase over optimum EOQ costs, probably negating the class *C* policy suggestion. Actually, the problem lies with constant storage costs per item—usually, class *C* items will have small storage charges.

TABLE 6.12   Class *C* Costs

Item	Q_c	TC_c	TAC_c
UR-10	4750	$0.22	$4180
ZP-40	11	7.46	328
BK-17	188	0.64	481
ZN-05	350	0.44	616
AN-54	125	0.86	430
AB-24	32	2.74	351
YA-16	6250	0.22	5500

TABLE 6.12 (*Continued*)

Item	Q_c	TC_c	TAC_c
PO-01	190	.74	559
XY-77	240	.60	576
XY-01	170	0.68	462
XE-41	125	0.85	425
GX-90	21	4.00	336
MB-10	4	21.65	346
XY-10	7000	0.22	6160
ZF-05	70	1.35	378
AY-03	25	3.42	342
AA-04	216	0.58	501
EY-60	3750	0.23	3450
DA-12	21,250	0.21	17,850
AY-16	500	0.37	740
LP-05	2500	0.24	2400
MN-01	3700	0.23	3404
LY-04	875	0.30	1050
DB-81	12,500	0.21	10,500
AA-81	500	0.37	740

Total annual costs: $62,105

Optimum EOQ annual costs for Class *C*
items: **$21,276.95**

The overall inventory cost for the *ABC* system is $80,121. If all items had been held to an EOQ policy, the total costs would have been $45,418.61, a considerable savings over the *ABC* system. Again, the recommended class *C* policy was poor, taking into account the high storage costs per item. This example should point out the need for careful analysis *before* policy implementation.

6.10 REFERENCES

1. *APICS Dictionary of Production and Inventory Control Terms*, American Production and Inventory Control Society, Chicago, 1966.

2. Buchan, J., and Koenigsberg E., *Scientific Inventory Management*, Prentice-Hall, Englewood Cliffs, N.J., 1963.

3. Love, S. F., *Inventory Control*, McGraw-Hill, New York, 1979.

4. MacNiece, E. H., *Production Forecasting, Planning and Control*, John Wiley, New York, 1961.

5. Magee, J., and Boodman D. M., *Production Planning and Inventory Control*, McGraw-Hill, New York, 1967.

6. Naddor, E., *Inventory Systems*, John Wiley, New York, 1966.

7. Stockton, R. S., *Basic Inventory Systems: Concepts and Analysis*, Allyn and Bacon, Boston, 1965.

6.11 EXERCISES

1. A production line has three production stations, *A*, *B*, and *C*. In-process storage is possible between the stations, but at the monthly cost of $100 for storage between *A* and *B* and $150 between *B* and *C*. The storage would offset any station downtime in the preceding station(s). Income per item produced is $5 per item and the maximum monthly production rate is 1000 units. If the downtimes for stations *A*, *B*, and *C* are 5%, 3%, and 7%, respectively, determine the optimum income-cost relationship from the four possible configurations of in-process inventory arrangement. Assume the station downtimes are statistically independent.

2. A particular product is being evaluated for its economic order quantity. Storage is charged at $2 per unit per month, and this product does not share the particular storage facility. Purchase order cost is $85, interest rate is 25% per year, and capital cost of the product is $200. The demand rate for the product is 3000 units per year. Determine the EOQ value.

3. Determine the total annual inventory cost for the product discussed in Problem 2.

4. At what time intervals should the product of Problem 2 be reviewed for reorder purposes?

5. The product given in Problem 2 is now one of many that utilize the same general storage area. Re-evaluate the EOQ, total annual inventory cost, and ordering time interval.

6. A certain product purchased for internal consumption is to be ordered so that delivery occurs three days before the expected runout of the previous order. Demand is considered deterministic and is linear. Derive the economic-order-quantity formula for this problem, using the symbols given in the text. Do it for both cases: one in which storage charges are based on average inventory and one in which the storage costs are based on maximum inventory.

7. Management decides that a safety stock is required for the product described in Problems 2 through 5. If this safety stock is equal to $Q_o/30$, determine the effect on total annual inventory costs under the assumption that the product is one of many utilizing the storage area.

8. For the situation given in Problem 7, specify values for s, S and T_R in

the three standard inventory policies: (s, S); (t, S); (t, s, S). Assume vendor shipment leadtime is 0.2 months.

9. Consider the inventory data given below.

Item	Item Cost	Demand per Year	Item	Item Cost	Demand per year
A	$10.00	1000	N	$1.50	500
B	0.20	750	O	3.00	30
C	1.00	820	P	0.50	2200
D	14.00	5	Q	0.01	1000
E	0.50	1620	R	0.05	1000
F	0.25	320	S	5.00	8
G	0.60	1000	T	3500.00	4
H	0.10	500	U	1.00	20
I	2.00	20	V	0.01	6000
J	200.00	85	W	0.02	4500
L	0.10	2000	Y	0.01	1000
M	0.90	200	Z	0.15	200

Also, interest charges, i, are set at 30% per year, storage charges are $1.50 per unit-year, and purchase order costs are $85 per order. Discounting the fact that an *ABC* inventory system should encompass hundreds of items and not just 24, as given above, suggest item classification into an *ABC* system. Do these data seem to follow Pareto's law?

10. Assuming random storage for the class *A* items of Problem 9, determine total inventory costs for class *A* assuming tight EOQ with no safety stock is maintained for each item. Ignore unit costs of the items.

11. Assume class *B* items in Problem 9 can be grouped on a *cyclic* ordering schedule if inventory costs (not counting capital costs) are allowed to increase above optimum by no more than 5%. Determine a cyclic ordering scheme and evaluate overall inventory costs for class *B*. Also, compare the "grouped policy" costs to optimum EOQ total costs.

12. Class *C* items in Problem 9 are delivered *once* a month against *one* blanket purchase-order made at the beginning of the year. The cost of this order is $350, which includes shipping costs through the year. Determine the class *C* costs under this policy and evaluate against optimum EOQ costs.

13. It is mentioned in the inventory material that the total unit cost for inventory with safety stock will differ from that of inventory with no safety stock, but that the EOQ value will stay the same. Verify Equation 6.19 and also prove that the EOQ values will not change.

14. An item is batched within a manufacturing facility with the following data being applicable:

> **Consumption rate**   500 items/month
>
> **Production rate**   1500 items/month
>
> **Storage costs** (based on average inventory) $10 per unit-year
>
> **Interest charges** $5 per unit-year
>
> **Setup charges per batch** $200

The batch is produced so that it is completed exactly when the previous batch is depleted. Determine the EMQ value and associated total costs per unit.

15. For the item given in Problem 14, assume that the batch is to be completed 0.2 months *before* the previous batch is depleted. Determine the EMQ value and associated total costs per unit.

16. Suppose the minimum total cost per unit for the item in Problem 14, not counting capital cost, is allowed to increase from TC_o to $2TC_o$. What is the allowable batch-quantity range? Display the costs and batch range pictorially.

17. A production facility has the peculiar production/consumption cycle given in Figure 6.11. Given

$$t_w = 2t_{p1}; \quad I = \text{interest charges; \$ per unit-time}$$
$$t_c = 4t_{p1}; \quad W = \text{storage costs; \$ per unit-time}$$
$$t_{p1} = 2t_{p2}; \quad A = \text{arrival rate}$$
$$D = \text{depletion rate}$$
$$P = \text{setup charges; \$/batch}$$

derive the formula for the batch quantity, Q_o, that minimizes unit inventory costs, assuming storage charges based on maximum inventory. Assume all stock is depleted during the cycle and use equation 6.4.

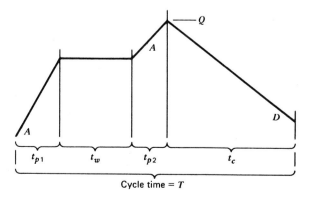

FIGURE 6.11   Unusual inventory pattern for Problem 17.

18. The following data are available for Problem 17 setup.

$$A = 200 \text{ units/day}$$
$$I = \$3 \text{ per unit-month}$$
$$W = \$2 \text{ per unit-month}$$
$$P = \$500/\text{batch}$$

Find TC_o', T_o', Q_o, knowing there are 22 working days a month.

19. An item has been ordered according to an EOQ evaluation. The item is stored according to random storage and has the following data.

Storage costs $3 per unit-month

Interest charges $2 per unit-month

Demand   3,000 units per year

Purchase order cost $70/order

Items can only be purchased in *multiples* of six, because of packaging. Determine the minimum-cost order quantity.

20. For the inventory item given in Problem 19, the vendor suggests an alternative scheme. Items will be delivered once a month. One annual charge of $300 will cover shipping and order costs. Show if the vendor's proposal should be considered.

SEVEN: MATERIALS REQUIREMENT PLANNING†

The Moving Finger writes; and having writ, Moves on; nor all your Piety nor Wit Shall lure it back to cancel half a Line, Nor all your Tears wash out a Word of it.

Omar Khayyam

One economic-order-quantity concept developed in Chapter 6 is formally referred to as an (s, S) approach to inventory management, where S represents a fixed order quantity without safety stock and s represents a fixed reorder level. There are significant problems associated with all (s, S) approaches. It is assumed, for example, that the expected value for the depletion rate is constant and continuous over time. In most realistic situations, demand is neither constant nor continuous, but occurs in discrete periodic bursts. Consider, as an illustration, demand over a six-week planning horizon to be 100 units in week 2, 200 in week 5 and 0 units in weeks 1, 3, 4, and 6. Calculating the order quantity would require the assumption of a 50 unit per week constant-depletion rate. Suppose the (s, S) approach led to a policy of ordering 120 units whenever the actual inventory fell below 25 units. Such a policy bears no resemblance to the reality of two periodic bursts of demand.

7.1 OVERVIEW

A better rule would be to order exactly the quantity needed to meet the demand, and to order so that the material arrives just prior to the need: in

---

† J. A. Orlicky's *Materials Requirement Planning* (New York: McGraw-Hill, 1975) is considered to be a fundamental authority and many of the concepts presented here can be traced to that text.

other words, to order enough to have exactly 100 units at the beginning of week 2 and 200 at the beginning of week 5. This idea is at the heart of the materials requirement planning (MRP) approach to inventory management.

Consider the effect of the (s, S) and MRP approaches when applied to the example problem. Suppose that 50 units were on hand at the beginning of week 1 and that the lead time for delivery is one week. Figure 7.1a shows the inventory history under the (s, S) approach, and 7.1b shows the history under the MRP approach. Integrating under the inventory curves of these two figures indicates that the (s, S) and MRP approaches resulted in average weekly inventories of 45 and 33 units, respectively. Thus, MRP reduced

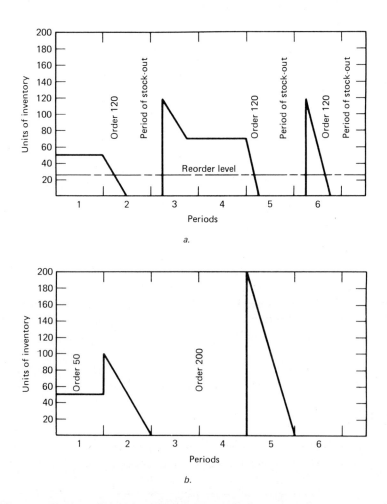

FIGURE 7.1   History of inventory for example problem using (s, S) and MRP approaches to inventory management. (a) (s, S) history. (b) MRP history.

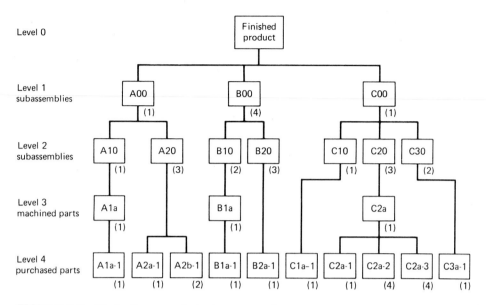

Level 0

Level 1
subassemblies

Level 2
subassemblies

Level 3
machined parts

Level 4
purchased parts

FIGURE 7.2 **Illustrative manufacturing process tree.**

average inventory by almost 27%. In addition, the (s, S) approach resulted in three stock-out situations that were avoided by MRP.

The clear need is for a materials-management information system that takes into account the specific timing of demands for materials at all levels of manufacture. MRP is such a computerized inventory planning and control system. MRP begins with a master schedule of demand for finished goods. For future planning periods, the gross demand for each finished product is listed. The MRP system utilizes a manufacturing-oriented explosion (as illustrated in Figure 7.2) to break the demand for the product into its primary subassemblies. These subassemblies are in turn broken into second, third, and so on levels of subassemblies until, at the lowest level, only purchased items exist. If more than one unit of a subassembly goes into the manufacture of the next highest parent item, appropriate multipliers are used to take this fact into account. Many of the subassemblies are interchangeably shared with several of the finished-goods products. The demand for these shared items is, therefore, the accumulation of the demand for all parent items. A *detailed* description of Figure 7.2 will be found in Section 7.3.

Using a time standard for the lead time between the completion of a process and the availability of its components, the system places the gross demand for each component item in some earlier planning period. Moving down the manufacturing-process tree, one level at a time, results in the period-by-period gross demand for all inventory items.

The gross requirements for the demand for each item can then be adjusted to account for inventories on hand and on order. This step in the analysis results in the net unfilled requirements against which production and purchase orders are generated. Therefore, the objective of the MRP system is to generate the gross and net unfilled requirements for all inventory items in all production periods so as to provide accurate information for the materials-ordering activity.

7.2 DEFINITIONS

In order better to understand the concepts of materials requirement planning, a few terms should be defined. A familiarity with the vocabulary is necessary to the intuitive understanding of the materials.

MRP
*M*aterials *R*equirement *P*lanning, a computer-based system for managing inventory and production schedules. This approach to materials management applies to large job-shop situations in which many products are manufactured in periodic lots via several processing steps. It does not apply to continuous flow-type manufacturing systems.

Manufacturing process tree
A hierarchical representation of the processing steps in the manufacture of a product. The nodes of the tree represent items that could be placed into or pulled from inventory. The branches between nodes represent manufacturing processes that transform a collection of items into a new, higher-level parent item.

Inventory item
A uniquely identifiable part or assembly that is used in the manufacturing process. Every item must have a unique part-number. Each item has an inventory record indicating period-by-period needs for and availability of the item.

Planning period
The unit of time utilized by the master schedule. It is likely to be one day or one week. The planning horizon is expressed in terms of the next N planning periods.

Production lead-time standard
The scheduling time required to manufacture one lot of a given item from its component items. The lead time is expressed in some number of planning periods. Essentially, the concept is that if one desires to process some quantity of an item, all components must be available prior to the due date of the item by a time equal to the lead-time standard. It is important to realize that this lead time is only an expected value and is subject to significant dynamic changes. In this chapter, production lead-time for item j is designated by ℓ_j.

Gross requirements
The total demand, from all sources, for an item in any given planning period. In this chapter, gross requirements for item j in period t are designated by $G_{t,j}$.

Schedule receipts	For an item in any given planning period, the total of all expected receipts for which purchase or manufacturing orders exist. In this chapter, scheduled receipts for item j in period t are designated by $R_{t,j}$.
Expected inventory	For an item at the beginning of any given planning period, the level of inventory that will exist if the materials requirement plan is accurate and utilized. In this chapter, expected inventory for item j in period t is designated by $I_{t,j}$.
Net unfilled requirements	For an item in any given planning period, the total demand for which purchase or manufacturing orders do not exist. In essence, it is the quantity which must be ordered if the materials requirement plan is to work. In this chapter, net unfilled requirements for item j in period t are designated by $N_{t,j}$.

7.3 HOW DOES MRP WORK?

Figure 7.3 represents the inputs, software, files, and outputs of a basic MRP system. In order better to understand how MRP works, each of the boxes in Figure 7.3 will be discussed in more detail. It should be noted that the following discussion presents the basic MRP concept, rather than a particular implementation package. Note first the five data-files indicated in the figure. As suggested by Donelson (1979),† these are the mandatory files of the MRP system. The inventory-item master file contains one record for each item maintained in inventory. The data in each record include part number, part description, quantity on hand, quantity on order, part location, and, if called for, various accounting data. Donelson suggests a typical size for this file would be 10,000–50,000 records of 100–500 bytes each. The order master file contains all customer, stock replenishment, shop, and purchase order records. The records would contain part number, order number, order quantity, due dates, vendor number, and other accounting data. The typical size of this file is 2000–20,000 records of 100–200 bytes each, where a byte is eight binary digits of computer storage. The manufacturing process file links the finished-product items to all of its components, as will be discussed in more detail later. The typical size here is two to four times the records of the inventory-item master file, depending on the complexity of the finished products; typical records are 40–100 bytes long. Linking the inventory-item master file to the order master file are the materials demand file and materials supply file. Each of these files typically contains 4000–40,000 records of 100 bytes each. Using Donelson's estimates, the typical MRP file system requires, on the average, 21 million bytes of mass storage. The *MRP Control System* is a driver or master control program. Its function

---

† W. S. Donelson, "MRP—Who Needs It?", *Datamation*, vol. 25, no. 5, May 1979, pp. 185, 194.

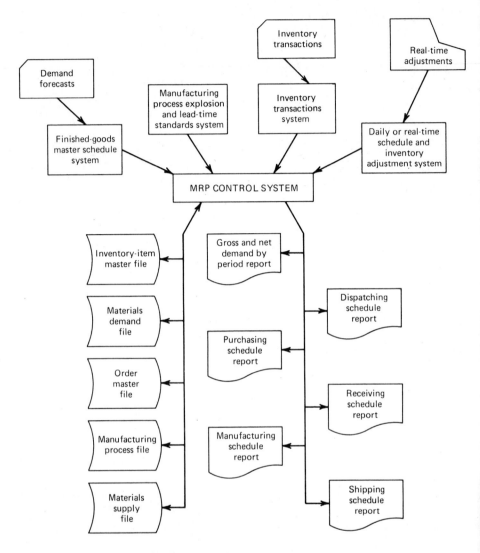

FIGURE 7.3 Input software systems, data files and output reports of a basic MRP system. (Adapted from W. S. Donelson, "MRP—Who Needs It?" *Datamation*, vol. 25, no. 5, May 1979).

is to control the input processing activities, update all data base files via the computer's database manipulator system, and generate the necessary reports.

The *finished-goods master schedule system* is equivalent to the aggregate planning system described in Chapter 3. Alternatively and perhaps more appropriately, this system merely presents the output of an independent aggregate-planning system that has been reviewed and modified by management in an off-line fashion. In either case, the system modifies the order master file for all finished-goods orders on a period-by-period basis. The operation of this system is the first step in the monthly or weekly update of the entire materials-requirement plan.

The first-step nature of the master schedule system makes its inputs extremely important. Without a reasonably accurate finished-goods forecast, the concept of planning closely to the forecasted material requirements is invalid. If the critical-path lead time of the finished goods is long, the forecast must be equally far into the future. When considering the feasibility of MRP, the availability of reasonably accurate forecasts is important.

The *manufacturing process explosion and lead-time system* follows the master schedule update and extends the finished-goods orders to purchasing and shop orders. The process explosion is not a bill of materials that merely lists the quantities of each item in the final product; rather, it is a manufacturing-process breakdown of the product. This breakdown is best envisioned as a manufacturing-process tree in which the finished product is the trunk. The first level of branches represents the major subassemblies that are put together at final assembly. The second level of branches represents the secondary subassemblies. The tree is further broken down until only purchased goods exist. The explosion recognizes multiple units of one subassembly required by its parent item. Figure 7.2 depicts an illustrative process tree for a very simple finished product. The numbers in the boxes represent part numbers. At level 4, the dashed part-numbers represent purchased items. The numbers in the parentheses represent the quantity of the item going into its parent item. Thus, the finished product is assembled from one each of subassemblies A00 and C00 and four of B00. These items are called level-1 subassemblies. Moving down the tree, we can see that level-1 items are assembled from level-2 subassemblies and that level-2 subassemblies are made from level-3 machined parts and level-4 purchased parts. At this last level, the complete list of all items in the final product appears in a fashion similar to the engineering bill of materials.

Each node in the manufacturing tree represents an inventory item in the inventory-item master file. Consider, for example, item A00 in Figure 7.2. In the manufacture of the final product, a shop order will have to be generated to assemble some quantity of item A00. In conjunction with that order, items A10 and A20 will be drawn out from inventory and assembled to become item A00. In turn, item A00 will be placed into inventory to await an order to assemble the final product. In reality, items need not physically enter and leave an inventory storage area, but a stock-control point and inventory transfer transaction must occur. When and how many units were removed from the stock of items A10 and A20, and subsequently entered into the stock of item A00, must be recorded. The primary intent of MRP is to know at any time how many of each item exist, how many are needed, and when they will be needed. This information requires accurate inventory record keeping even if individual items do not pass through a physical inventory-control station.

The lead-time aspect of the manufacturing process explosion makes MRP a valuable planning tool. In the example above, there is a purchasing, machining, or assembly step between each inventory node in the process tree. Associated with each step is a production lead-time standard. Using this standard as the lead-time, the production plan must call for the completion of all precedent steps prior to the start of the next step. For example, if the assembly lead-time of item A00, in Figure 7.2, is three days, all of the required units of items A10 and A20 must be completed at least three days prior to the completion of A00. The MRP system can start, therefore, with the due-date of the final product and work backwards to determine when the necessary stock levels of each item must exist and when orders to produce or purchase each item must be generated.

The lead-time in MRP is often dynamic and highly variable. In such situations, the statistic used for lead-time is, at best, the latest available value. As the lead-time changes, the entire materials plan changes. Thus, the lead-time statistic must be kept as accurate as possible. In situations in which the lead-time is hard to estimate, the system should be given a longer and safer estimate.

In brief summary, the manufacturing parts explosion and lead-time system translates the finished-goods demand schedule into a plan for when and how many of each item must be in the inventory. This system is, therefore, at the heart of MRP. It generates the materials requirement plan for all inventories, from purchased items through finished products.

The *inventory transactions system* is the vehicle used to update the actual inventory status for each item in the inventory-item master file. When purchased items are processed through receiving inspection, an inventory credit transaction is generated. Subsequently, when taken out of an in-process inventory status and placed in a manufacturing status, an inventory debit transaction is generated. Similarly, when each manufacturing step is completed, a credit transaction is generated for the next-higher-level inventory item. This process continues until the finished product is shipped.

It can be argued that MRP is simply a demand record-keeping system. A significant effort is needed to ensure that accurate and timely inventory transactions are generated as input to MRP. Anyone considering the implementation of MRP should understand the seriousness and magnitude of the problem of getting accurate and timely inventory transactions. The adage of "Garbage in—garbage out" applies here. The cost of a simple input data error can be significant, and the cost of minimizing such errors can be high.

The *schedule and inventory adjustment system* is operated on a daily or real-time basis to make minor corrections to either the planned inventory or the actual inventory records. This system thus interacts primarily with the inventory-item master file. External events may require the expediting or slippage of finished-product due dates. In addition, inventory at any level may be scrapped or pulled out for a period, to repair some defect. Finally, an *ABC*-type system for inventory review similar to that discussed in Chapter 6 may uncover, in the records of critical items, minor errors that need to be corrected. These nonplanned adjustments are handled by the schedule and inventory adjustment system.

Most of the outputs generated by an MRP system and depicted in Figure 7.3 are self-explanatory. They are, in effect, master schedules for manufacturing, purchasing, dispatching, shipping, and receiving. In manufacturing facilities, scheduling is a two-step process. In the first step, the production control department must decide what to manufacture in each scheduling period. The period can be as short as a day or as long as a month. The second step is to sequence the selected tasks in each period: that is, to determine the order in which the tasks are to be done. A significant role for the MRP system is to perform the first scheduling step. Consider, for example, a one-week scheduling period. The scheduling reports suggested in Figure 7.3 would list, therefore, everything that should be accomplished in the next two or three periods.

The *gross and net demand report* shown in Figure 7.3 is a facilitywide materials requirement plan designed to help production planners make the decisions needed to smoothly meet the demand for finished products. The report essentially contains a period-by-period plan for each item in the inventory list. Figure 7.4 illustrates a gross and net demand report. Recall that many of the items could best be described as subassemblies at different levels down from the finished products. For each item, four numbers are printed out for each future planning period. These four numbers represent the gross requirements, scheduled receipts, expected inventory, and net unfilled requirements. The expected inventory listed in any period can represent the level at the beginning or at the end of the period. In Figure 7.4, expected inventory is the quantity at the beginning of the period. The finished product used to generate Figure 7.4 is the one shown in Figure 7.2. Note that three levels of inventory are shown in the figure (i.e., level 0, level 1, and level 2).

The Mathematics of MRP

At level 0, the finished-product gross requirements are listed. The figure came from the master plan for finished goods. Note in Figure 7.4 that the plan begins period 1 with 53 units of finished-product inventory with a previously scheduled receipt of 40 units to arrive in period 3. It was arbitrarily decided that the lead time for the final assembly is two periods. (The lead time is shown on Figure 7.4 right after the level number.) Thus, referring to the level-1 items A00 and B00, 40 and 160 units will be required two periods prior to period 3 or at the beginning of period 1, or end of period 0. Item-A00 gross requirements are set at 40 because only one unit of A00 goes into the finished product. Item B00 requirements are set at 160 because four units are used in each finished product.

Note also that the expected inventory of finished products at the beginning of period 1 is 53 units. At the beginning of period 2, the expected

Finished prod. level 0 (2 periods)	1	2	3	4	Planning Period 5	6	7	8	9	10
Gross requirements	20	30	30	10	0	10	10	20	30	40
Scheduled receipts			40							
Expected inventory[a]	53	33	3	13	3	3	−7	−17	−37	−67
Net unfilled req'ts.				7	10	20	30			

Item A00, level 1 (2 period)

	1	2	3	4	5	6	7	8	9	10
Gross requirements	40	0	0	7	10	20	30	0	0	0
Scheduled receipts										
Expected inventory[a]	45	5	5	5	−2	−12	−32	−62	−62	−62
Net unfilled req'ts.			2	10	20	30				

Item B00, level 1 (1 period)

	1	2	3	4	5	6	7	8	9	10
Gross requirements	160	0	0	28	40	80	120	0	0	0
Scheduled receipts					100					
Expected inventory[a]	200	40	40	40	12	72	−8	−128	−128	−128
Net unfilled req'ts.					8	120				

:
:
:

Item B10, level 2 (3 period)

	1	2	3	4	5	6	7	8	9	10
Gross requirements	0	0	0	200	16	240	0	0	0	0
Scheduled receipts				250						
Expected inventory[a]	5	5	5	5	55	39	−201	−201	−201	−201
Net unfilled req'ts.				201						

[a] At beginning of period all other values are at end of period.

FIGURE 7.4 Illustrative gross and net requirements by period report.

inventory is reduced by 20 to become 33. The equation for calculating expected inventory is

$$I_{t,j} = I_{t-1,j} + R_{t-1,j} - G_{t-1,j} \tag{7.1}$$

where

$I_{t,j}$ = expected inventory of item j at beginning of period t

$R_{t-1,j}$ = receipts of item j during period $t - 1$

$G_{t-1,j}$ = expected gross requirements of item j during period $t - 1$

The bottom row for each item shows net unfilled demand. The expected inventory of finished product at the beginning of period 7 is minus seven units. Recall that the lead time for final assembly was two periods. To meet the shortage of seven units in period 7, the system must schedule seven units by the beginning of period 7–2, or period 5. Thus, the net unfilled requirements in period total seven units. In period 8, the figure shows–17 units of expected inventory. If, however, the seven units scheduled in period were assembled, a shortage of only 10 would exist in period 8. Thus, the net unfilled requirements filled by the end of period 5, total 10 units. The equation for calculating net unfilled requirements is

$$N_{t,j} = (-1)\min\{0, I_{t+} \ j+1, j\} - \sum_{k=1}^{t-1} N_{k,j} \qquad (7.2)$$

where

$N_{ij} =$ net unfilled requirements for item j at the end of period t

$I_{t+} \ j+1, j =$ expected inventory for item j at the beginning of period $t+ \ j+1$

$\ell_j =$ production lead-time for the operation that results in item j

Finally, note that the gross requirements for items other than the finished product equal in both quantity and period the net unfilled demand of the parent item multiplied by the quantity of the item going into its parent assembly. Recall that in Figure 7.4 the 40 and 160 gross requirements in period 1 for items A00 and B00 result from previous scheduling decisions. Therefore, the equation for calculating the gross requirements for items other than finished goods is

$$G_{t,j} = (R_{t+\ell_k,k} + N_{t,k})q_{j,k} \qquad (7.3)$$

where

$R_{t+\ell_k,k} =$ scheduled receipts of item k in period $t + \ell_k$

$k =$ parent item that uses item j

$q_{j,k} =$ quantity of item j required by parent item k

It is obvious that the mathematics of MRP are simple and easily programmed. Each finished product is associated with a simple tree of inventoried items that can easily be traversed. For each item a multiple-period set of records exists. The data values in each record can easily be calculated one level at a time. The required input data is the demand for the finished product, the starting inventories for each item, and the on-order quantities for each item.

7.4 THE MULTIPLE-PRODUCT CASE

In the example depicted in Figure 7.2, only one product was considered. Suppose the facility manufactured several versions of the same final product.

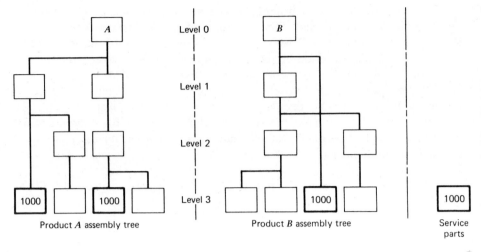

FIGURE 7.5   Illustration of multiple-product demand for an item at various stages in assembly or for service parts.

Although the final products are different, they may use many of the same subassemblies. The calculation of when and how many of the given items are needed then must consider the gross requirements from all parent items in which they are used. In addition, demand for service parts that is independent of final products must be added in. Thus, gross requirements for a given item in a given period represent the sum of all possible demands.

Typically, each item is assigned a level in which it will always occur. Consider for example, item 1000 as illustrated in Figure 7.5. This item occurs on level 3 in every finished-product tree and in its independent service demand. In order to accomplish this single-level requirement, the idea that the parent of an item is always at the next higher level has been relaxed. The purpose for this requirement is to reduce the computation time of the MRP system. If the computation procedure were to follow from one finished product to the next, it would have to calculate the net unfilled demand every time the given item occurred; for item 1000 in Figure 7.5, this would be four times. If, however, the item always occurred at the same level and the computation procedure were to complete all items at any level before moving down, the total gross demand for any item would be accumulated before the procedure of calculating net unfilled demand was accomplished. Thus, the system would deal with each item only once.

This simplification is not without its costs. The effect is to aggregate over all the demand for an item before dealing with the requirement for ordering more to be purchased or assembled. Unfortunately, this aggregation prevents the association of a given sales order with the many manufacturing orders required to produce the product. Typical accounting systems are designed to tag work orders to specific sales orders, so that the cost of the sale can be tracked and calculated. In cases in which nonstandard finished products are quoted and sold, this "lot-tracking" system may furnish the only way of knowing what the cost of manufacturing actually was. Since the MRP system is incompatible with the lot-tracking concept, the accounting needs of the firm must be taken into account if a decision to implement MRP is being considered.

7.5 LOT-SIZING CONCEPTS IN MRP

Unrelated to lot tracking, lot sizing is the MRP activity of translating into an order quantity the net unfilled requirements for a given item. As discussed in Chapter 6, order quantity is a question of minimizing the costs of ordering (or setup) plus the cost of carrying the item in stock. Certainly, one of the desires in materials requirement planning is to generate the least-cost purchasing and manufacturing orders.

There are many approaches to selecting the least-cost order quantity, several of which were discussed in Chapter 6. These and other approaches are discussed extensively in the MRP literature (Orlicky, 1975;† Berry, 1972;‡ Wagner and Whitin, 1958§). Consider again the example illustrated in Figure 7.4. Note that for the level-0 item, there are unfilled requirements in periods 5, 6, 7, and 8 for 7, 10, 20, and 30 units, respectively. Obviously, we would like to issue an order to assemble some quantity of this product in period 5. Suppose the least-cost quantity is 50 units. Note than an order of 50 significantly changes the gross requirements for items A00 and B00. Instead of being 7 and 28 units in period 5, the gross requirements are 50 and 200, respectively. In addition, the order for 50 units of the final product in period 5 will change the unfilled requirements at level 0 for periods 6, 7, and 8. The upshot of this example is that lot sizing must be accomplished on a level-by-level basis, because the order quantity significantly alters the MRP calculation for all subsequent levels within a given product tree. Therefore, the lot-sizing decision must be made automatically by the computer.

Automated lot-sizing and order-generation is a potential cause of difficulty for MRP. One ramification of the problem is that the quantity must be determined by some sort of mathematical model that may or may not consider all the factors incumbent on the decision. The ability to insert human review of model decisions is difficult when the computer is making decisions

---

† Orlicky, *Materials Requirements Planning*.
‡ W. L. Berry, "Lot Sizing Procedures for Requirements Planning Systems: A Framework for Analysis," *Production and Inventory Management*, 2nd quarter 1972, pp. 19, 34.
§ H. M. Wagner, and Whitin, T. M., "Dynamic Version of the Economic Lot Size Model," *Management Science*, vol. 5 no. 1, September 1958, pp. 89, 96. Reprinted by permission of H. M. Wagner and T. M. Whitin. Copyright © 1958 The Institute of Management Sciences.

in microseconds. Another ramification of tying the lot-size decision too closely to the computer is that it puts the production control staff in a position of serving the machine rather than being served by the computer. Good systems design would avoid such areas of potential psychological trauma. Finally, the lot-sizing decisions made are based on the concept that the order quantity must be at least as large as the net unfilled requirements. Thus, at each level the quantity tends to grow. It is easy to envision a situation in which at the lower levels, quantities far in excess of the actual need are being ordered and held for long periods. The establishment of upper and lower limits for order quantities, however, can reduce this last problem.

The concept of a computerized materials requirements planning system has been introduced in this chapter, but the idea is much too involved for one chapter. The memory requirements and the amount of computer capacity necessary to MRP have been suggested. The need for accurate forecasts and inventory transactions were pointed out. The cost of obtaining the needed software and implementing the system are very high. In summary, there is a strong appeal for operating a system that determines when to manufacture each item and how many to make. But the cost and demand of the system are high and should be carefully studied.

To conclude the chapter, we shall present a case study. The reader will note that the product in the case is very simple: there are only four versions of the finished product and each unit has only 18 parts in the most complex version. Yet, as one reads through the tables of data and attempts the exercise problems, the complexity of the case will readily become apparent. There is no way that a real-world MRP system could be operated by hand. MRP is a very demanding concept.

7.6 CASE STUDY

The following case study is offered to suggest the extent of computational effort inherent in MRP. As you read, realize that the case involves a relatively simple product: there are only 18 parts and three levels in the manufacturing tree, and only four simple variations of this product in the entire product line. Yet it would take considerable effort to operate a manual MRP system for the case. Problems in the next section based on this case can only be solved realistically by using a computer. Extend in your mind what it would take to operate an MRP system for a realistic manufacturer with thousands of parts and products. In such situations, large computers, many hours of time, and extensive mass storage is needed.

Although fictitious, this study is based on a realistic manufacturing problem. A small electronics firm is manufacturing a series of graphic writing tablets. These tablets connect to any telephone and have the capability of communicating written and coded messages to compatible printers or to a computer. The units are offered in two models and two options within those models.

FIGURE 7.6   Representation of the graphic writing tablet used in the case study and some problems. (Provided courtesy of the Kurta Corporation, Tempe, Arizona).

The models are a function of the size of the graphic writing surface. The options on each model are for units with and without the computer-connect capability. Figure 7.6 is a pictorial representation of a graphic writing tablet.

For the purposes of the case study, the following four models form the product line.

Model No.	Writing Surface	Computer Connect
A1000	8×10	No
A2000	8×10	Yes
B1000	5×8	No
B2000	5×8	Yes

The manufacturing processes tree for each model is essentially the same. The 2000-series tablet, which connects to a standard computer bus, has an additional printed circuit board and output strip connector. Thus, the processes tree represented by Figure 7.7 for the A2000 model can be used for all models. Note that some of the part numbers have an X prefix whereas others have the A prefix. The parts with X prefix are interchangeable for all models. The parts with A prefix are for the A models only, and similar part numbers with a B prefix would be used in the B models. Note also that all purchased items are represented at level 3 and can be recognized as having no zeros in their part numbers.

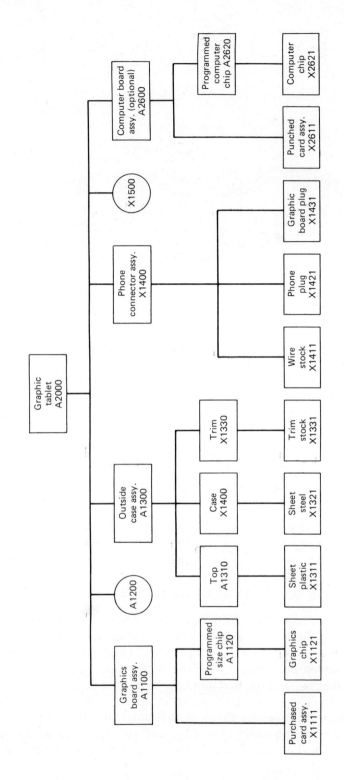

FIGURE 7.7 Manufacturing process tree for A2000 graphic tablet.

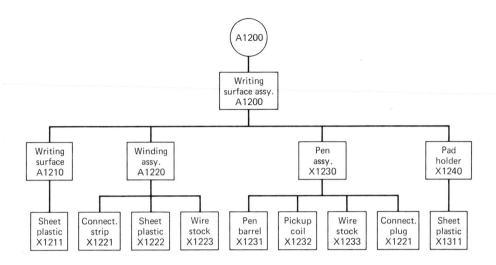

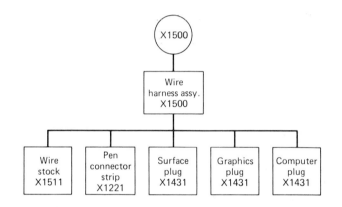

FIGURE 7.7 (*Continued*).

Problems 11–14 at the end of the chapter require the use of Tables 7.1 through 7.4. Table 7.1 is a shortened version of the inventory-item master file of Figure 7.3. It lists the part number, part name, inventory on hand, standard-order lot size, and standard-order lead time. Every part number needed to build the four products in the case study is listed in Table 7.1. Table 7.2 is a version of the manufacturing processes file in Figure 7.3. It contains an entry for each part number. Each record lists both the parents that require the part and the siblings that go into the manufacture of the part. After each parent and sibling part number, the quantity required is given in parentheses. Note in Tables 7.1 and 7.2 that the quantities for certain parts are decimal fractions—part X1223, for example. Fractional quantities indicate that only

TABLE 7.1 Inventory-Item Master File for Case Study

Part Number	Part Name	Inventory on hand	Std. Lot Size	Std. Lead Time
A1000	Tablet, 8 × 10	3	to order	2
B1000	Tablet, 5 × 8	2	to order	2
A2000	Tablet, 8 × 10, computer	5	to order	2
B2000	Tablet, 5 × 8, computer	6	to order	2
A1100	Graphic Card Assy.	20	5	3
B1100	Graphic Card Assy.	30	5	3
A1200	Writing Surface Assy.	10	10	3
B1200	Writing Surface Assy.	6	10	3
A1300	Outside Case Assy.	10	10	1
B1300	Outside Case Assy.	5	10	1
X1400	Phone Connect Assy.	25	50	4
X1500	Wire Harness Assy.	28	50	4
A2600	Computer Card Assy.	20	5	3
B2600	Computer Card Assy.	15	5	3
A1210	Writing Surface, 8 × 10	17	10	2
A1220	Windings Assy., 8 × 10	19	10	3
A1240	Pad Holder, 8 × 10	19	10	2
B1210	Writing Surface, 5 × 8	10	10	3
B1220	Windings Assy., 5 × 8	1	10	2
B1240	Pad Holder, 5 × 8	8	10	2
X1230	Pen Assy.	15	50	4
A1310	Plastic Top, 8 × 10	10	30	3
B1310	Plastic Top, 5 × 8	8	30	3
X1320	Metal Case	10	30	5
X1330	Plastic Trim	25	30	2
A1120	Graphics Chip Programmed	5	10	4
B1120	Graphics Chip Programmed	0	10	4
A2620	Computer Chip Programmed	5	10	4
B2620	Computer Chip Programmed	2	10	4
X1111	Graphics Card	5	10	4
X1121	Graphics Chip	3	20	3
X2611	Computer Card	5	10	4
X2621	Computer Chip	7	20	3
X1311	Sheet Plastic, Top	10	10	2
X1321	Sheet Steel, Case	5	10	1
X1331	Plastic Trim, Top	10	10	2
X1411	Wire, Phone Connect.	1	1	1
X1421	Plug, Phone End	5	20	2
X1431	Plug, Strip Std.	24	50	5

TABLE 7.1   (Continued)

Part Number	Part Name	Inventory on hand	Std. Lot Size	Std. Lead Time
X1211	Sheet Plastic, Surface	5	20	2
X1221	Connector, Strip Std.	38	50	5
X1222	Sheet Plastic	6	20	2
X1223	Wire Stock	0.5	2	1
X1231	Pen Barrel	22	50	4
X1232	Pickup Coil	8	12	3
X1233	Connect Wire, Pen	1.5	2	2
X1511	Wire Stock, Harness	0.7	2	2

TABLE 7.2   Manufacturing Process File for the Case Study

Part Number	Parent Part No. (Quant. Req'd.)	Sibling Part No. (Quant. Req'd.)
A1000	—	A1100(1), A1200(1), A1300(1), X1400(1), X1500(1)
B1000	—	B1100(1), B1200(1), B1300(1), X1400(1), X1500(1)
A2000	—	A1100(1), A1200(1), A1300(1), X1400(1), X1500(1), A2600(1)
B2000	—	B1100(1), B1200(1), B1300(1), X1400(1), X1500(1), B2600(1)
A1100	A1000(1), A2000(1)	X1111(1), A1120(1)
B1100	B1000(1), B2000(1)	X1111(1), B1120(1)
A1200	A1000(1), A2000(1)	A1210(1), A1220(1), X1230(1)
B1200	B1000(1), B2000(1)	B1210(1), B1220(1), X1230(1), B1240(1)
A1300	A1000(1), A2000(1)	A1310(1), X1320(1), X1330(1)
B1300	B1000(1), A2000(1)	B1310(1), X1320(1), X1330(1)
X1400	A1000(1), A2000(1), B1000(1), B2000(1)	X1411(0.05), X1421(1), X1431(1)
X1500	A1000(1), A2000(1), B1000(1), B2000(1)	X1511(0.05), X1221(1), X1431(3)
A2600	A2000(1)	X2611(1), A2620(1)

TABLE 7.2   (Continued)

Part Number	Parent Part No. (Quant. Req'd.)	Sibling Part No. (Quant. Req'd.)
B2600	B2000(1)	X2611(1), B2620(1)
A1210	A1200(1)	X1211(1)
A1220	A1200(1)	X1211(1), X1222(1), X1223(0.1)
A1240	A1200(1)	X1311(1)
B1210	B1200(1)	X1211(1)
B1220	B1200(1)	X1221(1), X1222(0.10), X1223(0.05)
B1240	B1200(1)	X1311(1)
X1230	A1200(1), B1200(1)	X1231(1), X1232(1), X1233(0.01), X1221(1)
A1310	A1300(1)	X1311(1)
B1310	B1300(1)	X1311(0.10)
X1320	A1300(1), B1300(1)	X1321(1)
X1330	A1300(1), B1300(1)	X1331(1)
A1120	A1100(1)	X1121(1)
B1120	B1100(1)	X1121(1)
A2620	A2600(1)	X2621(1)
B2620	B2600(1)	X2621(1)
X1111	A1100(1), B1100(1)	—
X1121	A1120(1), B1120(1)	—
X2611	A2600(1), B2600(1)	—
X2621	A2600(1), B2600(1)	—
X1311	A1310(1), B1310(0.10)	—
X1321	X1320(1)	—
X1331	X1330(1)	—
X1411	X1400(0.05)	—
X1421	X1400(1)	—
X1431	X1400(1), X1500(3)	—
X1211	A1210(1), B1210(1)	—
X1221	A1220(1), B1220(1), X1230(1), X1500(1)	—
X1222	A1220(1), B1220(0.10)	—
X1223	A1220(0.1), B1220(0.05)	—
X1231	X1230(1)	—
X1232	X1230(1)	—
X1233	X1230(0.01)	—
X1511	X1500(0.05)	—

TABLE 7.3 Materials Demand File for Case Study, Finished Products and Service Only

Part Number	Quantity Needed	Due Date	
A1000	20	5	
B1000	10	5	
A2000	15	4	
B2000	8	4	
A1100	10	15	Service part
B1100	10	15	Service part
A2600	3	10	Service part
B2600	3	10	Service part
X1230	20	2	Service part
A1000	15	10	
A1000	10	15	
B1000	10	10	
B1000	10	15	
A2000	20	9	
A2000	20	14	
B2000	5	9	
B2000	5	14	

TABLE 7.4 Materials Supply File and Order Master File for Case Study

Part Number	Quantity Ordered	Due Date
A1100	10	3
A1200	20	3
X1230	50	2
A1310	30	2
X1320	30	2
A1120	20	3
A1120	10	4

TABLE 7.4 (Continued)

Part Number	Quantity Ordered	Due Date
A2620	10	4
X1111	20	3
X1111	10	4
X2611	10	4
X1321	10	1
X1431	100	3
X1431	50	4
X1221	100	3
X1220	50	5
X1222	20	2

part of the inventory unit is required. For part X1223, which is wire, only 0.5 of a roll is in inventory, according to Table 7.1. According to Table 7.2, only 0.1 of a role is needed for each wire assembly A1220 and 0.05 of a roll for each B1220. Since the order quantity for X1223 is in terms of rolls of wire, all statistics for usage are in rolls or order quantity units. Table 7.3 is a version of the materials demand file. It contains the forecasted future demand for all finished products and service items. For each part number, Table 7.3 lists the quantity needed and the due date.

Finally, Table 7.4 is a shortened version of the materials supply file; it lists each part for which an outstanding purchase or shop order exists. For each listed part number, Table 7.4 gives the quantity ordered and the due date. As a whole, Tables 7.1 through 7.4 give a snapshot view of the materials activity at time-equals-zero in the case study.

7.7 REFERENCES

1. Berry, W. L., "Lot Sizing Procedures for Requirements Planning Systems: A Framework for Analysis," *Production and Inventory Management*, 2nd quarter 1972, pp. 19–34.

2. Donelson, W. S., "MRP—Who Needs It?" *Datamation*, vol. 25, no. 5, May 1979, pp. 185–197.

3. Orlicky, J. A., *Materials Requirement Planning*, McGraw-Hill Book Co., 1975.

4. Wagner, H. M., and Whitin, T. M., "Dynamic Version of the Economic Lot Size Model," *Management Science*, vol. 5, no. 1, September 1958, pp. 89–96.

7.8 EXERCISES

In order to offer realistic problems, consider the following simple product. If
you were a cub scout, you may remember building and racing a little wooden
race car. Such cars come 10 in a box. Each box has 10 preformed wood
blocks, 40 wheels, 40 nails for axles, and a sheet of 10 vehicle number
stickers. The problem is the manufacture and boxing of these racecar kits. An
assembly explosion and manufacturing tree are given in Figure 7.8.

Studying the tree indicates four operations. The first is to cut 50 rough
car bodies from a piece of lumber. The second is to plane and slot each car
body. The third is to bag 40 nails and wheels. The fourth is to box materials
for 10 racecars.

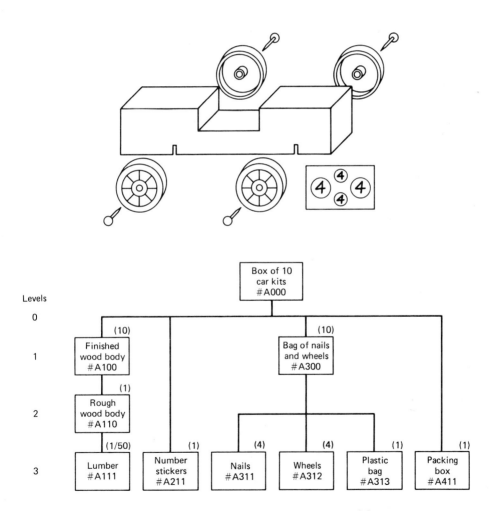

FIGURE 7.8 Assembly explosion and manufacturing tree for model car.

Table 7.5 is the inventory master file for this product. Note that there are 10 inventoried part numbers. Table 7.6 is the manufacturing process file (the required quantities are given in parentheses after the parent and sibling part numbers). Table 7.7 is the forecasted materials demand file for the next 15 periods.

TABLE 7.5 Inventory Master File for Problems

Part Number	Part Name	Inventory on hand	Standard lot size	Standard lead time
A000	Box of cars	20	50	1
A100	Finished body	100	50	1
A300	Bag of nails and wheels	150	50	1
A110	Rough wood body	200	100	1
A111	Lumber	5	10	3
A211	Number sticker	500	500	10
A311	Nails	300	500	2
A312	Wheels	200	500	2
A313	Plastic bag	30	500	3
A411	Packing box	40	500	5

TABLE 7.6 Manufacturing Process File

Part Number	Parent Part No. (Quantity Required)	Sibling Part No. (Quantity Required)
A000	—	A100(10), A211(1), A300(10), A411(1)
A100	A000(10)	A110(1)
A300	A000(10)	A311(4), A312(4), A313(1)
A110	A100(1)	A111(1/50)
A111	A110(1/50)	—
A211	A000(1)	—
A311	A300(4)	—
A312	A300(4)	—
A313	A300(1)	—
A411	A000(1)	—

TABLE 7.7 Forecasted Demand File

Part Number	Quantity Needed	Due Date
A000	25	3
A000	30	5
A000	30	8
A000	30	10
A000	40	12
A000	40	15

There are no supplies presently on order and no materials-supply file similar to Table 7.4 is given.
The following problems address this simple case.

1. Develop a 15-period gross and net requirements plan similar to Figure 7.4 for the present situation as given by Tables 7.5, 7.6, and 7.7.

2. Do Problem 1 for the following demand forecast.

Quantity	30	30	25	15	25	40
Due date	4	6	8	10	12	14

3. Do Problem 1 for the following demand forecast.

Quantity	15	15	20	25	30	25	20	20
Due date	3	4	5	7	9	11	13	15

4. Develop a gross and net requirements plan similar to Figure 7.4 if the forecasted demands in Table 7.7 were each to be increased by 10 units.

5. Suppose the sales department called and asked if you could handle an order for 30 boxes of cars in period 2. What would you say and what production plans would you make to meet the new demand?

6. The quality inspector has informed you that half of the 100 finished bodies (part A100) have to be scrapped. What actions would you recommend to overcome this unexpected news?

7. Suppose an inventory check discovered that instead of 30 plastic bags, there are only four. What would you do to minimize disruption from this error?

8. Suppose your box supplier calls to say that his inventory lead-time is being increased from five days to eight days. What would you do to overcome this change?

9. How many units of each part number exist at time $= 0$, including those in the process of being manufactured?

10. How many of each part number should exist in the plant, including inventory in various subassemblies after period 3?

Problems 11 through 14 refer to the graphic-writing-tablet case study. It may be necessary to employ a computerized MRP software package to do these problems.

11. For parts A1000, A2000, B1000, and B2000, calculate the net requirements for periods 1 through 15 in order to meet the forecasted demand shown in Table 7.3.

12. Suppose in the case study that the materials manager was told that all units of the graphics chip (part X1121) were bad when they came from the vendor. Using the data on Tables 7.1 and 7.2, account for all of those chips that exist anywhere in the shop. How many replacement chips should be ordered today to remedy this situation?

13. Create a materials requirement report similar to Figure 7.4 for the 14 parts on levels 0 and 1—that is, A1000 through B2600 on Table 7.1. Develop the report for the next 15 periods to satisfy the forecasted demand shown in Table 7.3.

14. As indicated in Table 7.1, the lead time for the purchased graphics card X1111 is four days. Suppose the vendor has just called to say that the present lead time is 10 days. What effects will this have on production and what action should be taken to soften the impact of this development?

15. Discuss the requirements for a computerized MRP system based on the Donelson article and others.

16. Using your library's Science Citation Index, discuss lot-sizing procedures as presented in Berry and others.

EIGHT: SCHEDULING WITH RESOURCE CONSTRAINTS

A man in earnest finds means, or, if he cannot find, creates them.

Channing

A construction project may be scheduled with techniques such as given in Chapter 3, but if limited availability of resources is not considered, it will doubtless not be feasible to complete the resulting schedule by the due date.

Typical limited resources that may elongate a theoretical schedule include raw materials, purchased and manufactured components, manpower by skill category, space in which to produce or store inventory, and available capital, and so on. Development of a schedule without consideration of limited or scarce resources will lead to a result that is infeasible to implement. Many scheduling techniques do not take into consideration the possibility of scarce resources. For example, CPM and PERT, as presented in Chapter 3, assume that sufficient resources will be available to allow the desired schedule to be achievable. Invariably this is not the case. Even if sufficient resources are available to allow a theoretical schedule to be achieved, how those resources are scheduled can affect the cost of implementation.

As an introductory example, consider the brief network and associated schedule given in Figure 8.1. Suppose that each of the four jobs requires laborers and that any laborer assigned to a job stays with that job until it is completed. The laborers required for each job are

A 2

B 2

C 3

D 2

Also, a total of four laborers are available at any one time. If the project is

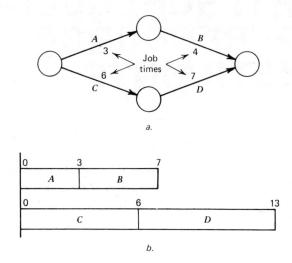

FIGURE 8.1   **Typical network and Gantt-chart schedule. (a) Network. (b) Gantt-chart schedule.**

scheduled as given in Figure 8.1, the amount of resources required over time, the *resource profile*, is as shown in Figure 8.2. Since five laborers are required until time period 6, it follows that the schedule given is infeasible, since only four laborers are available. Slipping jobs *A* and *B* six time-periods will allow the schedule to be completed in 13 time-periods, as shown in Figure 8.3. This iterative process is called the resource allocation problem. The first part of this chapter will be concerned with this resource allocation problem and with the associated resource-balancing problem—extremely complex problems when the number of activities rises into the hundreds. The second part of the chapter will be concerned with an exact production analog of the resource problems just specified, that of the *line-balancing* problem.

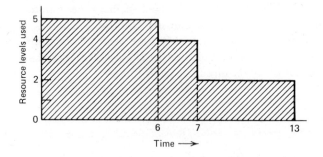

FIGURE 8.2   **Resource profile for the network of Figure 8.1.**

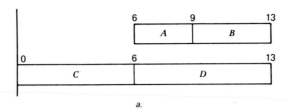

FIGURE 8.3 Revised schedule and resource profile for network of Figure 8.1. (*a*) Gantt chart. (*b*) Resource profile.

8.1 DEFINITIONS

As with earlier chapter definitions, only those with a somewhat broad application will be given in this section. Other definitions will be given in specific chapter sections.

Resource	Item required to allow project completion. Typical resources include manpower, equipment, space, money, parts, supplies, and so on.
Limited resource	A resource with an upper bound on the number of units available for a project. Needless to say, most resources fall in this category. Frequently, limited resources are called *critical resources*.
Resource allocation	The assignment of limited resources to a project's activities. An objective will be to minimize the project completion time, knowing that resources are limited and given the specific number of resource units available.
Resource balancing	Given a project completion time, resource balancing is the process of minimizing the number of resource units while meeting the required schedule time.

Scheduling criteria Criteria by which activities are sequenced into the schedule. Typical criteria might include scheduling the shortest available job first, scheduling the longest available job first, scheduling that available job with the largest resource requirement first, and so on.

Heuristic algorithm Sequence of scheduling steps, usually iterative in nature, that will allow a schedule to approach optimality but will not *guarantee* an optimal solution.

Cycle time The time, based on the rate of production, between which items are completed on a production line. If the production rate, for example, is 10 items per hour, the associated cycle time is six minutes.

Production station A grouping of production-line jobs, similar in skill and proximity requirements, that can be accomplished by a single operator or automated equipment in a given cycle time.

Line balance A schedule of production-line jobs that balances the work load for each production station. Similar in characteristics to resource allocation and resource balancing, *line balancing* may try to minimize production stations given a cycle time, or may try to minimize cycle time (maximize production rate) given the number of stations.

Float The length of time an activity may be delayed in starting time because it is not a critical-path activity. This slippage may not allow an increase in the critical-path time. *Slack* is synonymous with *float*.

8.2 ALLOCATION OF UNITS FOR A SINGLE RESOURCE

A project having only a single resource to be allocated would be rare indeed. Scheduling of multiple-resource projects is extremely complex, so discussion of single-resource allocation will allow scheduling procedures to be developed in a relatively simple manner, with later extension to the multiple-resource problem.

In allocating a limited resource to a network-oriented project, an obvious key attribute is always to try to schedule on time those activities that lie on a critical path. Another common approach is to determine the latest time at which activities may start and then schedule according to the sequence developed by the latest-time sort. A heuristic approach using those rules was developed by Lang.† The steps in this approach are as follows.

---

†Douglas W., Lang, *Critical Path Analysis*, David McKay, New York, 1977.

1. Order the activities according to the latest start-time.
2. When activities can start together, give priority according to
    a. Activity with least float.
    b. Activity with longest duration.
    c. Activity with largest resource requirement.

A simple example should clarify this procedure. Consider the network with associated activity-duration times and resource requirements given in Figure (8.4a). We need to determine, first of all, each activity's latest starting time. In Chapter 3, we developed a procedure for finding each *node's* latest starting time through a backwards pass approach (see Section 3.3). Each activity's latest starting time is found by subtracting its duration time from its ending-node latest time. The node latest times and activity latest start-times are given in Figure 8.4b. Activities 1–3, 1–5, and 3–4 show the fallacy in assuming that the latest time for an activity's beginning node would be the latest time that an

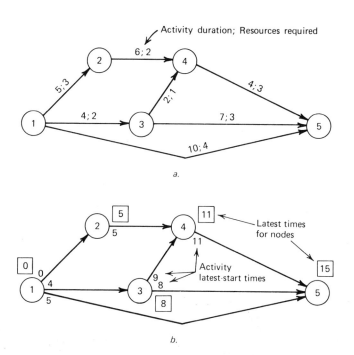

FIGURE 8.4 Finding activity and node latest-start times. (*a*) Network with activity and resource requirements. (*b*) Node and activity latest start times.

activity may start. Ranking of activities by latest start time is now as follows

Activity	Latest Start	Tie Broken By
1–2	0	
1–3	4	
2–4	5	Float is 0
1–5	5	Float is 5
3–5	8	
3–4	9	
4–5	11	

Scheduling activities according to Lang's steps are given in Figure 8.5 under the assumption that eight units of the resource are available at any one time. If a particular activity cannot be scheduled at a particular time-period

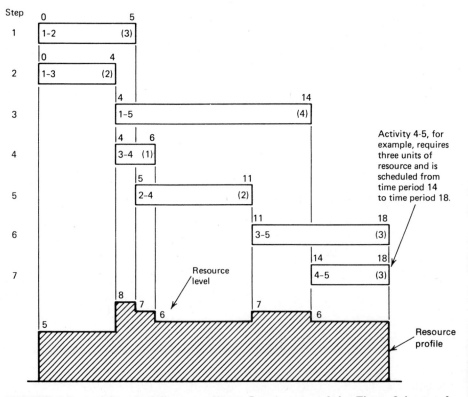

FIGURE 8.5   Activity scheduling according to Lang's approach for Figure 8.4 network.

because of resource constraints, all subsequent activities whose predecessors have been scheduled and completed are considered in priority order until no more available activities can be considered.

The first two activities, 1–2 and 1–3, follow the original priority list just developed. Activities 1–5 and 3–4 were scheduled before activity 2–4 at time period 4, since 2–4 had to wait for activity 1–2 to complete. Activity 3–4 was scheduled at time period 4 instead of activity 3–5, since activity 3–5 would have forced a violation of the requirement that resources at any period of time cannot exceed eight. The overall project time of 18 looks quite good and the resource profile looks quite smooth (though slipping 3–4 one time-period would allow the same project time but save a unit of resource). However, the completion time is not optimum. The Lang approach is heuristic and will not guarantee optimality, as Lang indicates in his presentation. A systematic way to approach the allocation of the resources will now be given, along with alternative criteria for activity-priority determination.

Brooks' Algorithm†

The Brooks' algorithm (BAG) is interesting in many ways, not the least of which is that it encompasses some of the attributes of digital computer simulation and also those of certain line-balancing heuristic algorithms (the latter are considered at the end of the chapter).

The line-balancing similarity comes through the manner utilized to determine which activities should receive limited resources first. The simulation similarity arises with the technique of looking ahead to when the next change in resource status will take place, rather than evaluating this status at every time-period. This minimizes the number of iterative steps required.

The steps required to assign the single resource with BAG are as follows (for convenience, Figure 8.6 gives a network and tabular results of these steps with three resources available)

1. Develop the project network as with the critical-path procedure, identifying activities and their required times.

2. Determine the maximum time each activity controls through the network on any one path. This would be like calculating the critical-path time through the network *assuming* that the starting node for each activity being analyzed is the network starting node. This activity control time will be designated ACTIM for convenience.

3. Rank these times in decreasing ACTIM sequence, as in Figure 8.6 (*G, A, C*, etc). Ties are broken by a secondary priority rule, as with Lang's earlier

---

†The material in this section is based on the original algorithmic approach developed by G. H. Brooks in "Algorithm for Activity Scheduling to Satisfy Constraints on Resource Availability," an unpublished paper dated September 17, 1963. Extensions and much of the material is from D. Bedworth, *Industrial Systems: Planning, Analysis, Control*, John Wiley, New York, 1973.

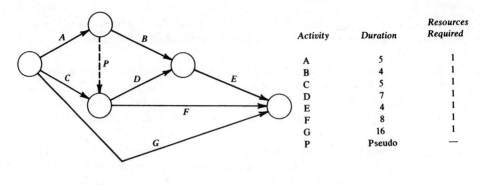

Activity	Duration	Resources Required
A	5	1
B	4	1
C	5	1
D	7	1
E	4	1
F	8	1
G	16	1
P	Pseudo	—

ACTIVITY DATA	Activity	G	A	C	D	B	F	E	
	Duration	16	5	5	7	4	8	4	
	ACTIM	16	16	16	11	8	8	4	
	Resources required	1	1	1	1	1	1	1	PROJECT COMPLETION TIME
	TEARL	0	0	0	5	5	5	12	
	TSTART	0	0	0	5	5	9	12	
	TFIN	16	5	5	12	9	(17)	16	

ALGORITHM ITERATION RESULTS				
TNOW	0	5	9	12
Resources available	3̶ 2̶ 1̶ 0	2̶ 1̶ 0	1̶ 0	1̶ 0
ACT. ALLOW.	G̶ A̶ C̶	D̶ B̶ F	F̶	E
Iteration No.	1	2	3	4

FIGURE 8.6   Brooks' algorithm sample network and solution—three available resource units. (*a*) Network. (*b*) BAG solution.

approach. ACTIM for activity *A* is found by summing the times for activities *A*, *D*, and *E*, to obtain a total of 16 days. The duration and resources required for each activity are self-explanatory. The rows titled TEARL, TSTART, TFIN, and TNOW need a little explanation.

a. TEARL is the earliest possible time, because of precedence and time limitations, to schedule each activity. The actual time will be equal to or later than TEARL. TEARL equals the latest TFIN time for all immediate predecessor activities.

b. TSTART is the actual start time of the activity. If there were no resource limitations, TSTART would always equal TEARL.

c. TFIN is the completion time of each activity. This equals the activity's TSTART added to the activity-duration time.

d. TNOW is the time at which resource assignments are now being considered. Initially TNOW equals zero, but subsequently it equals the lowest TFIN time for all activities currently being worked on.

4. We are now ready to sequence the activities according to resource constraints. TNOW is set at zero. The allowable activities (ACT. ALLOW.) to be considered for scheduling at TNOW of zero are those activities that would have a critical-path-method starting time of zero, namely activities G, A, and C. These are placed in the ACT. ALLOW. row, sequenced in decreasing ACTIM order. In this example, G, A, and C all have the same ACTIM, and so a secondary rule is needed. For this example we will choose longest duration first, which dictates schedule G first. Another rule is needed for A and C, since both are five time-units long. This rule will be to schedule alphabetically—thus, A before C. In the resources-available column, the resources initially available are placed—namely, three.

5. Determine if the first activity in ACT. ALLOW., G, can be assigned. It can, since three resources are available and G requires only one. Also, no predecessor limitations foul the picture. A line is struck through G to indicate assignment and the number of resources available is decreased by one to a value of two, since G required one resource. TSTART for activity G is set at the current TNOW and the TFIN is set at TSTART plus activity G's duration time. Now it is necessary to determine if activity G being completed will allow another activity to be feasible at some future time. With G it is not, since G is itself an entire critical path. This same process is repeated for the remainder of ACT. ALLOW. activities until the resources available are depleted. In our case, all activities G, A, and C could be assigned a TSTART of zero. From the network of Figure 8–6a it is seen that assigning activity A allows activity B to be scheduled a TEARL of five time-units later (activity A's TFIN). Similarly, activities D and F can be assigned a TEARL that is the latest of A's and C's TFIN times. Note that if activity A had required too many resources to allow assignment at TNOW of zero, we would still see if activity C could be assigned.

6. TNOW is raised to the next TFIN time, which happens to be five, the completion times of both activities A and C. The resources available at TNOW of five is set to the number remaining *after* assigning resources at TNOW equal to zero (zero in this case), added to the number of resources freed because of activity completion at the new TNOW (two in this case). ACT. ALLOW. we now set at those not assigned at the previous TNOW (none in our case), added to those that have a TEARL equal to or less than TNOW (D, B, and F).

7. Repeat this assignment process until all activities have been scheduled. The latest TFIN gives the duration of the project, which is 17 time-units—one more than the critical-path time.

As a further example, Table 8.1 gives the assignment if only two resource-units are available. The time assignment is found to be 25 days, quite an extension from 17 with three resources. It is left to the reader to determine whether or not the schedules realized are optimum.

The operation of the heuristic algorithm shows several pertinent points that may be helpful in designing such a procedure. First, it is logical—it just plain makes sense to assign activities on the basis of the time that they control

TABLE 8.1   Brooks' Algorithm Solution to Limited Resource Example with Two Units of Resource

	Activity	G	A	C	D	B	F	E	
Activity data	Duration	16	5	5	7	4	8	4	Project completion time
	ACTIM	16	16	16	11	8	8	4	
	Resources required	1	1	1	1	1	1	1	
	TEARL	0	0	0	10	5	10	20	
	TSTART	0	0	5	10	16	17	20	
	TFIN	16	5	10	17	20	㉕	24	
Algorithm iteration results	TNOW	0		5	10	16	17	20	
	Resources available	2̶1̶0		1̶0	1̶0	1̶0	1̶0	1̶0	
	ACT. ALLOW.	0̶A̶C		C̶B	D̶BF	B̶F	F	E	
	Iteration no.	1		2	3	4	5	6	

through the network. This ensures, for example, that critical-path activities are assigned first. Second, the next-event procedure of looking ahead to see when the next change in resource status will occur makes the actual work involved in using the algorithm as simple as possible. Third, it iteratively approaches a solution. This makes each stage of the solution relatively simple to apply, as well as orients the solution to possible computer manipulation. These three characteristics of logic, simplicity of application, and computer orientation should be paramount when designing heuristic algorithms for complex problem solution.

William Gleeson† suggested that optimality might be guaranteed if assignment were based on some criterion other than ACTIM, or the time each

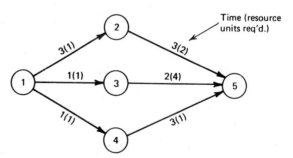

FIGURE 8.7   Network example for TIMRES solution.

†While a student at Arizona State University.

activity controls through the network. This certainly might be the case if another criterion dominates. Gleeson proposed that time and resource for an activity should be considered and suggested for each activity that the activity time multiplied by the resource requirement for the activity be considered in a manner analogous to ACTIM. For example, consider the network given in Figure 8.7, which we will schedule using ACTIM and also using each activity (time) multiplied by (resource) value, which will be designated as TIMRES. Table 8.2 gives the allocation by ACTIM, and Table 8.3 gives a similar allocation using TIMRES. For each case, five units of the resource are available.

The schedule using ACTIM gives a total duration of eight time-units, whereas by TIMRES an overall duration of six time-periods is achieved. First of all, it is now obvious that Brooks' algorithm with ACTIM is not necessarily optimum, as mentioned earlier. A rather significant improvement of 25% by TIMRES is achieved.

Now, a brief change in the network data given in Figure 8.7 has an interesting result. Change activity 4–5's time duration to seven time-units, rather than the original three. Leave everything else as given originally. The scheduling results using ACTIM and TIMRES are 8 and 10 time-units, respectively. Now ACTIM gives a more optimum solution, and only one data change was made. This pinpoints the complexity inherent in resource allocation optimization. Also, keep in mind that only one resource has been considered—usually a far from realistic condition. The Gantt schedules for the four resource-allocation results are given for comparison reasons in Figure 8.8. TIMRES places emphasis on early assignment of activities that

TABLE 8.2   Resource Allocation by ACTIM for Network Given in Figure 8.7; Total Resources Limited to Five Units

		Activity	1–2	1–4	1–3	2–5	4–5	3–5	
Activity data		Duration	3	1	1	3	3	2	
		ACTIM	6	4	3	3	3	2	
		Resources required	1	1	1	2	1	4	Project
		TEARL	0	0	0	3	1	1	completion
		TSTART	0	0	0	3	1	6	time
		TFIN	3	1	1	6	4	⑧ ↑	
Algorithm iteration results		TNOW		0		1	3	4	6
		Resources available		5̶4̶3̶2		4̶3	4̶2	3	5̶1
		ACT. ALLOW.		1̶–2̶; 1̶–4̶; 1̶–3̶		4̶–5̶; 3–5	2̶–5̶; 3–5	3–5	3̶–5̶
		Iteration no.		1		2	3	4	5

TABLE 8.3   Resource Allocation by TIMRES for Network Given in Figure 8.7; Total Resource Limited to Five Units

	Activity	1–2	1–3	3–5	2–5	1–4	4–5	
Activity data	Duration	3	1	2	3	1	3	
	TIMRES	9	9	8	6	4	3	
	Resources required	1	1	4	2	1	1	
	TEARL	0	0	1	3	0	1	Project
	TSTART	0	0	1	3	0	3	completion
	TFIN	3	1	3	⑥	1	⑥	time
Algorithm iteration Results	TNOW	0			1		3	
	Resources available	~~5~~,4,3,2			4,0		~~5~~,3,2	
	ACT. ALLOW.	~~1–2; 1–3; 1–4~~			~~3–5~~; 4–5		~~2–5; 4–5~~	
	Iteration no.	1			2		3	

have heavy resource-requirements for long periods of time. Although this is surely a highly practical consideration, it is certainly possible that *critical-path* activities may not be assigned in some optimal ordering using TIMRES. For the network in Figure 8.8, activity 4–5 was delayed in start for two time-units even though it was a critical-path item. These two time-units are exactly the time-length advantage ACTIM had over TIMRES. The reader can show this as a possible supplement to the problems at the end of this chapter. Without complete schedule enumeration—an impossibility for realistic projects even with digital computers—some optimal algorithm would have to incorporate a criteria-decision step to determine the best criterion for optimality. This is a very difficult task. Again, it should be recalled that we have not yet considered multiple-resource requirements.

Now, let's consider the project attacked earlier by Lang's sequence (Figure 8.4a). We will schedule the project using both ACTIM and TIMRES. Figure 8.9 repeats the original network and also shows both ACTIM and TIMRES computations. Obviously, once the individual (time) × (resources) values are computed for each activity, the cumulative TIMRES values are computed, as are the cumulative ACTIM values. Each activity's cumulative values are computed by adding its individual value to the *maximum* cumulative value for the activities that immediately succeed the activity in question. For example, activity 1–3 has two immediate successors, activities 3–4 and 3–5. The cumulative ACTIM values are six and seven, respectively, so seven is the maximum. The cumulative ACTIM for activity 1–3 is its individual value, four, added to the seven just determined. Logically, any project-terminating activity ACTIM value is just that activity's individual value.

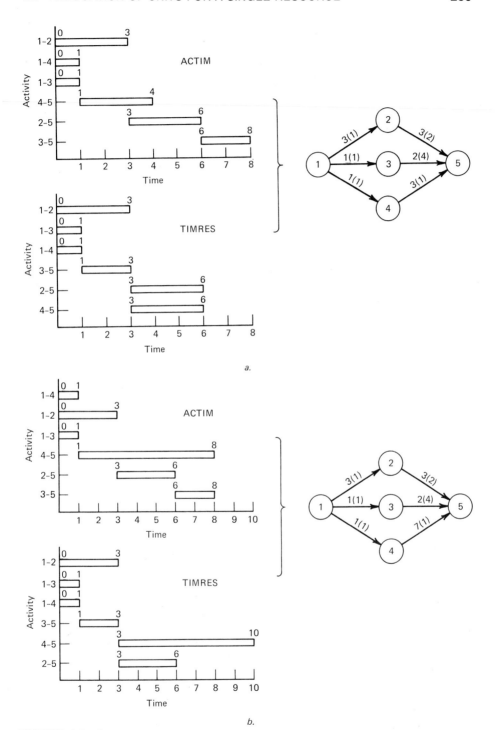

FIGURE 8.8 Schedules in Gantt-chart formats for example problem. (*a*) Time for activity 4-5 is 3. (*b*) Time for activity 4-5 is 7.

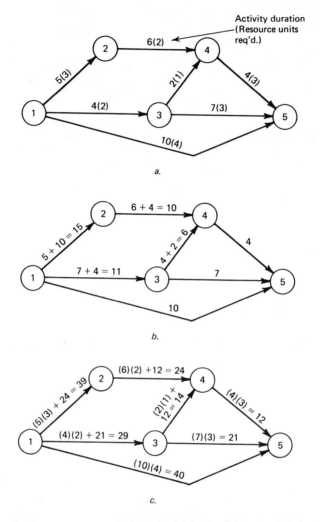

FIGURE 8.9 **Determination of ACTIM and TIMRES values. (a) Original network and data. (b) ACTIM determination. (c) TIMRES determination.**

Table 8.4 gives the schedule evolution using ACTIM. The project completion time is 18 time-units, the same as with Lang's schedule. Ties in ACTIM were broken with a secondary priority rule of scheduling activities according to the most resource units required. Table 8.5 gives the schedule development using the TIMRES criterion. Now a completion time of 17 time-units is realized. It should be apparent that a different network could reasonably have the better schedule realized through ACTIM or Lang—rather than TIMRES. Empirically, the ACTIM criterion has been found to

TABLE 8.4 ACTIM Solution for Lang's Problem

	Activity	1-2	1-3	1-5	2-4	3-5	3-4	4-5	
Activity data	Duration	5	4	10	6	7	2	4	
	ACTIM	15	11	10	10	7	6	4	
	Resources required	3	2	4	2	3	1	3	
	TEARL	0	0	0	5	4	4	11	Project
	TSTART	0	0	4	5	11	4	14	completion
	TFIN	5	4	14	11	(18)	6	(18)	time
Algorithm iteration results	TNOW	0	4	5		6	11	14	
	Resources available:	8, 8, 3	8, 8, 3; 1-5	8, X, 0	3, 1	2	4, 1	8, 2	
	ACT. ALLOW	1-2; 1-3; 1-5		1-5; 3-5; 3-4; 2-4; 3-5	2-4; 3-5	3-5	3-5; 4-5	4-5	
	Iteration no.	1		2	3	4	5	6	

257

TABLE 8.5 TIMRES Solution for Lang's Problem

	Activity	1-5	1-2	1-3	2-4	3-5	3-4	4-5	
Activity data	Duration	10	5	4	6	7	2	4	
	TIMRES	40	39	29	24	21	14	12	
	Resources required	4	3	2	2	3	1	3	
	TEARL	0	0	0	5	9	9	11	
	TSTART	0	0	5	5	10	9	11	
	TFIN	10	5	9	11	(17)	11	15	Project completion time
Algorithm iteration results	TNOW	0	5	9	10	11			
	Resources available:	8, 4, 1	4, 2, 0	2, 1	3, 2	3, 2			
	ACT. ALLOW	1-5; 1-2; 1-3	1-3; 2-4	3-5; 3-4	3-5	4-5			
	Iteration no.	1	2	3	4	5			

258

give consistently good results. It probably should be preferred to TIMRES on the ground that it forces early scheduling of critical-path activities.

8.3 ALLOCATION OF MULTIPLE RESOURCES

The multiple-resource allocation problem is obviously much more complex than the single-resource allocation problem. Considering different labor categories and different types of equipment, the number of *different* resources could be considerable. The same approach developed for single-resource allocation can be applied, but a digital computer would certainly be beneficial.†

It is recommended that only the ACTIM criterion be considered with multiple resources. How, for example, would multiple resources be incorporated into the TIMRES determination, since TIMRES is (time multiplied by number of resources)? Combining electricians with forklift trucks does not make sense, for example. An example for multiple-resource allocation is given in Table 8.6 for the network of Figure 8.10. A few comments pertaining to the steps used in this example are in order.

Step One   Test the resource requirements for each activity against resources available to see if any schedule is feasible. This step

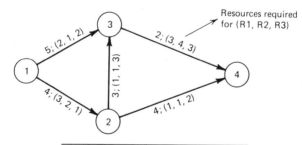

Activity	ACTIM
1–2	9
1–3	7
2–3	5
2–4	4
3–4	2

FIGURE 8.10   Network with data for three resource types.

---

†A computer program given in Appendix D will handle multiple-resource assignment. The philosophy embodied in this program is discussed in Section 8.5.

TABLE 8.6 Scheduling Multiple-Resource Project

Time	Activity	Duration	Start	Finish	Resources Available			ACTIM-Ranked (Left to Right)	
					R1	R2	R3	Allowable	Activities
0	—	—	—	—	5	4	4	1-2	1-3
0	1-2	4	0	4	2	2	3		
0	1-3	5	0	5	0	1	1		
4	1-2	—	—	—	3	3	2	2-3	2-4
4	2-4	4	4	8	2	2	0		
5	1-3	—	—	—	4	3	2	2-3	
8	2-4	—	—	—	5	4	4	2-3	
8	2-3	3	8	11	4	3	1		
11	2-3	—	—	—	5	4	4	3-4	
11	3-4	2	11	13	2	0	1		
13	3-4	—	—	—	5	4	4	Project complete	

should be obvious. If any activity requires more resources than are totally available, it is impossible to schedule that activity. In the example problem there are five units of resource R1 and four units each for resources R2 and R3. No activity requires more than these total levels. The requirements are feasible and we can continue.

Step Two Compute ACTIM or other decision criteria for each activity, working backwards from the terminal node of the network. This is accomplished in exactly the same manner as single-resource allocation.

Step Three Rank the activities according to ACTIM in a decreasing sequence. This ranking is given in Figure 8.10.

Step Four Construct work table and follow-through solution. The work table will be a little simpler than the tabular presentation used earlier for single-resource allocation. The allowable activities, TNOW, and certain other data will not be included. The solution will progress down the work table with respect to time until a final solution and project time have been achieved. This solution is given in Table 8.6. Given below are a few pertinent comments regarding this solution that correspond to the time column of the work table.

Time 0 Starting conditions are given in the first line. Activities 1–2 and 1–3 can be scheduled at this time period.

Time 4 First line gives starting resource conditions *after* activity 1–2 is completed. Activity 2–3, the next "ACTIM sequence" activity, cannot be scheduled because of insufficient resources available. Activity 2–4 can be scheduled.

Time 5 Resource levels are given *after* activity 1–3 is completed. No other activity can be scheduled at this time, since resource levels are too low.

Time 8 Completion of activity 2–4 allows sufficient resources for activity 2–3 to be scheduled.

The process continues until all activities are scheduled. A project duration of 13 time-units is realized, in contrast to the critical-path time of nine time-units.

8.4 RESOURCE BALANCING

A problem associated with resource allocation is that of resource balancing. Given the *time* required for a project, what is the *minimum number of resource units* required to meet that time? The *allocation* problem is the

TABLE 8.7   Two Iterations of the Resource Balancing Procedure

A)   Resource Units = 8

Activity	1–2	1–3	1–5	2–4	3–5	3–4	4–5	
Duration	5	4	10	6	7	2	4	
ACTIM	15	11	10	10	7	6	4	
Resources required	3	2	4	2	3	1	3	
TEARL	0	0	0	5	4	4	11	Project
TSTART	0	0	4	5	11	4	14	Completion
TFIN	5	4	14	11	⑱	6	⑱	Time

	Iter 1	Iter 2	Iter 3	Iter 4	Iter 5	Iter 6
TNOW	0	4	5	6	11	14
Resources available	8, 5, 3	5, 1, 0	3, 1	2	4, 1	5, 2
ACT. ALLOW	1–2; 1–3; 1–5	1–5; 3–5; 3–4	2–4; 3–5	3–5	3–5; 4–5	4–5
Iteration no.	1	2	3	4	5	6

B)   Resource Units = 9

Activity	1–2	1–3	1–5	2–4	3–5	3–4	4–5	
Duration	5	4	10	6	7	2	4	
ACTIM	15	11	10	10	7	6	4	
Resources required	3	2	4	2	3	1	3	
TEARL	0	0	0	5	4	4	11	Project
TSTART	0	0	0	5	6	4	11	Completion
TFIN	5	4	10	11	13	6	⑮	Time

	Iter 1	Iter 2	Iter 3	Iter 4	Iter 5	Iter 6
TNOW	0	4	5	6	10	11
Resources Available	9, 6, 4, 0	2, 1	4, 2	3, 0	4	6, 3
ACT. ALLOW	1–2; 1–3; 1–5	3–5; 3–4	2–4; 3–5	3–5	—	4–5
Iteration no.	1	2	3	4	5	6

complement of the balancing problem: given the *number of resource units*, what is the *minimum time* to complete the project?

An iteration of the allocation procedure that allows resource balancing is as follows:

Step One   Determine the maximum resource units required by any activity within the project. This is the starting level.

Step Two   Using the allocation procedure, determine the minimum project time with this resource level. If the time equals or is less than the required project time, the solution is complete. If not, go to step 3.

Step Three   Increase the resource units available by one and go to step 2. Iterate until time requirement can be met.

Whereas this procedure is quite satisfactory to single-resource balancing, multiple-resource balancing gets extremely cumbersome because of the need to determine which resources have to be increased in level. Logically, not all resource types would have to be increased in level at each iteration in the solution. As an example of single-resource balancing, consider the project presented in Figure 8.9a. Using ACTIM, a project duration time of 18 was realized. Suppose a project duration time of 15, the critical-path time, is mandatory because of extreme penalty costs. What resource level is required to allow this project duration time?

The first step normally would be to start with four resource units, the maximum required by any one activity—in this case, activity 1–5. But this step is not necessary, since we found in Table 8.4 that a resource level of eight units realized the schedule of 18 time-units. Starting with the resource level of eight units, the iterative solution is given in Table 8.7. It can be seen that an increase of one resource-unit, to nine units, allows the critical-path time to be achieved. As a point of interest, the computer program, described in the next section, computed the result of *all* the balancing iterations if we start with four resource units. The results are as follows.

Resource units	4	5	6	7	8	9
Project duration	32	26	25	18	18	15

It does not take much imagination to realize that the cost of resource units and the costs associated with the project duration can be implemented in a cost model to determine the optimum cost schedule. A simple approach to this cost model is presented in the next section.

8.5   RESOURCE ANALYSIS WITH THE DIGITAL COMPUTER

RESALL (RESource ALLocation of scarce resources) is a FORTRAN program developed at Arizona State University to schedule projects with multiple resources using the technique described in the previous sections with the ACTIM criterion.† A FORTRAN listing and directions for RESALL's use is given in Appendix D. A few brief comments are in order at this time, since the program will schedule up to 100 activities requiring up to 200 different resource-types—a situation that obviously would require the services of a computer, as would most real-world applications.

RESALL will compute *critical-path data* as this is required in the solution approach. Both *allocation* and *balance* options are available to the user. Normal and overtime operation can be handled with the allocation situation and cost analysis is available for *both* allocation and balance runs.

Costing	The user has to input fixed costs per unit time for each activity (normal and overtime), as well as resource costs. Accumulated costs for the project for *each period* are determined as follows.
Normal costs	Number of normal resources used in a period multiplied by the normal cost rate.
Overtime costs	Resource overtime costs multiplied by the number of overtime resources used in the particular period. An overtime resource is never considered in a particular period until *all* normal resources have been utilized in that period.
Idle costs	The number of *normal* resources not used in a particular period multiplied by the normal cost. Overtime resources are *never* considered idle, since they would not be utilized if not required.
	The sum of all period costs constitutes the total schedule cost. A small example will be used to demonstrate the output of the program and the cost analysis employed. Assume data is as given in Table 8.8.
Normal schedule	The normal schedule and associated costs are given in Figure 8.11. The project duration is 32 time-units and the total cost is $108,960. The utilization of resources is given in Figure 8.12 (resource 1) and Figure 8.13 (resource 2). For each of the resource profiles, the left side gives the utilization over time for the *normal* schedule and the right side gives the *normal and overtime* utilization for the overtime schedule.

The costs associated with the *normal* schedule are as follows.

Fixed costs	($1800) (32-period schedule) = $57,600

---

†RESALL was originally developed by Richard Mason under the direction of David D. Bedworth: See R. Mason, "*An Adaptation of the Brooks Algorithm for Scheduling Projects under Multiple Resource Constraints.*" unpublished MSE research paper in Industrial Engineering, Arizona State University, August 1970. Permission to use the RESALL material was graciously granted by Colonel Mason.

TABLE 8.8   Data for RESALL Example

	Resources Required		
Activity	Resource 1	Resource 2	Activity Duration
1–2	3	5	5
1–3	1	4	8
1–4	2	3	20
2–4	2	1	7
3–4	2	2	3

	Units Available		Resource Cost	
Resource	Normal	Overtime	Normal	Overtime
Resource 1	5	2	$125	$175
Resource 2	7	2	$140	$225

Project Fixed Costs: $1800 per time period

Resource normal costs	Add quantities used during the 32 periods for each resource and multiply by appropriate normal costs: Resource 1: (83) ($125) = $10,375 Resource 2: (130)($140) = $18,200 Total = $28,575
Resource idle costs	For each resource, the idle quantities over the 32 periods is (32) multiplied by (normal quantity available) minus quantities actually used over the 32 periods. Multiply by normal cost: Resource 1: [(32)(5) − 83][125] = $9625 Resource 2: [(32)(7) − 130][140] = $13,160 Total = $22,785

Costs associated with the overtime schedule are computed in the same manner, except that overtime costs are added. Figure 8.12, the profile for resource 1, shows that in no period were more than five resource-units ever used. Since five is the normal quantity, no overtime costs are incurred with *resource* 1. Figure 8.13 shows that overtime was utilized only in time periods 1 through 12, and only one unit at that. The overtime cost is then

$$(12)(225) = \$2700$$

a figure that can be confirmed in the overtime schedule and cost summary given in Figure 8.14. The overtime schedule is 20 time-units at a total cost of

NORMAL SCHEDULE

TOTAL PROJECT COSTS

FIXED	IDLE	NORMAL	OVERTIME	TOTAL
57600.	22785.	28575.	0.	108960.

A DETAILED SCHEDULE FOR THIS RUN IS GIVEN ON THE NEXT OUTPUT PAGE.

NORMAL SCHEDULE

PROJECT ACTIVITY SCHEDULE

CRITICAL PATH TERMINATION DATE   20

THESE ARE THE REVISED START AND FINISH TIMES

ACTIVITY TAIL HEAD	START	FINISH (END OF PERIOD)
1 - 2	20	25
1 - 3	0	8
1 - 4	0	20
2 - 4	25	32
3 - 4	8	11

MINIMUM PROJECT DURATION = 32 TIME UNITS

FIGURE 8.11 RESALL time and cost output for data given in Table 8.8—normal schedule.

$70,800, or $38,160 less than the normal schedule, along with a reduction of 12 time-units.

In conclusion, the cost model associated with RESALL may not be correct to every situation. What should be apparent is that once the schedule and resource profiles have been developed by the program, a cost analysis that is correct for a particular situation is quite easy to accomplish without a computer.

8.6 THE LINE-BALANCING PROBLEM

A manufacturing-oriented problem analogous to the resource-allocation and resource-balancing problems is that of line balancing. Historically, the line-balancing problem evolved from the mass-production assembly line, where

RESOURCE NUMBER 1 SUMMARY

RESOURCE ITEM IS RESOURCE 1
NORMAL QUANTITY IS: 5
NORMAL COST/PERIOD IS: 125

OVERTIME QUANTITY IS: 7. (NORMAL AND OVERTIME)
OVERTIME COST/PERIOD:175

UTILIZATION INFORMATION

TIME	NORMAL SCHEDULE QUANTITY USED	NORMAL SCHEDULE PERCENT UTILIZATION 0 1 2 3 4 5 6 7 8 9 10	OVERTIME SCHEDULE QUANTITY USED	OVERTIME SCHEDULE PERCENT UTILIZATION 0 1 2 3 4 5 6 7 8 9 10
1	3	NNNNNNNNNNNNN	5	0000000000000000
2	3	NNNNNNNNNNNN	5	0000000000000000
3	3	NNNNNNNNNNNN	5	0000000000000000
4	3	NNNNNNNNNNNN	5	0000000000000000
5	3	NNNNNNNNNNNN	5	0000000000000000
6	3	NNNNNNNNNNNN	5	0000000000000000
7	3	NNNNNNNNNNNN	5	0000000000000000
8	3	NNNNNNNNNNNN	5	0000000000000000
9	4	NNNNNNNNNNNNNNNN	5	0000000000000000
10	4	NNNNNNNNNNNNNNNN	5	0000000000000000
11	4	NNNNNNNNNNNNNNNN	5	0000000000000000
12	2	NNNNNNNN	5	0000000000000000
13	2	NNNNNNNN	3	0000000000
14	2	NNNNNNNN	4	0000000000000
15	2	NNNNNNNN	4	0000000000000
16	2	NNNNNNNN	4	0000000000000
17	2	NNNNNNNN	2	0000000
18	2	NNNNNNNN	2	0000000
19	2	NNNNNNNN	2	0000000
20	2	NNNNNNNN	2	0000000
21	3	NNNNNNNNNNNN		
22	3	NNNNNNNNNNNN		
23	3	NNNNNNNNNNNN		
24	3	NNNNNNNNNNNN		
25	3	NNNNNNNNNNNN		
26	2	NNNNNNNN		
27	2	NNNNNNNN		
28	2	NNNNNNNN		
29	2	NNNNNNNN		
30	2	NNNNNNNN		
31	2	NNNNNNNN		
32	2	NNNNNNNN		

FIGURE 8.12   Resource 1 profile developed by RESALL.

tasks required in the assembly process had to be apportioned to workers in such a fashion that worker effort was somewhat equalized and the number of workers minimized while maintaining a specified production rate.

This is similar to the resource-balancing problem. Conversely, *given* the number of assembly workers, what assignment of work maximizes production rate (minimizes assembly cycle time)? This would be the analog of the resource-allocation problem. The line-balancing problem is still significant in manufacturing. Even with automated production lines, the balancing of work in assembly stations and the minimization of transfer mechanisms within the line can be construed as a valid line-balancing problem.

Suppose we have eight jobs (elemental tasks) to be accomplished in an assembly line. The tasks and associated times in minutes to complete each task are as follows.

task	a_1	a_2	a_3	a_4	a_5	a_6	a_7	a_8
time	3	1	2	5	4	4	7	1

RESOURCE NUMBER 2 SUMMARY

RESOURCE ITEM IS RESOURCE 2
NORMAL QUANTITY IS: 7
NORMAL COST/PERIOD IS: 140

OVERTIME QUANTITY IS: 9. (NORMAL AND OVERTIME)
OVERTIME COST/PERIOD:225

UTILIZATION INFORMATION

TIME	NORMAL SCHEDULE QUANTITY USED	PERCENT UTILIZATION 0 1 2 3 4 5 6 7 8 9 10	OVERTIME SCHEDULE QUANTITY USED	PERCENT UTILIZATION 0 1 2 3 4 5 6 7 8 9 10
1	7	NNNNNNNNNNNNNNNNNNNNNN	8	OOOOOOOOOOOOOOOOOO
2	7	NNNNNNNNNNNNNNNNNNNNNN	8	OOOOOOOOOOOOOOOOOO
3	7	NNNNNNNNNNNNNNNNNNNNNN	8	OOOOOOOOOOOOOOOOOO
4	7	NNNNNNNNNNNNNNNNNNNNNN	8	OOOOOOOOOOOOOOOOOO
5	7	NNNNNNNNNNNNNNNNNNNNNN	8	OOOOOOOOOOOOOOOOOO
6	7	NNNNNNNNNNNNNNNNNNNNNN	8	OOOOOOOOOOOOOOOOOO
7	7	NNNNNNNNNNNNNNNNNNNNNN	8	OOOOOOOOOOOOOOOOOO
8	7	NNNNNNNNNNNNNNNNNNNNNN	8	OOOOOOOOOOOOOOOOOO
9	5	NNNNNNNNNNNNNNNN	8	OOOOOOOOOOOOOOOOOO
10	5	NNNNNNNNNNNNNNNN	8	OOOOOOOOOOOOOOOOOO
11	5	NNNNNNNNNNNNNNNN	8	OOOOOOOOOOOOOOOOOO
12	3	NNNNNNNNNN	8	OOOOOOOOOOOOOOOOOO
13	3	NNNNNNNNNN	7	OOOOOOOOOOOOOOOO
14	3	NNNNNNNNNN	5	OOOOOOOOOOOO
15	3	NNNNNNNNNN	5	OOOOOOOOOOOO
16	3	NNNNNNNNNN	5	OOOOOOOOOOOO
17	3	NNNNNNNNNN	3	OOOOOOOO
18	3	NNNNNNNNNN	3	OOOOOOOO
19	3	NNNNNNNNNN	3	OOOOOOOO
20	3	NNNNNNNNNN	3	OOOOOOOO
21	5	NNNNNNNNNNNNNNNN		
22	5	NNNNNNNNNNNNNNNN		
23	5	NNNNNNNNNNNNNNNN		
24	5	NNNNNNNNNNNNNNNN		
25	5	NNNNNNNNNNNNNNNN		
26	1	NNNN		
27	1	NNNN		
28	1	NNNN		
29	1	NNNN		
30	1	NNNN		
31	1	NNNN		
32	1	NNNN		

FIGURE 8.13   Resource 2 profile developed by RESALL.

The time to assemble *one* complete assembly is, of course, the time to complete all eight tasks—27 minutes.

The time between completion of assemblies can be much less than 27 minutes. For example, the cycle time could be as low as seven minutes, since that is the maximum elemental-task time. The cycle time is a function of *production rate*. A production rate of six parts per hour would require a cycle time of 10 minutes.

Suppose, for our simple example, that a cycle time of nine minutes is required. Further, it is given that the tasks can be accomplished in any sequence in the line (unordered). An optimum number of assemblers (or stations) would be three, as shown in Figure 8.15a.

In a more realistic situation, certain operations would be required to precede others: for example, a hole must be drilled before it is tapped. Now let's assume that the elemental tasks *have* to be sequenced as follows.

$$a_1 \rightarrow a_4 \rightarrow a_7 \rightarrow a_5 \rightarrow a_2 \rightarrow a_3 \rightarrow a_6 \rightarrow a_8$$

OVERTIME SCHEDULE

TOTAL PROJECT COSTS

FIXED	IDLE	NORMAL	OVERTIME	TOTAL
36000.	5205.	26895.	2700.	70800.

A DETAILED SCHEDULE FOR THIS RUN IS GIVEN ON THE NEXT OUTPUT PAGE.

OVERTIME SCHEDULE

PROJECT ACTIVITY SCHEDULE

CRITICAL PATH TERMINATION DATE   20

THESE ARE THE REVISED START AND FINISH TIMES

ACTIVITY		START	FINISH
TAIL	HEAD	(END OF	PERIOD)
1 -	2	0	5
1 -	3	5	13
1 -	4	0	20
2 -	4	5	12
3 -	4	13	16

MINIMUM PROJECT DURATION = 20 TIME UNITS

FIGURE 8.14   RESALL time and cost output for data given in Table 8.8—overtime schedule.

The cycle time requirement of nine minutes would realize a balance shown in Figure 8.15b. The number of assemblers has been increased to four. However, the production rate *would be increased* if all other factors are amenable, since the maximum *station* time is eight minutes. One measure of a balance is *station efficiency* and *line efficiency*. Line efficiency is the sum of *all* task times multiplied by 100, divided by (cycle time)(number of stations). Figure 8-15b has a line efficiency of

$$\frac{(27)(100)}{(9)(4)} = 75\%$$

The line efficiency for Figure 8.15a is of course 100%—much better. The station efficiency is the sum of the *station* task times multiplied by 100,

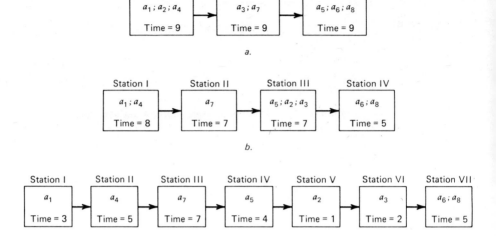

FIGURE 8.15   **Examples of task assignment in line balancing. (*a*) Tasks unordered. (*b*) Tasks sequenced—no other constraints. (*c*) tasks sequenced—zone constraints added.**

divided by the cycle time. Station I in Figure 8.15*b* has an efficiency of

$$\frac{(8)(100)}{(9)} = 88.9\%$$

Similarly, station II's efficiency is 77.8%, the same as station III's.

Now, union skill requirements dictate that no assembler can work on *both* even- and odd-numbered tasks (sometimes called a zone constraint). The cycle time of nine would realize the balance given in Figure 8.15*c*—seven assemblers. It should now be clear that adding constraints, precedence or zone, will lead to an inefficient line balance. It should be just as clear that any assembly line, such as a line to manufacture automobiles, will have thousands of tasks, both ordered and unordered, and many types of zone constraints. Zones will include skills, physical zoning such as right or left-hand side of the line, and so on. The actual economic balancing of the line according to some cycle-time requirement can be an almost unbelievable task. The solution approach, as with the resource problem, usually has to be heuristic in nature. Three heuristic approaches will be given in subsequent sections. Finally, an approach to the even more complicated problem of *multiple products* in the assembly line will be considered.

The rather complex line-balancing problem now boils down to the following: Knowing the operations required in a particular assembly task, and knowing their procedence and zone restrictions, determine an optimal worker/task(s) assignment to allow a particular cycle time to be met. As with resource allocation, this problem can be broken into two, one of which can be solved by iteratively solving the other.

1. Given a required cycle time, find the minimum number of workers required to perform the tasks in an assembly task, knowing each task's time, precedence, and zone status.

2. Given a specified number of workers, determine the minimum cycle time in which an assembly can be produced, knowing each task's time, precedence, or zone status.

To generalize further, a grouping of tasks will be classified as a work station at which usually one worker will be assigned. The following symbology will be used in the solutions to the line-balancing problem:

1. Let t_i be the time for the ith task (or operation), O_i, in the assembly, $i = 1, 2, 3, \ldots N$.

2. Let C be the cycle time.

3. Let S_k be the set of tasks in the kth work station, $k = 1, 2, 3, \ldots M$.

4. Let T be the overall time available for the sequence of assembly required.

5. Let Q be the production quantity required in T. Therefore, $C = T/Q$.

The restrictions for assignment of tasks to stations, other than precedence or zone, has to include

1. $1 \leq M \leq N$
The number of stations cannot be greater than the number of tasks. Also, the minimum number of stations is one.

2. $t_i \leq C$
No task time may be greater than the cycle time (unless multiple workers are allowed per task). Implicit in this restriction is that the accumulation of task times per station cannot exceed the cycle time.

Line efficiency is found by

$$\frac{100 \sum_{i=1}^{N} t_i}{(C)(M)}$$

and the kth station efficiency is found by

$$\frac{100 \sum_{j=1}^{J} t_j}{(C)}$$

where t_j is the jth task in the set of tasks, S_k.

8.7   HELGESON--BIRNIE APPROACH

The line-balancing approach generally cited as the foundation technique is the one developed by Helgeson and Birnie.† This approach assigns operations to stations in an order that corresponds to the length of time each controls through the remainder of the network. This is directly comparable to the resource-allocation ACTIM procedure. The only difference is that all succeeding operations are considered in the ranking, not just those on the longest path emanating from the operation in question. The sum of the times of those operations controlled in this manner by a particular operation is defined as the *positional weight*. Ranking operations in decreasing sequence according to their positional weights leads to the technique designation of ranked *positional weight technique*. Of course, as operations are assigned to stations, cognizance has to be taken of the precedence and zoning restrictions. The latter is very simple. Since a zone includes only operations that may be combined with each other, having separate line-balance solutions for each zone solves the restriction. One complication of this, however, occurs with operations that can be in one of several zones.

An example of the effect of physical zoning on the line-balancing solution is given in Figure 8.16. This example will not be worked in detail. The cathode ray tube (CRT) has certain operations that can only be done on one side of the production line. Obviously, operations on the front of the CRT cannot be combined with those on the left if the operator cannot jump the conveyor. So, for example, operation 1 cannot be in the same station as immediate subsequent operations 9 and 10. This type of arrangement, though realistic, certainly restricts the combinations of tasks within stations, which, in turn, minimizes the possibility of an efficient solution. Figure 8.16 points out another problem. The six tasks after the test station cannot be combined with any task that is *prior to* the test station. This forces *two* independent line-balancing problems, one before and one after the test station.

The line-balancing problem that will be carried through the two techniques presented in this and the subsequent section is given in Figure 8.17. The task *positional weight* is, as mentioned earlier, the length of time, in terms of accumulated task times, controlled by the task in question. Task 19 has no subsequent tasks and so has a positional weight of 2. Task 13 has subsequent tasks 17, 18, 19, and 20, so its positional weight, including the time for the task in question, is

$$5 + 13 + 5 + 2 + 3 = 28$$

The positional weights for all tasks are given in Table 8.9. Also given is a list

---

†W. B. Helgeson and D. P. Birnie, "Assembly Line Balancing Using the Ranked Positional Weight Technique," *The Journal of Industrial Engineering*, vol. 12, no. 6, November–December 1961.

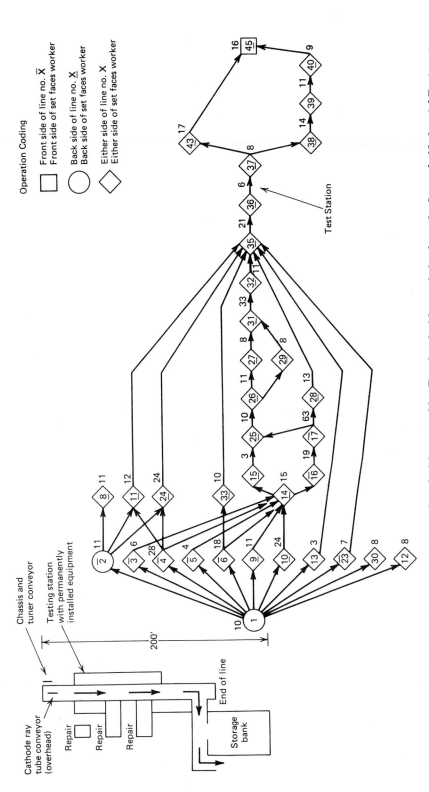

FIGURE 8.16 Schematic and associated network for television assembly. (Reprinted with permission from the *Journal of Industrial Engineering*, vol. 13, No. 3, May–June 1962, pages 140–41. Copyright © American Institute of Industrial Engineers, Inc., 25 Technology Park/Atlanta, Norcross, Ga. 30095.

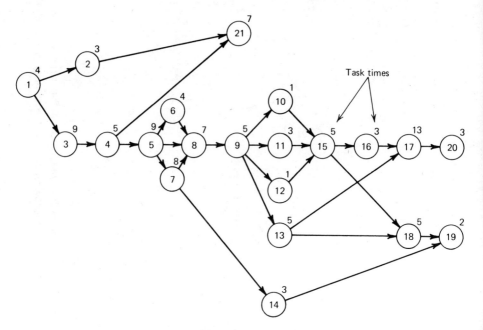

FIGURE 8.17 **Line-balancing precedence network. (Reprinted with permission from the *Journal of Industrial Engineering*, vol. 16, No. 1, January–February 1965, p. 25. Copyright © American Institute of Industrial Engineers, Inc., 25 Technology Park/Atlanta, Norcross, Ga. 30092.)**

of tasks ranked by positional weight, highest to lowest. This ranking is called the ranked positional weighting. Obviously, the highest ranked operation, 1, has to be a critical-path item. Therefore, this operation should be assigned first to the station arrangement. In fact, this is how the technique works. Activities are assigned according to the *ranked positional weighting*, assuming precedence and zone constraints have been satisfied. Assignments are made to a station as long as the cycle-time constraint is met. So the Helgeson-Birnie approach is not only logical, it is simple—a tremendous asset for a heuristic algorithm. The solution to the Figure 8.17 precedence network problem is given in Table 8.10, assuming a cycle time of 21 is required. We see that six stations result, with station 6 having a terrible efficiency

$$\frac{(2)(100)}{21} = 9.5\%$$

The line efficiency is not too bad:

$$\frac{(105)(100)}{(6)(21)} = 83.3\%$$

With an academic problem this small, switching tasks *after* the assignment might be feasible. However, with realistic problems such as an appliance manufacturing line, this would not be really feasible.

TABLE 8.9 Positional Weights for Network of Figure 8.17

Task	Positional Weight	Task	Ranked Positional Weight
1	105	1	105
2	10	3	98
3	98	4	89
4	89	5	77
5	77	7	64
6	57	6	57
7	64	8	53
8	53	9	46
9	46	11	34
10	32	12	32
11	34	10	32
12	32	15	31
13	28	13	28
14	5	16	19
15	31	17	16
16	19	2	10
17	16	18	7
18	7	21	7
19	2	14	5
20	3	20	3
21	7	19	2

The problem just tackled is that of approaching the minimum number of stations given a cycle time. The second problem gives the number of stations and asks for the minimum cycle time. Suppose for our problem that five stations were specified. We could now increment the cycle time by one time-unit at a time and iterate to determine the first five-station balance. If we raise C to 22, we get the balance given in Table 8.11. By increasing the cycle time by one, the stations can be decreased to five. A similar analysis would reveal that four stations can be achieved with a cycle time of 27.

A logical way to start the determination of cycle time given the number of stations, is to determine the *lower bound* on the cycle time. This is found by dividing the total of the task times—105 in the example problem—by the number of stations. Results that are not integers should always be rounded *up* to the closest integer. For four stations we should get the lower bound of

$$\frac{105}{4} = 26.25, \text{ or } 27$$

This is the value we found, but of course, if line efficiency is plotted against

TABLE 8.10   Line Balancing for Network Given in Figure 8.17 (Cycle Time = 21)

	Task	Task Time	Cumulative Station Time	Comments
Station 1	1	4	4	
	3	9	13	
	4	5	18	
	2	3	21	Cycle time achieved. Task 2 is next task after 4 that can be assigned.
Station 2	5	9	9	
	7	8	17	
	6	4	21	
Station 3	8	7	7	
	9	5	12	
	11	3	15	
	12	1	16	
	10	1	17	
	14	3	20	Next smallest task time is 2, which will force station time greater than the cycle time.
Station 4	15	5	5	
	13	5	10	
	16	3	13	
	21	7	20	
Station 5	17	13	13	
	18	5	18	
	20	3	21	
Station 6	19	2	2	

TABLE 8.11 Line Balance for Network Given in Figure 8.17 (Cycle Time = 22)

	Task	Task Time	Cumulative Station Time
Station 1	1	4	4
	3	9	13
	4	5	18
	2	3	21
Station 2	5	9	9
	7	8	17
	6	4	21
Station 3	8	7	7
	9	5	12
	11	3	15
	12	1	16
	10	1	17
	15	5	22
Station 4	13	5	5
	16	3	8
	17	13	21
Station 5	18	5	5
	21	7	12
	14	3	15
	20	3	18
	19	2	20

cycle times, a sawtooth relationship occurs, as shown in Figure 8.18. Peak efficiencies give the recommended cycle times for specific numbers of stations.

Table 8.10 showed that the Helgeson-Birnie technique can give a very poor solution, as can any heuristic approach. The question tackled in the next section relates to how we might improve on the heuristic procedure.

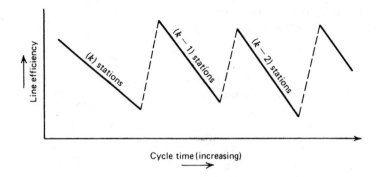

FIGURE 8.18   Line efficiency as a function of cycle time.

8.8   REGION APPROACH

An improvement on the Helgeson-Birnie approach that will guarantee optimality was suggested by Mansoor.† This approach involves interchanging tasks after an initial balance has been realized. Because the approach guarantees optimality, the combinations of tasks that qualify for interchange can become extremely cumbersome and thus nonfeasible for large networks.

A possible improvement developed by Bedworth‡ utilizes some of the ideas from Helgeson-Birnie, Mansoor, and an approach developed by Kilbridge and Wester.§ This procedure entails the following philosophy:

1. Operations that have heavy precedence responsibility (several operations dependent) should be scheduled early.

2. In line with proposition 1, a fallacy of the Helgeson-Birnie approach is that an operation with a large associated time might take precedence over one with heavy dependence responsibilities if several of the dependent operations are small in time. For example, in the previous problem, if operation 21 had a time of 47, it would have had an assignment capability over operation 9 even though the latter has 10 subsequent operations and operation 21 has none.

The steps involved in the new solution will be

1. Develop the precedence network in the normal manner.

---

†E. M. Mansoor, "Assembly Line Balancing—An Improvement on the Ranked Positional Weight Technique," *The Journal of Industrial Engineering*, Vol. 15 no. 2, March–April 1964.

‡Bedworth, *Industrial Systems: Planning, Analysis, Control.*

§M. D. Kilbridge and L. Wester, "A Heuristic Method of Line Balancing," *The Journal of Industrial Engineering*, Vol. 12, no. 4, July–August 1961.

2. Assign precedence regions from left to right. Redraw the network, assigning all tasks the latest precedence region possible; this will ensure that tasks with few dependencies will at least be considered for assignment late in the schedule.

3. Within each precedence region rank tasks from maximum to minimum duration times. This will ensure that the largest task will be considered first, giving the chance for a better combination of smaller tasks later. Assigning most of the small tasks early is one problem with some Helgeson-Birnie solutions.

4. Assign tasks by the following sequence, conforming to process zone restrictions.

   a. Leftmost region first.

   b. Within a region, assign according to largest task first.

5. At the end of each station assignment, decide if the time utilization is acceptable. If not, check all tasks whose predecessor relations have been satisfied. Determine if changing these for any task(s) within the station whose predecessor region(s) are equal to or earlier than the tasks being considered for entry into the station, will increase the utilization. If yes, make the change. This station assignment is now final.

The network given in Figure 8.17 now can be reevaluated, using a cycle time of 21, in light of the new procedure. The solution is given in the same order as the given procedural steps.

Step 1   The network was developed in Figure 8.17.

Step 2   The network, redrawn according to precedence regions, is given in Figure 8.19.

Step 3   Task priorities, according to decreasing task times within regions, are given in Table 8.12.

Step 4 ⎫ Assignment of tasks to stations are given in Table 8.13...

Step 5 ⎭ ... with appropriate comments.

This solution has to be optimum, since all stations now have a 100% station efficiency. The advantage of attempting to improve only the last station balance according to some acceptable utilization factor has to lie with the fact that each station should have only a few operations within it, and relatively few tasks should be eligible for switching into the station. Thus, possible improvements should be readily apparent, as in the example. A disadvantage in attempting to optimize each station as the balances are made stems from the fact that the good combinations of large and small tasks might be used early in the balance, forcing possible bad balances later in the line. Needless to say, the method just generated does not guarantee optimality, although its

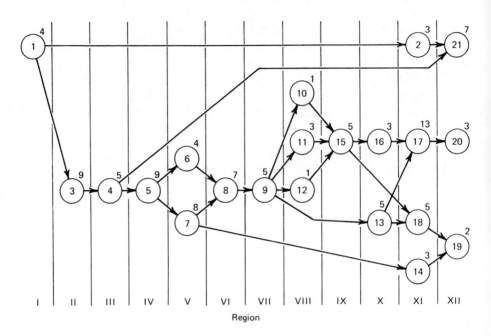

FIGURE 8.19   Network from Figure 8.17 redrawn into regions.

TABLE 8.12   Task Priorities

Region	Tasks (Within Regions, Priority Is Left-to-Right)
I	1
II	3
III	4
IV	5
V	7, 6
VI	8
VII	9
VIII	11, 10, 12
IX	15
X	13, 16
XI	17, 18, 14, 2
XII	21, 20, 19

TABLE 8.13 Region Method Balance

Station	Tasks (in order of assignment)
1	1, 3, 4, 2 [Station time = 21]
2	5, 7, 6 [Station time = 21]
3	8, 9, 11, 10, ~~12~~, ~~14~~, 13 [12 and 14 originally assigned for a station time of 20. Task 13 has predecessor assigned (9) and so was interchanged with 12 and 14 to give a station time of 21]
4	12, 15, 16, 18, ~~14~~, ~~19~~, 21 [Original Assignment did not include 21 (station time of 19): 21 was interchanged with 14 and 19 to give a station time of 21]
5	14, 17, 19, 20 [Station time = 21]

solutions should be good ones approaching optimal, and might well be optimal.

Even though production lines may be considered to have completely deterministic times, this may not be the case. The automatic line certainly may have deterministic times. Operator-controlled situations, such as stacking in the manufacture of semiconductor devices, would tend not to be deterministic. Also, many production lines have *multiproducts* being produced. The single-product discrete situation at least demonstrates how a *good* solution may be evolved for a highly complex problem by an almost common-sense approach. Now we will see how the multiproduct stochastis situation might be handled.

8.9 STOCHASTIC MIXED-PRODUCT LINE BALANCING— A COMPUTER APPROACH

Where different products utilize the same production line, it is assumed of course that a large percentage of the tasks within the line are common to most of the products. Since tasks are fixed within stations, once balanced, it should be apparent that station efficiencies will vary with the products being produced. A great variety in these efficiencies might dictate that separate lines be utilized. This section will assume that the mixed-product line is feasible and will start from that point.†

---

†This section is based on research performed by Dr. Don Deutsch in "A Branch and Bound Technique for Mixed-Product Assembly Line Balancing" (Ph.D. dissertation in Industrial Engineering, Arizona State University, 1971).

First of all, let's consider the precedence network. Since the products in the mixed-products line will undoubtedly have different precedence networks, even though they might only be slightly different, it follows that a *common* precedence diagram must be developed. Figure 8.20 shows precedence diagrams for two products and also the combined precedence diagram. If a task has *different* times for different products, the precedence diagram has to reflect all the times. It is certainly possible that tasks might have to be duplicated in the combined diagram. For example, if task 1 preceded task 2 for product *A* but followed task 2 for product *B*, there would have to be two task 2's in the combined diagram.

Perhaps it should be pointed out that if the tasks in the line are highly flexible and if product entry can be controlled by type, the mixed-product approach might not be needed. The random-entry, fixed production system definitely would require the mixed-product approach.

If the cycle time is 10 for the example in Figure 8.20 and the Helgeson-Birnie approach is used with the *combined network only*, we would get the balance shown in Figure 8.21*a* (the reader is warned that this result is incorrect). The overall line efficiency is

$$\frac{(39)(100)}{(5)(10)} = 78\%$$

This is a fallacy, since it would only be possible if both products were in all stations at the same time—an impossibility. The utilization with product 1 only is

$$\frac{(22)(100)}{(5)(10)} = 44\%$$

and for product 2 is

$$\frac{(30)(100)}{(5)(10)} = 60\%$$

In reality the two-product line efficiency is not correct since different products could occupy *different* stations simultaneously. For example, if product 1 was in stations II and IV while product 2 was in stations I, III, and V, the line efficiency for that one cycle would be

$$\frac{(39)(100)}{(5)(10)} = 78\%$$

Loss of efficiency over single-product lines but gain in equipment effectiveness is the trade-off that must be evaluated in the mixed-product line balance. Unfortunately, the Helgeson-Birnie results are *far* from optimum, as we can see when an optimal computer program evolves the balance.

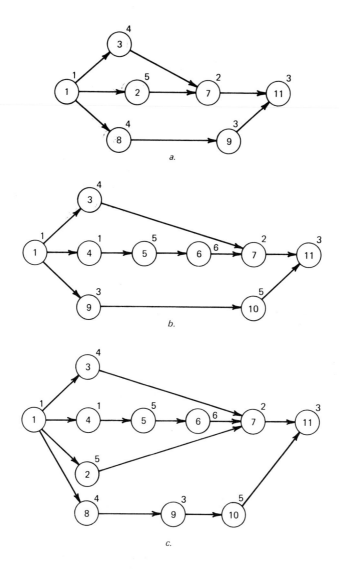

FIGURE 8.20 Precedence networks for two-product line. (*a*) Product 1. (*b*) Product 2. (*c*) Combined.

Computer Program

A computer program is available to allow *optimal* line balancing for the mixed-product, deterministic or stochastic situation. This program is called BABALB† for *B*ranch *A*nd *B*ound *A*ssembly *L*ine *B*alancing. "Optimal solution" refers to both station and workload assignment. The program first

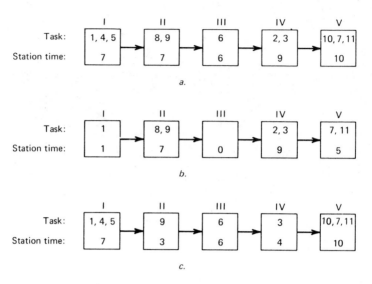

FIGURE 8.21   **Incorrect line balance and utilizations for the network given in Figure 8.20 (cycle time = 10). (a) Combined-product line balance. (b) Product 1 utilization. (c) Product 2 utilization.**

determines the *minimum* number of stations, given a user cycle time. Next, the program determines the operation balance that minimizes the cycle time for this minimum number of stations. This achieves the *optimum balance workload* for the given user cycle time. The user has to develop a composite precedence diagram specifying operations, immediate predecessors, operation times, and operation time variances if stochastic analysis is required, and the cycle time desired. In addition, if stochastic analysis is required, the user has to stipulate the percentage of times that a station must be equal to or less than the cycle time. This is input as the corresponding normal-distribution standardized variable Z. For example, a 99.87% probability for the stations to meet the cycle time would require a value of 3, a probability of 50% would require Z to be 0, and so on. The optimal balance is accomplished with the branch-and-bound optimization approach, and description of the procedure is not feasible in this text.

An example of the output is given in Figure 8.22 for the sample problem set given in Figure 8.20, using a cycle time of 10. Now we can see why the Helgeson-Birnie approach using *only* the combined precedence network was incorrect. A station can contain tasks whose cumulative times *exceed the cycle time* as long as *individual product* times do not exceed the cycle time.

†Developed as part of Dr. Deutsch's "A Branch and Bound Technique for Mixed-Product Assembly Line Balancing." Permission to include the program listing in Appendix E was kindly granted by Dr. Deutsch.

EXAMPLE TWO-PRODUCT BABALB PROBLEM.

CYCLE TIME = 10.000   Z = .000

OPERATION	PRODUCT	TIME/VARIANCE		
	1		2	
1	1.0 /	.0	1.0 /	.0
2	5.0 /	.0	.0 /	.0
3	4.0 /	.0	4.0 /	.0
4	.0 /	.0	1.0 /	.0
5	.0 /	.0	5.0 /	.0
6	.0 /	.0	6.0 /	.0
7	2.0 /	.0	2.0 /	.0
8	4.0 /	.0	.0 /	.0
9	3.0 /	.0	3.0 /	.0
10	.0 /	.0	5.0 /	.0
11	3.0 /	.0	3.0 /	.0

(a)

OPERATION	IMMEDIATE PREDECESSORS		
1	0	0	0
2	1	0	0
3	1	0	0
4	1	0	0
5	4	0	0
6	5	0	0
7	3	6	2
8	1	0	0
9	8	0	0
10	9	0	0
11	7	10	0

STATION	OPERATION
1	1
1	4
1	5
1	8
1	9
2	2
2	3
2	6
3	7
3	10
3	11

(b)

EXAMPLE TWO-PRODUCT BABALB PROBLEM.

LOAD SUMMARY   CYCLE TIME = 10.000

STATION	PRODUCT	
	1	2
1	8.00	10.00
2	9.00	10.00
3	5.00	10.00

FIGURE 8.22 **BABALB optimum solution for the two-product balancing problem.** *(a)* **Input data.** *(b)* **Three-station balance.**

TABLE 8.14   Computer Station Assignment

Station	Tasks	Product 1 Tasks	Product 1 Station Time	Product 2 Tasks	Product 2 Station Time
1	1, 4, 5, 8, 9	1, 8, 9	8	1, 4, 5, 9	10
2	2, 3, 6	2, 3	9	3, 6	10
3	7, 10, 11	7, 11	5	7, 10, 11	10

BABALB assigned elements to three stations as given in Table 8.14. For product 2 the line efficiency is 100% and for product 1 it is 73% – both are *far* superior to the incorrect five station balance shown in Figure 8.21.

One comment should be made to clarify the fact that BABALB optimizes *both* stations and *loading within stations*. A cycle time of 11 was requested instead of 10. As expected, three stations still resulted. However, BABALB then determined the *minimum cycle time* with the three stations. This proved to be 10, which gives the best loading (or balanced load) for a cycle of 11. When one product can have no more tasks assigned because of the cycle-time constraint, the other product can only have tasks assigned that are not used in the product just finished in that station. When the products exceed two, hand solutions are very difficult. A brief case problem will consider four products with an associated economic analysis assisted by line balancing—a concept not yet presented.

8.10 CASE STUDY

The MIXPROD Corporation is planning a four-product automatic assembly line. The Computer Aided Manufacturing (CAM) Department of MIXPROD has been given the task of determining the optimum arrangement for the automatic line.

Figure 8.23 gives the precedence relationships for each of the products, and these are summarized into a combined precedence chart in Figure 8.24. The times for each task in Figure 8.23 are given in minutes. It should be mentioned that the products are revolutionary microprocessors, with assembly operations for each product being very similar. Also, components are basically the same for each product, so automatic handling and assembly is feasible for this mixed-product situation. The task times are large, but it should be pointed out that each task comprises a complicated assembly task that is automated. MIXPROD has decreed that the analysis has to be for a one-year period, with no salvage value considered.

The CAM department, after several weeks of effort, came up with the

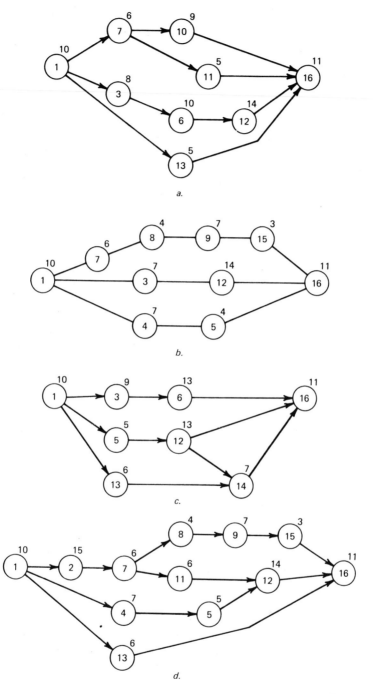

FIGURE 8.23 Precedence networks for four-product case problem. (*a*) Product I. (*b*) Product II. (*c*) Product III. (*d*) Product IV.

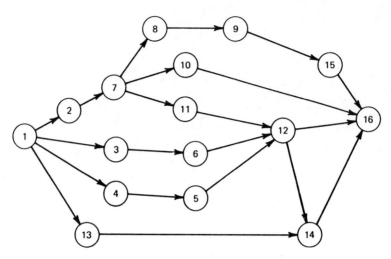

FIGURE 8.24 **Combined precedence diagram for case problem's four products.**

following data.

1. Line-operating costs per year:
   $200,000 + ($15,000 per station) + $50/unit produced.

2. Station development and implementation costs (per station):
   $250,000 + ($5,000) (number of tasks in station, squared)
   NOTE: The second term reflects "crowding" of operations.

3. Potential income:
   a. 0–2000 units/year: $300/unit.
   b. 2001–5000 units/year: $600,000 + ($275/unit over 2000 units).
   c. 5001–10,000 units/year: $1,425,000 + ($250/unit over 5000 units).
   d. Over 10,000 units/year: $2,675,000 + ($200/unit over 10,000 units).

      NOTE: Income is the same regardless of microprocessor. Because of similarity between products, price breaks are on cumulative production of *all* products.

   e. Cycle time range: 15 minutes to 60 minutes.
   f. Production time per year: 208,000 minutes.

The logical solution approach is to determine feasible station balances within the given cycle-time ranges. Following this, a potential-profit-per-year analysis can be accomplished for each allowable balance. Because of the company's proximity to Arizona State University, CAM contracted for the program BABALB to be used in the analysis.

Several BABALB runs were made within the given cycle-time range and

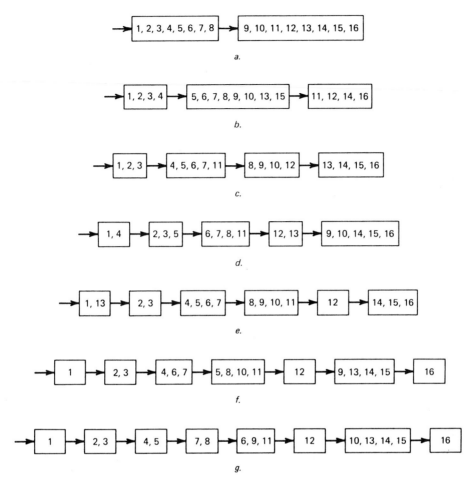

FIGURE 8.25 **Feasible balances for case problem (task numbers given within stations).** (*a*) **Two stations (*C* = 47 minutes). (*b*) Three stations (*C* = 32 minutes). (*c*) Four stations (*C* = 25 minutes). (*d*) Five stations (*C* = 21 minutes). (*e*) Six stations (*C* = 18 minutes). (*f*) Seven stations (*C* = 16 minutes). (*g*) Eight stations (*C* = 15 minutes).**

the optimized loading utilized for each station arrangement. The feasible station balances under the given constraints are shown in Figure 8.25, based on the computer runs. Actual product loading will eventually be given for the arrangement recommended by CAM.

We now have sufficient information to determine the potential profit for each station arrangement. This will be itemized for a cycle time of 47 minutes (balance a in Figure 8.25).

TABLE 8.15 Summary of Income and Costs for Each Station Loading

Number of Stations	Yearly Production (Units)	(A) Operating Costs	(B) Development Costs	(C) Income	Profit (C−A−B)
2	4426	$ 451,277	$1,140,000	$1,267,150	−$324,127
3	6500	570,000	1,230,000	1,800,000	0
4	8320	676,000	1,330,000	2,255,000	249,000
5	9905	770,238	1,540,000	2,651,250	341,012
6	11,556	940,000	1,750,000	2,986,200	296,200
7	13,000	955,000	1,990,000	3,275,000	330,000
8	13,867	1,013,333	2,200,000	3,448,400	235,067

```
CASE STUDY WITH BABALB.

CYCLE TIME =  21.000    Z =    .000

OPERATION   PRODUCT   TIME/VARIANCE
```

OPERATION	1		2		3		4	
1	10.0 /	.0	10.0 /	.0	10.0 /	.0	10.0 /	.0
2	.0 /	.0	.0 /	.0	.0 /	.0	15.0 /	.0
3	8.0 /	.0	7.0 /	.0	9.0 /	.0	.0 /	.0
4	.0 /	.0	7.0 /	.0	.0 /	.0	7.0 /	.0
5	.0 /	.0	4.0 /	.0	5.0 /	.0	5.0 /	.0
6	10.0 /	.0	.0 /	.0	13.0 /	.0	.0 /	.0
7	6.0 /	.0	6.0 /	.0	.0 /	.0	6.0 /	.0
8	.0 /	.0	4.0 /	.0	.0 /	.0	4.0 /	.0
9	.0 /	.0	7.0 /	.0	.0 /	.0	7.0 /	.0
10	9.0 /	.0	.0 /	.0	.0 /	.0	.0 /	.0
11	5.0 /	.0	.0 /	.0	.0 /	.0	6.0 /	.0
12	14.0 /	.0	14.0 /	.0	13.0 /	.0	14.0 /	.0
13	5.0 /	.0	.0 /	.0	6.0 /	.0	6.0 /	.0
14	.0 /	.0	.0 /	.0	7.0 /	.0	.0 /	.0
15	.0 /	.0	3.0 /	.0	.0 /	.0	3.0 /	.0
16	11.0 /	.0	11.0 /	.0	11.0 /	.0	11.0 /	.0

```
OPERATION   IMMEDIATE PREDECESSORS
```

OPERATION				
1	0	0	0	0
2	1	0	0	0
3	1	0	0	0
4	1	0	0	0
5	4	0	0	0
6	3	0	0	0
7	2	0	0	0
8	7	0	0	0
9	8	0	0	0
10	7	0	0	0
11	7	0	0	0
12	5	6	11	0
13	1	0	0	0
14	12	13	0	0
15	9	0	0	0
16	10	12	14	15

FIGURE 8.26   BABALB input data for case problem (cycle time = 21).

a. *Line-Operating Costs Per Year*:

$$\$200,000 + \$(15,000)(2 \text{ stations}) + \$(50)\left(\frac{208,000}{47}\right) = \$451,277$$

b. *Station Development and Implementation Costs*:
Station 1: (8 tasks), $\$250,000 + \$(5000)(8^2) = \$570,000$
Station 2: (8 tasks), $\$250,000 + \$(5000)(8^2) = \underline{\quad 570,000}$
$$\$1,140,000$$

CASE STUDY WITH BABALB.

LOAD SUMMARY   CYCLE TIME = 21.000

STATION	PRODUCT					STATION	OPERATION
	1	2	3	4			
1	10.00	17.00	10.00	17.00		1	1
2	8.00	11.00	14.00	20.00		1	4
3	21.00	10.00	13.00	16.00		2	2
4	19.00	14.00	19.00	20.00		2	3
5	20.00	21.00	18.00	21.00		2	5
						3	6
						3	7
						3	8
						3	11
						4	12
						4	13
THE MINIMUM NUMBER OF STATIONS IS			5			5	9
						5	10
THE BEST LOADING IS GIVEN FOR A CYCLE TIME OF			21.000			5	14
						5	15
						5	16

FIGURE 8.27   BABALB optimized five-station loading for a cycle time of 21.

C. *Income*:

Units produced: $\dfrac{208,000}{47} = 4,426$

Income for first 2000: (2000) (300) = \$600,000
Income for next 2426: (2426) (275) = \$667,150
$$\overline{\hspace{3cm}\$1,267,150}$$

Potential Profit $= C - A - B$
$= \$1,267,150 - \$451,277 - \$1,140,000$
$= -\$324,127$

This loss does not look too good. However, a summary for all balances is given in Table 8.15. Dramatic increases in potential profits are seen for balances with four or more stations. The CAM department recommended to MIXPROD that five stations be implemented. Samples of the computer output for this option are given in Figures 8.26 and 8.27.

This case study is of course not realistic—the cost structure was very simplistic. It does show, however, how a computer line-balancing program might be utilized for planning analysis. One final comment might be made. Since BABALB optimizes loading for a determined optimum number of stations, a cost analysis would have to be run for each loading formed. Since the development costs were dependent on the number of tasks per station it is possible (but doubtful) that a nonoptimum loading for a given station arrangement might accrue.

8.11 REFERENCES

1. Bedworth, David D., *Industrial Systems: Planning, Analysis, Control*, John Wiley, New York, 1973.

2. Brooks, G. H., "Algorithm for Activity Scheduling to Satisfy Constraints on Resource Availability," unpublished paper dated September 17, 1963.

3. Deutsch, Donald, "A Branch and Bound Technique for Mixed-Product Assembly Line Balancing," Ph.D. dissertation in Industrial Engineering, Arizona State University, February 1971.

4. Helgeson, W. B., and Birnie, D. P., "Assembly Line Balancing Using the Ranked Positional Weight Technique," *The Journal of Industrial Engineering*, vol. 12, no. 6, November–December 1961.

5. Kilbridge, M. D., and Wester, Leon, "A Heuristic Method of Line Balancing," *The Journal of Industrial Engineering*, vol. 12 no. 4, July–August 1961.

6. Lang, Douglas W., *Critical Path Analysis*, David McKay, New York, 1977.

7. Mansoor, E. M., "Assembly Line Balancing—An Improvement on the Ranked Positional Weight Technique," *The Journal of Industrial Engineering*, vol. 15, no. 2, March–April 1964.

8. Mason, Richard, "An Adaptation of the Brooks Algorithm for Scheduling Projects under Multiple Resource Constraints," unpublished MSE research paper, Arizona State University, August, 1970.

9. Moodie, C. L., and Young, H. H., "A Heuristic Method of Line Balancing for Assumption of Constant or Variable Work Element Times," *The Journal of Industrial Engineering*, vol. 16, no. 1, January–February 1965.

10. Wester, L. and Kilbridge, M. D., "Heuristic Line Balancing: A Case," *The Journal of Industrial Engineering*, vol. 13, no. 3, May–June 1962.

8.12 EXERCISES

1. A project requires activities, tasks, and resource units per activity as given in Figure 8.28. Determine the Gantt chart schedule from conventional CPM analysis that does not consider resource allocation.

2. For the network of Problem 1, six resource units are available for the project. Use the Brooks algorithm with ACTIM to determine if the CPM schedule from Problem 1 can be met.

3. The network in Problem 1 is for monthly maintenance on a city bus, with "resources" being mechanics and "times" being hours. A mechanic costs the city $15 per hour and an idle bus is evaluated as costing $65 per hour. If it is possible to assign *no more* than six mechanics to the project, determine the optimum number to assign to minimize the monthly maintenance costs.

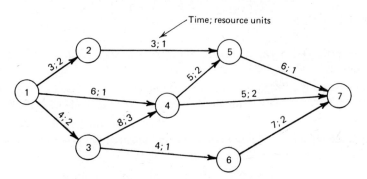

FIGURE 8.28   Limited-resource network for Problem 1.

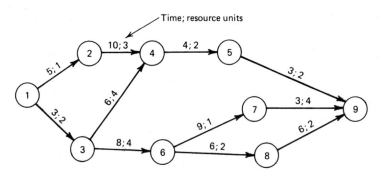

FIGURE 8.29   Limited-resource network for Problem 4.

4. Consider the limited-resource network given in Figure 8.29. If four resource units are available to the project at any period of time, determine the ACTIM minimum time schedule.

5. Repeat Problem 4 using the TIMRES criterion. If either ACTIM or TIMRES gives a better schedule, indicate why this might be so.

6. A time schedule of 27 time-periods for Problem 1 is mandatory. What is the minimum number of resource units to allow this?

7. A multiresource project has a network as given in Figure 8.30. Assuming

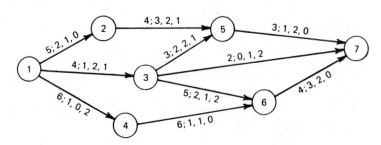

FIGURE 8.30   Multiple-resource network for Problem 7.

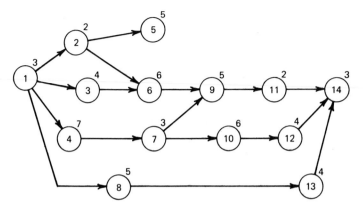

FIGURE 8.31 Line-balancing precedence networks for Problem 9.

that resources 1, 2, and 3 have three, two, and two units, respectively, what is the minimum time in which the project can be scheduled?

8. One way to take advantage of ACTIM and TIMRES is somehow to combine the two criteria. Suggest a way to accomplish this.

9. A line-balancing project has a precedence network as given in Figure 8.31. Given a cycle time of 10 minutes, determine the Helgeson-Birnie station arrangement.

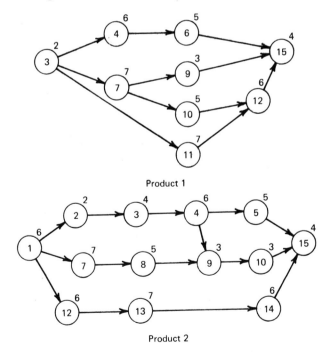

Product 1

Product 2

FIGURE 8.32 Multi-product precedence for Problem 13.

10. Given for Problem 9 that five stations are required, determine the cycle time that will maximize the production rate.

11. Redraw the network of Problem 9 for use by the REGION technique: that is, assign all tasks into the latest region possible.

12. Using the redrawn network from Problem 11, determine the balance obtained using the REGION approach. As with Problem 9, use a cycle time of 10 minutes.

13. Two products use a single assembly line in a particular facility. Precedence diagrams for the two products are given in Figure 8.32. Given a cycle time of 22 minutes, determine the balance using the REGION method on the combined precedence network.

14. For the solution to Problem 13, determine the line efficiency and station efficiencies for both products.

15. Realistically, it is doubtful that all products in a mixed-product line will each have the same *demand* requirement. Suggest ways to incorporate this into the mixed-product balance. Suppose product 2 in Problem 13 has three times the demand as product 1. Show how a better solution might be realized if demand is considered.

16. Verify that the ACTIM and TIMRES resource-allocations given in Figure 8.8*b* are correct by using the BAG iterative approach.

NINE: SEQUENCING AND SCHEDULING

Let all things be done decently and in order.

I Corinthians, XIV

An output of the materials requirement plan as presented in Chapter 7 is a master schedule. Such a schedule is broken down into planning periods, such as a day or a week, and lists all the production that is to be accomplished during that period. For a given production department, all the resources needed to meet the master schedule are available at the beginning of that period. The decisions that must be made at the department level concern what resources to assign to each production task and in what order the tasks should be performed. The sequencing of tasks to resources is the subject of this chapter. Some scheduling techniques are optimum, as with the branch-and-bound approach to solving the line-balancing problem used in the computer program BABALB discussed in Chapter 8. Frequently, as shall be seen, the approaches have to be heuristic in nature because of the complexity of the problem. In fact, a common-sense approach may often be the best solution.

When the supervisor of a department begins the scheduling period, he or she ascertains the availability of labor and equipment. In addition, the set of tasks that must be accomplished are reviewed. For each task, the supervisor must know the resources required and the processing time needed to finish the task. Any constraints as to when the task can be started and when it is due must also be considered. Finally, the supervisor may know of advantages that would accrue from running certain tasks together or in some specific order. With all this in mind, the supervisor allocates the resources to the various tasks so as to meet some scheduling objective. As time goes on, the availability of resources may change and rescheduling will become necessary. Thus, the schedule problem is a dynamic process. In this chapter we look at how the scheduling activity is accomplished.

9.1 OVERVIEW

The shop supervisor can deal with scheduling problems in a variety of ways. The simplest approach is to ignore the problem and accomplish the tasks in any random order. The most frequently used approach is to schedule heuristically according to predetermined "rules of thumb." In certain cases, scientifically derived scheduling procedures can be used to optimize the scheduling objective.

There are many possible scheduling objectives. The most obvious is to increase the utilization of the resources: that is to say, to reduce the resource idle time. For a finite set of tasks, the utilization of resources is inversely proportional to the time required to accomplish all the tasks. This time is referred to as the makespan or maximum flow time of the schedule. In a finite problem, resource utilization is improved by scheduling the set of tasks so as to reduce makespan.

Another important scheduling objective is to reduce in-process inventory: that is to say, to reduce the average number of tasks waiting in a queue while the resources are busy with other tasks. As shown by Baker,† if the makespan of a schedule is constant, that sequence which reduces mean flow-time also reduces mean in-process inventory.

One final objective for scheduling is to reduce some function of the tardiness. In many situations, some or all of the tasks have due dates and if a task is finished after that date a penalty is incurred. There are several ways that we might look at the tardiness objective. One can reduce the maximum tardiness, or one can reduce the number of tasks that are tardy. There is no general procedure for reducing the mean tardiness, but there are heuristics that tend to give good results in this regard.

Typical real-world scheduling problems are often very complex. It is not unusual to desire a solution that addresses all three of the objectives mentioned above. In addition, tasks typically require several steps that must be accomplished in a predefined order. Setup times are often sequence-dependent. Available equipment usually consists of a variety of resources with varying but overlapping capabilities. The scheduling rules and heuristics presented in this chapter are useful in pointing the way toward the solution of complex real-world problems, but they cannot be used with blind faith. With this admonition in mind, a good intuitive engineering approach is generally best. Such an approach can often lead to increased utilization, decreased in-process inventory, and reduced tardiness when compared with a seat-of-the-pants method.

Consider for a moment the seat-of-the-pants scheduling approach often used in manufacturing today. The scheduler has a set of tasks and a set of resources and has learned to prioritize tasks according to their importance and schedules according to that priority. A system of "red tagging" the highest-priority items assists in this regard. In addition, the scheduler may recognize that certain tasks ought to be run together to reduce setup time. In

---

†K. R. Baker, *Introduction to Sequencing and Scheduling*, John Wiley, New York, 1974, pp. 14–17.

some cases he or she may know that certain tasks are scheduled in a prescribed order. If all else is equal, the scheduler orders the tasks on a first-come, first-served basis.

There is a troublesome phenomenon related to the seat-of-the-pants approach. In most situations, the opportunity for improved performance through systematic scheduling is not obvious because the organization acts to adjust its production capacity and delivery lead-times to allow the seat-of-the-pants method to work satisfactorily. Consider a situation in which the order-entry activity uses some known standard lead-time to place orders into the master schedule. The lead time is sufficiently long so that due dates can easily be met. If demand goes up, the standard lead-time is allowed to increase. If deliveries get too far out, overtime is increased or more equipment is acquired. If resource idle time begins to climb, overtime is reduced or layoffs occur and delivery dates improve. In other words, the levels of performance for alternate objectives are relaxed to improve the one that is unsatisfactory. In this fashion the computationally difficult scheduling problems are avoided and the opportunity for an overall performance gain is lost.

The psychology of American management gets in the way when it comes to recognizing scheduling problems. Productive systems are designed essentially to meet demand in an efficient fashion. Whether the system meets the demand or not is easy to observe. Whether it does so in the efficient fashion is easy to hide. Thus, when demand is not satisfactorily met and the alternatives are to improve production control or to increase capacity, the latter is the easy way out. Grief comes to management when it fails to meet objectives, not when the objectives are too easily met.

9.2 DEFINITIONS

Most of the vocabulary in scheduling is self-explanatory. Only a few new terms need to be defined.

Processing time The forecasted estimate of how long it will take to complete a task. This estimate includes any setup time that might be required, which in this chapter is assumed to be relatively independent of which task was run before the task in question. Sometimes setup times are not sequence-independent. In addition, if there are alternative processors, this time may be processor-dependent. Finally, actual processing time is often a random variable and the value used in scheduling is a forecasted expected value. In this chapter, processing time for task i is denoted by t_i.

Due date The established deadline for a task beyond which it would be considered tardy. It is assumed that some kind of penalty for being tardy exists. In this chapter, due date is denoted by d_i.

Lateness   The deviation between a task's completion time and its due date. A task will have positive lateness if it is completed after its due date and negative lateness if completed before its due date. Lateness is denoted in this chapter by L_i.

Tardiness   The measure of positive lateness. If a task is early, it has negative lateness but zero tardiness. If a task has positive lateness, it has equal positive tardiness. Tardiness is denoted in this chapter by T_i, where T_i is the maximum of $\{0, L_i\}$.

Slack   A measure of the difference between the remaining time to a task's due date and its processing time. Slack is denoted by SL_i: $SL_i = d_i - t_i$.

Completion   The span between the beginning of work on the first job, which time is
time   referred to as $t = 0$, and the time when a task i is finished. This span is called C_i.

Flow time   The time span between the point at which a task is available for processing and the point at which it is completed. Thus, it equals the processing time plus the time that the task waits before being processed. Flow time is denoted by F_i.

9.3 SCHEDULING n TASKS ON ONE PROCESSOR

The most elementary scheduling problem occurs whenever there is a set of tasks waiting to be accomplished and only one processor available. The processing times and due dates of each task are known and are independent of the sequence in which the tasks are run. The scheduling problem in this situation is one of deciding which task to run first, second, third, and so forth. The choice of sequence will affect when each task will be completed. The makespan needed to complete the whole set of tasks is constant for all sequences. Makespan equals the sum of the processing times for all tasks.

$$M_s = \sum_{i=1}^{n} t_i \qquad (9.1)$$

where

M_s = the makespan for the n tasks in schedule S
t_i = the processing time of task i

If we assume that all tasks are available when the schedule is started (i.e., at $t = 0.0$), the flow time of each task equals its completion time

$$F_{i,s} = C_{i,s} \qquad (9.2)$$

where

$F_{i,s}$ = flow time for task i in schedule S
$C_{i,s}$ = completion time for task i in schedule S

and the mean flow-time of schedule S is

$$\bar{F}_s = \frac{1}{n} \sum_{i=1}^{n} F_{i,s} \tag{9.3}$$

If we assume that all due dates are measured from $t = 0.0$, the lateness and tardiness of each task are given by

$$L_{i,s} = C_{i,s} - d_i \tag{9.4}$$

$$T_{i,s} = \max\{0, C_{i,s} - d_i\} \tag{9.5}$$
$$\forall i \text{ in } n$$

Thus, the mean lateness and mean tardiness are given by

$$\bar{L}_s = \frac{1}{n} \sum_{i=1}^{n} L_{i,s} \tag{9.6}$$

$$\bar{T}_s = \frac{1}{n} \sum_{i=1}^{n} T_{i,s} \tag{9.7}$$

A related measure is the number of tardy jobs given by

$$N_T = \sum_{i=1}^{n} \delta_i \tag{9.8}$$

where

$$\delta_i = 1 \quad \text{if } T_i > 0$$

and

$$= 0 \quad \text{otherwise}$$

Further, we might be interested in the maximum lateness or tardiness, which is given by[†]

$$T_{\max} = \max\{0, L_{\max}\} \tag{9.9}$$
$$\forall i \text{ in } n$$

$$L_{\max} = \max\{L_{i,s}\} \tag{9.10}$$
$$\forall i \text{ in } n$$

Although we can't affect the makespan objective by selecting a good sequence, we can affect the mean flow-time, mean lateness, and mean tardiness.

Consider a set of two tasks, A and B. The processing times are given by t_A and t_B and neither task has a due date. Suppose task A is shorter than task B: that is, $t_A < t_B$. There are two options available to the scheduler: run task A first or run task B first. Figure 9.1 shows the Gantt chart of these two options. Note that the flow time of the task run first equals its processing time, whereas the flow time of the second task equals its processing time plus the processing time of its predecessor in the schedule. We shall denote the processing time of the task run first and second by $t_{[1]}$ and $t_{[2]}$, respectively,

---

[†]Note: The symbol $\forall$ is read "for all."

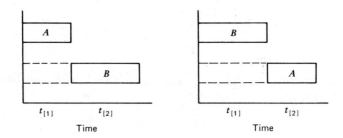

FIGURE 9.1 Two ways to schedule tasks A and B.

where the number in square brackets denotes the position in the schedule. For either schedule in Figure 9.1, the mean flow-time is given by

$$\bar{F}_s = \frac{1}{2}(F_{[1]} + F_{[2]}) = \frac{1}{2}(t_{[1]} + t_{[1]} + t_{[2]}) \qquad (9.11)$$

Note that the processing time of the task run first appears twice in Equation 9.11, whereas the processing time of the second task appears only once. The objective of minimizing mean flow-time is attained, therefore, by scheduling the shorter of the tasks first. This result holds for the general case, as can be seen in the following theorem. (This and later theorems appear in greater detail in Baker and elsewhere.†)

Theorem 9.1 The SPT Rule to Minimize Mean Flow-Time on One Processor

When scheduling n tasks on a single processor, the mean flow-time is minimized by sequencing the Shortest Processing Time (SPT) task first: that is, $t_{[1]} \leq t_{[2]} \leq \cdots \leq t_{[n]}$.

Proof

Consider two arbitrary sequences, S and S', of the same set of tasks. These sequences are identical except for two adjacent tasks i and j, which are reversed in S', and $t_i < t_j$. The tasks that occur before i and j are defined as being in set A and those occurring after are set B. The two sequences can be seen in Figure 9.2. Observe that the tasks in sets A and B start and complete at the same times in both sequences; thus, their flow-times are the same. The only difference in the flow-times of the two sequences occur for tasks i and j.

---

†Some material in this chapter is derived from Baker, *Introduction to Sequencing and Scheduling.* Copyright © 1974 by John Wiley and Sons, Inc. Used by permission.

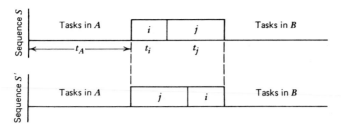

FIGURE 9.2 Two sequences, S and S', defined in proof of Theorem 9.1.

The mean flow-time for each sequence is given by

$$\bar{F}_s = \frac{1}{n}\left[\left(\sum_{\substack{\forall k \text{ in} \\ A \text{ and } B}} F_{k,s}\right) + F_{i,s} + F_{j,s}\right]$$

$$= \frac{1}{n}\left[\left(\sum_{\substack{\forall k \text{ in} \\ A \text{ and } B}} F_{k,s}\right) + (t_A + t_i) + (t_A + t_i + t_j)\right]$$

$$\bar{F}_{s'} = \frac{1}{n}\left[\sum_{\substack{\forall k \text{ in} \\ A \text{ and } B}} (F_{k,s'}) + F_{j,s'} + F_{i,s'}\right]$$

$$= \frac{1}{n}\left[\sum_{\substack{\forall k \text{ in} \\ A \text{ and } B}} (F_{k,s'}) + (t_A + t_j) + (t_A + t_j + t_i)\right]$$

Subtracting the mean flow of S' from that of S we get:

$$\bar{F}_S - \bar{F}_{S'} = \frac{1}{n}[t_i - t_j]$$

Recall that $t_i < t_j$; thus

$$\bar{F}_S - \bar{F}_{S'} = \frac{1}{n}[t_i - t_j] < 0.0$$

$$\bar{F}_S < \bar{F}_{S'}$$

That is to say, the mean flow-time of sequence S was less than the mean flow-time of S', because in S, tasks i and j were sequenced shortest processing-time first. This same pairwise interchange of adjacent tasks can be repeated whenever the change would place the shorter task ahead of the longer and each exchange would reduce the mean flow-time. Such improvements can be made until $t_{[1]} \leq t_{[2]} \leq \cdots \leq t_{[n]}$, which represents the minimum mean flow-time.

Using the SPT scheduling rule is obviously very simple. Calculating the mean flow of the sequence is also easy. Observe in Figure 9.3 that the processing time of the first of n tasks is added into the total flow-time n times, once for each task; and further, that the processing of the [i]th task is added

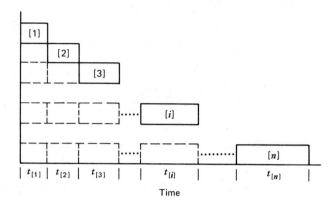

FIGURE 9.3   Example of an SPT sequence.

in $n - i + 1$ times. Thus, the calculation of the mean flow-time is given by

$$\bar{F}_s = \frac{1}{n}[nt_{[1]} + (n-1)t_{[2]} + \cdots + 2t_{[n-1]} + t_{[n]}] \tag{9.12}$$

Consider the following example problem with the objective of minimizing the mean flow-time.

Task	Processing Time (hours)
1	5
2	8
3	6
4	3
5	10
6	14
7	7
8	3

The SPT sequence is 4-8-1-3-7-2-5-6. The mean flow-time is

$$\bar{F}_s = \frac{1}{8}[(8 \times 3) + (7 \times 3) + (6 \times 5) + (5 \times 6) + (4 \times 7) + (3 \times 8) + (2 \times 10) + (1 \times 14)]$$

$$= \frac{1}{8}[24 + 21 + 30 + 30 + 28 + 24 + 20 + 14]$$

$$= 23.875 \text{ hours}$$

In addition to minimizing mean flow-time, the SPT scheduling rule minimizes the mean lateness, the mean waiting-time, and the mean number of tasks waiting as in-process inventory. Not only does SPT accomplish many desirable objectives, it also is a rather robust scheduling rule. The proof given above was for *n* tasks on one machine where all tasks were available at the start of the period. Scheduling research designed to find rules for more complicated situations consistently shows that SPT outperforms other scheduling rules, even though it may not guarantee the minimum of the objectives listed above. Thus, if the objective is to reduce in-process inventory and mean waiting-time of the tasks, the SPT scheduling rule can confidently be employed.

One caution is in order. If tasks continually arrive over time, the SPT rule will tend to avoid the longer task in favor of some newly arrived shorter one. Thus, it is possible to have very long flow-times for longer tasks. One simple solution to this difficulty is to look periodically for tasks that have been waiting a long time and run them next in spite of the existence of shorter tasks. Another solution is periodically to batch all tasks together and run them all before considering another batch of newly arrived tasks.

A variation of the SPT rule is the weighted-scheduling rule (WSPT), which is used when the importance of the tasks vary. The scheduler can assign an importance value, w_i, to each task. The larger the value, the more important the task. Then, by dividing the processing time by the weighting factor, the tendency is to move the more important task to an earlier position in the sequence. The weighted mean flow-time is given by

$$\bar{F}_{w,s} = \frac{\sum\limits_{i=1}^{n} w_i F_i}{\sum\limits_{i=1}^{n} w_i} \qquad (9.13)$$

Theorem 9.2   The WSPT Rule For Minimizing Weighted Mean Flow-Time on One Processor

When scheduling *n* tasks on a single processor where each task *i* has an importance weight w_i, the weighted mean flow-time is minimized by sequencing in order of

$$\frac{t_{[1]}}{w_{[1]}} \le \frac{t_{[2]}}{w_{[2]}} \le \cdots \le \frac{t_{[n]}}{w_{[n]}}$$

The proof of this theorem is accomplished exactly like that for Theorem 9.1 and is left to the reader. An example problem is, however, in order. Consider the previous set of tasks with the objective of minimizing weighted mean flow-time.

Task (i)	Processing Time (t_i), hours	Importance Weight (w_i)	$\dfrac{t_i}{w_i}$
1	5	1	5.0
2	8	2	4.0
3	6	3	2.0
4	3	1	3.0
5	10	2	5.0
6	14	3	4.7
7	7	2	3.5
8	3	1	3.0

The resulting sequence is 3-4-8-7-2-6-1-5. The mean flow-time as given by Equation 9.12 is 27.0 hours, and the weighted mean flow as given by Equation 9.13 is 27.47 hours.

Now consider the problem when due dates exist and the objective is to minimize some measure of lateness or tardiness as given by Equations 9.6 through 9.10. Mean lateness for the simple n task, one-processor problem is minimized by the SPT rule.

Theorem 9.3   The SPT Rule for Minimizing Mean Lateness on One Processor

When scheduling n tasks on a single processor, mean lateness is minimized by sequencing in order of

$$t_{[1]} \leq t_{[2]} \leq \cdots \leq t_{[n]}$$

Proof

Mean lateness is given by Equations 9.2, 9.4, and 9.6 to be

$$\bar{L}_s = \frac{1}{n} \sum_{i=1}^{n} (F_i - d_i)$$

$$= \frac{1}{n} \sum_{i=1}^{n} F_i - \frac{1}{n} \sum_{i=1}^{n} d_i$$

$$= \bar{F}_s - \bar{d}_s$$

Note that $\bar{d}_s$ is the average of the given set of due dates that are constant and independent of the sequence. Thus, to minimize $\bar{L}_s$, we need only minimize $\bar{F}_s$ using the SPT rule.

Consider once again the previous example problem, expanded now to include due dates.

Task (i)	Processing Time (t_i)	Due Date (d_i)
1	5	15
2	8	10
3	6	15
4	3	25
5	10	20
6	14	40
7	7	45
8	3	50

Recall that the SPT rule resulted in a sequence of 4-8-1-3-7-2-5-6. The lateness of each task is given below.

Task (i)	Completion Time (c_i)	Due Date (d_i)	Lateness ($L_{i,s}$)
4	3	25	−22
8	6	50	−44
1	11	15	−4
3	17	15	2
7	24	45	−21
2	32	10	22
5	42	20	22
6	56	40	16

Mean lateness is therefore −3.625 hours.

Another rule, first reported by Jackson (1955),[†] is referred to as the

†J. R. Jackson, "Scheduling a Production Line to Minimize Maximum Tardiness," research report no. 43, Management Science Research Project, University of California at Los Angeles, January 1955.

*E*arliest *Due-Date* (EDD) rule. It is used to minimize the maximum task lateness or maximum task tardiness. Unfortunately the rule tends to make more tasks tardy and increases the mean tardiness.

Theorem 9.4   The EDD Rule for Minimizing Max Lateness on One Processor

When scheduling n tasks on a single processor, maximum task lateness and maximum task tardiness are minimized by sequencing in EDD order, or such that

$$d_{[1]} \leq d_{[2]} \leq \cdots \leq d_{[n]}$$

The proof is similar to that for Theorem 9.1, except lateness is summed rather than flow time where the lateness of tasks i and j are given by their completion time less their due date.

Consider once again the example problem. Recall that the SPT rule resulted in four tasks being tardy, with a mean lateness of -3.625 hours and a maximum lateness of 22 hours. The EDD rule would give a sequence of 2-1-3-5-4-6-7-8.

The comparable lateness of the EDD rule is as follows:

Task i	Completion Time c_i	Due Date d_i	Lateness L_i
2	8	10	-2
1	13	15	-2
3	19	15	4
5	29	20	9
4	32	25	7
6	46	40	6
7	53	45	8
8	56	50	6

Thus the number of tasks late increased from four to six. The mean lateness increased from -3.625 hours to 4.5 hours. The maximum lateness and tardiness, however, were reduced from 22 hours to 9 hours.

Suppose the penalty for being tardy was the same for all tasks and was independent of how tardy they were. In this situation, the objective would be to minimize the number of tardy jobs. The EDD rule gives the desired schedule only if it results in zero or one tardy task. If more than one tardy task results, an algorithm attributed to Hodgson† will yield the desired objective. Hodgson's algorithm is given below:

Algorithm 9.1 Hodgson: Minimize the Number of Tardy Tasks for One Processor

Step 1 Order all tasks by the EDD rule; if zero or one tasks are tardy (positive lateness), then stop. Otherwise go to step 2.

Step 2 Starting at the beginning of the EDD sequence and working toward the end, identify the first tardy task. If no further tasks are tardy, go to step 4; otherwise go to step 3.

Step 3 Suppose that the tardy task is in the *i*th position in the sequence. Examine the first *i* tasks in the sequence and identify the one with the longest processing time. Remove that task and set it aside. Revise the completion time of the other tasks to reflect the removal, and return to step 2.

Step 4 Place all those tasks that were set aside in any order at the end of the sequence.

Consider the example problem in light of Hodgson's algorithm. The EDD rule used in step 1 resulted in the sequence 2-1-3-5-4-6-7-8 with six tardy tasks. Thus we move to step 2 and 3, as shown below.

Task i:	2	1	3	5	4	6	7	8
Processing time t_i:	8	5	6	10	3	14	7	3
Completion time c_i:	8	13	19	29	32	46	53	56
Due date d_i:	10	15	15	20	25	40	45	50
Lateness L_i:	−2	−2	4	9	7	6	8	6

Task 3 is the first tardy task. Task 2 has the longest processing time of the first three tasks, thus it is set aside.

Task i:	1	3	5	4	6	7	8
t_i:	5	6	10	3	14	7	3
c_i:	5	11	21	24	38	45	48
d_i:	15	15	20	25	40	45	50
L_i:	−10	−4	1	−1	−2	0	−2

Task 5 is the first tardy; and of tasks 1, 3, and 5, task 5 is the longest. Thus it

---

†Hodgson's algorithm appears as a note in J. M. Moore, "Sequencing *n* Jobs on One Machine to Minimize the Number of Tardy Jobs" (*Management Science*, vol. 17, no. 1, September 1968). Copyright © 1968 The Institute of Management Sciences.

is set aside.

Task i:	1	3	4	6	7	8
t_i:	5	6	3	14	7	3
c_i:	5	11	14	28	35	38
d_i:	15	15	25	40	45	50
L_i:	-10	-4	-11	-12	-10	-12

No more tasks are tardy. Thus, the first part of the sequence is 1-3-4-6-7-8 and the last part consists of tasks 2 and 5 in any order. Let us add these two on in an SPT order. Thus, the sequence is 1-3-4-6-7-8-2-5. The resulting sequence yields the following result.

Task i	Completion Time c_i	Due Date d_i	Lateness L_i
1	5	15	-10
3	11	15	-4
4	14	25	-11
6	28	40	-12
7	35	45	-10
8	38	50	-12
2	46	10	36
5	56	20	36

Thus the number of tasks late is two. The mean lateness is 1.625 hours, as compared with a minimum of -3.625. The maximum lateness for Hodgson is 36, as compared with a minimum of 9 hours.

Perhaps the most significant of the tardiness objectives is the desire to reduce mean tardiness. This is obviously the case if the penalty for tardiness is the same for all tasks and linear with respect to how tardy the task is. Unfortunately, there is no simple scheduling rule, even for n tasks and one processor, which minimizes mean tardiness. In specialized situations, as shown by Baker, simple rules do apply. Those cases are as follows.

Theorem 9.5   The EDD Rule for Minimizing Mean Tardiness on One Processor

If the EDD rule produces zero or one tardy jobs, then it minimizes mean tardiness.

Theorem 9.6   The SPT Rule for Minimizing Mean Tardiness on One Processor

If all tasks have the same due date, or if SPT results in all tasks being tardy, then the SPT rule minimizes mean tardiness.

Another scheduling rule that tends to address mean tardiness is the shortest SLACK time rule. Slack time for task i is defined as the time remaining before its due date less its processing time. If the schedule is to begin at $t = 0.0$ and the due date is expressed as units of time after the start time, slack time equals the due date less the processing time. Let us sequence the tasks in the example problem according to the shortest slack-time first.

Task i	Processing Time t_i	Due Date d_i	Slack Time SL_i
1	5	15	10
2	8	10	2
3	6	15	9
4	3	25	22
5	10	20	10
6	14	40	26
7	7	45	38
8	3	50	47

The resulting sequence is therefore 2-3-1-5-4-6-7-8, which results in the following sequence.

Task i	Completion Time c_i	Due Date d_i	Tardiness T_i
2	8	10	0
3	14	15	0
1	19	15	4
5	29	20	9
4	32	25	7
6	46	40	6
7	53	45	8
8	56	50	6

Step	α	β	γ	Step 2 Calculations $F_\alpha + \max(t_\beta, t_\gamma) \leq \max(d_\beta, d_\gamma)$	$t_\beta \leq t_\gamma$	Step 3 Calculations $F_\alpha - t_\alpha + \max(t_\alpha, t_\beta) \leq \max(d_\alpha, d_\beta)$	$t_\alpha \leq t_\beta$
2	2	1	3	$8 + 6 \leq 15$ yes	$5 \leq 6$ yes		
2	1	3	5	$13 + 10 \leq 20$ no	$6 \leq 10$ yes		
2	3	5	4	$19 + 10 \leq 25$ no	$10 \leq 3$ no		
3	3	4			$10 \leq 14$ yes	$19 - 6 + 6 \leq 25$ yes	$6 \leq 3$ no
2	4	5	6	$22 + 14 \leq 40$ yes	$10 \leq 14$ yes		
2	5	6	7	$32 + 14 \leq 45$ no	$14 \leq 7$ no		
3	5	7			$14 \leq 3$ no	$32 - 10 + 10 \leq 45$ yes	$10 \leq 7$ no
2	7	6	8	$39 + 14 \leq 50$ no			
3	7	8				$39 - 7 + 7 \leq 50$ yes	$7 \leq 3$ no

Sequence 2-1-3-4-5-7-8-6

FIGURE 9.4 Exercise of the Wilkerson–Irwin algorithm on the example problem.

The SLACK rule thus yields a mean tardiness of 5.00 hours. Correspondingly, the SPT, EDD, and Hodgson rules yielded mean tardiness values of 7.75, 5.00, and 9.0 hours, respectively.

An algorithm attributed to Wilkerson–Irwin† sometimes minimizes mean tardiness for the *n* task and one-processor problem. The algorithm presented here is discussed in more detail in Wilkerson–Irwin and in Baker. Before reading on, refer to Figure 9.4. Note the three columns headed α, β, and γ. Tasks of interest can be designated in three ways. They can be the last task on the list of scheduled tasks, the pivot task that is a candidate to join the scheduled list, or the next task on the list of unscheduled tasks. The task in the α column at any time is the last task on the scheduled list.

The order in which tasks appear in the α column is the resulting schedule. There exists in the algorithm a list of unscheduled tasks in EDD order. The task in the γ column is the highest task from the EDD list. The task in the β column is called the pivot task in that it is the candidate to become α and join the desired schedule.‡

Algorithm 9.2   Wilkerson–Irwin: Reduce or Minimize Mean Tardiness for One Processor

Step 1   Initialize the set of tasks in EDD order. Compare the first two tasks on the list, call these tasks *a* and *b*, respectively. If $\max(t_a, t_b) \leq \max(d_a, d_b)$, assign task *a* to the α column and *b* to the β column. Otherwise assign the shortest task to α and the other to β. The third task in the EDD order is assigned to the γ column.

Step 2   Compare β and γ to see if β will join α on the scheduled list. If $t_\beta \leq t_\gamma$ or if $F_\alpha + \max\{t_\beta, t_\gamma\} \leq \max\{d_\beta, d_\gamma\}$, move the task in the β column to α and the task in the γ column to β. The next task in the EDD list becomes γ. If there are no more tasks on the EDD list, add the α and β tasks to the schedule and stop. Otherwise repeat step 2. If both conditions listed above fail, go to step 3.

Step 3   Put β back in the EDD list and move the γ task to the β column. Compare α and β to see if β will join α on the scheduled list. If $t_\alpha \leq t_\beta$ or if $F_\alpha - t_\alpha + \max\{t_\alpha, t_\beta\} \leq \max\{d_\alpha, d_\beta\}$, move the task in the β column to the α column and select the next two tasks from the EDD list to be the new β and γ. Return to step 2. If both conditions above fail, then go to step 4.

Step 4   Put the task in the α column back on the EDD list and assign the

†J. L. Wilkerson and J. D. Irwin, "An Improved Method for Scheduling Independent Tasks," *AIIE Transactions*, vol. 3, no. 3, September 1971.

last task to go into the scheduled list as the new α. Return to step 3. If no task exists in the scheduled list, put β on the scheduled list and the first two tasks on the EDD list become β and γ. Then go to step 2.

Algorithm 9.2 does not always minimize mean tardiness. Define the tardy period for each tardy task to be that time period between its due date and its completion date. If we review the tardy periods for each tardy task and find that they do not overlap, the solution is optimal: that is, if no two tasks are tardy at the same time, the solution minimizes mean tardiness.

Consider once again the example problem in which the EDD rule gave a sequence of 2-1-3-5-4-6-7-8. Figure 9.4 is a step-by-step solution of this problem using the Wilkerson–Irwin algorithm. The resulting sequence is 2-1-3-4-5-7-8-6. This sequence results in the following tardiness.

Task i	Completion Time t_i	Due Date d_i	Tardiness T_i
2	8	10	0
1	13	15	0
3	19	15	4
4	22	25	0
5	32	20	12
7	39	45	0
8	42	50	0
6	56	40	16

This yields a minimum mean tardiness of 4.00 hours, which was minimum. Of the 40,320 possible sequences, only four had this minimum mean-tardiness result.

Unlike the SPT rule, the EDD and SLACK rules as well as the Hodgson and Wilkerson–Irwin algorithms are not exceptionally robust. For more complex problems the rules may perform well, but they should be utilized with care.

Let us pause for a brief summary. In this section we have discussed the problem of scheduling n tasks on one processor. All tasks are available at the beginning of the scheduling period and all processing times are known and are independent of the sequence chosen. The very desirable objective of minimizing makespan is accomplished by every sequence and equal to the sum of the processing time of all tasks. Other objectives are addressed as indicated in Table 9.1. The results of the example problem used in the section are given in the table for a simple comparison.

TABLE 9.1 Comparison of Six Scheduling Rules Relative to Their Intended Objective and Their Performance on the Example Problem in the Section.

Objective (To minimize)	Rule to Use	Mean Flow-Time	Weight Mean Flow	Mean Lateness	Max Tardiness	No. of Tardy Tasks	Mean Tardiness
Mean flow-time	SPT	23.9	29.0	-3.6	22	4	7.8
Weighted mean flow	WSPT	27.0	27.5	-0.5	36	4	10.6
Mean lateness	SPT	23.9	29.0	-3.6	22	4	7.8
Maximum tardiness	EDD	32.0	31.7	4.5	9	6	5.0
Number of tardy tasks	Hodgson	29.1	29.9	1.6	36	2	9.0
Mean tardiness	SLACK (does well)	32.1	31.1	4.6	9	6	5.0
Mean tardiness	Wilkerson–Irwin	31.1	59.0	1.4	16	3	4.0

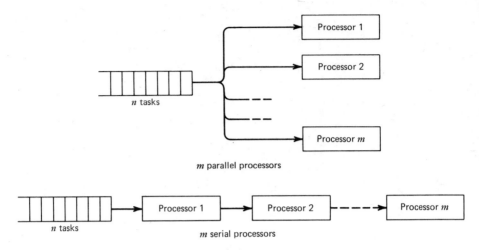

FIGURE 9.5   **Parallel- and serial-processor scheduling problems.**

9.4   SCHEDULING *n* TASKS ON *m* PROCESSORS

Scheduling problems become complex very fast. The last section presented simple rules or algorithms that deal effectively with single processors. In this section, the problem is complicated by considering several processors. First, the problem of *m* parallel processors will be examined; in this case, each task must visit only one of the processors. Subsequently, the problem of *m* processors in series will be presented; in this case, each task must visit each process in the same order. These two situations are illustrated in Figure 9.5. As shall be seen, even these simple increases in complexity make the problem considerably more difficult.

     Consider first the case in which *m* identical processors exist. The problem is to select both the processor to be used and the sequence for the tasks on each processor. If the objective is to minimize mean flow-time, a simple variation of the SPT scheduling rule can be used. The algorithm is given below.

Algorithm 9.3   **Minimize Mean Flow-Time on *m* Parallel Processors**

     Step 1   Sequence all tasks in SPT order.

     Step 2   Taking the tasks from the list one at a time, schedule them on the processor with the least amount of time already assigned. Break ties arbitrarily.

     To illustrate this procedure, consider the scheduling of the following 10 tasks on three identical processors.

Task *i*	Processing Time t_i (hours)
1	5
2	6
3	3
4	8
5	7
6	2
7	3
8	5
9	4
10	2

The SPT sequence is 6-10-3-7-9-1-8-2-5-4. Figure 9.6 illustrates the resulting schedule.

The mean flow-time of this schedule is 8.1 hours and the makespan is 18 hours. The first lesson to be learned from this algorithm is that the desire to reduce mean flow-time is best met by always scheduling the shortest task on the next available processor. The second lesson is how to handle scheduling situations with two or more identical processors in parallel. Such scheduling problems can generally be handled by first ordering all tasks using some appropriate single-processor rule and then allocating the tasks to the processors on a least scheduled-time first basis.

Once we get beyond the one-processor problem, the makespan of the schedule can no longer be considered independent of the sequence selected. Thus, if makespan and its corresponding processor-efficiency connotations

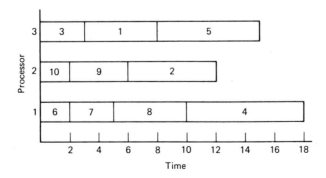

FIGURE 9.6 Illustrative schedule for Algorithm 9.3.

are the objective, an appropriate scheduling rule must be considered. There are no rules or algorithms that guarantee a minimum makespan schedule. A simple procedure has been shown to consistently perform well, however. Essentially, it is the reverse of the SPT rule used in Algorithm 9.3: that is, the algorithm is based on the *Longest Processing-Time* first (LPT) rule, as indicated below. Once the LPT rule is used to determine which processor to schedule each task upon, the tasks on each processor then are put in SPT order so that mean flow-time is minimized for that particular processor allocation scheme.

Algorithm 9.4   Reduce Makespan as well as Mean Flow-Times on *m* Processors

Step 1   Sequence the *n* tasks in LPT order.

Step 2   Schedule each task from the LPT list to that processor which has the least time already assigned. Break ties arbitrarily.

Step 3   After the tasks are scheduled, reverse their sequence on each machine, putting the tasks on each processor in SPT order.

To illustrate this algorithm, consider the previous problem of scheduling 10 tasks on three processors. The LPT order for the tasks is 4-5-2-1-8-9-3-7-6-10. Figure 9.7 shows the Gantt chart for the three processors scheduled according to step 2 of the algorithm. The reversal of this sequence on each processor is illustrated in Figure 9.8.

The mean flow-time of this schedule is 8.1 hours. The makespan is 16 hours. Although the algorithm cannot guarantee a minimum makespan, it does consistently yield a good schedule relative to this objective.

The essence of Algorithm 9.4 can be seen in Figures 9.7 and 9.8. Minimizing makespan is the same as minimizing the idle time found at the end of the schedule, as seen in Figure 9.7. In this example there are two hours of idle time on processor 1 and one hour on processor 2.

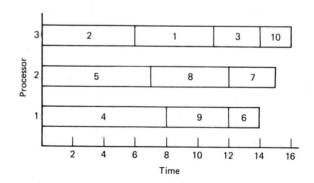

FIGURE 9.7   Illustrative schedule after step 2 of Algorithm 9.4.

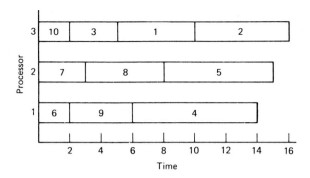

FIGURE 9.8 Illustrative schedule after step 3 of Algorithm 9.4.

When concerned about makespan, the desire is to leave as many short tasks as possible to the end so that they can fill in the remaining blocks of available time. The reversing of the sequence indicated in Figure 9.8 maintains the same processor loadings but puts each processor's tasks in an SPT order.

If the objective of the scheduling problems is one of the functions of tardiness discussed in Section 9.3, minimizing algorithms do not exist. Recall that the EDD (earliest due-date next) rule addressed the objective of reduced maximum lateness and the Hodgson algorithm addressed the objective of reducing the number of late tasks, whereas the SLACK rule and Wilkerson–Irwin algorithm addressed the objective of mean tardiness. The EDD, SLACK, and Wilkerson–Irwin rules can be adapted to algorithms similar to 9.3 with good results.

Algorithm 9.5 EDD Rule for Reducing Maximum Tardiness on m Parallel Processors

Step 1 Sequence the tasks in EDD order.

Step 2 Taking the tasks one at a time from the EDD list, schedule them on the processor with the least assigned time. Break ties arbitrarily.

To illustrate this algorithm, consider the previous problem with due dates added as shown on page 320.

The EDD sequence is therefore 6-10-1-7-2-8-5-4-3-9. The schedule given by Algorithm 9.5 is shown in Figure 9.9. The mean tardiness, maximum tardiness, and number of tardy tasks are 0.6 hours, four hours, and three tasks, respectively.

For the SLACK rule, the identical-parallel-processor equivalent is given by Algorithm 9.6.

Task i	Processing Time t_i	Due Date d_i	Slack time SL_i
1	5	8	3
2	6	9	3
3	3	14	11
4	8	12	4
5	7	11	4
6	2	5	3
7	3	8	5
8	5	10	5
9	4	15	11
10	2	7	5

Algorithm 9.6   SLACK for Reducing Tardiness on m Processors

Step 1   Sequence the tasks in SLACK order.

Step 2   Taking the tasks one at a time from the SLACK list, schedule them
on the processor with the least assign time. Break ties arbitrarily.

The SLACK-time sequence for the example problem is 1-2-6-4-5-7-8-10-3-9.
The schedule given by Algorithm 9.6 is shown in Figure 9.10. The resulting
mean tardiness, maximum tardiness, and number of tardy tasks are 1.3 hours,
five hours, and six tasks, respectively.

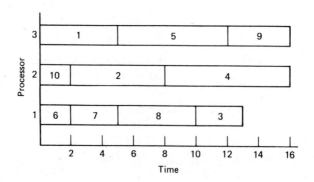

FIGURE 9.9   Illustration of example problem scheduled with Algorithm 9.5.

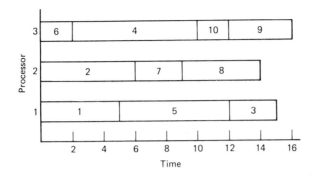

FIGURE 9.10 Illustration of example problem scheduled with Algorithm 9.6.

An algorithm suggested by Dagramici and Surkis† has proven to work well in reducing mean tardiness for the *m* parallel processor problem. In essence, the algorithm generates three different schedules using Algorithms 9.3 (SPT), 9.5 (EDD), and 9.6 (SLACK). It then applies the Wilkerson–Irwin procedure (Algorithm 9.2) to each individual processor. The schedule with the least mean tardiness is then implemented.

Algorithm 9.7   Reduce Mean Tardiness on *m* Parallel Processors

Conduct steps 1 through 3 three times, once each for the SPT, EDD, and SLACK initial priority rules. Select that schedule from step 3 with the least mean tardiness and implement.

Step 1   Arrange the unscheduled tasks according to the initial-priority rule.

Step 2   Taking the tasks from the list one at a time, assign them to the processor with the least assigned time. Repeat step 2 until all tasks are assigned.

Step 3   Take each processor separately and minimize the mean tardiness of those tasks assigned to it. This can be done using Algorithm 9.2 in this text.

To illustrate this algorithm, the example problem will again be solved. Recall

---

†A. Dagramici and J. Surkis, "Scheduling Independent Jobs on Parallel Identical Processors," *Management Science,* vol. 25, no. 12, December 1979. Reprinted by permission of A. Dagramici and J. Surkis. Copyright © 1979 The Institute of Management Sciences.

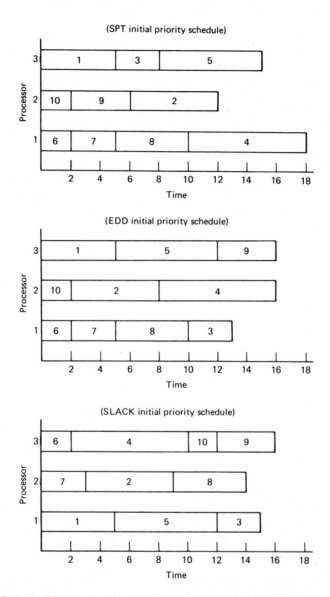

FIGURE 9.11   Illustration of example problem scheduled with Algorithm 9.7.

that the SPT schedule was represented in Figure 9.6, the EDD schedule in Figure 9.9, and the SLACK schedule in 9.10. For each of these schedules, the Wilkerson–Irwin algorithm was applied to each of the three processors. The three resulting schedules are represented in Figure 9.11. The Wilkerson–Irwin algorithm resulted in only minimal changes to the SPT and SLACK schedules. The mean tardy time of the SPT, EDD, and SLACK initial-priority schedules were 1.3, 0.6, and 1.2, respectively. Thus, the EDD schedule modified by Wilkerson–Irwin would be implemented.

Recall that the Hodgson algorithm first sequenced all tasks via the EDD rule. Then it looked for tardy tasks in the EDD sequence. If tardy tasks were found, the algorithm called for removing the longest task up to and including the first tardy task and placing it at the end of the sequence. For one processor, this minimized the number of tardy tasks. Algorithm 9.8 is the equivalent to Hodgson for *m* parallel processors.

Johnson's rule

Algorithm 9.8   Reduce Number of Tardy Tasks on *m* Parallel Processors

Step 1   Schedule all tasks using Algorithm 9.5.

Step 2   For each processor, review the tasks starting with the earliest in the sequence, until a tardy task is found. Suppose that task for processor *j* is in position *i*.

Step 3   Examine the first *i* tasks on processor *j* and identify the one with the longest processing time. Remove that task and place it last in the sequence of processor *j*. Revise the completion times of all tasks to reflect this change and return to step 2.

To illustrate Algorithm 9.8, consider the example problem. After step 1 we have the sequence given in Figure 9.9. Note that there were three tardy tasks; 4, 5, and 9. According to steps 2 and 3, there is nothing that can be done on processors 1 and 2. For processor 3, however, task 5 is the first tardy task and the one to be removed using step 3. The new sequence makes task 5 even more tardy, but task 9 will now be on time. The new schedule thus is given by Figure 9.12. The mean tardy, maximum tardy, and number of tardy tasks are 0.9 hours, 5.0 hours, and two tasks, respectively.

In summary, for *m* parallel processors we have complicated the scheduling process, but the rules and algorithms presented in Section 9.3 can be adapted to offer approaches to solving practical problems. Table 9.2 summarizes the algorithms and their use, as well as their performance on the example problem.

Consider now another simple extension of the "*n* tasks on one processor" scheduling problem. Suppose that there are *m* processors in series as indicated earlier in Figure 9.5. Once again, the objectives of scheduling are typically to reduce the makespan of the *n* tasks, reduce their mean flow, and reduce some measure of tardiness.

With regard to the makespan objective, an optimal schedule can be found for the two-processor cases. The algorithm to achieve minimum makespan is

TABLE 9.2   Rules for Scheduling *n* Tasks on *m* Parallel Processors

Objective (to Reduce)	Algorithm	Mean Flow	Make-span	Max. Tardy	No. of Tardy	Mean Tardy
Mean flow-time	9.3	8.1	18	6	3	1.3
Makespan	9.4	8.1	16	7	4	1.4
Max. Tardy	9.5	8.9	16	4	3	0.6
Tardiness	9.6	10.1	16	5	6	1.3
Mean Tardy	9.7	8.9	16	4	3	0.6
No. of Tardy	9.8	8.8	16	5	2	0.9

generally called Johnson's rule.† If *n* tasks are to be sequenced on two processors such that each task must visit each processor, the tasks should pass through each processor in the same order. In fact, for the more general *m*-processor case and for the makespan and mean-flow objectives, the tasks should pass through the first two processors in the same order. Although it may be different from the order on processors 1 and 2, the tasks should also pass through the last two processors in the same order. The algorithm for Johnson's rule is as given on page 325.

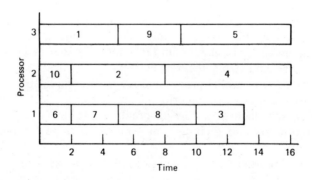

FIGURE 9.12   Illustration of example problem scheduled with Algorithm 9.8.

†S. M. Johnson, "Optimal Two- and Three-Stage Production Schedules with Setup Times Included," *Naval Research Logistics Quarterly*, vol. 1, no. 1, March 1954.

Algorithm 9.9   Johnson's Rule to Minimize Makespan on Two Serial Processors

Step 1   For all tasks i find the minimum of $t_{i,1}$ and $t_{i,2}$, the processing time on the first and second processors.

Step 2   If the minimum time is on processor 1, (i.e., $t_{i,1}$) then schedule the task to the next available position starting at the beginning of the sequence. Go to step 3. If the minimum time is on processor 2, (i.e., $t_{i,2}$), then schedule the task in the next available position starting from the end of the sequence. Ties may be broken arbitrarily.

Step 3   Remove the scheduled task from the list. If tasks remain, return to step 1; otherwise stop.

To illustrate Johnson's rule consider the following example containing 10 tasks.

Task i	Time on Proc. 1 (hours)	Time on Proc. 2 (hours)
1	3	5
2	6	2
3	2	8
4	7	6
5	6	6
6	5	9
7	5	4
8	3	2
9	6	8
10	10	4

The smallest time of the 10 tasks are the 2s found in $t_{2,2}$, $t_{3,1}$, and $t_{8,2}$. Thus, task 3 should be scheduled at the beginning of the schedule and tasks 2 and 8 at the end. We choose to break the tie between 2 and 8 by scheduling last that task with the longest $t_{i,1}$—that is, task 2. The schedule, so far, is thus

$$\underline{3} \, \_ \, \_ \, \_ \, \_ \, \_ \, \_ \, \underline{8} \, \underline{2}$$

With these tasks removed from the list, the minimum processing time is 3 for $t_{i,1}$ which puts task 1 in the number 2 scheduling position.

$$\underline{3} \, \underline{1} \, \_ \, \_ \, \_ \, \_ \, \underline{8} \, \underline{2}$$

Continuing on in this fashion leads to the sequence 3-1-6-9-5-4-7-10-8-2. Figure 9.13 represents this sequence. Note that the makespan is 56 hours. Also note that the first processor is working continuously until all tasks are

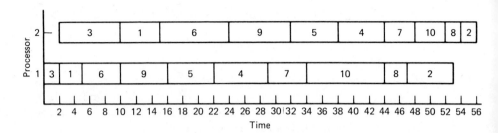

FIGURE 9.13   Illustrative problem scheduled with Algorithm 9.9.

finished on it. As for the second processor, it is possible to have tasks waiting until it becomes available or for the processor to wait until a task finishes processor 1. It is perfectly reasonable to include tasks in the schedule that require only one or the other of the two processors. In this case a processing time of zero is used and the tasks find themselves either at the very beginning or very end of the schedule.

The essence of Johnson's rule is simple to grasp. The desire is to get a few jobs through processor 1 quickly so as to give processor 2 something to do. At the end of the schedule the desire is to leave tasks with short time-needs on the last processors so that once the first processor is complete the last processor can quickly finish up.

A generalization of Johnson's rule for m processors was suggested by Campbell, Dudek, and Smith.† The idea is to use a Johnson-like rule to create $m - 1$ possible schedules and select the best of these for implementation. For the first schedule one applies Algorithm 9.9 to the $t_{i,1}^*$ and $t_{i,2}^*$ where

$$t_{i,1}^* = t_{i,1}$$

$$t_{1,2}^* = t_{i,m}$$

that is, the processing times on the first and last processors. For the second schedule,

$$t_{i,1}^* = t_{i,1} + t_{i,2}$$

$$t_{i,2}^* = t_{i,m} + t_{i,m-1}$$

that is, the processing time on the first two and last two processors. For the

---

† H. G. Campbell, R. A. Dudek, and M. L. Smith, "A Heuristic Algorithm for the n Job m Machine Sequencing Problem," Management Science, vol. 16, no. 10, June 1970. Reprinted by permission of H. G. Campbell, R. A. Dudek, and M. L. Smith. Copyright © 1970 The Institute of Management Sciences.

*K*th schedule,

$$t_{i,1}^* = \sum_{k=1}^{K} t_{i,k} \tag{9.14}$$

$$t_{i,2}^* = \sum_{k=1}^{K} t_{i,m-k+1} \tag{9.15}$$

Using this approach, $m - 1$ schedules are generated. That schedule that has the least makespan is then implemented. This approach does not guaranteee the minimum makespan schedule. In fact, depending on the nature of the processing times in any given problem, the approach may be very good one time and very poor the next. Research has shown, however, that the approach tends to be more effective than other simple heuristics presently available.

The following algorithm implements the Campbell, Dudek, and Smith approach.

TCJ calls this CDS heuristic

Algorithm 9.10   Reduce Makespan in the *m* Serial Processor Problem

Step 1   Let $K = 1$. Calculate $t_{i,1}^*$ and $t_{i,2}^*$ using Equations 9.14 and 9.15.

Step 2   Schedule the *m* tasks using Algorithm 9.9 where $t_{i,1} = t_{i,1}^*$ and $t_{i,2} = t_{i,2}^*$ as found in step 1. Record the sequence and calculate makespan. If the makespan is the least found so far, save the sequence and makespan values.

Step 3   If $K = (m - 1)$, stop; the most recently saved sequence is the one to implement. If $K \neq (m - 1)$, increase K by 1 and return to step 1.

To illustrate this algorithm and develop a method for calculating makespan for the *m*-processor situation, consider the following three-processor problem.

Task *i*	Time on Proc. 1 (hours)	Time on Proc. 2 (hours)	Time on Proc. 3 (hours)
1	4	3	5
2	3	3	4
3	2	1	6
4	5	3	2
5	6	4	7
6	1	8	3

For $K = 1$ and $K = 2$, the values of $t_{i,1}^*$ and $t_{i,2}^*$ are

Task	$K = 1$		$K = 2$	
i	$t_{i,1}^*$	$t_{i,2}^*$	$t_{i,1}^*$	$t_{i,2}^*$
1	4	5	7	8
2	3	4	6	7
3	2	6	3	7
4	5	2	8	5
5	6	7	10	11
6	1	3	9	11

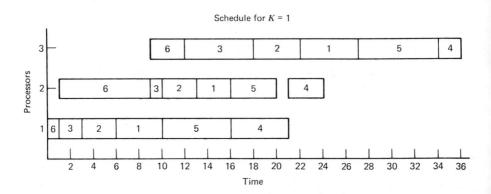

Schedule for $K = 1$

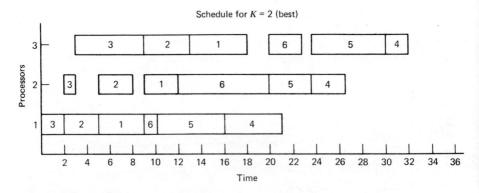

Schedule for $K = 2$ (best)

FIGURE 9.14   Illustrative example problem scheduled with Algorithm 9.10.

TABLE 9.3 Illustrative Calculation of Inserted Idle Time for Example Problem

Sequence Position	Task Number	Time on Proc. 1	Time on Proc. 2	Idle time Proc. 2
[1]	i	$t_{[i],1}$	$t_{[i],2}$	$I_{[i],2}$
[1]	3	2	1	2
[2]	2	3	3	2
[3]	1	4	3	1
[4]	6	1	8	0
[5]	5	6	4	0
[6]	4	5	3	0
			Totals 22	5

$I_{[1],2} = t_{[1],1} = 2$

$I_{[2],2} = \max\{0, (t_{[1],1} + t_{[2],1} - t_{[1],2} - I_{[1],2})\}$

$\quad = \max\{0, (2 + 3 - 1 - 2)\}$

$\quad = \max\{0, 2\} = 2$

$I_{[3],2} = \max\{0, (2 + 3 + 4 - 1 - 3 - 2 - 2)\} = 1$

$I_{[4],2} = \max\{0, (2 + 3 + 4 + 1 - 1 - 3 - 3 - 2 - 2 - 1)\} = 0$

$I_{[5],2} = \max\{0, (2 + 3 + 4 + 1 + 6 - 1 - 3 - 3 - 3 - 2 - 2 - 1 - 0)\} = 0$

$I_{[6],2} = \max\{0, (2 + 3 + 4 + 1 + 6 + 5 - 1 - 3 - 3 - 3 - 4 - 2 - 2 - 1 - 0 - 0)\} = 0$

Applying Algorithm 9.9 for $K = 1$ yields a sequence of 6-3-2-1-5-4. For $K = 2$ the corresponding sequence is 3-2-1-5-6-4. The resulting two schedules are seen in Figure 9.14. Note that for $K = 1$ makespan was 36 hours and for $K = 2$ the makespan was 33 hours. The sequence to implement is thus 3-2-1-5-6-4.

In order to understand how makespan is calculated, study for a moment the $K = 2$ schedule in Figure 9.14. Note that the makespan equals the time that the last task was completed on the last processor; and further, that the completion time of that last task equals the sum of the processing times of all tasks on the last processor plus the sum of all periods when that processor was idle.

To calculate makespan, we first must renumber the tasks according to their position in the sequence. That is, the first task in the sequence is denoted by [1] and the ith task in the sequence is denoted by [i]. In Figure 9.14 for $K = 2$, the first task in the sequence is task 3, thus [1] = 3. Similar renumberings are [2] = 2, [3] = 1, [4] = 6, [5] = 5, and [6] = 4. Now, let the inserted idle time just prior to the execution of task $[i]$ on processor j equal $I_{[i],j}$. Note that for processor $1: I_{[i],1} = 0$ for all tasks, there is no idle time on the first processor. Note also that the inserted idle times for various tasks on processor 2 are given by

$$I_{[1],2} = t_{[1],1}$$

$$I_{[2],2} = \max\{0, (t_{[1],1} + t_{[2],1} - t_{[1],2} - I_{[1],2})\}$$

$$I_{[3],2} = \max\{0, (t_{[1],1} + t_{[2],1} + t_{[3],1} - t_{[1],2} - t_{[2],2} - I_{[1],2} - I_{[2],2})\}$$

$$I_{[i],2} = \max\left\{0, \left(\sum_{k=1}^{i} t_{[k],1} - \sum_{k=1}^{i-1} t_{[k],2} - \sum_{k=1}^{i-1} I_{[k],2}\right)\right\} \qquad (9.16)$$

To illustrate the use of Equation 9.16, Table 9.3 shows the calculation of inserted idle time for all tasks in the $K = 2$ schedule shown in Figure 9.14. Note that the completion time of the last task on processor 2 equals the sum of the processing times of all tasks on processor 2 plus the sum of the inserted idle time. In the example covered in Table 9.3, this completion time is $22 + 5$ or 27 hours, which can be verified pictorially in Figure 9.14.

The next step in calculating the makespan for the m-processor problem is to calculate the inserted idle times for processor 3. Glance back at Figure 9.14 for $K = 2$ on the second processor. Visualize the redefining of the processing time for each task on processor 2 to equal its old processing time plus the inserted idle time. This redefinition essentially removes all inserted idle time from processor 2 while keeping the completion time of all tasks the same. With this accomplished, one can calculate inserted idle time on processor 3 exactly as calculated on processor 2. Formally, this redefinition is as follows.

$$t_{[i],2}^{New} = t_{[i],2} + I_{[i],2} \qquad (9.17)$$

$$I_{[1],3} = t_{[1],2}^{New}$$

$$I_{[2],3} = \max\left\{0, \left(t_{[1],2}^{New} + t_{[2],2}^{New} - t_{[1],3} - I_{[1],3}\right)\right\}$$

$$I_{[i],3} = \max\left\{0, \left(\sum_{k=1}^{i} t_{[k],2}^{New} - \sum_{k=1}^{i-1} t_{[k],3} - \sum_{k=1}^{i-1} I_{[k],3}\right)\right\} \qquad (9.18)$$

To illustrate this second step in the calculation, Table 9.4 shows the calculation of idle time on processor 3 for the $K = 2$ example of Figure 9.14.

As with the processor 2, the flow time of the last task on processor 3 equals the sum of the $t_{[i],3}$ and $I_{[i],3}$ columns from Table 9.4. This total is 33 hours. Since the illustrative example-problem was a three-processor situation, 33 hours is the makespan for the schedule.

In general, for the jth processor in an m-processor system, the following

TABLE 9.4 Illustrative Calculation of Inserted Idle Time for Example Problem

Sequence Position	Time on Proc. 2	Idle Time Proc. 2	New Time Proc. 2	Time on Proc. 3	Idle Time Proc. 3
	$t_{[1],2}$	$I_{[i],2}$	$t_{[i],2}^{New}$	$t_{[i],3}$	$I_{[i],3}$
[1]	1	2	3	6	3
[2]	3	2	5	4	0
[3]	3	1	4	5	0
[4]	8	0	8	3	2
[5]	4	0	4	7	1
[6]	4	0	3	2	0
				Totals 27	6

$I_{[1],3} = t_{[1],2}^{New} = 3$

$I_{[2],3} = \max\{0, (3 + 5 - 6 - 3)\} = 0$

$I_{[3],3} = \max\{0, (3 + 5 + 4 - 6 - 4 - 3 - 0)\} = 0$

$I_{[4],3} = \max\{0, (3 + 5 + 4 + 8 - 6 - 4 - 5 - 3 - 0 - 0)\} = 2$

$I_{[5],3} = \max\{0, (3 + 5 + 4 + 8 + 4 - 6 - 4 - 5 - 3 - 3 - 0 - 0 - 2)\} = 1$

$I_{[6],3} = \max\{0, (3 + 5 + 4 + 8 + 4 + 3 - 6 - 4 - 5 - 3 - 7 - 3 - 0 - 0 - 2 - 1)\} = 0$

equations hold.

$$t_{[i],j-1}^{New} = t_{[i],j-1} + I_{[i],j-1} \tag{9.19}$$

$$I_{[i],j} = \max\left\{0, \left(\sum_{k=1}^{i} t_{[k],j-1}^{New} - \sum_{k=1}^{i-1} t_{[k],j} - \sum_{k=1}^{i-1} I_{[k],j}\right)\right\} \tag{9.20}$$

$$F_{[n],j} = \sum_{i=1}^{n} t_{[i],j} + \sum_{i=1}^{n} I_{[i],j} \tag{9.21}$$

$$\text{M.S.} = F_{[n],m} = \sum_{i=1}^{n} t_{[i],m} + \sum_{i=1}^{n} I_{[i],m} \tag{9.22}$$

In summary, the heuristic to generate a reasonably low makespan schedule for the "*n* task on *m*-processor" problems is given by Algorithm 9.10. Essentially, one uses a computer to generate $m - 1$ possible schedules and calculates the makespan for each using Equations 9.19 through 9.22. The schedule with the lowest makespan then is implemented.

For the mean flow and mean tardy objectives, no good heuristic algorithms exist. Perhaps the best advice is to take the simplest approach: that is, to treat each processor as a separate single-processor and schedule it dynamically using rules suggested in Section 9.3. Dynamic scheduling problems exist when jobs are not all available at time equals zero, but arrive periodically. The scheduling rule thus is used, whenever a task is completed, to select which of the available tasks to run next.

To summarize this chapter, we repeat the adage that scheduling problems generally are not obvious. To spot them, one must look for situations in which delivery times tend to be increasing or overtime tends to be a regular practice; at the same time, various resources tend to be less than fully utilized. In such situations, sequencing may increase resource utilization while decreasing delivery times and overtime needs. That is to say, good scheduling can get the same work done at a higher level of productivity.

Technically, the scheduling problem is not simple. Chapter 8 covered the problem of scheduling when tasks must be accomplished in a given order. The Chapter 8 situation is called the precedent-constrained project scheduling problem. In this chapter we removed the precedent constraints and looked at the job-shop sequencing problem. Most job shops can be subdivided into subproblems in which the resources are viewed as either single processors or several relatively identical processors in parallel or several processors in series. Once the shop is broken down, each subproblem can be scheduled separately. Relatively simple algorithms were presented in this chapter. In the real world these algorithms applied to the many subproblems may not guarantee optimal results, but they should work well.

9.5 CASE STUDY

The complexity of realistic scheduling problems has already been suggested. This case study demonstrates how one might utilize scheduling heuristics in such situations. Typically, scheduling is not intended to find "optimal" sequences. Instead, the intent is to find "good" solutions that avoid gross errors that occur when haphazard sequences are used.

The case study is adapted from an actual problem that occurred in an aluminum extrusion facility. The plant has 10 extrusion presses of differing sizes and capabilities. These presses are essentially in parallel, since any given job passes through only one press. Different-size aluminum billets are extruded into 287 different shapes. Many of the shapes are limited to certain presses, because the required dies fit only those machines. Extrusion dies fit into specific die carriers. Machines are set up with one carrier at a time. The carriers can be changed as needed. Each press is manned by two-, three-, or four-man crews. The work force is sufficiently cross-trained so that the workers can run several presses and can trade activities within their crew. Typically, there are fewer crews than needed to run all the presses. The plant runs on a single-shift basis.

Orders for extrusions are booked in different quantities and have widely varying delivery lead-times. Marketing practices tend to offer faster deliveries to key customers. In general, marketing would like to reduce delivery lead-times to everyone in order to gain a competitive edge. However, work load fluctuations are smoothed by accepting longer delivery schedules. Manufacturing tries to maintain sufficient capacity to keep the booked orders between two and six weeks' worth of work. If the work load is approaching six weeks, overtime is scheduled or more people are hired to man additional presses. If the work load decreases to near two weeks, temporary layoffs are ordered. Since the labor force will not tolerate frequent shifts in hiring plus overtime and layoffs, manufacturing management wants to maintain large back orders and would like to increase the delivery lead-time.

When customers book orders, they typically request several different extrusion shapes and sizes. It is desirable to have all of these products ready at the same time so that they can all be shipped at once. Customer orders for different shapes are broken down into work orders. Work orders are grouped at two levels. First, orders for the same extrusion are grouped to run together. Secondly, extrusions requiring different dies but the same die carrier are grouped together to reduce the job change over time. Obviously, each set of orders has different due dates within the group. It is difficult, therefore, to determine what the lead time for a group of work orders ought to be. Work orders for critical customers are marked with a red "Do not delay" stamp.

The dies are designed to fit into specific die carriers and each machine is limited in the carriers it can accommodate. When a press is changed over from one job to another, the effort depends on whether the carrier needs to be changed along with the die. Setups that require only die changes are relatively quick and simple; the time standard for such changes is one hour. Setups that require the carrier be changed have a standard time of four hours. In addition to the machine crews, the plant employs four setup men, who typically work in pairs.

The scheduling objective is not clear. On the one hand, there is a desire to run tasks on a nearest-due-date-first basis. As we have seen, this would tend to result in fewer late deliveries. On the other hand, once a machine is set up to extrude a given product, it seems foolish not to make enough to satisfy all known orders. In addition, once a die carrier is set up, there is a desire to run orders requiring only die changes. These scheduling objectives would reduce the need for setup crews and idle time for work crews waiting for the machine. Such a policy, however, has negative impact on inventory costs. Items will be run well in advance of their due dates and have to be inventoried until the other parts of the customers's order are completed.

The selection of an appropriate scheduling objective is not easy. If the company's share of the market is falling because the competition has shorter delivery times, management likely would opt for a shorter-run/more-change-over scheduling objective. If the market share is holding firm and the cost of labor and inventory is getting too large, management likely would opt for a longer-run/few changeovers scheduling objective. The scheduling system should be designed to accommodate any balance between these two conflicting objectives.

A significant constraint placed on the solution to the problem was that it would have to be implemented so that all scheduling decisions were made by the production control people. Giving them a computer solution to follow would not work. Further, the heuristic to be used had to be obvious and require no sophisticated procedures.

The first step in the solution was to use group technology concepts and categorize all products that might be scheduled. Obviously, the first breakdown was by die carrier. A survey identified 27 different carriers. Thus, all products were placed into one of 27 groups. A study of past orders for products in each group indicated that for three groups, orders arrived faster than they could be produced on one press. Thus, it was decided to devote three presses exclusively and continuously to these three die carriers. The remaining 24 carriers and seven presses would be scheduled by a different rule, which will be discussed later.

The sequencing of the tasks in each of the three high-volume carrier groups was accomplished according to a modification of Hodgson's rule (Algorithm 9.1). Realize that the problem facing the scheduler is one of n orders and one machine. For each order the processing time is given by the quantity required multiplied by the standard time. Although the setup time may be zero if a die change is not needed, the scheduler assumes a change and increases the processing time of each job by one hour. The due date for each job is given on its work order.

The sequencing procedure given below is accomplished at the end of each shift for the next shift. This update is accomplished daily, even though the sequence may contain four or five days' work. The daily schedule is more sensitive to fluctuations caused by fewer die changes and occasional machine breakdowns. A special sequencing form (like the one in Figure 9.15) was used to write down the schedule. The scheduling steps for each of the three presses are as follows:

Step 1   Enter work orders on the form one at a time. Sequencing work orders by their due dates with the nearer due dates first.

Step 2   Accumulate the run times for this sequence and using an eight-hour day, estimate the completion date for each task.

Step 3   Do steps 1 and 2 one work order at a time until you have an order whose estimated completion time is later than its due date. When this occurs, go to steps 4 and 5. When all tasks are scheduled, go to steps 6 and 7.

Step 4   Review all sequenced work orders to see if any two or more call for the same part number. If you find the same parts, attempt to move the orders so they are adjacent to each other without causing intervening orders to become late. Count how many

Work-order number	Part number	Due date	Run time	Accumulated run time	Estimated completion date
3015	102	4/4	4.5	4.5	4/3
3127	104	4/4	5.0	9.5	4/4
3094	105	4/6	2.5	12.0	4/4
3112	104	4/7	10.0	22.0	4/7
3114	107	4/8	3.5	25.5	4/8
3114	106	4/8	4.5	30.0	4/8

FIGURE 9.15 Scheduling form for case study.

setups you saved and subtract that number of hours from the completion time of the order that was late in step 3. If the order is now on time, return to steps 1 and 2. Otherwise go to step 5.

Step 5 Of all the work orders sequenced so far, identify the one with the longest run time that is not stamped "Do not delay." Remove that work order from the schedule and reduce the completion time of the job that was late in step 3 by the run time of the removed work order. If the late job is now on time, return to steps 1 and 2; otherwise repeat this step.

Step 6 Once all the tasks are sequenced, attempt to reschedule in those tasks removed during step 5. Taking those tasks one at a time in order of their due date, note their run times. Working forward from the back end of the schedule, review the slack time of each scheduled work order. Slack time is the difference between the completion time and due date and indicates how early the work order will be. If the slack time is greater than the run time of the job being scheduled in, it will not be made tardy if the scheduled job is placed in front of it. Find the earliest time that the tardy job can be rescheduled without making other tasks tardy, and insert it.

Step 7 Once all tardy tasks are scheduled, if any are excessively tardy (three or more days), consider the possibility of pulling them out and running them on an alternative press.

Sequencing each of the remaining seven presses also was accomplished via a modified Hodgson procedure—in this case, a modified Algorithm 9.8. Recall that typically fewer than seven crews were brought in and not all presses are run every day. All the tasks for each of the remaining 24 carriers were grouped by part number. That is, all work orders for the same part number were grouped together.

By assuming that once a part number is started, all work orders for it will be completed, the processing time for each part number was calculated as the total number of units multiplied by the standard press time plus the four hours for carrier setup. As we shall see later, this assumption will not be true, but the error caused will be insignificant. The due date for each part number was established as the earliest due date of all the work orders requesting that part. Thus, we now have an "*n* order, *m* parallel machine" sequencing problem. The suggested procedure is given below. The same work form (Figure 9.15) is used with the procedure.

Step 1 Identify a copy of the sequencing form for each of the crews to be scheduled. Taking the jobs one part number at a time in order of the earliest due date first, schedule all of that part number to the crew form with the least assigned time. If the last part number on a form requires the same die carrier as the part being scheduled, its assigned time can be considered to be four hours less than given on the form. Enter the part number, due date, and run time on the appropriate form. Do this until all available part numbers are assigned. Accumulating the run times of each part number and using an eight-hour day, estimate the completion dates.

Step 2 For each crew form, starting at the earliest part in the sequence, identify the first part number whose estimated completion date is after its due date. Suppose that were part number I. When all forms have completed steps 3, 4, and 5, go to step 6.

Step 3 For all part numbers, preceding and including part number I, look for parts whose dies use the same carriers. If such parts exist, attempt to move them in the sequence so that they are adjacent and neither part number becomes late. For each time this is accomplished, reduce the completion time of the late job (and all jobs coming after it) by the four hours saved in carrier changeover time. If this makes the late part number finish on time, return to step 2; otherwise go to step 4.

Step 4 For each part number, preceding and including part number I, look at the individual due dates for all work orders requesting that part. Starting with the longest due date, remove that quantity of the part from the schedule. Reschedule these parts at the end of the form for that crew. Do this until either the tardy part (part number I) will finish on time or no further work orders can be removed without making them tardy. If part number I is now on time, return to step 1; otherwise go to step 5.

Step 5 If steps 3 and 4 do not make part number I complete on time, review work orders not stamped, "Do not delay." Remove the work order with the largest time requirement and reschedule it at the end of the form for that crew. Recalculate the completion of all part numbers after the one removed. Do this step until part number I is on time. Then return to step 2.

Step 6 Note that adjacent part numbers on given crew forms may require different die carriers. Setup time can be saved if these carrier changeovers can be made ahead of time on unused machines.

It is obvious, reading the scheduling procedures in this case study, that with some training they can be accomplished by hand. A computer graphics terminal could be programmed, however, to allow the moving of jobs and subsequent update of completion times. This would be a good example of computer-aided manufacturing.

In conclusion, the new scheduling rules were simulated by the analyst for a two-month period using historical data. The results of the simulation were measured in terms of the number of tardy work orders and the average lateness of all work orders. These results compared very favorably to the actual tardiness and lateness for the existing scheduling system. A report was presented to management, which authorized a six-month trial implementation. After this trial period, the new system was reviewed and made permanent.

9.6 REFERENCES

1. Baker, K. R., *Introduction to Sequencing and Scheduling*, John Wiley, New York, 1974.

2. Campbell, H. G., Dudek, R. A., and Smith, M. L., "A Heuristic Algorithm for the *n* Job *m* Machine Sequencing Problem," *Management Science*, vol. 16, no. 10, June 1970.

3. Dagramici, A., and Surkis, J., "Scheduling Independent Jobs on Parallel Identical Processors," *Management Science*, vol. 25, no. 12, December, 1979.

4. Jackson, J. R., "Scheduling a Production Line to Minimize Maximum Tardiness," research report no. 43, Management Science Research Project, UCLA, January 1955.

5. Johnson, S. M., "Optimal Two- and Three-Stage Production Schedules with Setup Times Included," *Naval Research Logistics Quarterly*, vol. 1, no. 1, March 1954.

6. Moore, J. M., "Sequencing *n* Jobs on One Machine to Minimize the Number of Tardy Jobs," *Management Science*, vol. 17, no. 1, September 1968.

7. Wilkerson, L. J., and Irwin, J. D., "An Improved Method for Scheduling Independent Tasks," *AIIE Transactions*, vol. 3, no. 3, September 1971.

9.7 EXERCISES

The following three data sets are used in conjunction with problems 1 through 20.

Task i	Processing time t_i	Importance weight w_i	Due Date d_i
Data Set A			
1	1	3	10
2	10	2	20
3	5	1	15
4	2	1	10
5	8	4	10
6	7	2	25
7	8	3	15
8	4	3	25
9	3	2	10
10	6	4	20
Data Set B			
1	5	3	30
2	6	2	30
3	11	1	40
4	8	3	80
5	12	2	100
6	14	1	70
7	7	3	90
8	10	2	80
9	6	1	40
10	12	3	90

Data Set C

Task i	Proc. Time t_i	Due Date d_i	Task i	Proc. Time t_i	Due Date d_i
1	2	100	26	1	180
2	6	240	27	4	90
3	5	180	28	5	200
4	8	200	29	9	50
5	4	50	30	8	170
6	4	30	31	6	140
7	1	190	32	1	200
8	9	110	33	7	250
9	6	150	34	7	160
10	7	210	35	6	50
11	7	200	36	3	100
12	1	130	37	2	150
13	4	250	38	2	250
14	7	20	39	3	220
15	9	170	40	1	180
16	3	230	41	5	20
17	9	30	42	7	120
18	9	110	43	6	140
19	8	80	44	8	50
20	3	70	45	5	100
21	5	150	46	9	50
22	9	50	47	5	200
23	4	250	48	4	250
24	3	210	49	6	150
25	5	240	50	8	110

1. Using Data Set A, develop the minimum mean flow-time schedule for one processor. What is the minimum mean flow-time?
2. Using Data Set A, develop the single-processor minimum-weighted mean flow-time schedule. What is the weighted mean flow-time for this schedule?
3. Using Data Set A, calculate the minimum mean lateness of all possible schedules if one processor is available.
4. Using Data Set A, develop the schedule that minimizes the lateness of the most-late task, given one processor.
5. Using Data Set A, find a schedule that minimizes the number of tardy tasks, given one processor.
6. Using Data Set A, find a schedule using the "least SLACK first" rule for one processor.

7. Using Data Set *A*, use the Wilkerson–Irwin algorithm to minimize (it is hoped) mean tardiness on one processor. Does the resulting sequence, in fact, minimize mean tardiness?

8. Compare the mean tardiness, maximum tardy time, and number of tardy tasks resulting from Problems 4, 5, and 6.

9. Suppose the processing times in Data Set *B* represent estimated minutes of execution for 10 batch-loaded computer programs. The objective of the computer center is to minimize turnaround time. How should the program loader feed the tasks to the computer?

10. Referring to Problem 9, suppose the importance of the tasks fall into three categories as given in Data Set *B*. What rule should the program loader use, and what schedule would result? Comment on the choice of values for weighting factor relative to an *ABC* category approach to prioritizing.

11. Suppose the tasks in Data Set *B* represent jobs in a one-man drafting shop. The processing times represent man-days of effort. Assume a charge of $100 per day for deliveries after the due date. How would you schedule the 10 drafting jobs to minimize total cost?

12. Suppose the chief engineer over the shop hypothesized in Problem 11 called to say that all jobs are now due immediately. How would you schedule the jobs, knowing this new information?

13. Do Problem 1 for the three-parallel-processor situations.

14. Do Problem 4 for the three-parallel-processor situations.

15. Do Problem 5 for the three-parallel-processor situations.

16. Do Problem 6 for the two-parallel-processor situations.

17. Do Problem 8 for the two-parallel-processor situations.

18. Write a Fortran program to implement Algorithms 9.5 for the two-parallel-processor cases and print out the mean tardy, maximum tardy, and number tardy statistics. Use Data Set *C* to test your program.

19. Do Problem 18 for Algorithm 9.6.

20. Do Problem 18 for Algorithm 9.7.

21. Calculate the minimum makespan for a schedule of the following tasks on two serial processors.

Task i	Time on Proc. 1, $t_{i,1}$	Time on Proc. 2, $t_{i,2}$
1	5	3
2	2	7
3	9	4
4	3	2
5	8	6
6	4	4
7	8	3

22. Using the following data, schedule the processors using Algorithm 9.10
    What is the resulting makespan for the six tasks?

Task i	Time on Proc. 1, $t_{i,1}$	Time on Proc. 2, $t_{i,2}$	Time on Proc. 3, $t_{i,3}$
1	4	3	5
2	6	8	2
3	2	3	5
4	3	4	8
5	8	6	5
6	5	6	7

23. Write a Fortran program to solve Problem 22.

TEN: PERSONNEL SCHEDULING

Let us then be up and doing,
With a heart for any fate; Still achieving, still pursuing,
Learn to labor and to wait.

Longfellow

Scheduling is a very critical problem in all areas of the endeavor, as we have seen especially in the last two chapters. Scheduling the human element itself presents a considerable problem. In Chapter 5, approaches to setting aggregate-production and labor-force levels in manufacturing were discussed. The objective was to satisfy a fluctuating demand for products in a least-cost fashion. The choices were trade-offs among the size of the work force, the size of inventory, and the extent of overtime. In Chapter 7, translation of the aggregate plan into a master schedule was discussed. The necessary tasks for each activity in each period were identified relative to the materials requirement plan. In Chapter 9, the problem of scheduling tasks onto existing facilities was discussed. The sequence of tasks was selected to satisfy some performance objective. Now let us face the problem of staffing the facility with people.

In manufacturing organizations, the option of building to inventory during slow periods and working from inventory during peaks tends to soften the people-scheduling problem. In service industries, such as banking and health, the product is often personal attention. Since it is impossible to perform such services ahead of time, the inventory option does not exist and the personnel-scheduling problem is magnified. In manufacturing as well as service industries, the problem of having people on hand when they are needed requires planning and scheduling. The purpose of this chapter is to cover the topics of personnel and associated shift scheduling.

10.1 INTRODUCTION

Personnel-scheduling problems have distinct characteristics that help identify them. The first trait is that demand tends to fluctuate widely in the short term

342

and to occur seven days a week. In restaurants and mass-transit industries, demand varies hourly but is predictable. In the machine repair department of a factory, demand is far less predictable but the high cost of delay requires immediate service. In a hospital, nursing and food must be provided around the clock, seven days a week. None of these examples fit the typical 8:30 a.m. to 5:00 p.m., forty-hour-a-week schedule that tradition and labor contracts call for.

The second attribute of personnel scheduling is that human effort cannot be inventoried. This is readily apparent in activities performed at a grocery checkout or by a telephone operator. It is possible to have the customer wait for service, but a worker cannot perform the service before the demand occurs. The production plan cannot flatten the fluctuations in demand by building and depleting inventories of people's time.

A third attribute of the problem is that customer convenience is critical. If the customer is willing to travel long distances, arrive when the facility is open, and wait in a queue, the problem disappears. If, however, competition exists or the demand for service is critical, personnel must be scheduled to the customer's convenience.

All of these characteristics make the personnel-scheduling problem more difficult. The solution to the problem takes several steps. First, the services provided are individually identified for study. Time studies are used to determine the average time required for each service. Forecasting studies are made to build models that forecast the demand for each service. Aggregate demand models are developed to forecast the total staffing requirements. These requirements are likely to vary in time. They may vary by the time of the day, day of the week, and/or week of the year.

With the forecast in hand, the next step is to smooth out the staffing needs and look for available staffing options. A number of approaches can be considered. For example, one should look for ways to reduce the service-time requirement once the customer arrives. Perhaps parts of the task can be automated; the use of microprocessor computers offers fantastic opportunities in this regard. Perhaps parts of the task can be done before the customer arrives. Such activities might be accomplished during slower periods or by support-type personnel. Another option that might work is to prescreen customers, either by service needs or by priority; the fast-line checkout counter is an example of this option. Finally, one might examine the possibility of having customers call in orders and pick them up at an agreed-upon later time. These ideas and others should be designed to reduce the service time once the customer arrives. Using them will allow the same degree of service with fewer "up front" people. In this way, the variations in demand affect fewer people.

In another approach, there may be ways to smooth out the work load of all the service people. In doctor's offices, for example, customer arrivals are smoothed by an appointment system. If customers are willing to schedule their arrivals rather than risk a long wait, this idea may work. Staffing to meet peak periods and providing other "fill in" tasks for slower times is another way to smooth the work load. All employees need breaks in their work day, and typically, breaks are scheduled to occur during slower periods. Finally, one might look for other business opportunities that have a complementary demand profile.

The last source of ideas for simplifying the scheduling problem is to find ways to vary the number of people employed. It may be possible to draw people from other parts of the organization to work for a few hours during peak periods. Hiring part-time personnel is often a simple solution if the policies of the Personnel Department permit. In larger communities, temporary people are available from organizations that specialize in satisfying these needs. Staggering shift times is another approach that will work if company policy will permit. Scheduling overtime in the form of longer and overlapping shifts would help if peak demands occur seasonally. One final idea is to establish a group of "on call" people who can come to work on short notice. Retired persons are a source of such workers.

There are many organizational ways to simplify the scheduling problem, ranging from reducing the service time by filling in slack periods to increasing the availability of short-period help. The scheduling problem, thus simplified, is still challenging, but there are some heuristic approaches for dealing effectively with it.

In the sections that follow, we shall present techniques to deal with the problem. Scheduling five-day workweeks into seven-day demand forecasts will be covered. Secondly, the problem of scheduling each shift to satisfy fluctuating hourly demands will be addressed. The history of research into personnel scheduling is still quite young. The algorithms presented below are not the final answer. Thus, a cautious and creative approach to personnel scheduling problems is very much in order.

10.2 DEFINITIONS

Most of the vocabulary used in this chapter is straightforward. Simple definitions of a few words and phrases might make the learning process a little easier, however,

> **Demand** In this chapter the numbers of people needed during some period in order to provide a predefined level of service. For example, demand might be for the number of bank tellers necessary to process 95% of the peak customer load within 10 minutes of arrival. Demand then is found by forecasting customer arrival rates and mean processing times. Queuing analysis can be used to translate the forecasts into numbers of people. A weekly demand forecast, then, is the number of people to be employed during each day of the week. An hourly demand profile is defined as the number of people required at different periods during a specific day.

Shift   In this chapter, has two meanings. In Section 10.3 it denotes the set of days during a given week when a person will be expected at work. One might say, for example, that shift number 5 is Monday through Friday, with Saturday and Sunday off. In many personnel-scheduling problems, the days that a person works will vary from week to week. In section 10.4, the word *shift* has a more traditional meaning: the time of day when a person begins work and when, during the day, rest and lunch breaks are to occur. Thus, one might say that shift number 10 starts at 8:00 a.m. with 15 minutes off at 10:00 a.m. and 2:00 p.m. and lunch from 12:15 p.m. to 12:45 p.m.

Schedule   In this chapter, the set of shifts that satisfies the demand criteria. In Section 10.3, a shift schedule is the collection of days-on/days-off shifts that staff the operation each day of the week. In Section 10.4, a schedule is the set of start times and breaks for the entire staff established to ensure that sufficient people are available during each period of the day.

In this chapter, we will look at two personnel-scheduling problems. The specific meanings of terms differ a bit for each problem. The first problem will be referred to as shift scheduling and the second problem as scheduling within each shift.

10.3 SHIFT SCHEDULING

When scheduling personnel to cover six- or seven-day workweeks, the objective is to provide an adequate number of people at a minimum labor cost. This problem occurs whenever a need for people cannot be made to fit the standard five day/40-hour workweek. Ways of smoothing out the problem with nonscheduling procedures, such as by overtime or by using part-time people, have already been introduced. Having exhausted these approaches, the question becomes one of scheduling shifts for the full-time people: that is, which days should they work and which days they will be off. In this section, we shall discuss three approaches to this problem.

All approaches to this problem begin with a forecast of needs over the seven-day period. Such forecasts are broken down according to people with the same capabilities. In a hospital, for example, different forecasts must be made for nurse's aides, practical nurses, and registered nurses. Specialized talents, such as training in cardiovascular or mental-health nursing, may require further breakdowns. Each of the three shifts requires a set of personnel-need forecasts. The establishment of the seven-day need profiles is a significant study in itself. With the profile in hand, the scheduler must allocate people to the need.

Figure 10.1 represents a very simple daily-demand forecast and shift schedule. Note that the forecast calls for a total of 28 people or shifts. Since each individual will work a five-day shift, the forecast requires at least six

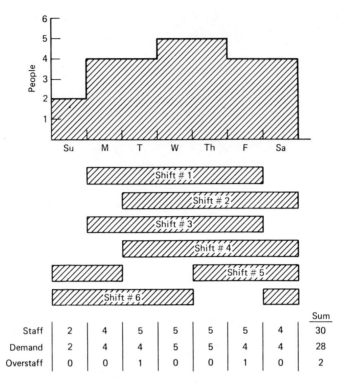

FIGURE 10.1   Simple daily-demand forecast with a shift schedule to satisfy the need.

shifts for six people. As shown in the figure, a satisfactory solution was found. The solution will contain overstaffing on Tuesday and Friday. The shop foreman can look for additional activities to fill those people's times. The solution contains only two Saturday/Sunday off-shifts, but everyone at least has consecutive days off. The solution is optimal in that it requires six people—the minimum feasible. Let us now turn to the procedure used to generate the solution to this simple problem.

The approach used was first published by Tibrewala, Philippe and Browne (1972).† The algorithm begins with a forecasted demand profile and assigns pairs of regular days off (RDOs), one person at a time. Each pair of consecutive days off establishes a shift, which is then assigned to a specific individual. The algorithm can be stated as the three-step procedure given at the top of page 347.

†R. Tibrewala, D. Philippe, and J. Browne, "Optimal Scheduling of Two Consecutive Idle Periods, "*Management Science*, vol, 19, no. 1, September 1972. Reprinted by permission of R. Tibrewala, D. Philippe, and J. Browne. Copyright © 1972 The Institute of Management Sciences.

Algorithm 10.1 Tibrewala, Philippe, and Browne

Step 1   Working from the largest manpower-need day to the second largest and so forth, do the following. Place all days with the same manpower need on the schedule until a unique two-consecutive-days period appears that identifies the five-on/two-off schedule. If a tie exists, go to step 2.

Step 2   If two identical two-days off periods occur, select the period with the smallest requirements on an adjacent day. If the tie cannot be broken, go to step 3.

Step 3   Select the most reasonable pair; for example, the one that has a Saturday or Sunday or the first pair in the week.

To illustrate the algorithm, an example problem is worked out. Suppose the seven-day demand forecast beginning with Sunday is for four, eight, seven, seven, seven, seven, six people. Demand totals 46, which will require a minimum of 10 people.† Thus, any set of 10 shift-schedules that meets the demand forecast will represent an optimum solution. The iterative solution procedure is represented in Figure 10.2 and the following discussion refers to that figure.

Consider the development of shift number 1 in Figure 10.2. Note that there are -1's on Monday through Friday and 0's on Saturday and Sunday. Using step 1 of the algorithm, one would first put a -1 on Monday as the day with the greatest demand (i.e., 8 people). Step 1 can then be used to put -1 on Tuesday through Friday, as days with the second highest demand. This leaves Saturday and Sunday as two consecutive days off. In this fashion, the first shift is generated. At this point the tableau would appear as follows.

Su	M	T	W	Th	F	Sa	
4	8	7	7	7	7	6	Initial Demand
0	-1	-1	-1	-1	-1	0	Shift #1
4	7	6	6	6	6	6	Residual Demand

The last line on the tableau represents the yet-unfilled needs. These figures are found by subtracting 1 from those days that have a -1.

---

†Five days per shift with a demand of 46 gives a minimum shift requirement of 9.2 shifts. Obviously, shifts or people have to be integers, so the minimum feasible number of shifts or people in this case is 10.

Su	M	T	W	Th	F	Sa	
4	8	7	7	7	7	6	Initial demand
0	-1	-1	-1	-1	-1	0	Shift #1
4	7	6	6	6	6	6	
0	-1	-1	-1	-1	-1	0	Shift #2
4	6	5	5	5	5	6	
-1	-1	0	0	-1	-1	-1	Shift #3
3	5	5	5	4	4	5	
-1	-1	-1	-1	0	0	-1	Shift #4
2	4	4	4	4	4	4	
0	-1	-1	-1	-1	-1	0	Shift #5
2	3	3	3	3	3	4	
0	0	-1	-1	-1	-1	-1	Shift #6
2	3	2	2	2	2	3	
-1	-1	0	0	-1	-1	-1	Shift #7
1	2	2	2	1	1	2	
-1	-1	-1	-1	0	0	-1	Shift #8
0	1	1	1	1	1	1	
0	-1	-1	-1	-1	-1	0	Shift #9
0	0	0	0	0	0	1	
0	0	-1	-1	-1	-1	-1	Shift #10
0	0	-1	-1	-1	-1	0	

FIGURE 10.2   Tableau for the Tibrewala, Phillipe, and Browne solution of the example problem.

We now repeat the process for the second shift. The seven-person demand on Monday places that day on the schedule, but a tie exists. Only four of the five days with a demand of six people can be given a -1. The question is resolved using step 2. One must select two consecutive days to be taken off; the desire is to find two that have the smallest combined need. The Saturday/Sunday pair have a combined need of 10 people, whereas all other combinations require 12 people. Of all the days with six-people needs, Saturday has the neighbor with the smallest need (i.e., Sunday, with four people). Thus, the -1's are placed on Tuesday through Friday and the tableau is altered as follows.

Su	M	T	W	Th	F	Sa	
4	8	7	7	7	7	6	Initial demand
0	-1	-1	-1	-1	-1	0	Shift #1
4	7	6	6	6	6	6	
0	-1	-1	-1	-1	-1	0	Shift #2
4	6	5	5	5	5	6	

In the development of the third shift, we first put a -1 on Monday and Saturday, as having the highest demand. The five people-days form a tie that cannot be broken using step 2. Thus we apply step 3. For lack of any better alternative, step 3 tells us to select Tuesday and Wednesdays as days off.

Using these cycles, we have developed shifts 1, 2, and 3. The entire solution is given in Figure 10.2. It would be wise to study the remaining shifts to satisfy yourself that they were all developed using Algorithm 10.1 properly.

The schedule represented by Figure 10.2 is optimal because it requires only 10 people. The negative numbers below shift number 10 represent idle days caused by overstaffing. There are four Saturday/Sunday off-schedules (i.e., 1, 2, 5, and 9). Two schedules have Tuesday/Wednesday off. Two schedules have Thursday/Friday off. Finally, two schedules have Sunday/Monday off. Obviously, one of the Sunday/Monday off-schedules could be replaced with a single day of overtime offered to one of the four people with Saturday off. The allocation of one day of overtime would thus save one person (shift #10) and eliminate all four idle days. This would therefore constitute a perfect schedule with no idle time.

The solution this time was lucky. It is often not possible to find an optimal schedule that contains only consecutive pairs of days off. To guarantee two consecutive days off, the algorithm often leads to solutions requiring more than the minimum number of people and containing many idle days of overstaffing.

In any case, the question now becomes one of matching work schedules to people. This can be done in any convenient way. Using seniority, each worker may in turn select the schedule of his or her choice. If the five-day need forecast repeats itself week after week, the schedules might be rotated over the entire staff.

The instructive value of the Tibrewala et al. approach lies in its general applicability. The first step is to break the work force into groups of similar talents. For each group, select shifts using some intelligent heuristic, one person at a time. For each schedule, attempt to satisfy the policies of the company as closely as possible. When the entire staffing need is satisfied, review the selected shifts to see if the use of overtime or transfers can overcome any glaring inefficiencies. Finally, go back to the employees and use their input to assign people to the various shift schedules. Without knowing any published heuristic, this procedure should result in reasonably good personnel schedules.

Another approach to the shift-scheduling problem was first published by Monroe (1970).† The objective is very similar to Tibrewala et al. in that it seeks two consecutive regular days off (RDOs). It differs, however, in that it guarantees a solution for the minimum number of people even if it has to create shifts with nonconsecutive days off.

As before, the approach begins with a forecasted demand profile; for example: four, eight, seven, seven, seven, seven, six people. The first step is to determine the minimum required staff size, which, as before, is 10 people. Knowing the size of the staff, the next step is to determine the RDOs for each day. If the staff size is 10 and four people are needed on Sunday, then there are six people with a RDO on Sunday. Regular days off for any given day comprise merely the difference between the staff size and the staff need for that day. For the example, the RDOs are

	Su	M	T	W	Th	F	Sa
Minimum staff	10	10	10	10	10	10	10
Forecasted demand	4	8	7	7	7	7	6
RDO		6	2	3	3	3	3	4

A simple constraint exists at this point. The sum of the forecasted demand must be a multiple of 5 to ensure that all people work five days a week. If this is not the case, demand can be increased on various days. The days to be increased should logically be those that can most easily absorb the excess capacity. In the example, the total demand is 46; thus, an extra demand of four must be entered. Arbitrarily, we put them on Tuesday, Wednesday, Thursday, and Friday. The RDOs are thereby changed as follows.

	Su	M	T	W	Th	F	Sa
Minimum staff	10	10	10	10	10	10	10
Forecasted demand	4	8	8	8	8	8	6
RDOs		6	2	2	2	2	2	4

†G. Monroe, "Scheduling Manpower for Service Operations," *Industrial Engineering*, August 1970. Presented with permission from *Industrial Engineering Magazine.* Copyright © American Institute of Industrial Engineers, Inc., 25 Technology Park/Atlanta Norcross, Ga., 30092.

	Su	M	T	W	Th	F	Sa	(Su)	(M)
RDOs	6	2	2	2	2	2	4	(6)	(2)
Day-off Pairs	SuM	MT	TW	WTh	ThF	FSa	SaSu	(SuM)	
First trial	1	1	1	1	1	1	3	(3)	
Second Trial	2	0	2	0	2	0	4	(2)	

FIGURE 10.3   Tableau using Monroe's approach to solving the staff scheduling problem.

Note that an alternative procedure would have been to reduce the demand by 1 on one day, perhaps Monday, and thereby have a total demand of 45 shifts. This would, however, have reduced the minimum staff need from 10 to 9.

The next step in the Monroe procedure is to look for consecutive pairs of RDOs. Since the process is best understood by studying an example, we have worked out the previous problem in Figure 10.3. Note that the number of days in the figure have been increased from seven to nine by repeating Sunday and Monday at the end. The reason for this will become clear in a moment. The process of finding consecutive pairs of RDOs requires two trials. Referring to Figure 10.3, note that the days have been paired: that is, Sunday and Monday are joined to form a SuM pair and Monday and Tuesday are joined to form a MT pair. In the first trial, the scheduler attempts to estimate the number of shift schedules that will have the first and second days (i.e., SuM) off for their consecutive pair of RDOs. Note that day 2 (Monday) requires a total of two RDOs; arbitrarily, half of these are assigned to the SuM pair. Thus, for the first trial in the example, an estimate of one shift schedule will have the SuM pair off. Obviously, if one person has Sunday and Monday off and Monday requires two RDOs, a second person must have Monday and Tuesday off: that is, the MT pair is calculated by subtracting the SuM trial value from the Monday RDO. This same arithmetic holds for all subsequent days off pairs. Note that this results in the second occurrence of a SuM of three, which differs from the first SuM pair. The difference indicates an inconsistency that is resolved with a second trial. Had the first and second SuM pair been equal, a second trial would be unnecessary. Obviously, the extension of the tableau by two days was done to accomplish this comparison.

To start the second trial, the average of the first and second pairs for SuM is used for the new SuM pair. This average in the example is two. Repeating the procedure to get all pairs, we note that the first and second SuM pairs are equal in the second trial. This will always be the case.

The tableau now contains scheduled days off for each of the 10 shifts. Two people will have Sunday/Monday off, two will have Tuesday/Wednesday off, two will get Thursday/Friday off, and four will get Saturday/Sunday off.

This is the same solution as that found with Algorithm 10.1. Also, as before, one person could be asked to work overtime on Saturday. As with the Tibrewala et al. procedure, the last step is to assign individuals to the selected shifts.

In order to formalize the procedure, the central steps of Monroe's approach are given below as an algorithm.

Algorithm 10.2   Monroe

Step 1   For each day of the week, calculate the regular days off (RDOs) by subtracting the daily staff need from the chosen staff size. The summed staff need must be an even multiple of 5 if five-day workweeks are to be scheduled. If this is not the case, add to the staff needs of one or more days until a multiple of 5 is reached.

Step 2   Beginning with the first two days of the week, establish pairs of RDOs until the first pair is repeated a second time.

Step 3   For a first trial at scheduling pairs of RDO, assign approximately half of the second-day's RDO to the first pair of days off. Subtracting this assignment from the second-days RDO, assign the remainder to the second pair of days off. Continue this procedure until all pairs have assignments. If the first and second occurrence of the first pair are equal, stop; otherwise go to step 4.

Step 4   Calculate the average of the assignment to the first and second occurrence of the first pair of days off. Use this as the second trial assignment for the first pair. Using the procedure in step 3, reassign all pairs of days off.

To illustrate the limitations of Tibrewala's and Monroe's approaches, a second variation of the example problem will be solved. The need profile for this problem is exactly as before, except that the Sunday need is set to zero. This is the typical six-day workweek problem. The solution of the problem using Algorithm 10.1 is shown in Figure 10.4 and the solution using Algorithm 10.2 is shown in Figure 10.5. Note that both approaches come up with strange results. A total of 42 people-days were needed, and Algorithm 10.1 scheduled 10 people. This represented a total of eight shifts of excess capacity. Four of those excess shifts are generated on Sundays by workers with shifts 3, 4, 7, and 8. Surely you would not have these people come in on Sunday to do nothing. Neither would it be wise to give them five days' pay for four days' work, staying home on Sunday. Figure 10.5 contains even stranger results, which suggest that four of the nine people be given Sunday/Monday off when eight people are needed on Monday. This results in a negative three people being given Monday/Tuesday off. The negative days-off might be translated to hiring in three temporary people to work just Mondays and Tuesdays while full-time people are home on their days off.

Su	M	T	W	Th	F	Sa	
0	8	7	7	7	7	6	Initial demand
0	-1	-1	-1	-1	-1	0	Shift #1
0	7	6	6	6	6	6	
0	-1	-1	-1	-1	-1	0	Shift #2
0	6	5	5	5	5	6	
-1	-1	0	0	-1	-1	-1	Shift #3
-1	5	5	5	4	4	5	
-1	-1	-1	-1	0	0	-1	Shift #4
-2	4	4	4	4	4	4	
0	-1	-1	-1	-1	-1	0	Shift #5
-2	3	3	3	3	3	4	
0	0	-1	-1	-1	-1	-1	Shift #6
-2	3	2	2	2	2	3	
-1	-1	0	0	-1	-1	-1	Shift #7
-3	2	2	2	1	1	2	
-1	-1	-1	-1	0	0	-1	Shift #8
-4	1	1	1	1	1	1	
0	-1	-1	-1	-1	-1	0	Shift #9
-4	0	0	0	0	0	1	
0	0	-1	-1	-1	-1	-1	Shift #10
-4	0	-1	-1	-1	-1	0	

FIGURE 10.4 Tableau for the Tibrewala, Phillipe, and Browne solution of second example problem.

	Su	M	T	W	Th	F	Sa	(Su)	(M)
Staff	9	9	9	9	9	9	9	(9)	(9)
Needs	0	8	8	8	8	7	6	(0)	(8)
RDO	9	1	1	1	1	2	3	(9)	(1)

Pairs	SuM	MT	TW	WTh	ThF	FSa	SaSu	(SuM)
First trial	1	0	1	0	1	1	2	(7)
Second trial	4	-3	4	-3	4	-2	5	(4)

FIGURE 10.5 Tableau for Monroe's solution to the second example problem.

The problem results from the requirement that all people be given two consecutive days off. If the consecutive stipulation were removed, a satisfactory solution could be found. If large negative values occur in the tableau when using Algorithm 10.1, the solution is to schedule nonconsecutive days whenever necessary. Referring to Figure 10.4, note that the creation of shift 3 required the assignment of a person to work on Sunday when there was nothing to do. Instead, the scheduler should have scheduled Sunday and another nonconsecutive day off. The rule for the second day off should be the first appearing day with the smallest need. For shift 3 in Figure 10.4, this would be Tuesday. Thus, shift 3 would have Sunday and Tuesday off. Figure 10.6 is the

```
Su  M   T   W  Th   F  Sa
───────────────────────────────────
 0   8   7   7   7   7   6     Initial demand
 0  -1  -1  -1  -1  -1   0     Shift #1
───────────────────────────────────
 0   7   6   6   6   6   6
 0  -1  -1  -1  -1  -1   0     Shift #2
───────────────────────────────────
 0   6   5   5   5   5   6
 0  -1   0  -1  -1  -1  -1     Shift #3
───────────────────────────────────
 0   5   5   4   4   4   5
 0  -1  -1   0  -1  -1  -1     Shift #4
───────────────────────────────────
 0   4   4   4   3   3   4
 0  -1  -1  -1   0  -1  -1     Shift #5
───────────────────────────────────
 0   3   3   3   3   2   3
 0  -1  -1  -1  -1   0  -1     Shift #6
───────────────────────────────────
 0   2   2   2   2   2   2
 0   0  -1  -1  -1  -1  -1     Shift #7
───────────────────────────────────
 0   2   1   1   1   1   1
 0  -1  -1  -1  -1  -1   0     Shift #8
───────────────────────────────────
 0   1   0   0   0   0   1
 0  -1   0  -1  -1  -1  -1     Shift #9
───────────────────────────────────
 0   0   0  -1  -1  -1   0
```

FIGURE 10.6 Revised Tibrewala, Phillipe, and Browne solution of second example problem.

solution to the second example, using this modification to Algorithm 10.1. Similarly, the modification to the Monroe algorithm is to select nonconsecutive days off in order to generate a satisfactory solution. The modification is to take the largest negative number in the tableau (-3 in Figure 10.5) and create that number of schedules with nonconsecutive days off. First subtract that number from the RDO of the day with the largest RDO needs; this is shown in Figure 10.7. The remaining days off are subtracted from other nonconsecutive days. Monroe suggests a trial-and-error procedure for locating these second days off. The suggestion here is to select those nonconsecutive days that tend to make the remaining RDOs as similar as possible. Once this subtraction is made, the remaining RDOs are distributed as before, using Algorithm 10.2. If this does not remove all the negative values in the second trial, increase the number of schedules with nonconsecutive RDOs. The solution of the example using the revision of Algorithm 10.2 is shown in Figure 10.7.

There is a linear-programming formulation of Monroe's algorithm that guarantees a feasible solution with a minimum of nonconsecutive days off.

	Su	M	T	W	Th	F	Sa	(Su)	(M)
Old RDO	9	1	1	1	1	2	3	(9)	(1)
Nonconsecutive	-3				-1	-2		(-3)	
Remaining RDO	6	1	1	1	0	0	3	(6)	(1)

Pairs	SuM	MT	TW	WTh	ThF	FSa	SaSu	(SuM)
First trial	1	0	1	0	0	0	3	(3)
Second trial	2	-1	2	-1	1	-1	4	(2)

	Su	M	T	W	Th	F	Sa	(Su)	(M)
Old RDO	6	1	1	1	0	0	3	(6)	(1)
Nonconsecutive	-1		-1					(-1)	
Remaining RDO	5	1	1	0	0	0	3	(5)	(1)

Pairs	SuM	MT	TW	WTh	ThF	FSa	SaSu	(SuM)
First trial	1	0	1	-1	1	-1	4	(1)
Second trial		not needed						

	Su	M	T	W	Th	F	Sa	(Su)	(M)
Old RDO	5	1	1	0	0	0	3	(5)	(1)
Nonconsecutive	-1		-1					(-1)	
Remaining RDO	4	1	0	0	0	0	3	(4)	(1)

Pairs	SuM	MT	TW	WTh	ThF	FSa	SaSu	(SuM)
First trial	1	0	0	0	0	0	3	(1)
Second trial		not needed						

FIGURE 10.7 Tableau for modified Monroe solution to second example problem.

This formulation is given by Rothstein (1972).† The formulation requires 15 constraints and 15 variables, as shown in Figure 10.8. Constraint 1 states that the number of consecutive pairs of days off scheduled for Sunday/Monday, (i.e. x_1) or for Monday/Tuesday (i.e., x_2) plus the number of nonconsecutive days off that contain a Monday (i.e., u_1) must equal the number of people who are to have Monday off (i.e., b_1). Constraints 2 through 7 are similar to constraint 1. Constraint 8 states that the number of scheduled pairs of days off, either consecutive or nonconsecutive, should equal the number of workers. Since each worker has two days off, the number of workers is $\frac{1}{2}\Sigma b_i$. Constraints 9 through 15 state that no value of a u_i can exceed the sum of all the other u values. This ensures that the nonconsecutive days off are not assigned to the same day. Such a solution is not possible, since one person cannot have two days off on the same day. The objective function of the LP formulation states that the number of consecutive days off should be maximized.

This linear programming formulation by its structure guarantees an integer solution. Therefore, any of the commonly available LP computer packages can be used to solve the problem. Variations on the basic theme can allow the scheduler to implement a variety of policy constraints. For example, if the desire was to have at least n people with a Saturday/Sunday-off schedule, one could add the constraint $x_7 \geq n$. If n is too large, however, the system will not provide a feasible solution. If the policy was to encourage Sundays off, the objective function could be changed to include u_7 and give a weight greater than 1 to x_1 and x_7. Thus, a scheduler could examine alternative schedules with a variety of additional constraints.

As suggested earlier, the use of part-time personnel can, in some organizations, greatly relieve the staff-scheduling problems. Mabert and Raedels (1977)‡ pointed to a simple heuristic for scheduling part-time people who will provide full eight-hour days but work fewer than five days a week. The heuristic begins with the daily staff needs forecast. Suppose, for example, the forecast were as follows.

Su	M	T	W	Th	F	Sa
0	11	6	8	6	10	0

Suppose further that there are five full-time employees and the policy is to use part-time people to fill in the remaining needs. The need for full- and

---

† M. Rothstein, "Scheduling Manpower by Mathematical Programming," *Industrial Engineering*, vol. 4, no. 4, April 1972. Presented with permission from *Industrial Engineering* magazine. Copyright © American Institute of Industrial Engineers, Inc., 25 Technology Park/Atlanta. Norcross, Ga. 30092.

‡ V. A. Mabert and A. R. Raedels, "The Detail Scheduling of a Part-Time Work Force: A Case Study of Teller Staffing," *Decision Sciences*, vol. 8, no. 1, January 1977. *Decision Sciences* is the quarterly journal of the American Institute for Decision Sciences.

Maximize $z = \sum_{i=1}^{7} x_i$

S.T.

1	$x_1 + x_2$	$+ u_1$			$= b_1$
2	$x_2 + x_3$	$+ u_2$			$= b_2$
3	$x_3 + x_4$	$+ u_3$			$= b_3$
4	$x_4 + x_5$	$+ u_4$			$= b_4$
5	$x_5 + x_6$	$+ u_5$			$= b_5$
6	$x_6 + x_7$	$+ u_6$			$= b_6$
7	$x_1 + x_7$	$+ u_7$			$= b_7$
8	$x_1 + x_2 + x_3 + x_4 + x_5 + x_6 + x_7$	$+ d = \frac{1}{2} \Sigma\, b_i$			
9	$u_1 - u_2 - u_3 - u_4 - u_5 - u_6 - u_7$	≤ 0			
10	$-u_1 + u_2 - u_3 - u_4 - u_5 - u_6 - u_7$	< 0			
11	$-u_1 - u_2 + u_3 - u_4 - u_5 - u_6 - u_7$	≤ 0			
12	$-u_1 - u_2 - u_3 + u_4 - u_5 - u_6 - u_7$	≤ 0			
13	$-u_1 - u_2 - u_3 - u_4 + u_5 - u_6 - u_7$	≤ 0			
14	$-u_1 - u_2 - u_3 - u_4 - u_5 + u_5 - u_7$	≤ 0			
15	$-u_1 - u_2 - u_3 - u_4 - u_5 - u_6 + u_7$	≤ 0			

$$d,\ u_i,\ x_i \leq 0 \text{ for all } i\text{'s}$$

where

x_1 = number of Sunday/Monday RDO pairs
x_2 = number of Monday/Tuesday RDO pairs
x_3 = number of Tuesday/Wednesday RDO pairs
x_4 = number of Wednesday/Thursday RDO pairs
x_5 = number of Thursday/Friday RDO pairs
x_6 = number of Friday/Saturday RDO pairs
x_7 = number of Saturday/Sunday RDO pairs

b_1 = required RDO for Monday
b_2 = required RDO for Tuesday
b_3 = required RDO for Wednesday
b_4 = required RDO for Thursday
b_5 = required RDO for Friday
b_6 = required RDO for Saturday
b_7 = required RDO for Sunday

u_1 = number of Mondays in nonconsecutive RDOs
u_2 = number of Tuesdays in nonconsecutive RDOs
u_3 = number of Wednesdays in nonconsecutive RDOs
u_4 = number of Thursdays in nonconsecutive RDOs
u_5 = number of Fridays in nonconsecutive RDOs
u_6 = number of Saturdays in nonconsecutive RDOs
u_7 = number of Sundays in nonconsecutive RDOs
d = number of workers who will be assigned nonconsecutive RDOs

FIGURE 10.8 Linear programming formulation of Monroe's algorithm as given by Rothstein.

part-time people is therefore

	Su	M	T	W	Th	F	Sa
Total Need	0	11	6	8	6	10	0
Full-time	0	5	5	5	5	5	0
Part-time	0	6	1	3	1	4	0

Mabert and Raedels point out that a minimum of six part-time individuals must be employed to meet the peak Monday need. Suppose these people were identified as persons 1, 2, 3, 4, 5, and 6, with lower ID numbers indicating greater seniority and desire to work more hours. Then the heuristic to schedule them would simply call for cycling people through the days in order of their ID number. The simple result is as follows.

> **Monday**   Persons 1, 2, 3, 4, 5, 6
>
> **Tuesday**   Persons 1
>
> **Wednesday**   Persons 2, 3, 4
>
> **Thursday**   Persons 5
>
> **Friday**   Persons 6, 1, 2, 3

   In summary, we have examined three solutions to the staffing problem in this section. All approaches to the problem require a forecast of staff needs by day of the week. This forecast is then modified to account for part-time or temporary people. The regular full-time staff is then allocated across the remaining needs. Tibrewala, Philippe, and Browne looked at the problem as one of finding one schedule at a time. Monroe viewed the problem as one of finding as many consecutive pairs of regular days off as possible. In many cases, the solution required a heuristic approach to allocate nonconsecutive days. Rothstein extended Monroe's concept to a linear-programming formulation that looked for the maximum consecutive days off while automatically allocating nonconsecutive days off. Finally, a technique suggested by Mabert and Raebels was presented for scheduling shifts to part-time people.

10.4 SCHEDULING TO VARIATIONS WITHIN EACH SHIFT

The last section covered the problem of scheduling on which days people should work. The objective was to satisfy variations in the day-to-day staff needs in an economical way. In this section, the problem of scheduling around variation within the day is addressed. Demand for services can vary significantly during the course of the day. In a restaurant, for example, the problem is to provide staffing during the traditional eating hours. City bus drivers must be scheduled to work during the two daily rush-hour periods. Figure 10.9 is an illustration of a demand profile for one shift in a factory cafeteria. The objective of the scheduling problem is to determine when people should start their shift and when their rest and lunch breaks should

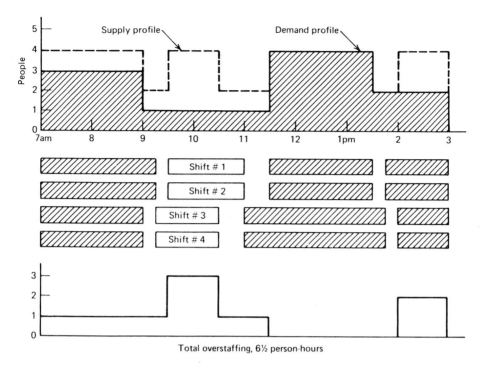

FIGURE 10.9 Typical eight hour staffing-needs profile in 15-minute periods.

occur so that the desired staffing level is maintained. For illustration purposes, several shifts are shown on the figure. The sum total of these sample shifts is shown as the staffing supply profile. In this section, we shall study a heuristic that intelligently identifies shifts to be included in the staffing schedule.

Luce† developed a heuristic that typifies the approach to this scheduling problem. Once again, the first step in the solution is to forecast the staff needs. In this case, the forecast should be in quarter-hour, half-hour, or hourly segments. Random sampling or time-lapse photographic studies of many days' activities can lead to profiles of the expected worker demand over given days. Such forecasts must be translated into the aggregate people needs on a period-by-period basis.

The shift schedule for each individual can be defined by the start time, stop time, and break periods during the day. In union shops, these times are often controlled by the labor contract. In any case, there are logical rules that describe an acceptable shift schedule. Figure 10.10 represents a reasonable set of day-shift scheduling rules. Note that rule 1 offers nine alternative start-times. In addition, rules 2 and 6 offer three alternative break-times each. Finally, rule 4 offers five alternative lunch-breaks. Counting the combinations,

---

†B. J. Luce, "A Shift Scheduling Algorithm," as reported in E. S. Buffa, *Modern Production/Operations Management*, 6th ed., John Wiley, New York, 1980.

Rule

1. Start time; $t_1 = 6:30, 6:45, 7:00, \ldots 8:15$, and $8:30$ a.m.
2. Morning break start; $t_2 = t_1 + 1:45, t_1 + 2:00, t_1 + 2:15$.
3. Morning break is 15 minutes long.
4. Lunch break start; $t_3 = t_1 + 3:30, t_1 + 3:45, t_1 + 4:00$ $t_1 + 4:15, t_1 + 4:30$.
5. Lunch break is 30 minutes long.
6. Afternoon break start; $t_4 = t_3 + 2:00, t_3 + 2:15, t_3 + 2:30$.
7. Afternoon break is 15 minutes long.
8. Quitting time; $t_5 = t_1 + 8:30$.

FIGURE 10.10   Typical rules for establishing day shift schedules.

these rules could be used to generate $9 \times 3 \times 5 \times 3 = 405$ possible day-shift schedules. In addition, there may also be 405 possible schedules for each of the other two shifts. Thus, the scheduler must solve his problem by selecting from these 1215 approved shift schedules.

The problem is now one of selecting which shift schedules to use. Luce proposed a computer program that selects shifts one at a time until the worker supply exceeds the demand during each period. For each selection cycle, the computer individually examines all approved shifts to find one that would minimize the absolute difference between the demand profile and the supply profile should the candidate schedule be included. (This rule is used in the computer program to be discussed shortly.)

Figure 10.11 illustrates a portion of the profiles of both worker supply and demand. A candidate shift is drawn into the figure. Visualize on the figure the meanings of the absolute deviation between the two profiles if the candidate were to be included. This is the Luce criterion for selecting which

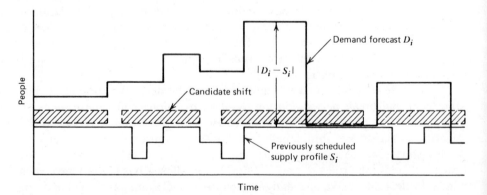

FIGURE 10.11   Worker supply and demand profile with a candidate schedule for in-clusion using Luce's approach to shift scheduling.

candidate to implement. If the candidate shift j were to begin in period k_j and last for L periods, an approximation to the Luce criterion is given by

$$J = \overset{min}{V_j} \left(b + \sum_{i=k_j}^{k_j+L} | D_i - S_i - 1| \right)$$ (10.1)

where

J = the shift schedule to be implemented
k_j = the starting period of candidate j
D_i = the total demand for work force in period i
S_i = the previously supplied work force in period i
b = the number of break periods in the candidate schedule

It is now time to translate Luce's approach into an algorithm.

Algorithm 10.3   Luce

Step 1   For each approved candidate schedule, do steps 2 and 3. If all candidates have been examined, go to step 4.

Step 2   For candidate j let the start time and number of periods included be k and $\mathscr{L}$ respectively. Calculate

$$\delta_j = \sum_{i=k}^{k+\mathscr{L}} | D_i - S_i - 1|$$

Step 3   If δ_j is the minimum value found so far, record as such and go to step 1; otherwise go directly to step 1.

Step 4   The minimum-value candidate found in step 3 is to be implemented. Record it as such. Add one to each value for supply from the kth to the $(k + \mathscr{L})$th value, except where breaks occur for the candidate. If $D_i - S_i \leq 0$ for all values of i, stop; otherwise return to step 1 and begin again.

Further to illustrate this algorithm, an example problem will be solved. The problem is given by the tabulated profile of demand given in Figure 10.12 and the set of candidates given in Figure 10.13. The solution was accomplished using a simple FORTRAN computer program. The solution to the example problem is tabulated in Figure 10.14. Note that the total absolute deviation is 321 fifteen-minute periods whereas the demand was totally satisfied utilizing 30 people. This number of people represents 900 periods of productive capacity. Thus, the 321 periods of idle capacity represents a 36% excess staffing.

Excessive idle capacity is going to occur whenever the variation in demand over the course of the day is large or when the duration of the

Period	Demand	Period	Demand	Period	Demand	Period	Demand	Period	Demand
1	5	2	5	3	6	4	7	5	10
6	15	7	15	8	15	9	15	10	15
11	20	12	20	13	20	14	20	15	20
16	18	17	18	18	18	19	18	20	18
21	18	22	18	23	15	24	15	25	15
26	10	27	10	28	10	29	10	30	15
31	15	32	15	33	15	34	15	35	15
36	10	37	10	38	10	39	10	40	8
41	8	42	6	43	6	44	6		

FIGURE 10.12 Demand profile for illustrative problem.

Schedule	Starting Period	Break Period	Lunch Periods		Break Period	Last Period
1	1	7	15	16	26	34
2	1	8	16	17	27	34
3	1	9	17	18	28	34
4	1	10	18	19	29	34
5	1	11	19	20	30	34
6	2	8	16	17	27	35
7	2	9	17	18	28	35
8	2	10	18	19	29	35
9	2	11	19	20	30	35
10	2	12	20	21	30	35
11	3	9	17	18	28	36
12	3	10	18	19	29	36
13	3	11	19	20	30	36
14	3	12	20	21	31	36
15	3	13	21	22	32	36

FIGURE 10.13 Set of candidate schedules for illustrative problem.

Schedule	Starting Period	Break Period	Lunch Period		Break Period	Last Period
16	4	10	18	19	29	37
17	4	11	19	20	30	37
18	4	12	20	21	31	37
19	4	13	21	20	32	37
20	4	14	22	23	33	37
21	5	11	19	20	30	38
22	5	12	20	21	31	38
23	5	13	21	22	32	38
24	5	14	22	23	33	38
25	5	15	23	24	34	38
26	6	12	20	21	31	39
27	6	13	21	22	32	39
28	6	14	22	23	33	39
29	6	15	23	24	34	39
30	6	16	24	25	35	39
31	7	13	21	22	32	40
32	7	14	22	23	33	40
33	7	15	23	24	34	40
34	7	16	24	25	35	40
35	7	17	25	26	36	40
36	9	15	23	24	34	42
37	9	16	24	25	35	42
38	9	17	25	26	36	42
39	9	18	26	27	37	42
40	9	19	27	28	38	42
41	10	16	24	25	35	43
42	10	17	25	26	36	43
43	10	18	26	27	37	43
44	10	19	27	28	38	43
45	10	20	28	29	39	43
46	11	17	25	26	36	44
47	11	18	26	27	37	44
48	11	19	27	28	38	44
49	11	20	28	29	39	44
50	11	21	29	30	40	44

FIGURE 10.13 (*Continued*)

Period	Supply	Demand	Deviation	Period	Supply	Demand	Deviation
1	9	5	4	2	9	5	4
3	10	6	4	4	11	7	4
5	18	10	8	6	21	15	6
7	17	15	2	8	18	15	3
9	22	15	7	10	22	15	7
11	27	20	7	12	29	20	9
13	27	20	7	14	29	20	9
15	22	20	2	16	21	18	3
17	18	18	0	18	27	18	9
19	26	18	8	20	26	18	8
21	26	18	8	22	26	18	8
23	26	15	11	24	27	15	12
25	23	15	8	26	17	10	7
27	29	10	19	28	29	10	19
29	29	10	19	30	27	15	12
31	29	15	14	32	27	15	12
33	29	15	14	34	27	15	12
35	21	15	6	36	14	10	4
37	19	10	9	38	19	10	9
39	12	10	2	40	9	8	1
41	8	8	0	42	8	6	2
43	7	6	1	44	7	6	1

Total absolute deviation = 321

Shifts Used in Schedule			
1	1	1	1
1	2	2	2
2	11	16	21
21	21	23	25
25	25	26	27
28	31	39	46
46	46	46	46
46	46		

FIGURE 10.14   Solution to illustrative example problem.

demand is significantly different from 8, 16, or 24 hours. In the example problem, demand varied from 5 to 20 people and the demand duration was 44 periods (10.25 hours). In such situations, it might be possible to add overtime to a few shifts so that poorly utilized shifts can be eliminated. The Luce algorithm does not guarantee an optimum solution. Reviewing the computer results to find possible shifts to eliminate from the schedule could yield significant improvements.

The significance of the Luce procedure lies in its instructive value. The design of a heuristic to schedule shifts into a widely varying demand-profile would follow the Luce procedure. Time studies can be used to create a process that will forecast service needs over the course of a day. Queuing theory analysis can then be applied to translate the forecast into personnel needs. Alternative shift schedules can be generated in consultation with the employees or their representative. The task then is one of fitting combinations of the acceptable schedules into the demand profile. Luce used a criterion of least absolute deviation to select the schedules for inclusion. Other criteria could also be used, such as the least resulting addition to idle capacity or the greatest contribution to periods of peak demand. After the demand profile is satisfied, an examination of the solution might reveal several shifts that generate far more excess capacity than they provide needed service. Overtime or part-time alternatives may allow for the elimination of these poorly utilized shifts. Finally, the set of chosen shifts is published and the personnel are involved in the processes of attaching names to each shift.

10.5 CASE STUDY

The following case study is presented to suggest a thorough analysis of a personnel scheduling problem. The facility in question is an outpatient HMO (Health Maintenance Organization) serving a metropolitan community.†

The sorts of service provided can be viewed in two ways. Some of the patients call for an appointment; their arrival times thus are controllable. Other patients are classed as "walk-ins," whose arrival times are predictable but uncontrollable. The clinic sees, on the average, 600 to 700 patients per day, seven days a week. Service needs fall into three categories. One group of patients requires only the services of a nurse under the doctor's supervision: perhaps for an immunization shot, TB test, or minor first aid. Another group of patients requires the doctor for consultation, diagnostic, and medication services. The remaining patients require the doctor followed by laboratory work.

The symptoms of scheduling problems were significant. At times, the

---

†The topic of this case was inspired by J. Rising, R. Baron and B. Averill, "A Systems Analysis of a University-Health-Service Outpatient Clinic," *Operations Research*, vol. 21, no. 5, 1973.

numbers of patients waiting for service was so great that they had to stand in the waiting room. Complaints about the long waits were becoming more frequent. The professional staff felt overworked and retention was becoming a problem. Physicians and nurses were often seeing patients long after closing time. Finally, physicians and nurses were sometimes idle for long periods because patients failed to keep appointments and walk-in traffic was low. The clear need was to find ways to smooth the work load and schedule the professional staff so that better service could be provided and employee morale could be improved.

The first step in the analysis was to gather data relating to arrival rates and service times. This was accomplished by means of the patient arrival form used to get necessary initial information when the patient enters the system. A time clock was used to stamp the arrival time. Temporary clerks were stationed at the entrances to various service areas. The arrival form was stamped in and out of each service until the visit was complete. This data collection activity was continued for three months. In addition, the past year's patient arrival forms without time stamps were used as data input.

The interarrival times and the service times for two weeks' data then were plotted. Chi-square tests were applied to see if these times fit the known queuing assumptions of negative exponential interarrival times and service times. Histograms of these times are shown in Figure 10.15. Note the means and standard deviations of distribution in the figure.

An analysis of week-of-the-year effects was conducted to see if the work load varied from week to week. Because the HMO was new and the number of families participating was growing steadily, it was not possible directly to correlate weekly patient visits. Instead, the percent variation in number of patient visits per participating family was plotted for each week of the year, for both walk-in and appointment visits. This plot is shown in Figure 10.16. The figures clearly show that the week of the year affected patient visits. The next question was to see if the day of the week affected patient loads. The average daily visits were therefore plotted for each day, and again a significant causal condition was observed. The plot of these averages are shown in Figure 10.17. Finally, the time of day was thought to be a factor. Several weeks' worth of data was therefore broken down by time of day and the average percent patient arrivals was plotted against the time of day. As Figure 10.18 suggests, predictable variations show up here also.

Using all of these factors, a model was built to forecast the walk-in patient demand on a daily basis. The model was based on the projected growth in subscribing families, the weekly variation factor, and the daily variation factor. The essence of that model is given in Figure 10.19.

In addition, a model to predict total weekly demand, walk-in plus appointment, was generated. This model is also presented in Figure 10.19. Using these two predictive models in combination, it is possible to plan the patient load so as to smooth out the load between days of the week. Suppose, for example, that the total weekly demand was forecasted to be 740 patient visits.

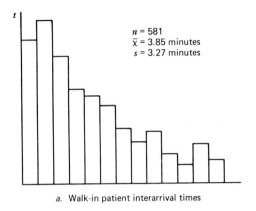

a. Walk-in patient interarrival times

n = 581
x̄ = 3.85 minutes
s = 3.27 minutes

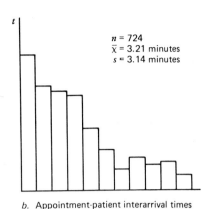

b. Appointment-patient interarrival times

n = 724
x̄ = 3.21 minutes
s = 3.14 minutes

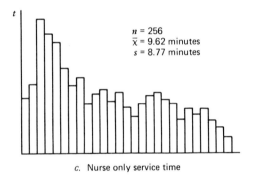

c. Nurse only service time

n = 256
x̄ = 9.62 minutes
s = 8.77 minutes

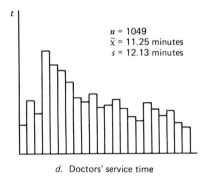

d. Doctors' service time

n = 1049
x̄ = 11.25 minutes
s = 12.13 minutes

FIGURE 10.15   Plots of interarrival and service times for case study.

Further, suppose that the decided breakdown is to have staff for 125 visits on each weekday, with the remainder on Saturday and Sunday. The policy is that all appointments be during the five weekdays. Then, knowing the daily walk-in forecast, the capacity for appointments is established as follows.

	Su	M	T	W	Th	F	Sa
Staff Demand	55	125	125	125	125	125	60
Walk-in	50	62	51	44	26	37	63
Appointments	—	63	74	81	99	88	—

In this fashion, the expected daily variation in demand is leveled by the use of the more-controllable appointments schedule.

Using queuing theory models for n parallel servers, it was determined that the customers would have to wait an average of about 20 minutes with

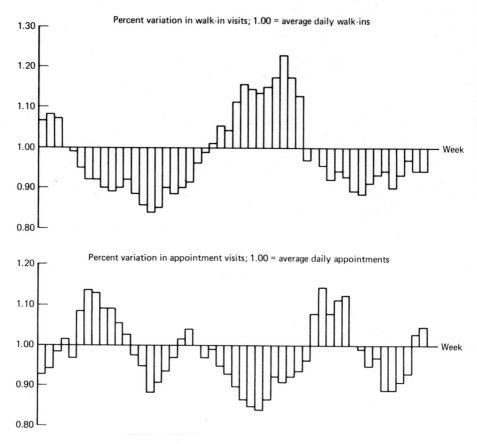

FIGURE 10.16   **Average percent variation in weekly walk-in and appointment patients per enrolled family as used in the case study.**

four doctors on hand during peak periods. The analysis for this conclusion follows the approach in Hillier and Lieberman.†

This wait was considered acceptable and the decision was made to have four doctors on hand during the weekdays and two doctors during the weekends. Because of other administrative and hospital responsibilities, doctors were scheduled for only five hours per shift and the HMO clinic was to be open 10 hours per day. Thus the demand profile for doctors was.

Su	M	T	W	Th	F	Sa
4	8	8	8	8	8	4

---

†F. S. Hillier and G. J. Lieberman, *Operations Research*, 2nd ed., Holden-Day, San Francisco, 1967, pp. 396, 401.

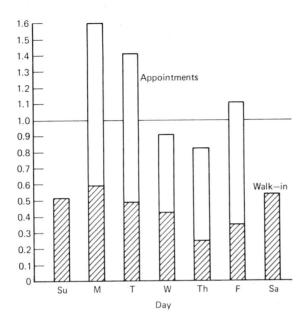

FIGURE 10.17 Average percent of total weekly visits occurring on each day and specified as walk-in or appointment for case study.

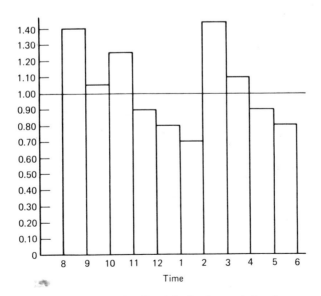

FIGURE 10.18 Average percent of daily visits by hour of the day as used in the case study.

$$W_d = TF_w \times P_{w,v/f} \times P_{w/y} \times P_{d/w}$$

$$D_w = TF_w \times (P_{w,v/f} + P_{a,v/f})$$

W_d = total walk-in demand for day d

D_w = total demand for week w

TF_w = total families enrolled in week w

$P_{w,v/f}$ = average percent walk-in visits per family per week

$P_{a,v/f}$ = average percent appointment visits per family per week

$P_{w/y}$ = average percent variation of week w of the year for walk-ins

$P_{d/w}$ = average percent variation of day d of the week for walk-ins

FIGURE 10.19   **Model to predict daily walk-in and total weekly patient visits in case study.**

With a total need of 48 doctor-shifts and each doctor working a five day week, a total of 10 doctors would be needed. The following is a schedule generation using Monroe's algorithm.

	Su	M	T	W	Th	F	Sa	(Su)	(M)	
Actual Demand	4	8	8	8	8	8	4	(4)	(8)	48
		+1				+1		+1		
Adjusted Demand	4	9	8	8	8	8	5	(4)	(9)	50
Total Staff	10	10	10	10	10	10	10	(10)	(10)	
Regular Days Off	6	1	2	2	2	2	5	(6)	1	
Pairs		SuM	MT	TW	WTh	ThF	FSa	SaSu	(SuM)	
First trial		1	0	2	0	2	0	5	1	

Doctor	Days Off	Doctor	Days OFF
1	Su/M	6	Sa/Su
2	T/W	7	Sa/Su
3	T/W	8	Sa/Su
4	Th/F	9	Sa/Su
5	Th/F	10	Sa/Su

It was decided permanently to assign the doctor with administrative responsibilities and his assistant to the #9 and #1 shift schedules above and to rotate the remaining eight doctors through the other eight schedules, changing schedules every week.

A similar analysis was made for the nursing staff. In this case, personnel had to be supplied for the types of customer services that required only a nurse as well as making nurse time available for doctors. Nurses, however, work eight-hour shifts, and fitting their time into the 10 hours per day of service caused concern. An analysis similar to that made for doctors resulted in the following staff schedules:

Nurse	Days Off	Nurse	Days Off
1	Su/M	8	Sa/Su
2	T/W	9	Sa/Su
3	T/W	10	Sa/Su
4	W/Th	11	Sa/Su
5	Th/F	12	Sa/Su
6	Th/F	13	Sa/Su
7	F/Sa		

However, scheduling when their shifts should start and end required an analysis of the daily demand profile. The analysis very quickly led to the decision to have about two-thirds of the daily nurse staff work from 8:00 a.m. to 4:30 p.m. and the remaining third work from 9:30 a.m. to 6:00 p.m. The choice of start times was selected by the nurses themselves on a seniority basis.

This personnel scheduling system was implemented for a two-month trial period. After the trial, interviews with the staff indicated that the approach was readily accepted. The regularity of the schedule and the smoother inflow of patients tended to remove the cycles of hectic and slow periods that had caused dissatisfaction. A re-study of the arrival and departure times of one week's patient load indicated a reduction in both the mean and variance of the average time in the system.

It was decided to review the plan every six months. Three statistics were to be developed for each review: the average customer wait-time, the ratio of walk-in over appointment patients, and the average day's wait to get an appointment. If any of these statistics increased by more than 20%, a study would be conducted to see if additional personnel were needed.

In summation, the problem was solved in part by making use of the controllable appointments schedule to flatten demand peaks. Once this was done, simple queuing analysis identified the size of doctor and nurse staffs needed to meet the flattened peak loads. Finally, the application of simple staff-scheduling heuristics gave a regularity to each individual's schedule.

10.6 REFERENCES

1. Hillier, F. S., and Lieberman, G. J., *Operations Research*, 2nd ed., Holden-Day, San Francisco, 1967.

2. Luce, B. J., "A Shift Scheduling Algorithm," as reported in E. S. Buffa,

Modern Production/Operations Management, 6th ed., Wiley, New York, 1980.

3. Mabert, V. A. and Raedels, A. R., "The Detail Scheduling of a Part-Time Work Force: A Case Study of Teller Staffing," *Decision Science*, vol. 8, no. 1, January 1977.

4. Monroe, G., "Scheduling Manpower for Service Operations," *Industrial Engineering*, August 1970.

5. Rising, J., Baron, R., and Averill, B., "A Systems Analysis of a University-Health-Service Outpatient Clinic," *Operations Research*, vol. 21, no. 5, 1973.

6. Rothstein, M., "Scheduling Manpower by Mathematical Programming," *Industrial Engineering*, vol. 4, no. 4, April 1972.

7. Tibrewala, R., Philippe, D., and Browne, J., "Optimal Scheduling of Two Consecutive Idle Periods," *Management Science*, vol. 19, no. 1, September 1972.

10.7 EXERCISES

The following demand forecasts are intended for use with Problems 1 through 18.

Data Set	Su	M	T	W	Th	F	Sa
A	6	6	6	6	6	6	6
B	2	6	7	6	7	6	4
C	1	6	7	7	7	6	1
D	2	9	10	10	9	9	2
E	7	4	4	4	4	4	8
F	5	5	5	5	5	5	5

(header: Personnel Demand)

1. Using Algorithm 10.1, determine a schedule for staffing Data Set *A*. Is the schedule optimal?
2. Do Problem 1 for data set *B*.
3. Do Problem 1 for data set *C*.
4. Using Algorithm 10.1, adjusted to handle shifts of four days and 10 hours per day, determine a schedule for Data Set *D*.
5. Using Algorithm 10.1, determine schedules for Data Sets *C*, *E*, and *F*. Note that all require 35 man-shifts but have different profiles. Discuss the results and the robost nature of the algorithm.
6. Write a FORTRAN program to implement Algorithm 10.1 and test it using Data Sets *A* through *F*.
7. Using Algorithm 10.2, determine a schedule for staffing Data Set *A*. Is the schedule optimal?

8. Do Problem 7 for data set *B*.

9. Do problem 7 for Data Set *C*.

10. Do Problem 7 adjusting Algorithm 10.2 to yield three regular days off with a maximum of the shifts having at least two of those days off consecutive. Use Data Set *D*.

11. Do Problem 5 using Algorithm 10.2.

12. Write a FORTRAN program to implement Algorithm 10.2 and test it using Data Sets *A* through *F*.

13. Using the linear-programming software available to you, find a schedule for Data Set *A*.

14. Do Problem 13 using Data Set *B*.

15. Do Problem 13 using Data Set *C*.

16. Do Problem 13 using Data Set *D*.

17. Do Problem 13 using Data Set *E*.

18. Do Problem 5 using a computerized linear-programming package.

19. Write a program that implements the Luce approach to personnel scheduling that would contain a section to sort the schedules before they are printed out. Alter the program to print the shift schedules unsorted. Then plot them into a graph of the demand forecast. Finally, remove shifts in the reverse order of their selection until the total overstaffing is just greater than 200 periods. How many periods of understaffing result from this reduction and how many shifts were removed? Was this a reasonable trade-off?

20. Alter the stopping criteria used in the program written for implementing the Luce algorithm. The present criterion is that the demand in all periods is satisfied. The desired criterion is that the total overstaffing exceeds 200 periods. How many periods of understaffing result from this reduction and how many shifts were saved from the 40 given in the illustrative problem?

21. Note that Problems 19 and 20 are intended to accomplish the same objective. Using the modified program suggested in either problem, tabulate the overstaffed periods and understaffed periods for schedules using 40, 39, 38, 37, 36, ... shifts. Suppose the cost of understaffing was twice the cost of overstaffing. What number of shifts minimizes the sum of these two costs?

22. Alter the shift selection criteria used in the program for implementing Algorithm 10.3. At present the criterion is to select that shift which minimizes the sum of the absolute deviations. The new criterion is to be the greatest number of periods that will be under the demand profile or, conversely, the fewest number of periods during times at which the demand is already satisfied. Compare the results to the illustrative problem solution.

APPENDIX A:

Z	0.00	0.01	0.02	0.03	0.04	Z
0.0	0.500 00	0.503 99	0.507 98	0.511 97	0.515 95	0.0
0.1	0.539 83	0.543 79	0.547 76	0.551 72	0.555 67	0.1
0.2	0.579 26	0.583 17	0.587 06	0.590 95	0.594 83	0.2
0.3	0.617 91	0.621 72	0.625 51	0.629 30	0.633 07	0.3
0.4	0.655 42	0.659 10	0.662 76	0.666 40	0.670 03	0.4
0.5	0.691 46	0.694 97	0.698 47	0.701 94	0.705 40	0.5
0.6	0.725 75	0.729 07	0.732 37	0.735 65	0.738 91	0.6
0.7	0.758 03	0.761 15	0.764 24	0.767 30	0.770 35	0.7
0.8	0.788 14	0.791 03	0.793 89	0.796 73	0.799 54	0.8
0.9	0.815 94	0.818 59	0.821 21	0.823 81	0.826 39	0.9
1.0	0.841 34	0.843 75	0.846 13	0.848 49	0.850 83	1.0
1.1	0.864 33	0.866 50	0.868 64	0.870 76	0.872 85	1.1
1.2	0.884 93	0.886 86	0.888 77	0.890 65	0.892 51	1.2
1.3	0.903 20	0.904 90	0.906 58	0.908 24	0.909 88	1.3
1.4	0.919 24	0.920 73	0.922 19	0.923 64	0.925 06	1.4
1.5	0.933 19	0.934 48	0.935 74	0.936 99	0.938 22	1.5
1.6	0.945 20	0.946 30	0.947 38	0.948 45	0.949 50	1.6
1.7	0.955 43	0.956 37	0.957 28	0.958 18	0.959 07	1.7
1.8	0.964 07	0.964 85	0.965 62	0.966 37	0.967 11	1.8
1.9	0.971 28	0.971 93	0.972 57	0.973 20	0.973 81	1.9
2.0	0.977 25	0.977 78	0.978 31	0.978 82	0.979 32	2.0
2.1	0.982 14	0.982 57	0.983 00	0.983 41	0.983 82	2.1
2.2	0.986 10	0.986 45	0.986 79	0.987 13	0.987 45	2.2
2.3	0.989 28	0.989 56	0.989 83	0.990 10	0.990 36	2.3
2.4	0.991 80	0.992 02	0.992 24	0.992 45	0.992 66	2.4
2.5	0.993 79	0.993 96	0.994 13	0.994 30	0.994 46	2.5
2.6	0.995 34	0.995 47	0.995 60	0.995 73	0.995 85	2.6
2.7	0.996 53	0.996 64	0.996 74	0.996 83	0.996 93	2.7
2.8	0.997 44	0.997 52	0.997 60	0.997 67	0.997 74	2.8
2.9	0.998 13	0.998 19	0.998 25	0.998 31	0.998 36	2.9
3.0	0.998 65	0.998 69	0.998 74	0.998 78	0.998 82	3.0
3.1	0.999 03	0.999 06	0.999 10	0.999 13	0.999 16	3.1
3.2	0.999 31	0.999 34	0.999 36	0.999 38	0.999 40	3.2
3.3	0.999 52	0.999 53	0.999 55	0.999 57	0.999 58	3.3
3.4	0.999 66	0.999 68	0.999 69	0.999 70	0.999 71	3.4
3.5	0.999 77	0.999 78	0.999 78	0.999 79	0.999 80	3.5
3.6	0.999 84	0.999 85	0.999 86	0.999 86	0.999 86	3.6
3.7	0.999 89	0.999 90	0.999 90	0.999 90	0.999 91	3.7
3.8	0.999 93	0.999 93	0.999 93	0.999 94	0.999 94	3.8
3.9	0.999 95	0.999 95	0.999 96	0.999 96	0.999 96	3.9

AREAS UNDER
THE NORMAL CURVE

Z	0.05	0.06	0.07	0.08	0.09	Z
0.0	0.519 94	0.523 92	0.527 90	0.531 88	0.535 86	0.0
0.1	0.559 62	0.563 56	0.567 49	0.571 42	0.575 34	0.1
0.2	0.598 71	0.602 57	0.606 42	0.610 26	0.614 09	0.2
0.3	0.636 83	0.640 58	0.644 31	0.648 03	0.651 73	0.3
0.4	0.673 64	0.677 24	0.680 82	0.684 38	0.687 93	0.4
0.5	0.708 84	0.712 26	0.715 66	0.719 04	0.722 40	0.5
0.6	0.742 15	0.745 37	0.748 57	0.751 75	0.754 90	0.6
0.7	0.773 37	0.776 37	0.779 35	0.782 30	0.785 23	0.7
0.8	0.802 34	0.805 10	0.807 85	0.810 57	0.813 27	0.8
0.9	0.828 94	0.831 47	0.833 97	0.836 46	0.838 91	0.9
1.0	0.853 14	0.855 43	0.857 69	0.859 93	0.862 14	1.0
1.1	0.874 93	0.876 97	0.879 00	0.881 00	0.882 97	1.1
1.2	0.894 35	0.896 16	0.897 96	0.899 73	0.901 47	1.2
1.3	0.911 49	0.913 08	0.914 65	0.916 21	0.917 73	1.3
1.4	0.926 47	0.927 85	0.929 22	0.930 56	0.931 89	1.4
1.5	0.939 43	0.940 62	0.941 79	0.942 95	0.944 08	1.5
1.6	0.950 53	0.951 54	0.952 54	0.953 52	0.954 48	1.6
1.7	0.959 94	0.960 80	0.961 64	0.962 46	0.963 27	1.7
1.8	0.967 84	0.968 56	0.969 26	0.969 95	0.970 62	1.8
1.9	0.974 41	0.975 00	0.975 58	0.976 15	0.976 70	1.9
2.0	0.979 82	0.980 30	0.980 77	0.981 24	0.981 69	2.0
2.1	0.984 22	0.984 61	0.985 00	0.985 37	0.985 74	2.1
2.2	0.987 78	0.988 09	0.988 40	0.988 70	0.988 99	2.2
2.3	0.990 61	0.990 86	0.991 11	0.991 34	0.991 58	2.3
2.4	0.992 86	0.993 05	0.993 24	0.993 43	0.993 61	2.4
2.5	0.994 61	0.994 77	0.994 92	0.995 06	0.995 20	2.5
2.6	0.995 98	0.996 09	0.996 21	0.996 32	0.996 43	2.6
2.7	0.997 02	0.997 11	0.997 20	0.997 28	0.997 36	2.7
2.8	0.997 81	0.997 88	0.997 95	0.998 01	0.998 07	2.8
2.9	0.998 41	0.998 46	0.998 51	0.998 56	0.998 61	2.9
3.0	0.998 86	0.998 89	0.998 93	0.998 97	0.999 00	3.0
3.1	0.999 18	0.999 21	0.999 24	0.999 26	0.999 29	3.1
3.2	0.999 42	0.999 44	0.999 46	0.999 48	0.999 50	3.2
3.3	0.999 60	0.999 61	0.999 62	0.999 64	0.999 65	3.3
3.4	0.999 72	0.999 73	0.999 74	0.999 75	0.999 76	3.4
3.5	0.999 81	0.999 81	0.999 82	0.999 83	0.999 83	3.5
3.6	0.999 87	0.999 87	0.999 88	0.999 88	0.999 89	3.6
3.7	0.999 91	0.999 92	0.999 92	0.999 92	0.999 92	3.7
3.8	0.999 94	0.999 94	0.999 95	0.999 95	0.999 95	3.8
3.9	0.999 96	0.999 96	0.999 96	0.999 97	0.999 97	3.9

APPENDIX B:
BEDSEAS PROGRAM

FURPUR 27R3-U4   E33 SL73R1 03/25/80 12:47:13

IEE461*LIBRARY(1).BEDSEAS

```
 1     C***********************************************************************      5
 2     C***********************************************************************     10
 3     C***********************************************************************     15
 4     C                                                                            20
 5     C                         THE BEDSEAS PROGRAM                                25
 6     C                                                                            30
 7     C                    (BEDWORTH SEASONAL INDEXES)                             35
 8     C                                                                            40
 9     C                   FOR FURTHER INFORMATION CONTACT                          45
10     C                        DAVID D. BEDWORTH                                   50
11     C               INDUSTRIAL ENGINEERING DEPARTMENT                            55
12     C                     ARIZONA STATE UNIVERSITY                               60
13     C                       TEMPE, ARIZONA 85281                                 65
14     C                                                                            70
15     C***********************************************************************     75
16     C***********************************************************************     80
17     C***********************************************************************     85
18     C                                                                            90
19     C          BEDSEAS ANALYZES  INPUT DATA TO DETERMINE SEASONAL                95
20     C          INDECES USING THE METHOD GIVEN IN THE TEXT: PRODUCTION           100
21     C          CONTROL SYSTEMS BY BEDWORTH AND BAILEY - JOHN WILEY              105
22     C          AND SONS - NEW YORK. THE SEASONAL INDEXES ARE USED IN            110
23     C          PREDICTING VALUES OVER A USER-SPECIFIED LEAD-TIME.               115
24     C                                                                           120
25     C***********************************************************************    125
26     C***********************************************************************    130
27     C***********************************************************************    135
28     C                                                                           140
29     C          INPUT REQUIREMENTS, USING CARD FORMATS, ARE AS FOLLOWS:          145
30     C          CARD J REPRESENTS TYPE J. THERE SHOULD BE MORE THAN 1 CARD OF    150
31     C          TYPE 3 FOR THIS PROGRAM.                                         155
32     C             (ALL INTEGER-FORMAT DATA IS RIGHT-JUSTIFIED IN FIELD)         160
33     C             CARD 1, COLS 1 - 78: FORMAT 13A6, USER TITLE INFORMATION.     165
34     C             CARD 2, COLS 1 - 10: INTEGER INDICATING NUMBER OF DATA        170
35     C                                  VALUES TO BE INPUT BY USER.              175
36     C                     COLS 11- 20: INTEGER INDICATING NUMBER OF SEASONAL    180
37     C                                  TIME UNITS WITHIN A TOTAL PERIOD.        185
38     C                                  IF MONTHS IN A YEAR-12;IF QUARTERS       190
39     C                                  IN A YEAR-4; IF DAYS IN A WEEK-7 OR      195
40     C                                  MAYBE 5.                                 200
41     C                     COLS 21- 30: INTEGER INDICATING NUMBER OF TOTAL       205
42     C                                  PERIODS FOR WHICH FORECAST REQUIRED.     210
43     C             CARD 3+; DATA CARDS. EACH DATA VALUE IS INPUT IN SEQUENCE     215
44     C                                  IN 6F10.3 FORAMT (COLS 1 - 60). EACH     220
45     C                                  CARD (OR PAIR OF CARDS) HOLDS THE        225
```

```
46    C                              SEASONAL TIME UNITS FOR ONE TOTAL          230
47    C                              PERIOD. FOR EXAMPLE:                        235
48    C                              SEASONAL TIME UNITS NUMBER IS 5.            240
49    C                              EACH DATA CARD WILL HOLD 5 VALUES.          245
50    C                              SEASONAL TIME UNITS NUMBER IS 10.           250
51    C                                1ST, 3RD, 5TH DATA CARD, ETC.,            255
52    C                                WILL HOLD SIX VALUES.                     260
53    C                                2ND, 4TH, 6TH DATA CARD, ETC.,            265
54    C                                WILL HOLD FOUR VALUES.                    270
55    C                                                                         275
56    C       AFTER THE LAST DATA CARD EITHER SET-UP A NEW DECK OR INSERT        280
57    C       TWO BLANK CARDS TO SIGNIFY TERMINATION.                           285
58    C                                                                         290
59    C                                                                         295
60    C       EXAMPLE WILL FOLLOW OF SET-UP. TWO RUNS ARE TO BE MADE.   THE      300
61    C       FIRST IS FOR 7 SEASONAL DAYS IN A WEEK AND THE SECOND IS FOR       305
62    C       4 QUARTERS INDICATING SEASONALS PER YEAR.                          310
63    C                                                                         315
64    C                                                                         320
65    C       TEST 1 - SEASONALS ARE 7 WITH 21 VALUES INPUT.                     325
66    C          21        7         1                                          330
67    C       15.200    3.600    145.300     8.000    12.600     3.000           335
68    C       80.900                                                            340
69    C       18.500    5.000    193.600    12.600    17.600     4.000           345
70    C       92.300                                                            350
71    C       13.600    4.200    147.000    11.000    10.300     3.600           355
72    C       84.600                                                            360
73    C       TEST 2 -  SEASONALS ARE   4  WITH   20 VALUES INPUT.               365
74    C          20        4         3                                          370
75    C        5.000    2.000    10.000    12.000                                375
76    C        8.000    3.000    18.000    23.000                                380
77    C       15.000   10.000    34.000    35.000                                385
78    C       45.000   21.000    93.000   102.000                                390
79    C       73.000   32.000   151.000   162.000                                395
80    C                                                                         400
81    C************************************************************************  405
82    C************************************************************************  410
83    C************************************************************************  415
84    C                                                                         420
85    C          BEDSEAS  WAS COMPILED IN ASCII-FORTRAN ON A UNIVAC-1110.        425
86    C          BOUNDS ON PROBLEMS TO BE RUN ARE                                430
87    C          1. NUMBER OF SEASONAL TIME UNITS WITHIN A TOTAL PERIOD          435
88    C             ARE EQUAL TO OR LESS THAN 12.                                440
89    C          2. MAXIMUM NUMBER OF DATA VALUES IS THE NUMBER OF               445
90    C             SEASONAL TIME UNITS (FOR A PARTICULAR PROBLEM)               450
91    C             MULTIPLIED BY 99.                                            455
92    C          3. NUMBER OF TOTAL PERIODS FORECAST SHOULD BE NO MORE           460
93    C             THAN 6.                                                      465
94    C************************************************************************  470
95    C************************************************************************  475
96    C************************************************************************  480
97    C************************************************************************  485
98    C          BEDSEAS WAS DEVELOPED BY DAVID D. BEDWORTH IN CONJUNCTION WITH   490
99    C          THE COURSE IEE 461 AT ARIZONA STATE UNIVERSITY.                 495
100   C                                                                         500
101   C************************************************************************  505
102   C************************************************************************  510
103   C************************************************************************  515
104   C************************************************************************  520
105         CHARACTER*6 TITLE(13)                                               525
106         DIMENSION DATA(99,12), SEAS(99,12), SEASJ(12), SUM3(99), PREDIC(99   530
107        1,12), PRETOT(99), DESEAS(99,12), PERTOT(99), ERROR(99,12), PRCNT(9   535
108        29,12), PFORE(1200), PDATA(1200)                                     540
109         READ 5,TITLE                                                        545
110       5 FORMAT (13A6)                                                       550
111         READ 10,ITOT,IPER,IFORE                                             555
112      10 FORMAT (3I10)                                                       560
```

```
113      15 N=ITOT/IPER                                              565
114         DO 35 I=1,N                                              570
115         IF (IPER-6) 20,20,30                                     575
116      20 READ 25,(DATA(I,J),J=1,IPER)                             580
117      25 FORMAT (6F10.3)                                          585
118         GO TO 35                                                 590
119      30 READ 25,(DATA(I,J),J=1,6)                                595
120         READ 25,(DATA(I,J),J=7,IPER)                             600
121      35 CONTINUE                                                 605
122      C     *COMPUTE SEASONAL FACTORS*                            610
123         DO 50 I=1,N                                              615
124         SUM=0.                                                   620
125         DO 40 J=1,IPER                                           625
126         SUM=SUM+DATA(I,J)                                        630
127      40 CONTINUE                                                 635
128         PERTOT(I)=SUM                                            640
129         DO 45 J=1,IPER                                           645
130         SEAS(I,J)=((DATA(I,J))*(IPER))/SUM                       650
131      45 CONTINUE                                                 655
132      50 CONTINUE                                                 660
133      C     *COMPUTE SEASONAL FACTOR J*                           665
134         DO 60 J=1,IPER                                           670
135         SUM=0.                                                   675
136         DO 55 I=1,N                                              680
137         SUM=SUM+SEAS(I,J)                                        685
138      55 CONTINUE                                                 690
139         SEASJ(J)=((SUM)*(IPER))/(ITOT)                           695
140      60 CONTINUE                                                 700
141      C     NORMALIZE SEASONALS                                   705
142         SUMS=0.                                                  710
143         DO 65 J=1,IPER                                           715
144      65 SUMS=SUMS+SEASJ(J)                                       720
145         DO 70 J=1,IPER                                           725
146      70 SEASJ(J)=(IPER*SEASJ(J))/(SUMS)                          730
147      C     *DESEASONALIZE DATA*                                  735
148         DO 80 I=1,N                                              740
149         DO 75 J=1,IPER                                           745
150         DESEAS(I,J)=(DATA(I,J))/(SEASJ(J))                       750
151      75 CONTINUE                                                 755
152      80 CONTINUE                                                 760
153         DO 90 I=1,N                                              765
154         SUM3(I)=0.                                               770
155         DO 85 J=1,IPER                                           775
156      85 SUM3(I)=SUM3(I)+DESEAS(I,J)                              780
157      90 CONTINUE                                                 785
158         DO 100 I=1,N                                             790
159         DO 95 J=1,IPER                                           795
160         DESEAS(I,J)=(DESEAS(I,J)*PERTOT(I))/SUM3(I)              800
161      95 CONTINUE                                                 805
162     100 CONTINUE                                                 810
163      C     *PRINT DATA(I,J), SEAS(J), DESEAS(I,J)*               815
164         PRINT 105,TITLE                                          820
165     105 FORMAT (1H1,1X,13A6)                                     825
166         PRINT 110,ITOT                                           830
167     110 FORMAT (//,2X,32HNUMBER OF DATA POINTS INPUT    =,2X,I3,//)   835
168         PRINT 115,IPER                                           840
169     115 FORMAT (//,2X,32HNUMBER OF SEASONALS PER PERIOD =,2X,I3,//)   845
170         PRINT 120,IFORE                                          850
171     120 FORMAT (//,2X,32HNUMBER OF PERIODS FOR FORECAST =,2X,I3,//)   855
172         PRINT 125                                                860
173     125 FORMAT (3X,34HORIGINAL INPUT DATA IS AS FOLLOWS:,///)    865
174         PRINT 130                                                870
175     130 FORMAT (40X,16HSEASONAL SEGMENT,/)                       875
176         PRINT 135,(J,J=1,IPER)                                   880
177     135 FORMAT (3X,6HPERIOD,12(8X,I2),//)                        885
178         DO 145 I=1,N                                             890
179         PRINT 140,I,(DATA(I,J),J=1,IPER)                         895
```

```
180        140 FORMAT (4X,I3,3X,12(1X,F8.2))                              900
181        145 CONTINUE                                                    905
182            PRINT 150                                                   910
183        150 FORMAT (1H1,3X,36HTHE SEASONAL INDEXES ARE AS FOLLOWS:,///)  915
184            PRINT 155                                                   920
185        155 FORMAT (30X,16HSEASONAL INDEXES,//)                        925
186            PRINT 160,(J,J=1,IPER)                                      930
187        160 FORMAT (8X,12(6X,I2))                                       935
188            PRINT 165,(SEASJ(J),J=1,IPER)                               940
189        165 FORMAT (13X,12(F6.4,2X))                                    945
190            PRINT 170                                                   950
191        170 FORMAT (///,3X,34HDESEASONALIZED DATA IS AS FOLLOWS:,//)    955
192            PRINT 175                                                   960
193        175 FORMAT (7X,6HPERIOD,28X,16HSEASONAL SEGMENT)                965
194            PRINT 180,(J,J=1,IPER)                                      970
195        180 FORMAT (7X,12(8X,I2))                                       975
196            DO 190 I=1,N                                                980
197            PRINT 185,I,(DESEAS(I,J),J=1,IPER)                          985
198        185 FORMAT (8X,I2,12(3X,F7.1))                                  990
199        190 CONTINUE                                                    995
200      C     *COMPUTE PERIOD PREDICTIONS ASSUMING QUADRATIC FIT*        1000
201      C     *MINIMUM OF 4 PERIODS OF DATA REQUIRED FOR FITTING*        1005
202            IF (N.LT.4) GO TO 360                                      1010
203            SUMI1=0.                                                   1015
204            SUMI2=0.                                                   1020
205            SUMI3=0.                                                   1025
206            SUMI4=0.                                                   1030
207            SUMDA=0.                                                   1035
208            SUMIY=0.                                                   1040
209            SUMI2Y=0.                                                  1045
210            DO 195 I=1,N                                               1050
211            SUMDA=SUMDA+PERTOT(I)                                      1055
212            SUMIY=SUMIY+(PERTOT(I)*I)                                  1060
213            SUMI2Y=SUMI2Y+(PERTOT(I)*I*I)                              1065
214            SUMI1=SUMI1+I                                              1070
215            SUMI2=SUMI2+I*I                                            1075
216            SUMI3=SUMI3+I*I*I                                          1080
217            SUMI4=SUMI4+I*I*I*I                                        1085
218        195 CONTINUE                                                   1090
219            SUMNI2=N*SUMI2                                             1095
220            SUMNI3=N*SUMI3                                             1100
221            SUMNI4=N*SUMI4                                             1105
222            ALPH=(SUMI1*SUMI2)-SUMNI3                                  1110
223            BETA=(SUMI1*SUMI1)-SUMNI2                                  1115
224            GAMA=(SUMI2*SUMI2)-SUMNI4                                  1120
225            DELT=(SUMI1*SUMDA)-(N*SUMIY)                               1125
226            THET=(SUMI2*SUMDA)-(N*SUMI2Y)                              1130
227            B=(GAMA*DELT-THET*ALPH)/(GAMA*BETA-ALPH*ALPH)              1135
228            C=(THET-B*ALPH)/GAMA                                       1140
229            A=(SUMDA/N)-(B*(SUMI1/N))-((C*SUMI2)/N)                    1145
230            K=N+1                                                      1150
231            IFORE=IFORE+N                                              1155
232            DO 205 L=1,IFORE                                           1160
233            PRETOT(L)=(A)+(B*L)+(C*L*L)                                1165
234            DO 200 J=1,IPER                                            1170
235        200 PREDIC(L,J)=((PRETOT(L))*(SEASJ(J)))/(IPER)               1175
236        205 CONTINUE                                                   1180
237      C     *PRINT PREDICTIONS FOR DESIRED LEAD-TIME VALUES*           1185
238            PRINT 210                                                  1190
239        210 FORMAT (1H1,2X,38HPREDICTION EQUATION THROUGH TOTALS IS:,///) 1195
240            IF (B.GE.0.AND.C.GE.0.) GO TO 220                          1200
241            IF (B.LT.0.AND.C.LT.0.) GO TO 230                          1205
242            IF (B.LT.0.) GO TO 240                                     1210
243            PRINT 215,A,B,C                                            1215
244        215 FORMAT (/,9H    (L)=,F10.3,1H+,F10.3,4H(L) ,F10.3,6H(L)(L),//) 1220
245            GO TO 250                                                  1225
```

```
246       220 PRINT 225,A,B,C                                                        1230
247       225 FORMAT (/,9H       (L)=,F10.3,1H+,F10.3,4H(L)+,F10.3,6H(L)(L),//)       1235
248           GO TO 250                                                              1240
249       230 PRINT 235,A,B,C                                                        1245
250       235 FORMAT (/,9H       (L)=,F10.3,1H ,F10.3,4H(L) ,F10.3,6H(L)(L),//)       1250
251           GO TO 250                                                              1255
252       240 PRINT 245,A,B,C                                                        1260
253       245 FORMAT (/,9H       (L)=,F10.3,1H ,F10.3,4H(L)+,F10.3,6H(L)(L),//)       1265
254       250 PRINT 255                                                              1270
255       255 FORMAT (2X,9HLEAD TIME,8X,5HTOTAL)                                      1275
256           K=N+1                                                                  1280
257           DO 265 I=K,IFORE                                                       1285
258           PRINT 260,I,PRETOT(I)                                                  1290
259       260 FORMAT (5X,I2,5X,F12.2)                                                1295
260       265 CONTINUE                                                               1300
261           PRINT 270                                                              1305
262       270 FORMAT (1H1,3X,36HSEASONAL PREDICTIONS ARE AS FOLLOWS:,///)             1310
263           PRINT 275                                                              1315
264       275 FORMAT (3X,8HFORECAST,30X,16HSEASONAL SEGMENT)                          1320
265           PRINT 280,(I,I=1,IPER)                                                 1325
266       280 FORMAT (4X,6HPERIOD,12(8X,I2),//)                                       1330
267           DO 285 I=1,N                                                           1335
268           PRINT 300,I,(PREDIC(I,J),J=1,IPER)                                     1340
269       285 CONTINUE                                                               1345
270           PRINT 290                                                              1350
271       290 FORMAT (//40(2X,1H*)//)                                                1355
272           PRINT 295                                                              1360
273       295 FORMAT (12X,43HFORECAST VALUES BEYOND GIVEN DATA ARE BELOW)             1365
274           DO 305 I=K,IFORE                                                       1370
275           PRINT 300,I,(PREDIC(I,J),J=1,IPER)                                     1375
276       300 FORMAT (4X,I2,9X,12(1X,F8.1))                                          1380
277       305 CONTINUE                                                               1385
278     C     DETERMINE MEAN ABS DEVIATION OF ERRORS THROUGH HISTORICAL DATA          1390
279           DO 315 I=1,N                                                           1395
280           DO 310 J=1,IPER                                                        1400
281           ERROR(I,J)=ABS(PREDIC(I,J)-DATA(I,J))                                  1405
282           PRCNT(I,J)=(ERROR(I,J)*100.)/DATA(I,J)                                 1410
283       310 CONTINUE                                                               1415
284       315 CONTINUE                                                               1420
285           SUMS1=0.                                                               1425
286           SUMS2=0.                                                               1430
287           DO 325 I=1,N                                                           1435
288           DO 320 J=1,IPER                                                        1440
289           SUMS1=SUMS1+ERROR(I,J)                                                 1445
290           SUMS2=SUMS2+PRCNT(I,J)                                                 1450
291       320 CONTINUE                                                               1455
292       325 CONTINUE                                                               1460
293           ERMN=(SUMS1)/(N*IPER)                                                  1465
294           PCTMN=(SUMS2)/(N*IPER)                                                 1470
295           PRINT 330,ERMN                                                         1475
296       330 FORMAT (//,3X,45HMEAN ABSOLUTE ERROR DEVIATION THROUGH DATA IS,F10      1480
297          1.4)                                                                    1485
298           PRINT 335,PCTMN                                                        1490
299       335 FORMAT (//,3X,38HMEAN PERCENT DEVIATION THROUGH DATA IS,F10.4)          1495
300     C     *SET UP FOR PLOT OF DATA VERSUS FORECASTING*                            1500
301           K=1                                                                    1505
302           DO 345 I=1,N                                                           1510
303           DO 340 J=1,IPER                                                        1515
304           PDATA(K)=DATA(I,J)                                                     1520
305           PFORE(K)=PREDIC(I,J)                                                   1525
306           K=K+1                                                                  1530
307       340 CONTINUE                                                               1535
308       345 CONTINUE                                                               1540
309           L=N+1                                                                  1545
310           DO 355 I=L,IFORE                                                       1550
311           DO 350 J=1,IPER                                                        1555
312           PFORE(K)=PREDIC(I,J)                                                   1560
```

```
313              K=K+1                                                      1565
314        350 CONTINUE                                                    1570
315        355 CONTINUE                                                    1575
316            M=(N*IPER)                                                  1580
317            N=(IFORE*IPER)                                              1585
318            CALL BLARGE (PDATA,M,BIG,SMALL)                             1590
319            CALL BLARGE (PFORE,N,BIGA,SMALLA)                           1595
320            IF (SMALLA.LT.SMALL) SMALL=SMALLA                          1600
321            IF (BIG.LT.BIGA) BIG=BIGA                                   1605
322            CALL BPLOT (PDATA,PFORE,M,N,BIG,SMALL)                      1610
323            GO TO 370                                                   1615
324     C      NOT ENOUGH DATA FOR PREDICTION - ERROR                     1620
325        360 PRINT 365                                                   1625
326        365 FORMAT (///,2X,48HTOTAL PERIODS LESS THAN 4, FORECAST NOT POSSIBLE  1630
327          1)                                                           1635
328        370 PRINT 375                                                   1640
329        375 FORMAT (///,7(3X,3H***),34HTHIS PROBLEM SET ANALYSIS COMPLETE,7(3X  1645
330          1,3H***))                                                    1650
331            READ 5,TITLE                                                1655
332            READ 10,ITOT,IPER,IFORE                                     1660
333            IF (ITOT.GT.0) GO TO 15                                     1665
334            STOP                                                        1670
335            END                                                        1675
336            SUBROUTINE BLARGE (ARRAY,M,BIG,SMALL)                         5
337            DIMENSION ARRAY(M)                                           10
338            BIG=ARRAY(1)                                                 15
339            SMALL=ARRAY(1)                                               20
340            DO 10 K=1,M                                                  25
341            IF (ARRAY(K).LT.BIG) GO TO 5                                 30
342            BIG=ARRAY(K)                                                 35
343          5 IF (SMALL.LT.ARRAY(K)) GO TO 10                             40
344            SMALL=ARRAY(K)                                               45
345         10 CONTINUE                                                     50
346            RETURN                                                       55
347            END                                                         60
348            SUBROUTINE BPLOT (POINT,ARRAY,M,N,BIG,SMALL)                  5
349            DIMENSION LIND(105), POINT(M), ARRAY(N), NAME(1)            10
350            INTEGER X, FORE, DATA, BLANK, EQUAL                         15
351            DATA X/1H*/, FORE/1HF/, DATA/1HD/, BLANK/1H /, EQUAL/1H=/   20
352            IPRNT=6                                                      25
353            RANGE=BIG-SMALL                                             30
354            IF (RANGE) 5,15,25                                          35
355          5 WRITE (IPRNT,10)                                            40
356         10 FORMAT (1H1,40HSMALL BIGGER THAN LARGEST DATA - NO PLOT)    45
357            GO TO 105                                                    50
358         15 WRITE (IPRNT,20)                                            55
359         20 FORMAT (1H1,38HPLOT IS JUST A CONSTANT - NO PLOT MADE)      60
360            GO TO 105                                                    65
361         25 DO 30 J=1,105                                               70
362         30 LIND(J)=X                                                    75
363            WRITE (IPRNT,35)                                            80
364         35 FORMAT (1H1)                                                 85
365            WRITE (IPRNT,40) LIND                                       90
366         40 FORMAT (1H ,105A1)                                          95
367            WRITE (IPRNT,45)                                           100
368         45 FORMAT (1H ,1H*,51X,1H*,51X,1H*)                           105
369            WRITE (IPRNT,50)                                           110
370         50 FORMAT (1H ,1H*,14X,7HPLOT OF,30X,1H*,16X,18HFORECAST SYMBOL: F,17  115
371          1X,1H*)                                                      120
372            WRITE (IPRNT,45)                                           125
373            WRITE (IPRNT,55)                                           130
374         55 FORMAT (1H ,1H*,19X,8HFORECAST,24X,1H*,16X,18HDATA SYMBOL IS:  D,1  135
375          17X,1H*)                                                     140
376            WRITE (IPRNT,45)                                           145
377            WRITE (IPRNT,60)                                           150
378         60 FORMAT (1H ,1H*,24X,11HVERSUS DATA,16X,1H*,16X,18HCOMMON POINT IS:  155
379          1 =,17X,1H*)                                                 160
```

```
380          WRITE (IPRNT,45)                                        165
381          WRITE (IPRNT,40) LIND                                   170
382          WRITE (IPRNT,65)                                        175
383          WRITE (IPRNT,65)                                        180
384       65 FORMAT (4X,1H*,48X,1H*,48X,1H*)                         185
385          WRITE (IPRNT,70)                                        190
386       70 FORMAT (1H ,7HMINIMUM,40X,9HMID-VALUE,42X,7HMAXIMUM)    195
387          FMID=(BIG+SMALL)/2.0                                    200
388          WRITE (IPRNT,75) SMALL,FMID,BIG                         205
389       75 FORMAT (1H ,F9.2,39X,F9.2,39X,F9.2)                     210
390          WRITE (IPRNT,65)                                        215
391          WRITE (IPRNT,65)                                        220
392          DO 80 J=1,105                                           225
393       80 LIND(J)=BLANK                                           230
394          DO 90 J=1,M                                             235
395          IPT=(((POINT(J)-SMALL)/RANGE)*98.0)+5.0                 240
396          JPT=(((ARRAY(J)-SMALL)/RANGE)*98.0)+5.0                 245
397          LIND(IPT)=DATA                                          250
398          LIND(JPT)=FORE                                          255
399          IF (IPT.EQ.JPT) LIND(IPT)=EQUAL                         260
400          WRITE (IPRNT,85) J,(LIND(K),K=5,103),J                  265
401       85 FORMAT (1H ,I3,99A1,I3)                                 270
402          LIND(IPT)=BLANK                                         275
403          LIND(JPT)=BLANK                                         280
404       90 CONTINUE                                                285
405          MK=M+1                                                  290
406          DO 95 J=MK,N                                            295
407          JPT=(((ARRAY(J)-SMALL)/RANGE)*98.0)+5.0                 300
408          LIND(JPT)=FORE                                          305
409          WRITE (IPRNT,85) J,(LIND(K),K=5,103),J                  310
410          LIND(JPT)=BLANK                                         315
411       95 CONTINUE                                                320
412          DO 100 J=1,105                                          325
413      100 LIND(J)=X                                               330
414          WRITE (IPRNT,40) LIND                                   335
415          WRITE (IPRNT,40) LIND                                   340
416          WRITE (IPRNT,40) LIND                                   345
417      105 RETURN                                                  350
418          END                                                     355
```

APPENDIX C: PREDICTS PROGRAM

FURPUR 27R3-U4   E33 SL73R1 03/24/80 14:40:08

```
IEE461*LIBRARY(1).PREDICTS
  1   C*******************************************************************    5
  2   C*******************************************************************   10
  3   C*******************************************************************   15
  4   C                                                                      20
  5   C                    THE PREDICTS PROGRAM                              25
  6   C                                                                      30
  7   C               (PREDICTION OF DISCRETE TIME SERIES)                   35
  8   C                                                                      40
  9   C                  FOR FURTHER INFORMATION CONTACT                     45
 10   C                       DAVID D. BEDWORTH                              50
 11   C                 INDUSTRIAL ENGINEERING DEPARTMENT                    55
 12   C                    ARIZONA STATE UNIVERSITY                          60
 13   C                      TEMPE, ARIZONA 85281                            65
 14   C                                                                      70
 15   C*******************************************************************   75
 16   C*******************************************************************   80
 17   C*******************************************************************   85
 18   C                                                                      90
 19   C         PREDICTS ANALYZES HISTORICAL DATA FOR GROWTH AND CYCLIC      95
 20   C         PATTERNS FOR PREDICTIVE PURPOSES. OPTIONS AVAILABLE         100
 21   C         INCLUDE:                                                    105
 22   C           1. GROWTH ONLY - REGRESSION FIT. PROGRAM WILL FIT UP      110
 23   C              TO A QUADRATIC MODEL, AT USER'S REQUEST, AND PREDICT   115
 24   C              OVER A USER-SPECIFIED LEAD-TIME.                       120
 25   C           2. GROWTH AND GROWTH WITH CYCLES - EXPONENTIAL SMOOTHING  125
 26   C              FOR THE GROWTH. UP TO A QUADRATIC GROWTH FIT CAN BE    130
 27   C              OPTIMALLY  DETERMINED. CYCLE FITS ARE BY A SPECTRAL    135
 28   C              ANALYSIS. MULTIPLE CYCLIC FITS MAY EVALUATE SEASONAL   140
 29   C              CHARACTERISTICS.                                       145
 30   C                                                                     150
 31   C*******************************************************************  155
 32   C*******************************************************************  160
 33   C*******************************************************************  165
 34   C                                                                     170
 35   C         INPUT REQUIREMENTS, USING CARD FORMATS, ARE AS FOLLOWS:     175
 36   C         CARD J REPRESENTS TYPE J. THERE SHOULD BE MORE THAN 1       180
 37   C         CARD OF TYPE 5.                                             185
 38   C         (ALL INTEGER-FORMAT DATA IS RIGHT-JUSTIFIED IN FIELD)       190
 39   C         CARD 1, COLS 1 - 80: FORMAT 20A4, USER TITLE INFORMATION.   195
 40   C         CARD 2, COLS 1 -  5: AN INTEGER(0,1,2,3) INDICATING ORDER   200
 41   C                              OF EXPONENTIAL SMOOTHING. IF 0,        205
 42   C                              TYPE WHICH MINIMIZES ERRORS SQUARED    210
 43   C                              IS DETERMINED. 1,2 OR 3 WILL FORCE     215
 44   C                              CONSTANT, LINEAR OR QUADRATIC MODEL.   220
 45   C              COLS 6 - 10: FORECAST LEAD TIME,USUALLY 1, I5.         225
```

```
 46    C                  COLS 11- 15: FORECAST HORIZON, I5.                     230
 47.   C                  COLS 16- 20: INTEGER INDICATING NUMBER OF FORCED        235
 48.   C                               CYCLES TO BE FIT BETWEEN 0 AND 5.          240
 49.   C                  COLS 21- 25: INTEGER INDICATING NUMBER OF CYCLES TO     245
 50.   C                               BE TRIED - CAN BE NO SMALLER THAN          250
 51.   C                               FORCED CYCLES NUMBER                       255
 52.   C                  COLS 26- 30: INTEGER INDICATING IF POLYNOMIAL TO        260
 53.   C                               BE REMOVED PRIOR TO CYCLE ANALYSIS.        265
 54.   C                               IF GROWTH SUSPECTED, POLYNOMIAL            270
 55.   C                               SHOULD BE REMOVED. 0 INDICATES NO          275
 56.   C                               REMOVAL AND 1, 2 OR 3 INDICATE             280
 57.   C                               CONSTANT, LINEAR OR QUADRATIC.             285
 58.   C                                                                         290
 59.   C                               NOTE: IF ONLY REGRESSION FIT WANTED,       295
 60.   C                               INDICATE TYPE BY 1, 2 OR 3.                300
 61.   C                  COLS 31 -35: INTEGER INDICATING SEARCH FOR OPTIMAL      305
 62.   C                               SMOOTHING CONSTANT. 1 WILL SEARCH,         310
 63.   C                               0 WILL NOT.                                315
 64.   C                  COL     55: A 1 INDICATES REGRESSION FIT ONLY. A        320
 65.   C                               ZERO OR BLANK, EXPONENTIAL SMOOTHING.      325
 66.   C                               IF REGRESSION ONLY, SKIP ALL DATA ON       330
 67.   C                               THIS CARD EXCEPT COLS 11-15,26-30, &55.    335
 68.   C          CARD 3, COLS  1 -80: 8F10.0, SMOOTHING CONSTANTS. IF USER       340
 69.   C                               SPECIFIED IN CARD 2 NON-OPTIMIZATION       345
 70.   C                               OF SMOOTHING, AT LEAST ONE VALUE HAS       350
 71.   C                               TO BE GREATER THAN 0.0. THE LAST           355
 72.   C                               VALUE HAS TO BE 0.0 (IF 4 VALUES ARE       360
 73.   C                               INPUT THEN COLS 51-60 HAVE TO CONTAIN      365
 74.   C                               0.0)                                       370
 75.   C                               NOTE: CARD NOT NEEDED IF REGRESSION        375
 76.   C                               ONLY.                                      380
 77.   C          CARD 4, COLS  1 -12:FORMAT FOR DATA INPUT, LEFT-JUSTIFIED,      385
 78.   C                               IN PARENTHESES. EXAMPLES: (F10.0),         390
 79.   C                               (8F10.3) ETC.                              395
 80.   C                  COLS 18-20:INTEGER REPRESENTING NUMBER OF PIECES        400
 81.   C                               OF DATA.                                   405
 82.   C                  COL     25:IF A DATA SET HAS BEEN INPUT AND             410
 83.   C                               ANOTHER ANALYSIS NEEDED WITH NEW           415
 84.   C                               PARAMETERS, INSERT *. THIS WILL            420
 85.   C                               REPLACE DATA CARDS - GO TO CARD 6.         425
 86.   C          CARD 5, DATA CARDS - USE FORMAT SPECIFIED IN PREVIOUS CARD.     430
 87.   C                               FOLLOW LAST ONE WITH STOP TYPED IN COLS    435
 88.   C                               1-4.                                       440
 89.   C                                                                         445
 90.   C          TWO EXAMPLES OF SETUP FOLLOW. THE FIRST IS FOR RESRESSION ONLY  450
 91.   C          AND THE SECOND IS FOR GROWTH + CYCLE. A SECOND RUN ON GROWTH    455
 92.   C          IS MADE.                                                        460
 93.   C     TEST 1 -  QUADRATIC REGRESSION, 14DATA VALUES  7F8.2, LEADTIME 4     465
 94.   C             4              3                   1                         470
 95.   C(7F8.2)          14                                                       475
 96.   C5.69     11.71     14.32     18.61     23.79     30.54     38.39          480
 97.   C60.23    72.40     85.61     99.31    115.21    135.30    160.19          485
 98.   C     TEST 2 - GROWTH AND CYCLES                                           490
 99.   C  3   1    4    2         3   0                                           495
100.   C0.1      0.2       0.0                                                    500
101.   C(6F10.0)          12                                                      505
102.   C      2.        4.        8.        10.       15.       21.              510
103.   C     70.       90.      115.       140.      170.      210.              515
104.   C     TEST 3 - GROWTH ON PREVIOUS DATA                                     520
105.   C  3   1    4    0         3   0                                           525
106.   C(8F10.0)          20    *                                                 530
107.   CSTOP                                                                      535
108.   C                                                                         540
109.   C                                                                         545
110.   C*********************************************************************     550
```

```
111.    C*********************************************************************    555
112.    C*********************************************************************    560
113.    C*********************************************************************    565
114.    C                                                                        570
115.    C          PREDICTS WAS COMPILED IN ASCII-FORTRAN ON A UNIVAC-1110.      575
116.    C          NUMBER OF DATA VALUES SHOULD BE LESS THAN 500.                580
117.    C                                                                        585
118.    C                                                                        590
119.    C*********************************************************************    595
120.    C*********************************************************************    600
121.    C*********************************************************************    605
122.    C                                                                        610
123.    C          PREDICTS WAS ORIGINALLY DEVELOPED BY CHESTER BRADLEY AND PETER 615
124.    C          REESE IN THE FORECASTING CLASS IEE 579 AT ARIZONA STATE       620
125.    C          UNIVERSITY. SUBSEQUENT CHANGES AND ADDITIONS WERE MADE BY     625
126.    C          DAVID D. BEDWORTH.                                            630
127.    C                                                                        635
128.    C*********************************************************************    640
129.    C*********************************************************************    645
130.    C*********************************************************************    650
131.    C*********************************************************************    655
132.          CHARACTER*6 NAME(13), NAME                                         660
133.          DIMENSION X(500), Y(500), Z(500), R(251), AT(4,5), A(500), XTX(4,4 665
134.         1), XTY(4), PERIOD(5), ALFA(8), S1(500), S2(500), S3(500), XF(500), 670
135.         2 IFMT(3),NAME(20)                                                  675
136.          INTEGER CYCLE, REGR                                                680
137.          COMMON S1, S2, S3, COEF1, COEF2, COEF3, COEF4, COEF5, SDEV         685
138.          DATA AC/1H$/, AB/1H*/, NAME1/4HSTOP/                               690
139.    C                                                                        695
140.    C     INITIALIZATION AND INPUT OF DATA -*-*-*-*-*-*-*-*-*-*-*-*-*--*-*   700
141.    C                                                                        705
142.          IPRNT=6                                                            710
143.          IREAD=5                                                            715
144.          PI=3.14159265358979                                               720
145.        5 READ (IREAD,10) NAME                                              725
146.       10 FORMAT (20A4)                                                      730
147.          IF (NAME(1).EQ.NAME1) GO TO 1105                                   735
148.          WRITE (IPRNT,15) NAME                                             740
149      15 FORMAT (1H1,13A6,37HASU INDUSTRIAL ENGINEERING - PREDICTS)           745
150         N2=0                                                                 750
151         ISWTCH=1                                                             755
152         DO 20 I=1,4                                                          760
153         DO 20 J=1,5                                                          765
154         PERIOD(J)=0.                                                         770
155      20 AT(I,J)=0.                                                           775
156         DO 25 I=1,500                                                        780
157      25 Y(I)=0.                                                              785
158         NCY=0                                                                790
159         READ (IREAD,30) ITYPSM,LDTM,IFORHZ,NFCYC,NCYCLS,ITREND,IOPT,KPFCYC   795
160        1,MXLG,CYCLE,REGR                                                     800
161      30 FORMAT (16I5)                                                        805
162         ISWC=0                                                               810
163         IF (REGR.EQ.0) GO TO 40                                             815
164         WRITE (IPRNT,35)                                                    820
165      35 FORMAT (//,2X,50HTHIS RUN WILL FORECAST USING A REGRESSION FIT ONL   825
166        1Y,//)                                                               830
167         GO TO 210                                                           835
168      40 IF (KPFCYC) 45,45,60                                                840
169      45 IF (NCYCLS) 50,50,60                                                845
170      50 IF (NFCYC) 55,55,60                                                 850
171      55 ISWC=1                                                              855
172      60 READ (IREAD,65) (ALFA(J),J=1,8)                                     860
173      65 FORMAT (8F10.0)                                                     865
174         IF (CYCLE) 80,80,70                                                 870
175      70 WRITE (IPRNT,75)                                                    875
176      75 FORMAT (//,2X,92HTHIS RUN WILL DETERMINE CYCLIC FITS ONLY - NO SMO   880
```

```
177         10THING OR FORECASTING WILL BE ACCOMPLISHED.,//)                    885
178            GO TO 195                                                         890
179      80 IF (ITYPSM-3) 95,95,90                                              895
180      85 FORMAT (1H0,23HILLEGAL SMOOTHING TYPE=,I10)                         900
181      90 WRITE (IPRNT,85) ITYPSM                                             905
182            CALL EXIT                                                        910
183      95 IF (ITYPSM) 90,110,100                                             915
184     100 WRITE (IPRNT,105) ITYPSM                                           920
185     105 FORMAT (1H0,4HTYPE,I3,2X,24HSMOOTHING WILL BE FORCED)              925
186     110 WRITE (IPRNT,115) LDTM                                             930
187     115 FORMAT (1H0,10HLEAD TIME=,I6)                                      935
188            WRITE (IPRNT,120) IFORHZ                                        940
189     120 FORMAT (1H0,17HFORECAST HORIZON=,I6)                              945
190            IF (NFCYC-NCYCLS) 135,135,125                                  950
191     125 WRITE (IPRNT,130) NFCYC,NCYCLS                                    955
192     130 FORMAT (1H0,31HILLEGAL NUMBER OF FORCED CYCLES,I3,2X,41HIS GREATER 960
193          1 THAN NUMBER OF CYCLIC ANALYSES,I3)                             965
194            CALL EXIT                                                      970
195     135 ICOMP=5                                                           975
196            IF (NCYCLS-ICOMP) 150,150,140                                  980
197     140 WRITE (IPRNT,145) NCYCLS,ICOMP                                    985
198     145 FORMAT (1H0,33HILLEGAL NUMBER OF CYCLIC ANALYSIS,I3,2X,20HMAXIMUM  990
199          1ALLOWABLE IS,I3)                                                995
200            CALL EXIT                                                      1000
201     150 WRITE (IPRNT,155) NFCYC,NCYCLS                                   1005
202     155 FORMAT (1H0,24HNUMBER OF FORCED CYCLES=,I3,2X,26HNUMBER OF CYCLIC 1010
203          1ANALYSES=,I3)                                                   1015
204            IF (ITREND) 160,160,170                                        1020
205     160 WRITE (IPRNT,165)                                                1025
206     165 FORMAT (1H0,69HPOLYNOMIAL FIT WILL NOT BE EXTRACTED FROM DATA BEFO 1030
207          1RE CYCLIC ANALYSES)                                             1035
208            GO TO 180                                                      1040
209     170 WRITE (IPRNT,175)                                                1045
210     175 FORMAT (1H0,65HPOLYNOMIAL FIT WILL BE EXTRACTED FROM DATA BEFORE C 1050
211          1YCLIC ANALYSES)                                                 1055
212     180 IF (IOPT) 195,195,185                                            1060
213     185 WRITE (IPRNT,190)                                                1065
214     190 FORMAT (1H0,79HPREDICTS PROGRAM WILL SELECT OPTIMAL SMOOTHING CONS 1070
215          1TANT,ALPHA,WITHIN + OR - .01)                                   1075
216     195 IF (KPFCYC) 210,210,200                                          1080
217     200 WRITE (IPRNT,205) KPFCYC                                          1085
218     205 FORMAT (1H0,9HPERIOD OF,I5,2X,22HWILL BE FORCED ON DATA)          1090
219            NCY=1                                                          1095
220            PERIOD(1)=KPFCYC                                              1100
221            NFCYC=NFCYC+1                                                 1105
222     210 WRITE (IPRNT,215)                                                1110
223     215 FORMAT (1H0,50H*******************INPUT DATA*******************)  1115
224            WRITE (IPRNT,220)                                            1120
225     220 FORMAT (/,1X,70HTIME        DATA SERIES        BASE SERIES    RE  1125
226          1SULTING INPUT SERIES)                                          1130
227            N=0                                                           1135
228            READ (IREAD,225) IFMT,N,ASTER                                1140
229     225 FORMAT (3A4,5X,I3,4X,A1)                                         1145
230            IF (N) 255,255,230                                           1150
231     230 IF (ASTER.EQ.AB) GO TO 240                                      1155
232            READ (IREAD,IFMT) (X(I),I=1,N)                               1160
233            N2=N+IFORHZ                                                   1165
234            DO 235 I=1,N2                                                1170
235     235 Y(I)=0.0                                                        1175
236            GO TO 240                                                    1180
237     240 DO 245 I=1,N                                                    1185
238            Z(I)=X(I)-Y(I)                                               1190
239     245 WRITE (IPRNT,265) I,X(I),Y(I),Z(I)                             1195
240            AN=N                                                         1200
241            IF (ASTER.NE.AB) GO TO 295                                   1205
242            WRITE (IPRNT,250)                                            1210
```

```
243        250 FORMAT (/,3X,51HDATA 'READ' FROM A PREVIOUS FILE AS USER REQUESTED   1215
244            1.,//)                                                              1220
245            GO TO 295                                                           1225
246        255 N=N+1                                                               1230
247            READ (IREAD,260) A1,X(N),Y(N)                                       1235
248        260 FORMAT (A1,3F20.0)                                                  1240
249            Z(N)=X(N)-Y(N)                                                      1245
250            WRITE (IPRNT,265) N,X(N),Y(N),Z(N)                                  1250
251        265 FORMAT (2X,I3,2X,3F20.4)                                            1255
252            IF (AC-A1) 270,290,270                                             1260
253        270 IF (AB-A1) 255,275,255                                             1265
254        275 N2=N+1                                                             1270
255        280 READ (IREAD,260) A1,X(N2),Y(N2)                                    1275
256            IF (AC-A1) 285,290,285                                             1280
257        285 N2=N2+1                                                            1285
258            GO TO 280                                                          1290
259        290 AN=N                                                               1295
260            IF (N2) 295,295,300                                                1300
261        295 N2=N                                                               1305
262        300 WRITE (IPRNT,305) N,N2                                             1310
263        305 FORMAT (1H0,28H NUMBER OF DATA POINTS READ=,I5,2X,34HNUMBER OF BAS  1315
264            1E SERIES POINTS READ=,I5)                                          1320
265      C                                                                         1325
266      C                                                                         1330
267      C     MAXIMUM LAG = N/2 OR MXLG INPUT BY USER                             1335
268      C                                                                         1340
269      C                                                                         1345
270            IF (REGR.EQ.0) GO TO 315                                            1350
271            CALL POLY (N,ITREND,BETA1,BETA2,BETA3,Z)                            1355
272            IT=ITREND-1                                                         1360
273            WRITE (IPRNT,310) IT,BETA1,BETA2,BETA3                              1365
274        310 FORMAT (//,2X,I3,3X,49HORDER POLYNOMIAL FIT TO THE DATA FOR FORECA  1370
275            1STING.,//,2X,23HPOLYNOMIAL EQUATION IS:,//,4X,28HY = A + B(Y) + C( 1375
276            2T-SQUARED).,//,4X,3HA =,F20.4,5H, B =,F20.4,11H,  AND C =,F20.4,/  1380
277            3/)                                                                 1385
278            GO TO 885                                                           1390
279        315 LAGP1=N/2                                                           1395
280            IF (MXLG) 330,330,320                                              1400
281        320 IF (MXLG-LAGP1) 325,330,330                                         1405
282        325 LAGP1=MXLG                                                          1410
283        330 WRITE (IPRNT,335) LAGP1                                             1415
284        335 FORMAT (///,2X,39HMAXIMUM LAG SIZE FOR CYCLIC ANALYSIS IS,I5,1H.)   1420
285            LAGP1=LAGP1+1                                                       1425
286      C     CALCULATE LEAST SQUARES FIT AND SUBTRACT FROM DATA.                 1430
287      C         ITREND = 1 CONSTANT MODEL POLYNOMIAL DELETED FROM THE DATA.     1435
288      C         ITRENS = 2 LINEAR MODEL POLYNOMIAL DELETED FROM THE DATA.       1440
289      C         ITREND = 3 QUADRATIC MODEL POLYNOMIAL DELETED FROM THE DATA.    1445
290      C                                                                         1450
291            IF (ITREND-1) 375,340,340                                          1455
292        340 CALL POLY (N,ITREND,BETA1,BETA2,BETA3,Z)                            1460
293            IT=ITREND-1                                                         1465
294            WRITE (IPRNT,345)                                                   1470
295        345 FORMAT (///,94H* * * * * * * * * * * * * * * * * * * * * * * * *    1475
296            1 * * * * * * * * * * * * * * * * * * *,//,10X,97HINITIAL POLY      1480
297            2NOMIAL WILL BE REMOVED FROM DATA AT USERS REQUEST. THIS FACILITAT  1485
298            3ES CYCLIC ANALYSES.,//,98H* * * * * * * * * * * * * * * * * * *    1490
299            4* * * * * * * * * * * * * * * * * * * * * * * * *,///)             1495
300            WRITE (IPRNT,350) IT,BETA1,BETA2,BETA3                              1500
301        350 FORMAT (//,2X,I3,3X,75HORDER POLYNOMIAL REMOVED FROM THE DATA. BAS  1505
302            1IC  POLYNOMIAL EQUATION FOLLOWS:,//,31H   Y = A + B(T) + C(T-SQUAR 1510
303            2ED).,//,8H,    A = ,F20.4,7H   B = ,F20.4,7H,  C = ,F20.4,1H.)     1515
304            IF (ITREND-1) 375,355,355                                          1520
305        355 WRITE (IPRNT,360)                                                   1525
306        360 FORMAT (1H1,3X,4HTIME,3X,13HORIGINAL DATA,6X,14HPOLYNOMIAL FIT,6X,  1530
307            113HADJUSTED DATA)                                                  1535
308            DO 370 I=1,N                                                        1540
```

```
309            AI=I                                                           1545
310            AI2=AI**2                                                      1550
311            FIT=BETA1+BETA2*AI+BETA3*AI2                                   1555
312            A(I)=Z(I)-FIT                                                  1560
313            WRITE (IPRNT,365) I,Z(I),FIT,A(I)                             1565
314        365 FORMAT (3X,I3,1F16.4,4F20.4)                                   1570
315        370 Z(I)=A(I)                                                      1575
316      C                                                                    1580
317      C     REMOVE FORCED CYCLE -*-*-*-*-*-*-*-*-*-*-*-*-*-*-*-*-*-*-*     1585
318      C                                                                    1590
319        375 IF (KPFCYC) 380,380,385                                       1595
320        380 IF (NCYCLS) 550,550,400                                       1600
321        385 WRITE (IPRNT,390) KPFCYC                                      1605
322        390 FORMAT (///,2X,24HA FORCED CYCLE OF PERIOD,I5,35H WILL BE REMOVED  1610
323           1AT   USERS REQUEST.,//)                                       1615
324            ISWTCH=2                                                      1620
325            GO TO 485                                                     1625
326        395 ISWTCH=1                                                      1630
327            IF (NCYCLS.GT.0) NCYCLS=NCYCLS-1                              1635
328            IF (NFCYC.GT.0) NFCYC=NFCYC-1                                 1640
329            IF (NCYCLS) 550,550,400                                       1645
330      C                                                                    1650
331      C     CALCULATE AUTOCOVARIANCES -*-*-*-*-*-*-*-*-*-*-*-*-*-*-*-*     1655
332      C                                                                    1660
333        400 CALL ACOVAR (Z,N,LAGP1,R)                                     1665
334            WRITE (IPRNT,405)                                            1670
335        405 FORMAT (//,2X,85HTHE FOLLOWING AUTOCORRELATION AND SPECTRAL RESULT  1675
336           1S   WERE USED IN THE DETERMINATION OF,/,3X,83HSIGNIFICANT CYCLE FRE
337           2QUENCIES   BUT   NOT CYCLE AMPLITUDES. THEREFORE, ONLY RAW POWER,/,2  1685
338           3X,97H VALUES ARE GIVEN.   THE MAXIMUM OF THESE MIGHT DENOTE SIGNIFI  1690
339           4CANT FREQUENCIES.   ACTUAL AMPLITUDES,/,2X,39H ARE FOUND THROUGH RE  1695
340           5GRESSION ANALYSIS.,//)                                        1700
341            IOUT=NCY+1                                                    1705
342            WRITE (IPRNT,410) IOUT                                       1710
343        410 FORMAT (1H0,15HCYCLIC ANALYSIS,I3,70H++++++++++++++++++++++++++++  1715
344           1+++++++++++++++++++++++++++++++++++++++++)                    1720
345            WRITE (IPRNT,415)                                           1725
346        415 FORMAT (1H0,15HAUTOCOVARIANCES,27X,28HAUTOCORRELATION COEFFICIENTS  1730
347           1)                                                            1735
348            POSUM=0.0                                                    1740
349            POSQ=0.0                                                     1745
350            DO 420 I=1,LAGP1                                             1750
351            K=I-1                                                        1755
352            ROE=R(I)/R(1)                                                1760
353        420 WRITE (IPRNT,425) K,R(I),ROE                                 1765
354        425 FORMAT (1H ,2HR(,I3,2H)=,F20.4,15X,F10.6)                    1770
355      C                                                                    1775
356      C     CALCULATE POWER SPECTRUM OF X -*-*-*-*-*-*-*-*-*-*-*-*-*-*     1780
357      C                                                                    1785
358            IF (NCYCLS) 590,590,430                                      1790
359        430 NCYCLS=NCYCLS-1                                              1795
360            WRITE (IPRNT,435)                                           1800
361        435 FORMAT (1H0,14HPOWER SPECTRUM)                              1805
362            J=3                                                         1810
363            BIGEST=0.                                                   1815
364            AJ=2.                                                       1820
365        440 POWER=R(1)                                                   1825
366            OMEGA=PI*2./AJ                                              1830
367            AJ=J                                                        1835
368            DO 445 I=2,LAGP1                                            1840
369            AI=I-1                                                      1845
370            POWER=POWER+2.*R(I)*COS(AI*OMEGA)                           1850
371        445 CONTINUE                                                     1855
372            POWER=POWER/PI                                              1860
373            POSUM=POSUM+POWER                                           1865
374            POSQ=POSQ+POWER*POWER                                       1870
```

```
375              K=J-1                                                        1875
376              WRITE (IPRNT,450) K,OMEGA,POWER                              1880
377         450 FORMAT (1H ,7HPERIOD=,I3,2X,6HOMEGA=,F10.4,2X,6HPOWER=,F20.4) 1885
378    C                                                                     1890
379    C         SELECT MAXIMUM FROM SPECTRAL DENSITY FUNCTION -*-*-*-*-*-*-*-* 1895
380    C                                                                     1900
381              IF (POWER-BIGEST) 460,460,455                               1905
382         455 BIGEST=POWER                                                 1910
383              KSAVE=J                                                     1915
384         460 J=J+1                                                        1920
385              IF (J-LAGP1) 440,440,465                                    1925
386    C                                                                     1930
387    C         REMOVE CYCLIC TREND FROM DATA -*-*-*-*-*-*--*-*-*--*-*-*-*-*-*-*-* 1935
388    C                                                                     1940
389         465 IOUT=KSAVE-1                                                 1945
390              WRITE (IPRNT,470) BIGEST,IOUT                               1950
391         470 FORMAT (1H0,26HMAXIMUM OF POWER SPECTRUM=,F20.6,2X,12HAT A PERIOD= 1955
392        1,I10)                                                           1960
393              LAG=LAGP1-2                                                 1965
394              FLAG=LAG                                                    1970
395              POMEAN=POSUM/FLAG                                           1975
396              POSTDE=((POSQ-(FLAG*POMEAN**2))/(FLAG-1.))**0.5             1980
397              UPLIM=POMEAN+2.*POSTDE                                      1985
398              WRITE (IPRNT,475) UPLIM                                     1990
399         475 FORMAT (1H0,46HUPPER CONTROL LIMIT FOR POWER, MEAN + 2(SE),= ,F12. 1995
400        12,58H. IF MAXIMUM POWER IS BELOW THIS VALUE THEN THIS CYCLE AND,/, 2000
401        2124H ANY SUBSEQUENT CYCLES SHOULD PROBABLY NOT BE INCLUDED. IF THI 2005
402        3S IS THE CASE, ANOTHER RUN SHOULD BE MADE WITH REDUCED CYCLES.)  2010
403         480 FORMAT (///,2X,44HTIME    CYCLE ADJUSTED DATA    CYCLE FIT DATA) 2015
404    C                                                                     2020
405    C        FIT CURVE Y=A1*SIN(  W *T)+A2*T*SIN(  W* T)+A3*COS(  W *T)    2025
406    C        +A4*T*COS(    W*T)  AND REMOVE FROM DATA -*-*-*-*-*-*-*-*-*-*-*-*-* 2030
407    C                                                                     2035
408              NCY=NCY+1                                                   2040
409              PERIOD(NCY)=KSAVE-1                                         2045
410         485 TPIOP=2.*PI/PERIOD(NCY)                                      2050
411              DO 490 I=1,4                                                2055
412              DO 490 J=1,4                                                2060
413              XTY(I)=0.                                                   2065
414         490 XTX(I,J)=0.                                                  2070
415              SMALL=1.0E-10                                               2075
416              DO 515 I=1,N                                                2080
417              T=I                                                         2085
418              OMEG=(T)*(TPIOP)                                            2090
419              SINA=SIN(OMEG)                                              2095
420              SDIFF=ABS(SINA-SMALL)                                       2100
421              IF (SDIFF) 495,495,500                                      2105
422         495 SINA=0.0                                                     2110
423         500 SINA2=SINA**2                                                2115
424              COSA=COS(OMEG)                                              2120
425              CDIFF=ABS(COSA-SMALL)                                       2125
426              IF (CDIFF) 505,505,510                                      2130
427         505 COSA=0.0                                                     2135
428         510 COSA2=COSA**2                                                2140
429              XTY(1)=XTY(1)+Z(I)*SINA                                     2145
430              XTY(2)=XTY(2)+T*Z(I)*SINA                                   2150
431              XTY(3)=XTY(3)+Z(I)*COSA                                     2155
432              XTY(4)=XTY(4)+T*Z(I)*COSA                                   2160
433              XTX(1,1)=XTX(1,1)+SINA2                                     2165
434              XTX(1,2)=XTX(1,2)+T*SINA2                                   2170
435              XTX(1,3)=XTX(1,3)+SINA*COSA                                 2175
436              XTX(1,4)=XTX(1,4)+T*SINA*COSA                               2180
437              XTX(2,2)=XTX(2,2)+T**2*SINA2                                2185
438              XTX(2,4)=XTX(2,4)+T**2*SINA*COSA                            2190
439              XTX(3,3)=XTX(3,3)+COSA2                                     2195
440              XTX(3,4)=XTX(3,4)+T*COSA2                                   2200
441         515 XTX(4,4)=XTX(4,4)+T**2*COSA2                                 2205
```

```
442            XTX(2,3)=XTX(1,4)                                                    2210
443            XTX(2,1)=XTX(1,2)                                                    2215
444            XTX(3,1)=XTX(1,3)                                                    2220
445            XTX(4,1)=XTX(1,4)                                                    2225
446            XTX(3,2)=XTX(2,3)                                                    2230
447            XTX(4,2)=XTX(2,4)                                                    2235
448            XTX(4,3)=XTX(3,4)                                                    2240
449            CALL INVERT (XTX,4)                                                  2245
450            DO 520 J=1,4                                                         2250
451            DO 520 I=1,4                                                         2255
452        520 AT(J,NCY)=AT(J,NCY)+XTX(J,I)*XTY(I)                                  2260
453            WRITE (IPRNT,525)                                                    2265
454        525 FORMAT (//,3X,113HTHE FOLLOWING CYCLE ADJUSTED VALUES ARE FORMED B   2270
455           1Y:  (ORIGINAL DATA MINUS ANY POLYNOMIAL REMOVED MINUS CYCLE FIT).,   2275
456           2//)                                                                  2280
457            WRITE (IPRNT,480)                                                    2285
458            DO 530 I=1,N                                                         2290
459            T=I                                                                  2295
460            FIT=(AT(1,NCY)+AT(2,NCY)*T)*SIN(T*TPIOP)+(AT(3,NCY)+T*AT(4,NCY))*C   2300
461            FIT=(AT(1,NCY)+AT(2,NCY)*T)*SIN(T*TPIOP)+(AT(3,NCY)+T*AT(4,NCY))*C   2305
462           1OS(T*TPIOP)                                                          2310
463            Z(I)=Z(I)-FIT                                                        2315
464        530 WRITE (IPRNT,365) I,Z(I),FIT                                         2320
465            WRITE (IPRNT,535) AT(1,NCY),AT(2,NCY),AT(3,NCY),AT(4,NCY),TPIOP      2325
466        535 FORMAT (//,2X,95HCYCLE FIT IS OF THE FORM: Y = (A1 + A2(T))SIN(WT)   2330
467           1 +  (A3 + A4(T))COS(WT). FOR THIS FIT WE HAVE:,//,8H    A1 = ,F15.4  2335
468           2,2X,7H, A2 = ,F15.4,7H, A3 = ,F15.4,7H, A4 = ,F15.4,10H, AND W = ,   2340
469           3F15.4)                                                               2345
470            WRITE (IPRNT,540)                                                    2350
471        540 FORMAT (//,3X,86H* * * * * * * * * * * * * * * * * * * * * * * *      2355
472           1 * * * * * * * * * * * * * * * * * ,//)                              2360
473            GO TO (545,395), ISWTCH                                              2365
474        545 IF (NCYCLS) 550,550,400                                             2370
475      C                                                                          2375
476      C       REBUILD INPUT DATA VECTOR                                          2380
477      C                                                                          2385
478        550 DO 555 I=1,N                                                         2390
479        555 Z(I)=X(I)-Y(I)                                                       2395
480      C                                                                          2400
481      C       REMOVE CALCULATED CYCLES FROM RAW DATA -*-*-*-*-*-*-*-*-*-*-*-*-   2405
482      C                                                                          2410
483            IF (NFCYC) 560,560,565                                              2415
484        560 IF (CYCLE) 590,590,5                                                 2420
485        565 WRITE (IPRNT,570)                                                    2425
486        570 FORMAT (//,3X,85HTHE FOLLOWING CYCLE ADJUSTED VALUES ARE FORMED BY   2430
487           1:  (ORIGINAL DATA MINUS CYCLIC FIT).,//)                            2435
488            DO 585 K=1,NFCYC                                                     2440
489            WRITE (IPRNT,575) K,PERIOD(K)                                        2445
490        575 FORMAT (1H0,12HFORCED CYCLE,I4,2X,7HPERIOD=,F10.6)                   2450
491            WRITE (IPRNT,580)                                                    2455
492        580 FORMAT (///,2X,38HTIME   CYCLE ADJUSTED DATA    CYCLE FIT,/)         2460
493            TPIOP=2.*PI/PERIOD(K)                                                2465
494            DO 585 I=1,N                                                         2470
495            T=I                                                                  2475
496            FIT=(AT(1,K)+AT(2,K)*T)*SIN(T*TPIOP)+(AT(3,K)+T*AT(4,K))*COS(T*TPI   2480
497           1OP)                                                                  2485
498            Z(I)=Z(I)-FIT                                                        2490
499        585 WRITE (IPRNT,365) I,Z(I),FIT                                         2495
500            IF (CYCLE) 590,590,5                                                 2500
501      C                                                                          2505
502      C       PERFORM EXPONENTIAL SMOOTHING -*-*-*-*-*-*-*-*-*-*-*-*-*-*-*-*     2510
503      C                                                                          2515
504      C       USE INPUT SPECIFIED ALPHAS                                         2520
505      C                                                                          2525
506        590 IF (ISWC) 605,605,595                                               2530
507        595 WRITE (IPRNT,600)                                                    2535
508        600 FORMAT (//,2X,110HNO CYCLIC ANALYSIS HAS BEEN REQUESTED FOR THIS R   2540
```

```
509          1UN. GROWTH ANALYSIS WILL NOW BE MADE BY EXPONENTIAL SMOOTHING.,///   2545
510          2)                                                                   2550
511          GO TO 615                                                            2555
512     605 WRITE (IPRNT,610)                                                     2560
513     610 FORMAT (//,2X,95HCYCLIC ANALYSIS IS NOW COMPLETE. GROWTH ANALYSIS     2565
514          1WILL BE ACCOMPLISHED BY EXPONENTIAL SMOOTHING.,///)                 2570
515     615 WRITE (IPRNT,620)                                                     2575
516     620 FORMAT (1H0,14HSMOOTHING TYPE,12X,5HALPHA,5X,26HSUM OF ABSOLUTE DE     2580
517          1VIATIONS,2X,23HMEAN ABSOLUTE DEVIATION,2X,17HSUM OF DEVIATIONS)     2585
518          DEVMIN=1.0E30                                                        2590
519          DO 665 ITYPE=1,3                                                     2595
520          IN=0                                                                 2600
521          IF (ITYPSM) 630,630,625                                              2605
522     625 IF (ITYPSM-ITYPE) 665,630,665                                         2610
523     630 IN=IN+1                                                               2615
524          IF (ALFA(IN)) 635,635,640                                            2620
525     635 IF (IN-8) 630,665,665                                                 2625
526     640 CALL EXPSMO (Z,N,ALFA(IN),BETA1,BETA2,BETA3,SABDEV,ITYPE,LDTM,DEVM     2630
527          1,SDEVSQ)                                                            2635
528          WRITE (IPRNT,645) ITYPE,ALFA(IN),SABDEV,DEVM,SDEV                    2640
529     645 FORMAT (1H ,7X,I3,4X,F20.4,2X,F20.4,2X,F20.4,2X,F20.4)                2645
530          IF (DEVMIN-SABDEV) 635,635,650                                       2650
531     650 IF (ITYPSM) 660,660,655                                               2655
532     655 IF (ITYPSM-ITYPE) 635,660,635                                         2660
533     660 SALFA=ALFA(IN)                                                        2665
534          ISTYPE=ITYPE                                                         2670
535          DEVMIN=SABDEV                                                        2675
536          SMIN=SDEV                                                            2680
537          DEVMI=DEVM                                                           2685
538          GO TO 635                                                            2690
539     665 CONTINUE                                                              2695
540          SMALL1=1.0E-8                                                        2700
541          SMALL=1.0E30                                                         2705
542          IF (IOPT-1) 670,680,680                                             2710
543     670 WRITE (IPRNT,675)                                                     2715
544     675 FORMAT (//,3X,107HRESULTS WERE BASED ON USER REQUESTED SMOOTHING O    2720
545          1R ORDER CHARACTERISTICS SO *OPTIMAL* IS ONLY LOCAL OPTIMAL.,//)     2725
546          GO TO 785                                                            2730
547   C                                                                          2735
548   C      SEARCH FOR OPTIMAL SMOOTHING TYPE AND CONSTANT -*-*-*-*-*-*-*-*-*-   2740
549   C                                                                          2745
550     680 DO 750 ITYPE=1,3                                                      2750
551          DALPHA=.1                                                            2755
552          ALCOMP=1.0E30                                                        2760
553          ALPHA=0.1                                                            2765
554          IF (ITYPSM) 690,690,685                                              2770
555     685 IF (ITYPSM-ITYPE) 750,690,750                                         2775
556     690 CALL EXPSMO (Z,N,ALPHA,BETA1,BETA2,BETA3,SABDEV,ITYPE,LDTM,DEVM,SD    2780
557          1EVSQ)                                                               2785
558          IF (ALCOMP-SABDEV) 715,695,695                                       2790
559   C      MAXIMUM ALLOWABLE ALPHA = 0.5                                        2795
560     695 IF (ALPHA-0.5) 700,700,735                                            2800
561     700 ALSAVE=ALPHA                                                          2805
562          ISAVE=ITYPE                                                          2810
563          ALCOMP=SABDEV                                                        2815
564          OMIN=SDEV                                                            282
565          ODEVMI=DEVM                                                          2825
566          IF (SABDEV-SMALL1) 705,705,710                                       2830
567     705 IF (ALPHA-0.01) 755,745,745                                           2835
568     710 ALPHA=ALPHA+DALPHA                                                    2840
569          GO TO 690                                                            2845
570     715 IF (DALPHA*2.-.01) 730,730,720                                        2850
571     720 ALPHA=ALPHA-DALPHA*2.                                                 2855
572          ALCOMP=1.0E30                                                        2860
573          DALPHA=DALPHA/2.                                                     2865
574   C      MINIMUM VALUE OF ALPHA ALLOWED = .01 -*-*-*-*-*-*-*-*-*-*-*-*-*-*-   2870
575          IF (ALPHA-0.01) 725,690,690                                          2875
```

```
576    725 ALPHA=0.01                                                        2880
577        GO TO 690                                                         2885
578    730 IF (SMALL-ALCOMP) 750,750,735                                     2890
579    735 IF (ITYPSM) 745,745,740                                           2895
580    740 IF (ITYPSM-ITYPE) 750,745,750                                     2900
581    745 SMALL=ALCOMP                                                      2905
582        KSAVE=ISAVE                                                       2910
583        SAVEA=ALSAVE                                                      2915
584        SOMIN=OMIN                                                        2920
585        SODEVM=ODEVMI                                                     2925
586    750 CONTINUE                                                          2930
587    755 SALFA=SAVEA                                                       2935
588        ISTYPE=KSAVE                                                      2940
589        DEVMIN=SMALL                                                      2945
590        SMIN=SOMIN                                                        2950
591        DEVMI=SODEVM                                                      2955
592        CALL EXPSMO (Z,N,SALFA,BETA1,BETA2,BETA3,SABDEV,ISTYPE,LDTM,DEVM,S 2960
593       1DEVSQ)                                                           2965
594        WRITE (IPRNT,760) ISTYPE,SALFA,SABDEV,DEVM,SDEV                   2970
595    760 FORMAT (8X,I3,4X,F20.4,2X,F20.4,2X,F20.4,2X,F20.4)                2975
596        WRITE (IPRNT,765)                                                 2980
597    765 FORMAT (///,3X,105HNOTE - THE FINAL ALPHA VALUE WAS FOUND USING A S 2985
598       1EARCH TECHNIQUE. ALL OTHERS WERE FOUND AS USER REQUESTED.)       2990
599        IF (ITYPSM) 775,775,770                                          2995
600    770 WRITE (IPRNT,675)                                                 3000
601    775 WRITE (IPRNT,780)                                                 3005
602    780 FORMAT (///,3X,105HWARNING - OPTIMAL SEARCH RESTRICTED TO A MAXIMU 3010
603       1M   ALPHA OF 0.5. ANY HIGHER VALUE INDICATES INVALID MODEL)      3015
604  C                                                                       3020
605  C       FINAL OUTPUT OF SMOOTHED DATA AND FORECAST OVER LEAD TIME -*-*-*-* 3025
606  C                                                                       3030
607    785 IF (ISTYPE) 790,790,795                                          3035
608    790 ISTYPE=ITYPE                                                      3040
609    795 CALL EXPSMO (Z,N,SALFA,BETA1,BETA2,BETA3,SABDEV,ISTYPE,LDTM,DEVM,S 3045
610       1DEVSQ)                                                           3050
611        WRITE (IPRNT,800) ISTYPE,SALFA                                    3055
612    800 FORMAT (//,3X,24HOPTIMAL SMOOTHING TYPE =,I3,2X,7HALPHA =,F15.4)  3060
613        SMALL1=1.0E-2                                                     3065
614        IF (SALFA-.3) 810,810,805                                        3070
615    805 IF (SABDEV-SMALL1) 840,840,820                                   3075
616    810 IF (SALFA-.01) 815,815,840                                       3080
617    815 IF (SABDEV-SMALL1) 840,840,830                                   3085
618    820 WRITE (IPRNT,825)                                                 3090
619    825 FORMAT (//,3X,61HOPTIMAL ALPHA GREATER THAN 0.3 MAY INDICATE AN IN 3095
620       1VALID MODEL.)                                                    3100
621        GO TO 840                                                         3105
622    830 WRITE (IPRNT,835)                                                 3110
623    835 FORMAT (//,3X,67HOPTIMAL ALPHA EQUAL TO 0.01 MAY INDICATE NEED FOR 3115
624       1 PROBABILITY MODEL,//)                                          3120
625  C                                                                       3125
626  C       PRINT CURRENT GROWTH EQUATION.                                  3130
627  C                                                                       3135
628    840 WRITE (IPRNT,845)                                                 3140
629    845 FORMAT (//,3X,45HTHE OPTIMAL GROWTH EQUATION FROM SMOOTHING IS)   3145
630        IF (ISTYPE-2.) 850,860,875                                       3150
631  C                                                                       3155
632  C       CONSTANT MODEL OPTIMUM.                                         3160
633  C                                                                       3165
634    850 WRITE (IPRNT,855) S1(N)                                          3170
635    855 FORMAT (//,3X,15HCONSTANT MODEL ,3X,11HFORECAST = ,F20.3)        3175
636        GO TO 925                                                         3180
637  C                                                                       3185
638  C       LINEAR MODEL.                                                   3190
639  C                                                                       3195
640    860 ALIN=2.*S1(N)-S2(N)                                              3200
641        SBETA=1.-SALFA                                                    3205
642        BLIN=(SALFA/SBETA)*(S1(N)-S2(N))                                 3210
```

```
643                 WRITE (IPRNT,865) ALIN,BLIN                                3215
644             865 FORMAT (2X,32H    A LINEAR MODEL: Y = A + B(L).,//,6H  A = ,F20.3,7   3220
645                1H,  B = ,F20.3,1H.)                                        3225
646                 WRITE (IPRNT,870)                                          3230
647             870 FORMAT (//,3X,111HL  REPRESENTS NUMBER OF PERIODS LEAD-TIME FOR WH   3235
648                1ICH FORECAST IS BEING MADE FROM THE LATEST PIECE OF INPUT DATA.,/,   3240
649                22X,90H MINIMUM VALUE FOR (L) IN THIS EQUATION IS THE FORECAST LEAD   3245
650                3 TIME   INPUT BY USER AS LDTM.)                            3250
651                 GO TO 925                                                  3255
652       C                                                                    3260
653       C         QUADRATIC MODEL OPTIMUM.                                   3265
654       C                                                                    3270
655             875 SBETA=1.-SALFA                                             3275
656                 AQUA=3.*S1(N)-3.*S2(N)+S3(N)                               3280
657                 BQUA=(((6.-5.*SALFA)*S1(N))-2.*(5.-4.*SALFA)*S2(N)+(4.-3.*SALFA)*S   3285
658                13(N))*((SALFA/(SBETA**2.*2.)))                             3290
659                 CQUA=((SALFA**2./SBETA**2.)*(S1(N)-2.*S2(N)+S3(N)))/2.0     3295
660                 WRITE (IPRNT,880) AQUA,BQUA,CQUA                           3300
661             880 FORMAT (2X,50H    A QUADRATIC MODEL: Y = A + B(L) + C(L-SQUARED).,/   3305
662                1/,7H   A = ,F20.3,6H, B = ,F20.3,9H AND C = ,F20.3,1H.)    3310
663                 WRITE (IPRNT,870)                                          3315
664       C       FORECAST OVER PAST DATA -*-*-*-*-*-*-*-*-*-*-*-*-*-*-*-*-*-*   3320
665       C                                                                    3325
666             885 IF (REGR.EQ.0) GO TO 925                                   3330
667       C                                                                    3335
668       C             FORECAST FOR REGRESSION FIT ONLY.                      3340
669       C                                                                    3345
670                 WRITE (IPRNT,890)                                          3350
671             890 FORMAT (1H1,3X,48HDATA FIT AND FORECASTS FOR REGRESSION MODEL ONLY   3355
672                1,////)                                                     3360
673                 WRITE (IPRNT,895)                                          3365
674             895 FORMAT (5X,60HTIME        FORECAST        ACTUAL DATA      MEAN ABSOL   3370
675                1UTEERROR,//)                                               3375
676                 APERR=0.0                                                  3380
677                 SFMAD=0.0                                                  3385
678                 BERR=0.0                                                   3390
679                 BERRS=0.0                                                  3395
680                 DO 905 I=1,N                                               3400
681                 AI=I                                                       3405
682                 AI2=AI*AI                                                  3410
683                 FOR=BETA1+BETA2*AI+BETA3*AI2                               3415
684                 FORMAD=ABS(X(I)-FOR)                                       3420
685                 BERR=BERR+X(I)-FOR                                         3425
686                 BERRS=BERRS+(X(I)-FOR)**2                                  3430
687                 SFMAD=FORMAD+SFMAD                                         3435
688                 APERR=APERR+(FORMAD/X(I))                                  3440
689                 WRITE (IPRNT,900) I,FOR,X(I),FORMAD                        3445
690             900 FORMAT (6X,I3,F14.3,3X,F15.3,3X,F15.3)                     3450
691             905 CONTINUE                                                   3455
692       C                                                                    3460
693       C       FORECAST OVER HORIZON.                                       3465
694       C                                                                    3470
695                 IF (IFORHZ) 5,5,910                                        3475
696             910 N1=N+1                                                     3480
697                 N2=N+IFORHZ                                                3485
698                 DO 915 I=N1,N2                                             3490
699                 AI=I                                                       3495
700                 AI2=AI*AI                                                  3500
701                 FOR=BETA1+BETA2*AI+BETA3*AI2                               3505
702                 WRITE (IPRNT,900) I,FOR                                    3510
703             915 CONTINUE                                                   3515
704                 FN=N                                                       3520
705                 AVMAD=SFMAD/FN                                             3525
706                 VAR=((FN*BERRS)-(BERR*BERR))/(N*(N-1))                     3530
707                 AVPERR=(APERR/FN)*100.                                     3535
708                 WRITE (IPRNT,920)                                          3540
709             920 FORMAT (///,4X,30HSUMMARY OF REGRESSION ANALYSIS,//)       3545
```

```
710              WRITE (IPRNT,1090) VAR                                      3550
711              WRITE (IPRNT,1095) AVMAD                                    3555
712              WRITE (IPRNT,1100) AVPERR                                   3560
713              GO TO 5                                                     3565
714          925 IF (NFCYC) 960,960,930                                     3570
715          930 WRITE (IPRNT,935)                                          3575
716          935 FORMAT (//,3X,102HNOTE - FORECAST ADDS ANY EARLIER CYCLIC FITS DET  3580
717             1ERMINED AND SPECIFIED TO USER. THE FORCED CYCLES WERE:)    3585
718              WRITE (IPRNT,940)                                          3590
719          940 FORMAT (//,3X,73HCYCLE FIT IS OF THE FORM: Y = (A1 + A2(T))SIN(WT)  3595
720             1 +  (A3 + A4(T))COS(WT).)                                  3600
721              WRITE (IPRNT,945)                                          3605
722          945 FORMAT (//,3X,104HCYCLE          A1                  A2    3610
723             1        A3              A4              W,/)               3615
724              DO 950 K=1,NFCYC                                           3620
725              TPIOP=(2.*PI)/PERIOD(K)                                    3625
726          950 WRITE (IPRNT,955) K,AT(1,K),AT(2,K),AT(3,K),AT(4,K),TPIOP  3630
727          955 FORMAT (3X,I3,5F20.8)                                      3635
728          960 CALL EXPSMO (Z,N,SALFA,BETA1,BETA2,BETA3,SABDEV,ISTYPE,LDTM,DEVM,S  3640
729             1DEVSQ)                                                     3645
730              NM1=N-LDTM                                                 3650
731              NM5=NM1-1.                                                 3655
732              STERET=(((NM1*SDEVSQ)-(SDEV)**2.)/(NM1*NM5))**0.5          3660
733              NM6=N-1.                                                   3665
734              VARET=STERET*STERET                                        3670
735              WRITE (IPRNT,965)                                          3675
736          965 FORMAT (1H1,//,67X,58HFORECAST CONTROL LIMITS(+,- 2 STANDARD ERROR  3680
737             1S OF ESTIMATE))                                           3685
738              WRITE (IPRNT,970)                                          3690
739          970 FORMAT (/,3X,95HTIME    FORECAST          ACTUAL DATA      3695
740             1DEVIATION          LOWER              UPPER,/)             3700
741              SAPERR=0.0                                                 3705
742              DO 1025 I=1,NM6                                            3710
743              M=LDTM                                                     3715
744              T=I+M                                                      3720
745              L=T                                                        3725
746              GO TO (975,980,985), ISTYPE                                3730
747          975 FOR=S1(I)                                                  3735
748              GO TO 990                                                  3740
749          980 FOR=COEF1*S1(I)+COEF2*S2(I)                                3745
750              GO TO 990                                                  3750
751          985 FOR=COEF3*S1(I)+COEF4*S2(I)+COEF5*S3(I)                    3755
752          990 IF (NFCYC) 1005,1005,995                                   3760
753          995 DO 1000 K=1,NFCYC                                          3765
754              TPIOP=2.*PI/PERIOD(K)                                      3770
755              FIT=(AT(1,K)+AT(2,K)*T)*SIN(T*TPIOP)+(AT(3,K)+T*AT(4,K))*COS(T*TPI  3775
756             1OP)                                                        3780
757         1000 FOR=FOR+FIT                                                3785
758         1005 FOR=FOR+Y(L)                                               3790
759              XF(L)=FOR                                                  3795
760              SLOWR=FOR-(2.*STERET)                                      3800
761              UPPR=FOR+(2.*STERET)                                       3805
762              IF (T-N) 1015,1015,1010                                    3810
763         1010 WRITE (IPRNT,1075) L,FOR,SLOWR,UPPR                        3815
764              GO TO 1025                                                 3820
765         1015 DEV=X(L)-FOR                                               3825
766              SAPERR=SAPERR+ABS(DEV/X(L))                                3830
767              WRITE (IPRNT,1020) L,FOR,X(L),DEV,SLOWR,UPPR               3835
768         1020 FORMAT (2X,I3,F16.4,4F20.4)                                3940
769         1025 CONTINUE                                                   3845
770    C                                                                    3850
771    C        FORECAST OVER HORIZON   -*-*-*-*-*-*-*-*-*-*-*-*-*-*-*-*-*-* 3855
772    C                                                                    3860
773              IF (IFORHZ) 5,5,1030                                       3865
774         1030 N3=N+IFORHZ-M                                              3870
775              ITAU=M-1                                                   3875
776              DO 1070 I=N,N3                                             3880
```

```
777              ITAU=ITAU+1                                          3885
778              CALL COEF (SALFA,ITAU)                               3890
779              T=I+M                                                3895
780              L=T                                                  3900
781              GO TO (1035,1040,1045), ISTYPE                       3905
782         1035 FOR=S1(N)                                            3910
783              GO TO 1050                                           3915
784         1040 FOR=COEF1*S1(N)+COEF2*S2(N)                          3920
785              GO TO 1050                                           3925
786         1045 FOR=COEF3*S1(N)+COEF4*S2(N)+COEF5*S3(N)              3930
787         1050 IF (NFCYC) 1065,1065,1055                            3935
788         1055 DO 1060 K=1,NFCYC                                    3940
789              TPIOP=2.*PI/PERIOD(K)                                3945
790              FIT=(AT(1,K)+AT(2,K)*T)*SIN(T*TPIOP)+(AT(3,K)+T*AT(4,K))*COS(T*TPI  3950
791         10P)                                                      3955
792         1060 FOR=FOR+FIT                                          3960
793         1065 FOR=FOR+Y(L)                                         3965
794              XF(L)=FOR                                            3970
795              SLOWR=FOR-(2.*STERET)                                3975
796              UPPR=FOR+(2*STERET)                                  3980
797         1070 WRITE (IPRNT,1075) L,FOR,SLOWR,UPPR                  3985
798         1075 FORMAT (2X,I3,F16.4,40X,2F20.4)                      3990
799              MM1=N-M                                              3995
800              APERR=(SAPERR/MM1)*100.                              4000
801              WRITE (IPRNT,1080)                                   4005
802         1080 FORMAT (//,3X,50HSTATISTICAL SUMMARY OF *OPTIMAL* FORECAST RESULTS  4010
803         1:)                                                       4015
804              WRITE (IPRNT,1085) STERET                            4020
805         1085 FORMAT (//,3X,33HTHE STANDARD ERROR OF ESTIMATE IS,F19.4)          4025
806              WRITE (IPRNT,1090) VARET                             4030
807         1090 FORMAT (//,3X,30HVARIANCE OF FORECAST ERRORS IS,F22.4)             4035
808              WRITE (IPRNT,1095) DEVM                              4040
809         1095 FORMAT (//,3X,26HMEAN ABSOLUTE DEVIATION IS,F26.4)                 4045
810              WRITE (IPRNT,1100) APERR                             4050
811         1100 FORMAT (//,3X,33HAVERAGE ABSOLUTE PERCENT ERROR IS,F19.4)          4055
812              N4=N3+M                                              4060
813              CALL BLARGE (X,N,BIG,SMALL,LDTM)                     4065
814              CALL BLARGE (XF,N4,BIGA,SMALLA,LDTM)                 4070
815              IF (SMALLA.LT.SMALL) SMALL=SMALLA                    4075
816              IF (BIG.LT.BIGA) BIG=BIGA                            4080
817              CALL BPLOT (X,XF,N,N4,BIG,SMALL,LDTM,NAME)           4085
818              GO TO 5                                              4090
819         1105 CALL EXIT                                            4095
820              END                                                  4100
821         SUBROUTINE BLARGE (ARRAY,M,BIG,SMALL,LDTM)                   5
822         DIMENSION ARRAY(M)                                          10
823              L=LDTM+1                                                15
824              SMALL=ARRAY(L)                                          20
825              BIG=ARRAY(L)                                            25
826              DO 10 K=L,M                                             30
827              IF (ARRAY(K).LT.BIG) GO TO 5                            35
828              BIG=ARRAY(K)                                            40
829            5 IF (SMALL.LT.ARRAY(K)) GO TO 10                         45
830              SMALL=ARRAY(K)                                          50
831           10 CONTINUE                                                55
832              RETURN                                                  60
833              END                                                     65
834         SUBROUTINE ACOVAR (X,N,LAG,R)                                5
835         DIMENSION X(N), R(LAG)                                       10
836    C                                                                 15
837    C          SUBROUTINE TO CALCULATE AUTOCOVARIANCES R, FOR SERIES X  20
838    C                                                                 25
839              IF (N-LAG) 5,5,15                                       30
840            5 R(1)=0.                                                 35
841              PRINT 10,LAG,N                                          40
842           10 FORMAT (1H1,11HILLEGAL LAG,I6,2X,7HFOR N =,I6)          45
843              RETURN                                                  50
```

```
844    C                                                                        55
845    C           CALCULATE MEAN OF X -*-*-*-*-*-*-*-*-*-*-*-*-*-*-*-*-*-       60
846    C                                                                        65
847      15 XBAR=0.                                                             70
848         DO 20 I=1,N                                                         75
849      20 XBAR=XBAR+X(I)                                                       80
850         AN=N                                                                85
851         XBAR=XBAR/AN                                                        90
852    C                                                                        95
853         DO 30 I=1,LAG                                                      100
854         K69=N-I+1                                                          105
855         SAVER=0.                                                           110
856         DO 25 J=1,K69                                                      115
857         J69=I+J-1                                                          120
858      25 SAVER=SAVER+(X(J)-XBAR)*(X(J69)-XBAR)                              125
859         AJ69=K69                                                          130
860      30 R(I)=SAVER/AJ69                                                    135
861         RETURN                                                            140
862         END                                                               145
863         SUBROUTINE COEF (ALPHA,ITAU)                                         5
864         DIMENSION S1(500), S2(500), S3(500)                                 10
865         COMMON S1, S2, S3, COEF1, COEF2, COEF3, COEF4, COEF5, SDEV          15
866         TAU=ITAU                                                            20
867         TAU2=TAU**2                                                         25
868         BETA=1.-ALPHA                                                       30
869         BETA2=BETA**2                                                       35
870         ALPHA2=ALPHA**2                                                     40
871         COEF1=2.+ALPHA/BETA*TAU                                             45
872         COEF2=-1.-ALPHA/BETA*TAU                                            50
873         COEF3=-(6.*BETA2+(6.-5.*ALPHA)*ALPHA*TAU+ALPHA2*TAU2)/(2.*BETA2)    55
874         COEF4=-(6.*BETA2+(10.-8.*ALPHA)*ALPHA*TAU+2.*ALPHA2*TAU2)/(2.*BETA  60
875        12)                                                                  65
876         COEF5=(2.*BETA2+(4.-3.*ALPHA)*ALPHA*TAU+ALPHA2*TAU2)/(2.*BETA2)     70
877         RETURN                                                              75
878         END                                                                 80
879         SUBROUTINE INVERT (A,N)                                              5
880         DIMENSION A(N,N), S(10,10)                                          10
881         DO 5 I=1,N                                                          15
882         DO 5 J=1,N                                                          20
883       5 S(I,J)=0.0                                                          25
884         DO 10 I=1,N                                                         30
885      10 S(I,I)=1.0                                                          35
886         DO 35 I=1,N                                                         40
887         DIV=A(I,I)                                                          45
888         DO 15 J=1,N                                                         50
889         A(I,J)=A(I,J)/DIV                                                   55
890      15 S(I,J)=S(I,J)/DIV                                                   60
891         DO 30 I1=1,N                                                        65
892         IF (I1-I) 20,30,20                                                  70
893      20 BUFF=A(I1,I)                                                        75
894         DO 25 J=1,N                                                         80
895         A(I1,J)=A(I1,J)-BUFF*A(I,J)                                         85
896      25 S(I1,J)=S(I1,J)-BUFF*S(I,J)                                         90
897      30 CONTINUE                                                            95
898      35 CONTINUE                                                           100
899         DO 40 I=1,N                                                        105
900         DO 40 J=1,N                                                        110
901      40 A(I,J)=S(I,J)                                                      115
902         RETURN                                                             120
903         END                                                                125
904         SUBROUTINE BPLOT (POINT,ARRAY,M,N,BIG,SMALL,LDTM,NAME)               5
905         DIMENSION LIND(105), POINT(N), ARRAY(N), NAME(1)                    10
906         INTEGER X, FORE, DATA, BLANK, EQUAL                                 15
907         DATA X/1H*/, FORE/1HF/, DATA/1HD/, BLANK/1H /, EQUAL/1H=/           20
908         IPRNT=6                                                             25
909         RANGE=BIG-SMALL                                                     30
910         IF (RANGE) 5,15,25                                                  35
```

```
911            5 WRITE (IPRNT,10)                                                   40
912           10 FORMAT (1H1,40HSMALL BIGGER THAN LARGEST DATA - NO PLOT)            45
913              GO TO 105                                                           50
914           15 WRITE (IPRNT,20)                                                    55
915           20 FORMAT (1H1,38HPLOT IS JUST A CONSTANT - NO PLOT MADE)              60
916              GO TO 105                                                           65
917           25 DO 30 J=1,105                                                       70
918           30 LIND(J)=X                                                           75
919              WRITE (IPRNT,35)                                                    80
920           35 FORMAT (1H1)                                                        85
921              WRITE (IPRNT,40) LIND                                               90
922           40 FORMAT (1H ,105A1)                                                  95
923              WRITE (IPRNT,45)                                                   100
924           45 FORMAT (1H ,1H*,51X,1H*,51X,1H*)                                   105
925              WRITE (IPRNT,50)                                                   110
926           50 FORMAT (1H ,1H*,14X,7HPLOT OF,30X,1H*,16X,13HFORECAST SYMBOL: F,17 115
927             1X,1H*)                                                             120
928              WRITE (IPRNT,45)                                                   125
929              WRITE (IPRNT,55)                                                   130
930           55 FORMAT (1H ,1H*,19X,8HFORECAST,24X,1H*,16X,18HDATA SYMBOL IS:   D,1 135
931             17X,1H*)                                                            140
932              WRITE (IPRNT,45)                                                   145
933              WRITE (IPRNT,60)                                                   150
934           60 FORMAT (1H ,1H*,24X,11HVERSUS DATA,16X,1H*,16X,18HCOMMON POINT IS: 155
935             1 =,17X,1H*)                                                        160
936              WRITE (IPRNT,45)                                                   165
937              WRITE (IPRNT,40) LIND                                              170
938              WRITE (IPRNT,65)                                                   175
939              WRITE (IPRNT,65)                                                   180
940           65 FORMAT (4X,1H*,48X,1H*,48X,1H*)                                    185
941              WRITE (IPRNT,70)                                                   190
942           70 FORMAT (1H ,7HMINIMUM,40X,9HMID-VALUE,42X,7HMAXIMUM)               195
943              FMID=(BIG+SMALL)/2.0                                               200
944              WRITE (IPRNT,75) SMALL,FMID,BIG                                    205
945           75 FORMAT (1H ,F9.2,39X,F9.2,39X,F9.2)                                210
946              WRITE (IPRNT,65)                                                   215
947              WRITE (IPRNT,65)                                                   220
948              DO 80 J=1,105                                                      225
949           80 LIND(J)=BLANK                                                      230
950              L=LDTM+1                                                           235
951              DO 90 J=L,M                                                        240
952              IPT=(((POINT(J)-SMALL)/RANGE)*98.0)+5.0                            245
953              JPT=(((ARRAY(J)-SMALL)/RANGE)*98.0)+5.0                            250
954              LIND(IPT)=DATA                                                     255
955              LIND(JPT)=FORE                                                     260
956              IF (IPT.EQ.JPT) LIND(IPT)=EQUAL                                    265
957              WRITE (IPRNT,85) J,(LIND(K),K=5,103),J                             270
958           85 FORMAT (1H ,I3,99A1,I3)                                            275
959              LIND(IPT)=BLANK                                                    280
960              LIND(JPT)=BLANK                                                    285
961           90 CONTINUE                                                           290
962              MK=M+1                                                             295
963              DO 95 J=MK,N                                                       300
964              JPT=(((ARRAY(J)-SMALL)/RANGE)*98.0)+5.0                            305
965              LIND(JPT)=FORE                                                     310
966              WRITE (IPRNT,85) J,(LIND(K),K=5,103),J                             315
967              LIND(JPT)=BLANK                                                    320
968           95 CONTINUE                                                           325
969              DO 100 J=1,105                                                     330
970          100 LIND(J)=X                                                          335
971              WRITE (IPRNT,40) LIND                                              340
972              WRITE (IPRNT,40) LIND                                              345
973              WRITE (IPRNT,40) LIND                                              350
974          105 RETURN                                                             355
975              END                                                               360
976              SUBROUTINE EXPSMO (Z,N,ALPHA,BETA1,BETA2,BETA3,SABDEV,ITYPE,LDTM,D   5
977             1EVM,SDEVSQ)                                                         10
```

```
978              DIMENSION S1(500), S2(500), S3(500), Z(N)                       15
979              COMMON S1, S2, S3, COEF1, COEF2, COEF3, COEF4, COEF5, SDEV       20
980              BETA=1.-ALPHA                                                    25
981              SABDEV=0.                                                        30
982              SDEV=0.                                                          35
983              SDEVSQ=0.                                                        40
984              ISAVY=ITREND                                                     45
985              ITREND=ITYPE                                                     50
986              CALL POLY (N,ITREND,BETA1,BETA2,BETA3,Z)                          55
987              ITREND=ISAVY                                                     60
988              GO TO (5,10,15), ITYPE                                           65
989      C                                                                        70
990      C           INITIAL CONDITIONS -*-*-*-*-*-*-*-*-*-*-*-*-*-*-*            75
991      C                                                                        80
992        5 S1(1)=BETA1                                                          85
993          GO TO 20                                                             90
994      C                                                                        95
995      C      UPDATE COEFS TO T1 FROM T0                                       100
996      C                                                                       105
997       10 BETA1=BETA1+BETA2                                                   110
998          S1(1)=BETA1-BETA/ALPHA*BETA2                                        115
999          S2(1)=BETA1-2.*BETA/ALPHA*BETA2                                     120
1000         GO TO 20                                                            125
1001     C      UPDATE COEFS TO T1 FROM T0                                       130
1002     C                                                                       135
1003     C                                                                       140
1004      15 BETA1=BETA1+BETA2+BETA3                                             145
1005         BETA2=BETA2+2.*BETA3                                                150
1006         S1(1)=BETA1-BETA/ALPHA*BETA2+BETA*(2.-ALPHA)/(ALPHA**2.)*BETA3      155
1007         S2(1)=BETA1-2.*BETA/ALPHA*BETA2+BETA*(3.-2.*ALPHA)/(ALPHA**2.)*BET  160
1008     1A3*2.                                                                  165
1009         S3(1)=BETA1-3.*(BETA/ALPHA)*BETA2+(3.0*BETA*(4.-3.*ALPHA)*BETA3)/(  170
1010     1ALPHA**2.)                                                             175
1011     C           SINGLE SMOOTHING                                            180
1012      20 DO 25 I=2,N                                                         185
1013      25 S1(I)=ALPHA*Z(I)+BETA*S1(I-1)                                       190
1014         GO TO (50,30,30), ITYPE                                             195
1015     C           DOUBLE SMOOTHING                                            200
1016      30 DO 35 I=2,N                                                         205
1017      35 S2(I)=ALPHA*S1(I)+BETA*S2(I-1)                                      210
1018         GO TO (50,50,40), ITYPE                                             215
1019     C           TRIPLE SMOOTHING                                            220
1020      40 DO 45 I=2,N                                                         225
1021      45 S3(I)=ALPHA*S2(I)+BETA*S3(I-1)                                      230
1022     C                                                                       235
1023     C           CALCULATE THE SUM OF THE ABSOLUTE DEVIATIONS BETWEEN        240
1024     C           FORECAST AND ACTUAL DATA                                    245
1025     C                                                                       250
1026      50 M=LDTM                                                              255
1027         NM1=N-M                                                             260
1028         CALL COEF (ALPHA,M)                                                 265
1029         DO 75 I=1,NM1                                                       270
1030         I69=M+I                                                             275
1031         GO TO (55,60,65), ITYPE                                             280
1032      55 FOR=S1(I)                                                           285
1033         GO TO 70                                                            290
1034      60 FOR=COEF1*S1(I)+COEF2*S2(I)                                         295
1035         GO TO 70                                                            300
1036      65 FOR=COEF3*S1(I)+COEF4*S2(I)+COEF5*S3(I)                             305
1037      70 SDEV=SDEV+Z(I69)-FOR                                                310
1038     C                                                                       315
1039     C      COMPUTE STANDARD ERROR OD ESTIMATE FOR CONTROL LIMITS            320
1040     C                                                                       325
1041         SDEVSQ=SDEVSQ+(Z(I69)-FOR)**2.                                      330
1042      75 SABDEV=SABDEV+ABS(Z(I69)-FOR)                                       335
1043         DEVM=SABDEV/NM1                                                     340
1044         RETURN                                                              345
```

```
1045              END                                                      350
1046              SUBROUTINE POLY (N,ITREND,BETA1,BETA2,BETA3,Z)             5
1047              DIMENSION Z(500)                                         10
1048              AN=N                                                     15
1049              GO TO (5,15,25), ITREND                                  20
1050          5   A=0.0                                                    25
1051              DO 10 I=1,N                                              30
1052              A=A+Z(I)                                                 35
1053         10   CONTINUE                                                 40
1054              BETA1=A/N                                                45
1055              BETA2=0.0                                                50
1056              BETA3=0.0                                                55
1057              RETURN                                                   60
1058         15   AN=N                                                     65
1059              E=0.                                                     70
1060              F=0.                                                     75
1061              A=AN*(AN+1.)/2.                                          80
1062              B=AN*(AN+1.)*(2.*AN+1.)/6.                               85
1063              DO 20 I=1,N                                              90
1064              AI=I                                                     95
1065              E=E+Z(I)                                                100
1066              F=F+Z(I)*AI                                             105
1067         20   CONTINUE                                               110
1068              BETA2=((AN*F)-(E*A))/((AN*B)-(A*A))                     115
1069              BETA1=(E/AN)-BETA2*(A/AN)                               120
1070              BETA3=0.                                                125
1071              RETURN                                                 130
1072         25   A=AN*(AN+1.)/2.                                        135
1073              B=AN*(AN+1.)*(2.*AN+1.)/6.                             140
1074              C=A**2                                                 145
1075              D=AN*(6.*AN**4+15.*AN**3+10.*AN**2-1.)/30.             150
1076              DETXTX=(AN*B*D+B*A*C*2.)-(B**3+AN*C**2+A**2*D)         155
1077              E=0.                                                   160
1078              F=0.                                                   165
1079              G=0.                                                   170
1080              DO 30 I=1,N                                            175
1081              AI=I                                                   180
1082              AI2=AI**2                                              185
1083              E=E+Z(I)                                               190
1084              F=F+Z(I)*AI                                            195
1085         30   G=G+Z(I)*AI2                                           200
1086              BETA1=((B*D-C**2)*E+(B*C-A*D)*F+(A*C-B**2)*G)/DETXTX    205
1087              BETA2=((B*C-A*D)*E+(AN*D-B**2)*F+(A*B-AN*C)*G)/DETXTX   210
1088              BETA3=((A*C-B**2)*E+(A*B-AN*C)*F+(AN*B-A**2)*G)/DETXTX  215
1089              RETURN                                                 220
1090              END                                                   225
```

APPENDIX D: RESALL PROGRAM

FURPUR 27R3-U4   E33 SL73R1 03/25/80 09:23:35

IEE461*LIBRARY(1).RESALL

```
    1    C**********************************************************************    A     5
    2    C**********************************************************************    A    10
    3    C**********************************************************************    A    15
    4    C**********************************************************************    A    20
    5    C                                                                         A    25
    6    C                      THE RESALL PROGRAM                                 A    30
    7    C                                                                         A    35
    8    C                     (RESOURCE ALLOCATION)                              A    40
    9    C                                                                         A    45
   10    C                  FOR FURTHER INFORMATION CONTACT                       A    50
   11    C                         DAVID D. BEDWORTH                              A    55
   12    C                INDUSTRIAL ENGINEERING DEPARTMENT                       A    60
   13    C                   ARIZONA STATE UNIVERSITY                             A    65
   14    C                     TEMPE, ARIZONA 85281                               A    70
   15    C                                                                         A    75
   16    C**********************************************************************    A    80
   17    C**********************************************************************    A    85
   18    C**********************************************************************    A    90
   19    C                                                                         A    95
   20    C          RESALL USES A HEURISTIC APPROACH TO ASSIGNING SCARCE           A   100
   21    C          RESOURCES ON A CRITICAL PATH (CPM) TYPE PROJECT.              A   105
   22    C             1. ASSIGNMENT OPTION: DETERMINES THE SHORTEST SCHEDULE     A   110
   23    C                UNDER LIMITED MULTIPLE-RESOURCE CONSTRAINTS. A          A   115
   24    C                MODIFICATION OF THE BROOKS ALGORITHM IS UTILIZED -      A   120
   25    C                SEE PRODUCTION SYSTEMS CONTROL BY BEDWORTH AND BAILEY - A   125
   26    C                JOHN WILEY AND SONS - NEW YORK.                         A   130
   27    C                                                                         A   135
   28    C             2. BALANCE OPTION: GIVEN A REQUIRED TIME SCHEDULE, THE     A   140
   29    C                PROGRAM WILL DETERMINE THE MINIMUM AMOUNT OF A SINGLE   A   145
   30    C                SCARCE RESOURCE TO ALLOW THE TIME SCHEDULE TO BE        A   150
   31    C                MAINTAINED.AN ITERIVE APPROACH USING OPTION ALLOCATION  A   155
   32    C                IS UTILIZED.                                            A   160
   33    C                                                                         A   165
   34    C          RESALL ALLOWS FOR BOTH NORMAL AND OVERTIME OPERATION AND      A   170
   35    C          COSTING FOR AN ASSIGNMENT RUN ONLY. ONLY A NORMAL RUN IS      A   175
   36    C          ALLOWED FOR A BALANCING PROBLEM.                              A   180
   37    C                                                                         A   185
   38    C          RESALL WILL COMPUTE BASIC CPM DATA IF DESIRED BUT WILL NOT    A   190
   39    C          PERFORM A CRASHING COST OPTIMIZATION.                         A   195
   40    C                                                                         A   200
   41    C**********************************************************************    A   205
   42    C**********************************************************************    A   210
   43    C**********************************************************************    A   215
   44    C**********************************************************************    A   220
   45    C                                                                         A   225
```

400

```
46      C      INPUT REQUIREMENTS, USING CARD FORMATS, ARE AS FOLLOWS:      A  230
47      C      CARD J REPRESENTS TYPE J. THERE SHOULD BE MORE THAN 1 CARD OF A  235
48.     C      TYPES 3 AND 8 FOR THIS PROGRAM.                                  240
49.     C         (ALL INTEGER-FORMAT DATA IS RIGHT JUSTIFIED IN FIELD)         245
50.     C      CARD 1, COLS 1 - 78: FORMAT 20A4, USER TITLE INFORMATION.        250
51.     C      CARD 2, COLS 1 - 10: TOTAL NUMBER OF ACTIVITIES IN THE           255
52.     C                           PROJECT, BETWEEN 3 AND 100 INCLUSIVE,       260
53.     C                           FORMAT F10.0.                               265
54.     C              COLS 11- 20: TOTAL NUMBER OF RESOURCE TYPES,             270
55.     C                           BETWEEN 1 AND 20 INCLUSIVE, F10.0.          275
56.     C              COLS 21- 30: CRITICAL PATH TIME FROM CPM PROGRAM         280
57.     C                           RUN. IF 0. IS INPUT, CPM DATA WILL          285
58.     C                           BE COMPUTED.                                290
59.     C              COLS 31- 40: FIXED (INDIRECT) COST PER TIME PERIOD,      295
60.     C                           F10.0. THIS MAY BE 0. FOR NO COSTING.       300
61.     C              COLS 41- 50: STARTING TIME FOR NORMAL SCHEDULE           305
62.     C                           (USUALLY 0.), F10.0.                        310
63.     C              COLS 51- 60: STARTING TIME FOR OVERTIME SCHEDULE         315
64.     C                           (USUALLY 0.), F10.0.                        320
65.     C              COL  61:     IF 0, INHIBITS DETAILED PRINTING FOR        325
66.     C                           EACH ITERATION. IF 1, GIVES DETAILED        330
67.     C                           PRINTING.                                   335
68.     C              COL  62:     IF 0, INHIBITS PRINTING OF FINAL            340
69.     C                           RESOURCE PROFILES OVER TIME. IF 1,          345
70.     C                           ALLOWS RESOURCE PROFILE PRINTING.           350
71.     C              COLS 63- 67: IF 0, THIS IS ASSIGNMENT OPTION. IF         355
72.     C                           1., BALANCE - F5.0.                         360
73.     C              COLS 68- 77: TIME REQUIRED FOR PROJECT BALANCE           365
74.     C                           RUN - F10.0.                                370
75.     C                                                                       375
76.     C      CARD 3+, COLS. 1-32, FORMAT 8A4, DESCRIPTION OF RESOURCE         380
77.     C         - ONE CARD NEEDED FOR EACH RESOURCE - PUT IN SAME             385
78.     C         SEQUENCE AS GIVEN ON TIME AND COST CARDS                      390
79.     C                                                                       395
80.     C      CARD 4, NORMAL RESOURCE QUANTITIES, 20I4 FORMAT. RESOURCE        400
81.     C         1 IN COLS 1-4; RESOURCE 2 IN COLS 5-8 ETC. LEAVE              405
82.     C                   NON-USED RIGHT-JUSTIFIED RESOURCE                    410
83.     C                   COLUMNS BLANK.                                       415
84.     C                                                                       420
85.     C      CARD 5, OVERTIME RESOURCE QUANTITIES - SAME PROCESS AS           425
86.     C         FOR CARD 4 - FORMAT IS 20I4.                                  430
87.     C                                                                       435
88.     C      CARD 6, NORMAL RESOURCE COSTS, 20I4 - SAME PROCESS AS            440
89.     C         FOR CARD 1. THESE ARE DIRECT COSTS.                           445
90.     C                                                                       450
91.     C      CARD 7, OVERTIME RESOURCE COSTS, 20I4 - SAME PROCESS AS          455
92.     C         FOR CARD 4. THESE ARE DIRECT COSTS.                           460
93.     C                                                                       465
94.     C      CARD 8+, ACTIVITY CARDS - ONE PER ACTIVITY:                      470
95.     C              COLS 1 - 3: TAIL NODE NUMBER, I3.                         475
96.     C              COLS 4 - 6: HEAD NODE NUMBER, I3.                         480
97.     C              COLS 7 - 9: EARLIEST START TIME FOR ACTIVITY             485
98.                          - NOT NEEDED IF CRITICAL PATH                       488
99      C                      FOUND IN THIS RUN. (I3)                       A  495
100     C              COLS 10- 12: DURATION TIME FOR ACTIVITY, I3.          A  500
101     C              COLS 13- 15: TOTAL FLOAT FOR ACTIVITY, I3. NOT        A  505
102     C                           NEEDED IF CRITICAL PATH FOUND IN         A  510
103     C                           THIS RUN.                                A  515
104     C              COLS 16- 18: FREE FLOAT FOR ACTIVITY, I3. NOT         A  520
105     C                           NEEDED IF CRITICAL PATH FOUND IN         A  525
106     C                           THIS RUN.                                A  530
107     C              COLS 19- 78: RESOURCE QUANTITIES NEEDED FOR THIS      A  535
108     C                           ACTIVITY, 20I3. RESOURCE 1 IN COLS       A  540
109     C                           19-21, RESOURCE 2 IN COLS 22-24,         A  545
110     C                           ETC. UNUSED RIGHT-JUSTIFIED              A  550
111     C                           RESOURCES LEAVE BLANK.                   A  555
```

```
112   C                                                                        A 560
113   C          ANOTHER SETUP MAY FOLLOW. TWO BLANK CARDS SIGNIFY LAST        A 565
114   C          SETUP                                                         A 570
115   C          AN EXAMPLE OF DECK SET-UP FOLLOWS WHERE USER DOES NOT         A 575
116   C          FURNISH DATA FROM CPM RUN. TWO SCARCE RESOURCES ANALYZED:     A 580
117   C                                                                        A 585
118   C                                                                        A 590
119   C      RESALL ASSIGNMENT RUN - TEST.                                     A 595
120   C          5.      2.      0.      0.      0.      0.00  0.              A 600
121   C      RESOURCE 1                                                        A 605
122   C      RESOURCE 2                                                        A 610
123   C 3   4                                                                  A 615
124   C 2   2                                                                  A 620
125   C 25  30                                                                 A 625
126   C 40  60                                                                 A 630
127   C 1  2  0  5  0  0  2  3                                                 A 635
128   C 2  4  0  7  0  0  1  1                                                 A 640
129   C 1  3  0  3  0  0  3  2                                                 A 645
130   C 3  4  0 10  0  0  2  0                                                 A 650
131   C                                                                        A 655
132   C                                                                        A 660
133   C************************************************************************ A 665
134   C************************************************************************ A 670
135   C************************************************************************ A 675
136   C                                                                        A 680
137   C          RESALL WAS COMPILED IN ASCII-FORTRAN ON A UNIVAC - 1110.     A 685
138   C                                                                        A 690
139   C************************************************************************ A 695
140   C************************************************************************ A 700
141   C************************************************************************ A 7 5
142   C************************************************************************ A 710
143   C          BOUNDS ON RESALL PROBLEMS INCLUDE:                            A 715
144   C             1. A MINIMUM OF 3 PROJECT ACTIVITIES AND A MAXIMUM OF 100. A 720
145   C             2. A MINIMUM OF 1 RESOURCE AND A MAXIMUM OF 20.            A 725
146   C             3. ONLY 1 RESOURCE ALLOWED FOR A BALANCE RUN.             A 730
147   C             4. NO OVERTIME CONDITIONS ALLOWED FOR A BALANCE RUN.       A 735
148   C************************************************************************ A 740
149   C************************************************************************ A 745
150   C************************************************************************ A 750
151   C************************************************************************ A 755
152   C                                                                        A 760
153   C          RESALL WAS ORIGINALLY DEVELOPED BY RICHARD MASON, WORKING     A 765
154   C          WITH DAVID BEDWORTH, FOR PART OF THE MS RESEARCH PAPER        A 770
155   C          TITLED AN ADAPTATION OF THE BROOKS ALGORITHM FOR SCHEDULING   A 775
156   C          PROJECTS UNDER MULTIPLE RESOURCE CONSTRAINTS - INDUSTRIAL     A 780
157   C          ENGINEERING DEPARTMENT, ARIZONA STATE UNIVERSITY, TEMPE:1970  A 785
158   C          SUBSEQUENT CHANGES AND ADDITIONS WERE MADE BY DAVID BEDWORTH  A 790
159   C                                                                        A 795
160   C************************************************************************ A 800
161   C************************************************************************ A 805
162   C************************************************************************ A 810
163   C************************************************************************ A 815
164         CHARACTER*6 TITLE(13), RTIT(20,30)                                A 820
165         DIMENSION ESX(100), TEMP(100), MRPL(100), POOL(22), USED(22), SP(2 A 825
166        212), IPOOL(22), IUSED(22), ISP(22), IT(100), IH(100), IASST(100), K A 830
167        2RES(20), KORES(20), KCSTN(20), LINE(110), NRCEN(200,20), KCSTO(20) A 835
168        3, NRCEO(200,20), IASFT(100), ITEMP(100)                           A 840
169         COMMON T(100), H(100), DUR(100), ES(100), TF(100), FF(100), CPTD,  A 845
170        1SNORM, NACT, KEXIT, ASST(100), ASFT(100), RM(100,20), NRES         A 850
171         INTEGER OVERT, BLANK, RES(20), ORES(20), CSTN(20), CSTO(20), T, H,  A 855
172        1 ES, DUR, TF, FF, RM                                              A 860
173         DATA NORM/1HN/, OVERT/1HO/, BLANK/1H /                            A 865
174   C                                                                        A 870
175   C*****READ PROJECT HEADER - REQUIRED                                     A 875
176   C                                                                        A 880
177      5 READ 10,TITLE                                                       A 885
```

```
178        10 FORMAT (13A6)                                                   A  890
179     C                                                                     A  895
180     C*****READ PARAMETER CARD--TOTAL NUMBER OF ACTIVITIES, TOTAL          A  900
181     C*****TYPES OF RESOURCES, CRITICAL PATH TERMINATION DATE,             A  905
182     C*****FIXED COST RATE, START TIME OF NORMAL SCHEDULE, AND             A  910
183     C*****START TIME OF OVERTIME SCHEDULE.                                A  915
184     C                                                                     A  920
185           READ 15,TACT,TRES,CPTD,FIX,SNORM,SOVER,IPPD,IRSM,BALNC,TREQ    A  925
186        15 FORMAT (6F10.0,2I1,F5.0,F10.0)                                  A  930
187           IF (TACT.EQ.0.) CALL EXIT                                       A  935
188           NACT=TACT                                                       A  940
189           NRES=TRES                                                       A  945
190           OUT=0.                                                          A  950
191           IVERTP=0                                                        A  955
192           KEXIT=1                                                         A  960
193     C                                                                     A  965
194     C*****READ RESOURCE HEADERS - ONE REQUIRED/RESOURCE                   A  970
195     C                                                                     A  975
196           DO 20 I=1,NRES                                                  A  980
197           READ 25,(RTIT(I,J),J=1,5)                                       A  985
198        20 CONTINUE                                                        A  990
199        25 FORMAT (5A6)                                                    A  995
200     C                                                                     A 1000
201     C*****READ NORMAL AND OVERTIME RESOURCE QUANTITITY CARDS,             A 1005
202     C                                                                     A 1010
203           READ 30,(RES(I),I=1,20)                                         A 1015
204           READ 30,(ORES(J),J=1,20)                                        A 1020
205        30 FORMAT (20I4)                                                   A 1025
206     C                                                                     A 1030
207     C*****READ NORMAL AND OVERTIME RESOURCE COST CARDS.                   A 1035
208     C                                                                     A 1040
209           READ 30,(CSTN(J),J=1,20)                                        A 1045
210           READ 30,(CSTO(K),K=1,20)                                        A 1050
211           DO 35 I=1,20                                                    A 1055
212           KRES(I)=RES(I)                                                  A 1060
213           KORES(I)=ORES(I)                                                A 1065
214           KCSTN(I)=CSTN(I)                                                A 1070
215           KCSTO(I)=CSTO(I)                                                A 1075
216        35 CONTINUE                                                        A 1080
217     C                                                                     A 1085
218     C*****INITIALIZE PERIOD RESOURCE VALUES.                              A 1090
219     C                                                                     A 1095
220           DO 40 I=1,200                                                   A 1100
221           DO 40 J=1,NRES                                                  A 1105
222           NRCEN(I,J)=0                                                    A 1110
223        40 NRCEO(I,J)=0                                                    A 1115
224     C                                                                     A 1120
225     C*****READ ACTIVITY CARDS--TAIL, HEAD, EARLIEST START TIME,           A 1125
226     C*****DURATION, TOTAL FLOAT, FREE FLOAT--ALL DETERMINED BY            A 1130
227     C*****A PREVIOUS CPM ANALYSIS,                                        A 1135
228     C                                                                     A 1140
229           DO 45 I=1,NACT                                                  A 1045
230        45 READ 50,T(I),H(I),ES(I),DUR(I),TF(I),FF(I),(RM(I,J),J=1,NRES)   A 1150
231        50 FORMAT (26I3)                                                   A 1155
232     C                                                                     A 1160
233     C*****PRINT INPUT INFORMATION                                         A 1165
234     C                                                                     A 1170
235           INFLAG=1                                                        A 1175
236           IF (CPTD.NE.0.) GO TO 55                                        A 1180
237           INFLAG=0                                                        A 1185
238           CALL CRITIC                                                     A 1190
239        55 PRINT 60                                                        A 1195
240        60 FORMAT (1H1,2X,67HTHIS IS THE BEDWORTH-MASON ADAPTATION OF BROOKS A 1200
241          1RESOURCE ALGORITHM.,///,2X,29HTHE DATA INPUT IS AS FOLLOWS:,///) A 1205
242           PRINT 65,TITLE                                                  A 1210
243        65 FORMAT (///,2X,14HPROJECT TITLE:,13A6,//)                       A 1215
```

```
244          IF (INFLAG.EQ.0) GO TO 75                                    A 1220
245          PRINT 70                                                     A 1225
246       70 FORMAT (//,4X,38HCRITICAL PATH AND FLOATS INPUT BY USER,///) A 1230
247          GO TO 85                                                     A 1235
248       75 PRINT 80                                                     A 1240
249       80 FORMAT (//,4X,42HCRITICAL PATH AND FLOATS NOT INPUT BY USER,///) A 1245
250       85 PRINT 90,TACT                                                A 1250
251       90 FORMAT (//,4X,21HNUMBER OF ACTIVITIES:,F14.0)                A 1255
252          PRINT 95,TRES                                                A 1260
253       95 FORMAT (//,4X,25HNUMBER OF RESOURCE TYPES:,F10.0)            A 1265
254          PRINT 100,CPTD                                               A 1270
255      100 FORMAT (//,4X,19HCRITICAL PATH TIME:,F16.0)                  + 1275
256          PRINT 105,FIX                                                A 1280
257      105 FORMAT (//,4X,25HFIXED COST PER TIME UNIT:,F10.0)            A 1285
258          PRINT 110,SNORM                                              A 1290
259      110 FORMAT (//,4X,26HSTART TIME (NORMAL SCHED):,F9.0)            A 1295
260          PRINT 115,SOVER                                              A 1300
261      115 FORMAT (//,4X,26HSTART TIME (OVERTIME SCH):,F9.0)            A 1305
262          IF (BALNC.GT.0.) GO TO 125                                   A 1310
263          PRINT 120                                                    A 1315
264      120 FORMAT (//,4X,26HTHIS IS AN ALLOCATION RUN.)                 A 1320
265          GO TO 135                                                    A 1325
266      125 PRINT 130,TREQ                                               A 1330
267      130 FORMAT (//,4X,43HTHIS IS A BALANCING RUN. TIME REQUESTED IS:,F5.0) A 1335
268      135 PRINT 140                                                    A 1340
269      140 FORMAT (//,4X,35HRESOURCE INFORMATION IS AS FOLLOWS:,/)      A 1345
270          PRINT 145                                                    A 1350
271      145 FORMAT (/,4X,8HRESOURCE,35X,8HQUANTITY,19X,4HCOST)           A 1355
272          PRINT 150                                                    A 1360
273      150 FORMAT (2X,13HNUMBER  TITLE,30X,15HNORMAL OVERTIME,9X,15HNORMAL OV A 1365
274     1ERTINE,/)                                                        A 1370
275          DO 155 I=1,NRES                                              A 1375
276      155 PRINT 160,I,(RTIT(I,J),J=1,5),RES(I),ORES(I),CSTN(I),CSTO(I) A 1380
277      160 FORMAT (4X,I3,3X,5A6,3X,I5,5X,I5,10X,I5,4X,I5)               A 1385
278          PRINT 265                                                    A 1390
279          PRINT 165                                                    A 1395
280      165 FORMAT (//,3X,21HACTIVITY INFORMATION:,/)                    A 1400
281          PRINT 170                                                    A 1405
282      170 FORMAT (/,1X,14HIDENTIFICATION,1X,6HEARLY.,5X,5HTOTAL,2X,4HFREE,20 A 1410
283     1X,18HRESOURCES REQUIRED)                                         A 1415
284          PRINT 175                                                    A 1420
285      175 FORMAT (4X,9HTAIL-HEAD,3X,5HSTART,1X,4HTIME,1X,5HFLOAT,1X,86HFLOAT A 1425
286     1  R1  R2  R3  R4  R5  R6  R7  R8  R9  R10 R11 R12 R13 R14 R15 R16 A 1430
287     2R17 R18 R19 R20,/)                                               A 1435
288          DO 180 I=1,NACT                                              A 1440
289      180 PRINT 185,T(I),H(I),ES(I),DUR(I),TF(I),FF(I),(RM(I,J),J=1,NRES) A 1445
290      185 FORMAT (4X,I3,2X,I3,4X,I3,3X,I3,3X,I3,3X,I3,1X,9I4,1X,11I4)  A 1450
291          IF (NACT.LT.3) GO TO 960                                     A 1455
292    C                                                                  A 1460
293    C*****TEST FOR RESTRICTIONS ON RESOURCE BALANCING                  A 1465
294    C                                                                  A 1470
295          IF (BALNC.EQ.0.) GO TO 195                                   A 1475
296          IF (NRES.GT.1) GO TO 940                                     A 1480
297          IF (CPTD.GT.TREQ) GO TO 950                                  A 1485
298    C                                                                  A 1490
299    C*****DETERMINE STARTING RESOURCE LEVEL - MAXIMUM FOR ANY ACTIVITY A 1495
300    C                                                                  A 1500
301          MAXR=0                                                       A 1505
302          DO 190 I=1,NACT                                              A 1510
303          IF (RM(I,1).GT.MAXR) MAXR=RM(I,1)                            A 1515
304      190 CONTINUE                                                     A 1520
305          RES(1)=MAXR                                                  A 1525
306          KCSTO(1)=0                                                   A 1530
307          ORES(1)=0.                                                   A 1535
308          KORES(1)=0                                                   A 1540
309          KRES(1)=RES(1)                                               A 1545
310          JRES=KRES(1)                                                 A 1550
```

```
311      C                                                                           A 1555
312      C*****TEST FOR PROJECT FEASIBILITY.  DETERMINE IF THE RESOURCE              A 1560
313      C*****REQUIREMENTS FOR ANY ACTIVITY EXCEED THOSE AVAILABLE.                 A 1565
314      C                                                                           A 1570
315        195 DO 200 M=1,NRES                                                       A 1575
316        200 POOL(M)=RES(M)+ORES(M)                                                A 1580
317            DO 205 I=1,NACT                                                       A 1585
318            DO 205 J=1,NRES                                                       A 1590
319            IF (POOL(J)-RM(I,J)) 775,205,205                                      A 1595
320        205 CONTINUE                                                              A 1600
321      C                                                                           A 1605
322      C*****COMPUTE MAXIMUM REMAINING PATH PENGTHS.                               A 1610
323      C                                                                           A 1615
324            DO 210 I=1,NACT                                                       A 1620
325            SUM=ES(I)+TF(I)                                                       A 1625
326        210 MRPL(I)=CPTD-SUM                                                      A 1630
327      C                                                                           A 1635
328      C*****ARRANGE ACTIVITY DATA IN ORDER OF LONGEST REMAINING PATH              A 1640
329      C*****LENGTH,  BREAK TIES BY RANKING THE ACTIVITY WITH THE                  A 1645
330      C*****LONGEST DURATION FIRST.                                               A 1650
331      C                                                                           A 1655
332        215 KRUD=0                                                                A 1660
333            NL1=NACT-1                                                            A 1665
334            DO 240 I=1,NL1                                                        A 1670
335            IP1=I+1                                                               A 1675
336            DO 235 J=IP1,NACT                                                     A 1680
337            IF (MRPL(I)-MRPL(J)) 225,220,235                                      A 1685
338        220 IF (DUR(I).GE.DUR(J)) GO TO 235                                       A 1690
339            KRUD=1                                                                A 1695
340        225 DO 230 L=1,NRES                                                       A 1700
341            TEMP(L)=RM(I,L)                                                       A 1705
342            RM(I,L)=RM(J,L)                                                       A 1710
343        230 RM(J,L)=TEMP(L)                                                       A 1715
344            SORT=MRPL(I)                                                          A 1720
345            MRPL(I)=MRPL(J)                                                       A 1725
346            MRPL(J)=SORT                                                          A 1730
347            SORT=T(I)                                                             A 1735
348            T(I)=T(J)                                                             A 1740
349            T(J)=SORT                                                             A 1745
350            SORT=H(I)                                                             A 1750
351            H(I)=H(J)                                                             A 1755
352            H(J)=SORT                                                             A 1760
353            SORT=ES(I)                                                            A 1765
354            ES(I)=ES(J)                                                           A 1770
355            ES(J)=SORT                                                            A 1775
356            SORT=DUR(I)                                                           A 1780
357            DUR(I)=DUR(J)                                                         A 1785
358            DUR(J)=SORT                                                           A 1790
359            SORT=FF(I)                                                            A 1795
360            FF(I)=FF(J)                                                           A 1800
361            FF(J)=SORT                                                            A 1805
362            SORT=TF(I)                                                            A 1810
363            TF(I)=TF(J)                                                           A 1815
364            TF(J)=SORT                                                            A 1820
365        235 CONTINUE                                                              A 1825
366        240 CONTINUE                                                              A 1830
367            IF (KRUD) 245,245,215                                                 A 1835
368      C                                                                           A 1840
369      C*****INITIALIZE TEMPORARY STORAGE LOCATIONS.                              A 1845
370      C                                                                           A 1850
371        245 PTIME=SNORM                                                           A 1855
372            IF (OUT.GT.0.0) PTIME=SOVER                                           A 1860
373            CORR=0.0                                                              A 1865
374            TIME=0.                                                               A 1870
375            OUT=0.                                                                A 1875
376            IACT=0.                                                               A 1880
377            PSFT=0.                                                               A 1885
```

```
378             SUPP=0.                                               A 1890
379             OVER=0.                                               A 1895
380             TOT=0.                                                A 1900
381             COST=0.                                               A 1905
382             CNORM=0.                                              A 1910
383             TFIX=0.                                               A 1915
384             TIDLE=0.                                              A 1920
385             TNORM=0.                                              A 1925
386             TOVER=0.                                              A 1930
387             TOTAL=0.                                              A 1935
388             KOUNT=6                                               A 1940
389             DO 250 J=1,22                                         A 1945
390         250 SP(J)=0.                                              A 1950
391             DO 255 I=1,NACT                                       A 1955
392             ESX(I)=ES(I)                                          A 1960
393             ASFT(I)=0.                                            A 1965
394             TEMP(I)=0.                                            A 1970
395         255 USED(I)=0.                                            A 1975
396     C                                                             A 1980
397     C*****COMPUTE THE COST OF NORMAL AND OVERTIME RESOURCES.       A 1985
398     C*****PRINT APPROPRIATE OUTPUT TITLES.                         A 1990
399     C                                                             A 1995
400             DO 260 N=1,NRES                                       A 2000
401             CN=CSTN(N)*RES(N)                                     A 2005
402             CO=CSTO(N)*ORES(N)                                    A 2010
403             OUT=OUT+CO                                            A 2015
404         260 COST=COST+CN                                          A 2020
405             PRINT 265                                             A 2025
406         265 FORMAT (1H1)                                          A 2030
407             IF (BALNC.GT.0.) GO TO 270                            A 2035
408             IF (IPPD.NE.1) GO TO 345                              A 2040
409             PRINT 275                                             A 2045
410             GO TO 290                                             A 2050
411         270 PRINT 280                                             A 0055
412             PRINT 285                                             A 2060
413         275 FORMAT (/,56X,25HTHIS IS AN ALLOCATION RUN)            A 2065
414         280 FORMAT (/,56X,23HTHIS IS A BALANCING RUN)              A 2070
415         285 FORMAT (///,4X,91HOVERTIME RESOURCES ARE OF NO BENEFIT IN A BALANC A 2075
416            1ING RUN.  IF AN OVERTIME QUANTITY WAS INPUT,/,4X,68HBY THE USER IT A 2080
417            2 WILL BE SET TO ZERO BY THIS PROGRAM BEFORE BALANCING.,//)         A 2085
418         290 IF (OUT) 305,305,295                                  A 2090
419         295 PRINT 300                                             A 2095
420         300 FORMAT (59X,17HOVERTIME SCHEDULE,/)                    A 2100
421             GO TO 325                                             A 2105
422         305 PRINT 310                                             A 2110
423         310 FORMAT (60X,15HNORMAL SCHEDULE,/)                      A 2115
424             IF (BALNC.EQ.0.) GO TO 325                            A 2120
425             PRINT 315,JRES                                        A 2125
426         315 FORMAT (/,10X,27HSTARTING RESOURCE LEVEL IS ,I3,6H UNITS) A 2130
427             KREQ=TREQ                                             A 2135
428             PRINT 320,KREQ                                        A 2140
429         320 FORMAT (/,10X,26HMAXIMUM TIME REQUESTED IS ,I4,11H TIME UNITS) A 2145
430             GO TO 360                                             A 2150
431         325 PRINT 330                                             A 2155
432         330 FORMAT (46X,35HPERIOD RESOURCES CONSUMED AND COSTS,8H SUMMARY,/) A 2160
433             PRINT 335                                             A 2165
434         335 FORMAT (7X,8HACTIVITY,30X,15HRESOURCE VALUES)          A 2170
435             PRINT 340                                             A 2175
436         340 FORMAT (2X,11HPERIOD SLIP,2X,118HR1  R2  R3  R4   R5  R6  R7  R8  R A 2180
437            19  R10 R11 R12 R13 R14 R15 R16 R17 R18 R19 R20    FIXED     IDLE  N A 2 85
438            2ORMAL    OVER  TOTAL)                                 A 2190
439         345 DO 350 J=1,20                                         A 2195
440         350 IPOOL(J)=POOL(J)                                      A 2200
441             IF (IPPD.NE.1) GO TO 360                              A 2205
442             PRINT 355,(IPOOL(J),J=1,20)                           A 2210
443         355 FORMAT (2X,11HQUANTITY: (,2OI4,1H),//)                 A 2215
```

```
444     C                                                                    A 2220
445     C*****COMPUTE FIXED COSTS, AND IDLE, NORMAL, AND OVERTIME            A 2225
446     C*****RESOURCE COSTS, AND SUM TO FIND THE TOTAL COST FOR A           A 2230
447     C*****GIVEN TIME PERIOD.                                             A 2235
448     C                                                                    A 2240
449       360 DO 565 L=1,1000                                                A 2245
450           IF (IACT) 455,455,365                                          A 2250
451       365 DO 380 I=1,NRES                                                A 2255
452           USED(I)=RES(I)+ORES(I)-POOL(I)                                 A 2260
453           OT=USED(I)-RES(I)                                              A 2265
454           IF (OT) 375,380,370                                           A 2270
455       370 COT=CSTO(I)*OT                                                 A 2275
456           OVER=OVER+COT                                                  A 2280
457           GO TO 380                                                      A 2285
458       375 UU=RES(I)-USED(I)                                             A 2290
459           SP(1)=CSTN(I)*UU                                              A 2295
460           SUPP=SUPP+SP(1)                                                A 2300
461       380 CONTINUE                                                       A 2305
462           CNORM=COST-SUPP                                               A 2310
463           IF (NACT-IACT) 385,385,390                                     A 2315
464       385 IF (PSFT-TIME) 570,390,390                                     A 2320
465       390 TOT=FIX+SUPP+CNORM+OVER                                        A 2325
466           IF (BALNC.GT.0.) GO TO 400                                     A 2330
467           IF (IPPD.NE.1) GO TO 400                                       A 2335
468           IF (KOUNT-20) 400,400,395                                      A 2340
469     C                                                                    A 2345
470     C*****PRINT FOR THE CURRENT TIME PERIOD THE RESOURCES CONSUMED       A 2350
471     C*****AND COST SUMMARY INFORMATION.                                  A 2355
472     C                                                                    A 2360
473       395 PRINT 500                                                      A 2365
474           PRINT 265                                                      A 2370
475           PRINT 340                                                      A 2375
476           KOUNT=0                                                        A 2380
477       400 DO 415 J=1,NRES                                                A 2385
478           IUSED(J)=USED(J)                                               A 2390
479           IF (OUT) 405,405,410                                           A 2395
480       405 NRCEN(L,J)=IUSED(J)                                            A 2400
481           GO TO 415                                                      A 2405
482       410 NRCEO(L,J)=IUSED(J)                                            A 2410
483       415 CONTINUE                                                       A 2415
484           ITIME=PTIME                                                    A 2420
485           JTIME=L                                                        A 2425
486           IF (BALNC.GT.0.) GO TO 430                                     A 2430
487           IF (IPPD.NE.1) GO TO 430                                       A 2435
488           PRINT 420,ITIME,(IUSED(J),J=1,NRES)                            A 2440
489       420 FORMAT (/,1H+,I3,9H *******,20I4)                              A 2445
490           PRINT 425,FIX,SUPP,CNORM,OVER,TOT                             A 2450
491       425 FORMAT (71X,26HCOSTS FOR THIS PERIOD ARE:,5F7.0,/)             A 2455
492           KOUNT=KOUNT+2                                                  A 2460
493       430 TFIX=TFIX+FIX                                                  A 2465
494           TIDLE=TIDLE+SUPP                                               A 2470
495           TNORM=TNORM+CNORM                                              A 2475
496           TOVER=TOVER+OVER                                               A 2480
497           TOTAL=TOTAL+TOT                                                A 2485
498           SUPP=0.                                                        A 2490
499           CNORM=0.                                                       A 2495
500           OVER=0.                                                        A 2500
501           TOT=0.                                                         A 2505
502     C                                                                    A 2510
503     C*****DETERMINE IF ANY ACTIVITIES END AT THE END OF THE             A 2515
504     C*****CURRENT TIME PERIOD.  IF SO, PLACE THEIR RESOURCES BACK        A 2520
505     C*****INTO THE POOL.                                                 A 2525
506     C                                                                    1 2530
507           DO 450 I=1,NACT                                                A 2535
508           ETIME=ASFT(I)-CORR                                            A 2540
509           IF (TIME-ETIME) 450,435,450                                    A 2545
```

```
510        435 IF (ASFT(I)) 450,450,440                              A 2550
511        440 DO 445 J=1,NRES                                       A 2555
512            POOL(J)=POOL(J)+RM(I,J)                               A 2560
513        445 CONTINUE                                              A 2565
514        450 CONTINUE                                              A 2570
515      C                                                           A 2575
516      C*****DETERMINE IF ANY ACTIVITIES ARE SCHEDULED TO START AT A 2580
517      C*****THE END OF THE CURRENT TIME PERIOD.  IF SO, DETERMINE A 2585
518      C*****THE ORDER IN WHICH RESOURCES ARE TO BE ALLOCATED.     A 2590
519      C*****PRIORITY IS GIVEN TO THE ACTIVITY WITH THE LONGEST    A 2595
520      C*****REMAINING PATH LENGTH.  IF THERE ARE INSUFFICIENT     A 2600
521      C*****RESOURCES, SLIP THE ACTIVITY ONE TIME UNIT FOR        A 2605
522      C*****CONSIDERATION IN THE NEXT TIME PERIOD.                A 2610
523      C                                                           A 2615
524        455 DO 535 I=1,NACT                                       A 2620
525            SHORT=0.                                              A 2625
526            IF (TIME-ESX(I)) 535,460,460                          A 2630
527        460 DO 470 J=1,NRES                                       A 2635
528            POOL(J)=POOL(J)-RM(I,J)                               A 2640
529            IF (POOL(J)) 465,470,470                              A 2645
530        465 SHORT=SHORT+POOL(J)                                   A 2650
531        470 CONTINUE                                              A 2655
532            IF (SHORT) 475,520,520                                A 2660
533        475 DO 480 M=1,NRES                                       A 2665
534            SP(M)=POOL(M)                                         A 2670
535        480 POOL(M)=POOL(M)+RM(I,M)                               A 2675
536            ESX(I)=ESX(I)+1.                                      A 2680
537            DO 490 MM=1,NRES                                      A 2685
538            IF (SP(MM)) 490,490,485                               A 2690
539        485 SP(MM)=0.                                             A 2695
540        490 CONTINUE                                              A 2700
541            IF (BALNC.GT.0.) GO TO 505                            A 2705
542            IF (IPPD.NE.1) GO TO 505                              A 2710
543            IF (KOUNT-20) 505,505,495                             A 2715
544        495 PRINT 500                                             A 2720
545        500 FORMAT (5X,26HFOR THE ABOVE INFORMATION:,/,3X,101H1. ******* FOR A  A 2725
546           1CTIVITY SLIP MEANS THAT THE FOLLOWING RESOURCES WERE CONSUMED DURI  A 2730
547           2NGTHAT TIME PERIOD.,/,3X,107H2. WHERE ACTIVITY IS LISTED UNDER ACT  A 2735
548           3IVITY SLIP, IT MEANS THAT ACTIVITY COULD NOT BE SCHEDULED IN THAT   A 2740
549           4TIME,/,5X,93HPERIOD BECAUSE OF A RESOURCE SHORTAGE. THE RESOURCE C  A 2745
550           5AN BE IDENTIFIED BY A NEGATIVE QUANTITY.)             A 2750
551            PRINT 265                                             A 2755
552            PRINT 340                                             A 2760
553            KOUNT=0                                               A 2765
554      C                                                           A 2770
555      C*****PRINT THE ELIGIBLE ACTIVITY THAT HAS BEEN SLIPPED DUE TO  A 2775
556      C*****A LACK OF RESOURCES AND IDENTIFY THE RESOURCE SHORTAGES,  A 2780
557      C                                                           A 2785
558        505 TYME=PTIME+1.                                         A 2790
559            ITYME=TYME                                            A 2795
560            IT(I)=T(I)                                            A 2800
561            IH(I)=H(I)                                            A 2805
562            DO 510 J=1,NRES                                       A 2810
563        510 ISP(J)=SP(J)                                          A 2815
564            IF (BALNC.GT.0.) GO TO 530                            A 2820
565            IF (IPPD.NE.1) GO TO 530                              A 2825
566            PRINT 515,ITYME,IT(I),IH(I),(ISP(NN),NN=1,NRES)       A 2830
567        515 FORMAT (/,1X,I3,1X,I3,2H -,I3,20I4)                   A 2835
568            KOUNT=KOUNT+1                                         A 2840
569            GO TO 530                                             A 2845
570      C                                                           A 2850
571      C*****SCHEDULE THE ACTIVITY, AND THEN REMOVE IT FROM FUTURE A 2855
572      C*****CONSIDERATION.  COUNT ACTIVITIES SCHEDULED.  COMPUTE  A 2860
573      C*****CURRENT LATEST PROJECT SHCEDULED FINISH TIME.         A 2865
574      C                                                           A 2870
575        520 ASST(I)=PTIME                                         A 2875
```

```
576              ASFT(I)=PTIME+DUR(I)                                     A 2880
577              ES(I)=ES(I)+9999.                                        A 2885
578              ESX(I)=ES(I)                                             A 2890
579              IACT=IACT+1                                              A 2895
580              IF (ASFT(I)-PSFT) 530,530,525                           A 2900
581          525 PSFT=ASFT(I)                                            A 2905
582          530 TEMP(I)=ASFT(I)                                         A 2910
583          535 CONTINUE                                                A 2915
584  C                                                                   A 2920
585  C***** TEST ACTIVITIES TO SEE IF SLIPPAGE CAN BE ABSORBED WITH      A 2925
586  C*****FREE FLOAT,  IF NOT, COMPUTE ACTIVITY DELAY, AND THEN         A 2930
587  C*****ADJUST ACCORDINGLY THE EARLIEST START TIME OF THE             A 2935
588  C*****ACTIVITY AND THE EARLIEST START TIMES OF ANY IMMEDIATE        A 2940
589  C*****DEPENDENT ACTIVITIES.                                         A 2945
590  C                                                                   A 2950
591              DO 560 I=1,NACT                                         A 2955
592              IF (ES(I)-ESX(I)) 540,560,560                           A 2960
593          540 DIFF=ESX(I)-ES(I)                                       A 2965
594              IF (FF(I)-DIFF) 545,560,560                             A 2970
595          545 DLAY=DIFF-FF(I)                                         A 2975
596              HEAD=H(I)                                               A 2980
597              DO 555 K=1,NACT                                         A 2985
598              IF (T(K)-HEAD) 555,550,555                              A 2990
599          550 ESX(K)=ES(K)+DLAY                                       A 2995
600          555 CONTINUE                                                A 3000
601          560 CONTINUE                                                A 3005
602              TIME=TIME+1.                                            A 3010
603              IF (IACT.GT.0) PTIME=PTIME+1.                           A 3015
604              IF (IACT.GT.0) CORR=PTIME-TIME                          A 3020
605          565 CONTINUE                                                A 3025
606              IF (BALNC.GT.0.) GO TO 605                              A 3030
607              IF (IPPD.NE.1) GO TO 575                                A 3035
608              IF (KOUNT.GT.0) PRINT 500                               A 3040
609              IF (KOUNT-20) 590,590,575                               A 3045
610          570 IF (BALNC.GT.0.) GO TO 580                              A 3050
611              IF (IPPD.NE.1) GO TO 575                                A 3055
612              IF (KOUNT.GT.0) PRINT 500                               A 3060
613              IF (KOUNT-16) 590,590,575                               A 3065
614          575 PRINT 265                                               A 3070
615              GO TO 590                                               A 3075
616          580 PRINT 585,KRES(1)                                       A 3080
617          585 FORMAT (/,10X,39HRESOURCE FOR THIS ITERATION WAS SET AT ,I3,7H UNI A 3085
618             1TS.)                                                    A 3090
619          590 IF (OUT) 620,620,595                                    A 3095
620          595 PRINT 600                                               A 3100
621          600 FORMAT (////)                                           A 3105
622              PRINT 300                                               A 3110
623              GO TO 630                                               A 3115
624          605 PRINT 265                                               A 3120
625              PRINT 610,TITLE                                         A 3125
626          610 FORMAT (13A6,//)                                        A 3130
627              PRINT 615,KRES(1)                                       A 3135
628          615 FORMAT (/,10X,39HRESOURCE FOR THIS ITERATION WAS SET AT ,I3,7H UNI A 3140
629             1TS.)                                                    A 3145
630              GO TO 655                                               A 3150
631          620 PRINT 625                                               A 3155
632          625 FORMAT (////)                                           A 3160
633              PRINT 310                                               A 3165
634          630 PRINT 635                                               A 3170
635          635 FORMAT (//,58X,19HTOTAL PROJECT COSTS,//)               A 3175
636              PRINT 640                                               A 3180
637          640 FORMAT (35X,5HFIXED,11X,4HIDLE,9X,6HNORMAL,7X,8HOVERTIME,10X,5HTOT A 3185
638             1AL,/)                                                   A 3190
639              PRINT 645,TFIX,TIDLE,TNORM,TOVER,TOTAL                  A 3195
640          645 FORMAT (25X,5F15.0)                                     A 3200
641              PRINT 650                                               A 3205
```

```
642       650 FORMAT (//,35X,66HA DETAILED SCHEDULE FOR THIS RUN IS GIVEN ON THE   A 3210
643         1 NEXT OUTPUT PAGE.)                                                   A 3205
644       C                                                                        A 3220
645       C*****PRINT PROJECT ACTIVITY SCHEDULE, WHICH CONSISTS OF A               A 3225
646       C*****LISTING OF THE REVISED ACTIVITY START AND FINISH TIMES,            A 3230
647       C                                                                        A 3235
648         655 PRINT 265                                                          A 3240
649             KKK=13                                                             A 3245
650             IF (OUT) 670,670,660                                               A 3250
651         660 PRINT 665                                                          A 3255
652         665 FORMAT (//,28X,17HOVERTIME SCHEDULE,/)                             A 3260
653             GO TO 680                                                          A 3265
654         670 PRINT 675                                                          A 3270
655         675 FORMAT (//,29X,15HNORMAL SCHEDULE,/)                               A 3275
656         680 PRINT 685                                                          A 3280
657         685 FORMAT (//,24X,26H PROJECT ACTIVITY SCHEDULE,/)                    A 3285
658             ICPTD=CPTD                                                         A 3290
659             PRINT 690,ICPTD                                                    A 3295
660         690 FORMAT (19X,30HCRITICAL PATH TERMINATION DATE,I5,///)              A 3300
661             PRINT 695                                                          A 3305
662         695 FORMAT (14X,38HTHESE ARE THE REVISED START AND FINISH,6H TIMES,/)  A 3310
663             PRINT 700                                                          A 3315
664         700 FORMAT (/,21X,32H ACTIVITY      START     FINISH)                  A 3320
665             PRINT 705                                                          A 3325
666         705 FORMAT (20X,10HTAIL   HEAD,8X,15H(END OF PERIOD),//)               A 3330
667       C                                                                        A 3335
668       C*****USE CRITIC SUBROUTINE TO REORDER ACTIVITIES                        A 3340
669       C*****PRIOR TO PRINTING THE FINAL SCHEDULE.                              A 3345
670       C                                                                        A 3350
671             KEXIT=0                                                            A 3355
672             CALL CRITIC                                                        A 3360
673             DO 720 I=1,NACT                                                    A 3365
674             KKK=KKK+1                                                          A 3370
675             IF (KKK-53) 715,715,710                                            A 3375
676         710 PRINT 265                                                          A 3380
677             PRINT 700                                                          A 3385
678             PRINT 705                                                          A 3390
679             KKK=0                                                              A 3395
680         715 IT(I)=T(I)                                                         A 3400
681             IH(I)=H(I)                                                         A 3405
682             IASST(I)=ASST(I)                                                   A 3410
683             IASFT(I)=ASFT(I)                                                   A 3415
684         720 PRINT 725,IT(I),IH(I),IASST(I),IASFT(I)                            A 3420
685         725 FORMAT (20X,I3,3H - ,I3,7X,I3,9X,I3)                               A 3425
686             DO 735 I=1,NL1                                                     A 3430
687             IP1=I+1                                                            A 3435
688             DO 735 J=IP1,NACT                                                  A 3440
689             IF (TEMP(I)-TEMP(J)) 730,735,735                                   A 3445
690         730 SORT=TEMP(I)                                                       A 3450
691             TEMP(I)=TEMP(J)                                                    A 3455
692             TEMP(J)=SORT                                                       A 3460
693         735 CONTINUE                                                           A 3465
694             ITEMP(1)=TEMP(1)                                                   A 3470
695             IF (OUT.GT.0.) IVERTP=ITEMP(1)                                     A 3475
696             PRINT 740,ITEMP(1)                                                 A 3480
697         740 FORMAT (//,15X,27HMINIMUM PROJECT DURATION = ,I3,11H TIME UNITS)    A 3485
698             IF (BALNC.GT.0.) GO TO 790                                         A 3490
699       C                                                                        A 3495
700       C*****TEST TO DETERMINE IF THE SCHEDULE JUST PRINTED WAS AN              A 3500
701       C*****OVERTIME SCHEDULE.  IF SO, ZERO THE OVERTIME RESOURCE              A 3505
702       C*****AND COST ARRAYS, AND THEN REPEAT THE PROGRAM TO COMPUTE            A 3510
703       C*****THE NORMAL SCHEDULE.                                               A 3515
704       C                                                                        A 3520
705         745 IF (OUT) 785,785,750                                              A 3525
706         750 IF (BALNC.EQ.0.) GO TO 755                                         A 3530
707             KORESL=KRES(1)                                                     A 3535
```

```
708          KRES(1)=JRES-ORES(1)                                          A 3540
709          JRES=KRES(1)                                                 A 3545
710      755 DO 760 KO=1,NRES                                             A 3550
711          ORES(KO)=0.                                                  A 3555
712      760 CSTO(KO)=0.                                                  A 3560
713      765 DO 770 NO=1,NACT                                             A 3565
714      770 ES(NO)=ES(NO)-0.                                             A 3570
715          GO TO 195                                                    A 3575
716      775 PRINT 780                                                    A 3580
717      780 FORMAT (///,10X,98HPROJECT COULD NOT BE COMPLETED AS RESOURCES REQ  A 3585
718        1UIRED EXCEEDED AVAILABLE RESOURCES ON THE NEXT RUN.)          A 3590
719          GO TO 5                                                      A 3595
720      785 IF (BALNC.GT.0.) GO TO 795                                   A 3600
721          GO TO 810                                                    A 3605
722      790 IF (ITEMP(1).GT.TREQ) GO TO 805                              A 3610
723          GO TO 745                                                    A 3615
724      795 KNRESL=KRES(1)                                               A 3620
725          PRINT 800                                                    A 3625
726      800 FORMAT (//,50X,17HBALANCE COMPLETE.)                         A 3630
727          GO TO 810                                                    A 3635
728      805 RES(1)=KRES(1)+1.0                                           A 3640
729          KRES(1)=RES(1)                                               A 3645
730          GO TO 765                                                    A 3650
731     C                                                                 A 3655
732     C*****PRINT RESOURCE  UTILIZATION PROFILES                        A 3660
733     C                                                                 A 3665
734      810 K=1                                                          A 3670
735          IF (IRSM.NE.1) GO TO 5                                       A 3675
736          KTIME=JTIME                                                  A 3680
737          JTIME=JTIME-1                                                A 3685
738      815 PRINT 820,K                                                  A 3690
739      820 FORMAT (1H1,50X,15HRESOURCE NUMBER,1X,I2,1X,7HSUMMARY,//)    A 3695
740          PRINT 825,(RTIT(K,J),J=1,5)                                  A 3700
741      825 FORMAT (20X,16HRESOURCE ITEM IS,1X,5A6)                      A 3705
742          IF (BALNC.GT.0.) GO TO 830                                   A 3710
743          KTOT=KRES(K)+KORES(K)                                        A 3715
744          GO TO 835                                                    A 3720
745      830 KTOT=0                                                       A 3725
746          KRES(1)=KNRESL                                               A 3730
747      835 PRINT 840,KRES(K),KTOT                                       A 3735
748      840 FORMAT (20X,23HNORMAL QUANTITY IS:    ,I3,20X,21HOVERTIME QUANTITY  A 3740
749        1 IS:,I3,23H. (NORMAL AND OVERTIME))                           A 3745
750          PRINT 845,KCSTN(K),KCSTO(K)                                  A 3750
751      845 FORMAT (20X,23HNORMAL COST/PERIOD IS: ,I3,20X,21HOVERTIME COST/PER  A 3755
752        1IOD:,I3,/)                                                    A 3760
753          PRINT 850                                                    A 3765
754      850 FORMAT (52X,23HUTILIZATION INFORMATION,/)                    A 3770
755          PRINT 855                                                    A 3775
756      855 FORMAT (20X,15HNORMAL SCHEDULE,25X,17HOVERTIME SCHEDULE)     A 3780
757          PRINT 860                                                    A 3785
758      860 FORMAT (14X,8HQUANTITY,6X,19HPERCENT UTILIZATION,9X,8HQUANTITY,6X,  A 3790
759        119HPERCENT UTILIZATION)                                       A 3795
760          PRINT 865                                                    A 3800
761      865 FORMAT (5X,4HTIME,7X,4HUSED,7X,22HO 1 2 3 4 5 6 7 8 9 10,9X,4HUSED  A 3805
762        1,7X,22HO 1 2 3 4 5 6 7 8 9 10,//)                             A 3810
763          DO 870 M=1,110                                               A 3815
764      870 LINE(M)=BLANK                                                A 3820
765          DO 930 L=2,KTIME                                             A 3825
766          IPT=(((NRCEN(L,K))*21.)/(KRES(K)))+28.                       A 3830
767          JPT=((NRCEO(L,K))*21.)/(KRES(K)+KORES(K))+70.                A 3835
768          DO 875 N=28,IPT                                              A 3840
769      875 LINE(N)=NORM                                                 A 3845
770          KFLAG=0                                                      A 3850
771          DO 890 N=70,JPT                                              A 3855
772          IF (L-IVERTP-1) 880,880,885                                  A 3860
773      880 LINE(N)=OVERT                                                A 3865
```

```
774            GO TO 890                                                          A 3870
775      885 KFLAG=1                                                              A 3875
776      890 CONTINUE                                                             A 3880
777            LT=L-1                                                             A 3885
778            IF (KFLAG) 895,895,905                                             A 3890
779      895 PRINT 900,LT,NRCEN(L,K),(LINE(I),I=28,49),NRCEO(L,K),(LINE(I),I=70   A 3895
780         1,91)                                                                A 3900
781      900 FORMAT (5X,I3,8X,I3,8X,22A1,8X,I3,9X,22A1)                           A 3905
782            GO TO 915                                                          A 3910
783      905 PRINT 910,LT,NRCEN(L,K),(LINE(I),I=28,49),(LINE(I),I=70,91)          A 3915
784      910 FORMAT (5X,I3,8X,I3,8X,22A1,20X,22A1)                               A 3920
785      915 DO 920 N=28,IPT                                                      A 3925
786      920 LINE(N)=BLANK                                                        A 3930
787            DO 925 N=70,JPT                                                    A 3935
788      925 LINE(N)=BLANK                                                        A 3940
789      930 CONTINUE                                                             A 3945
790            PRINT 935                                                          A 3950
791      935 FORMAT (//,58X,59HPARTIAL OVERTIME UTILIZATION ASSUMES NORMAL QUAN   A 3955
792         1TITIES USED,/,58X,72HFULLY BEFORE OVERTIME FOR COSTING. FOR EXAMPL   A 3960
793         2E, IF THE OVERTIME QUANTITY,/,58X,60H(NORMAL AND OVERTIME) IS 2 AN   A 3965
794         3D ONLY 1 UNIT IS USED, THEN THE,/,58X,53HUTILIZATION COST IS NORMA   A 3970
795         4L AND THE IDLE COST IS ZERO.)                                       A 3975
796            K=K+1                                                              A 3980
797            IF (NRES.GE.K) GO TO 815                                           A 3985
798            GO TO 5                                                            A 3990
799      940 PRINT 945                                                            A 3995
800      945 FORMAT (1H0,2X,73HNO BALANCE AS NUMBER OF RESOURCE TYPES IS GREATE   A 4000
801         1R THAN 1 - RUN TERMINATED)                                          A 4005
802            GO TO 5                                                            A 4010
803      950 PRINT 955                                                            A 4015
804      955 FORMAT (1H0,2X,72HNO BALANCE AS TIME REQUIRED IS LESS THAT CRITICA   A 4020
805         1L  PATH TERMINATION DATE)                                           A 4025
806            GO TO 5                                                            A 4030
807      960 PRINT 965                                                            A 4035
808      965 FORMAT (1H0,2X,78HA RUN CANNOT BE MADE AS THE NUMBER OF ACTIVITIES   A 4040
809         1 IS LESS THAN A MINIMUM THREE.)                                      A 4045
810            GO TO 5                                                            A 4050
811            END                                                               A 4055
812            SUBROUTINE CRITIC                                                         5
813            DIMENSION EF(100), LS(100), LF(100)                                      10
814            COMMON T(100), H(100), DUR(100), ES(100), TF(100), FF(100), CPTD,        15
815         1SNORM, NACT, KEXIT, ASST(100), ASFT(100), RM(100,20), NRES               20
816            INTEGER TACT, T, H, TF, FF, ES, DUR, RM                                 25
817            REAL LS, LF                                                            30
818    C ***  CPM SUBROUTINE  TO FIND OUT CRITICAL PATH                               35
819    C                                                                              40
820    C *** TACT=TOTAL NUMBER OF ACTIVITIES.                                         45
821    C *** SNORM=START TIME FOR PROJECT.                                            50
822    C *** T(I)=TAIL NODE NUMBER FOR ACTIVITY I.                                    55
823    C *** H(I)=HEAD NODE NUMBER;H(I)>T(I).                                         60
824    C *** DUR(I)=DURATION TIME OF ACTIVITY I.                                      65
825    C *** CPTD=CRITICAL PATH TIME                                                  70
826    C *** ES(I)=EARLIEST START TIME FOR ACTIVITY I.                                75
827    C *** EF(I)=EARLIEST FINISH TIME FOR I.                                        80
828    C *** LS(I)=LATEST START TIME FOR I.                                           85
829    C *** LF(I)=LATEST FINISH TIME FOR I.                                          90
830    C *** TF(I)=TOTAL FLOAT FOR ACTIVITY I.                                        95
831    C *** FF(I)=FREE FLOAT FOR I.                                                 100
832    C *** ASST(I)=SCHEDULE START FOR ACTIVITY I.                                  105
833    C *** ASFT(I)=SCHEDULE FINISH FOR ACTIVITY I.                                 110
834    C                                                                             115
835    C                                                                             120
836    C *** CHECK THE INPUT DATA                                                    125
837    C                                                                             130
838            TACT=NACT                                                            135
839            DO 5 I=1,TACT                                                        140
840            IF (H(I).LE.T(I)) GO TO 125                                          145
```

```
841        5 CONTINUE                                      150
842    C                                                   155
843    C *** PRIMARY SORTING ON TAIL NODES.                160
844    C                                                   165
845           NX=TACT-1                                    170
846           DO 25 N=1,NX                                 175
847           NX=N+1                                       180
848       10 IF (T(N).LE.T(NX)) GO TO 20                   185
849           DO 15 L=1,NRES                               190
850           ITEMP=RM(NX,L)                               195
851           RM(NX,L)=RM(N,L)                             200
852       15 RM(N,L)=ITEMP                                 205
853           JT=T(NX)                                     210
854           JA=H(NX)                                     215
855           JB=DUR(NX)                                   220
856           AC=ASST(NX)                                  225
857           AD=ASFT(NX)                                  230
858           T(NX)=T(N)                                   235
859           H(NX)=H(N)                                    240
860           DUR(NX)=DUR(N)                               245
861           ASST(NX)=ASST(N)                             250
862           ASFT(NX)=ASFT(N)                             255
863           T(N)=JT                                       260
864           H(N)=JA                                       265
865           DUR(N)=JB                                     270
866           ASST(N)=AC                                    275
867           ASFT(N)=AD                                    280
868       20 NX=NX+1                                        285
869           IF (NX.GT.TACT) GO TO 25                     290
870           GO TO 10                                      295
871       25 CONTINUE                                      300
872    C                                                   305
873    C *** SECONDARY SORTING ON HEAD NODE.               310
874    C                                                   315
875           KX=TACT-1                                    320
876           DO 50 K=1,KX                                 325
877           KR=K+1                                        330
878       30 IF (T(K).NE.T(KR)) GO TO 50                   335
879           IF (H(K).GT.H(KR)) GO TO 35                  340
880           GO TO 45                                      345
881       35 JX=H(K)                                        350
882           JY=DUR(K)                                     355
883           AX=ASST(K)                                    360
884           AY=ASFT(K)                                    365
885           H(K)=H(KR)                                    370
886           DUR(K)=DUR(KR)                               375
887           ASST(K)=ASST(KR)                             380
888           ASFT(K)=ASFT(KR)                             385
889           H(KR)=JX                                      390
890           DUR(KR)=JY                                    395
891           ASST(KR)=AX                                   400
892           ASFT(KR)=AY                                   405
893           DO 40 L=1,NRES                               410
894           ITEMP=RM(K,L)                                415
895           RM(K,L)=RM(KR,L)                             420
896       40 RM(KR,L)=ITEMP                                425
897       45 KR=KR+1                                        430
898           IF (KR-TACT) 30,30,50                        435
899       50 CONTINUE                                      440
900    C                                                   445
901    C *** CRITICAL PATH CALCULATIONS: FORWARD PASS.     450
902    C                                                   455
903           ES(1)=SNORM                                  460
904           EF(1)=ES(1)+DUR(1)                           465
905           N=1                                           470
906           NX=N+1                                        475
907       55 IF (T(NX).NE.T(N)) GO TO 60                   480
908           ES(NX)=ES(1)                                  485
```

```
909              EF(NX)=ES(NX)+DUR(NX)                                      490
910              NX=NX+1                                                    495
911              GO TO 55                                                   500
912           60 CONTINUE                                                   505
913              DO 75 N=NX,TACT                                            510
914              XB=0.0                                                     515
915              MA=T(N)                                                    520
916              DO 70 I=1,TACT                                            525
917              IF (H(I).NE.MA) GO TO 70                                   530
918              IF (EF(I).LT.XB) GO TO 65                                  535
919              XB=EF(I)                                                   540
920           65 ES(N)=XB                                                   545
921           70 CONTINUE                                                   550
922              EF(N)=ES(N)+DUR(N)                                         555
923           75 CONTINUE                                                   560
924     C *** CRITICAL PATH LENGTH                                          565
925     C                                                                   570
926              KA=H(TACT)                                                 575
927              RB=0.0                                                     580
928              DO 85 K=1,TACT                                            585
929              IF (H(K).NE.KA) GO TO 85                                   590
930              IF (EF(K).LT.RB) GO TO 80                                  595
931              RB=EF(K)                                                   600
932           80 CPTD=RB                                                    605
933           85 CONTINUE                                                   610
934     C                                                                   615
935     C *** FINDING OUT TOTAL FLOAT,FREE  FLOAT BY BACKWARD PASS.          620
936     C                                                                   625
937              LF(TACT)=CPTD                                              630
938              LS(TACT)=CPTD-DUR(TACT)                                    635
939              NT=TACT-1                                                  640
940              NX=TACT                                                    645
941              DO 100 N=1,NT                                             650
942              NX=NX-1                                                    655
943              IF (H(NX).NE.H(TACT)) GO TO 90                             660
944              LF(NX)=CPTD                                                665
945              LS(NX)=CPTD-DUR(NX)                                        670
946              GO TO 100                                                  675
947           90 XL=9999999.                                               680
948              KR=NX+1                                                    685
949              DO 95 K=KR,TACT                                           690
950              IF (T(K).NE.H(NX)) GO TO 95                                695
951              IF (LS(K).GT.XL) GO TO 95                                  700
952              XL=LS(K)                                                   705
953           95 CONTINUE                                                   710
954              LF(NX)=XL                                                  715
955              LS(NX)=LF(NX)-DUR(NX)                                      720
956          100 CONTINUE                                                   725
957     C                                                                   730
958     C *** FINAL CALCULATIONS                                            735
959     C                                                                   740
960              DO 120 J=1,TACT                                           745
961              TF(J)=LF(J)-EF(J)                                          750
962              JN=H(J)                                                    755
963              DO 105 K=J,TACT                                           760
964              IF (JN.EQ.H(TACT)) GO TO 110                               765
965              IF (T(K).NE.JN) GO TO 105                                  770
966              ESX=ES(K)                                                  775
967              GO TO 115                                                  780
968          105 CONTINUE                                                   785
969          110 ESX=CPTD                                                   790
970          115 FF(J)=ESX-EF(J)                                            795
971          120 CONTINUE                                                   800
972              RETURN                                                     805
973          125 WRITE (6,130) T(I),H(I),I                                  810
974          130 FORMAT (10X,48HERROR: HEAD NODE EQUAL OR GREATER THAN TAIL NODE,10   815
975             1H T(I) IS  ,I2,13H AND H(I) IS ,I2,10H WITH I = ,I2,/)     820
976              CALL EXIT                                                  825
977              END                                                       830
```

APPENDIX E:
BABALB PROGRAM

IEE461*LIBRARY(1).BABALB

```
  1    C*****************************************************************************  A     5
  2    C*****************************************************************************  A    10
  3    C*****************************************************************************  A    15
  4    C                                                                              A    20
  5    C                                                                              A    25
  6    C                        THE BABALB PROGRAM                                    A    30
  7    C                                                                              A    35
  8    C            (BRANCH AND BOUND ASSEMBLY-LINE BALANCING)                        A    40
  9    C                                                                              A    45
 10    C                  FOR FURTHER INFORMATION CONTACT                            A    50
 11    C                       DAVID D. BEDWORTH                                      A    55
 12    C                INDUSTRIAL ENGINEERING DEPARTMENT                            A    60
 13    C                    ARIZONA STATE UNIVERSITY                                 A    65
 14    C                      TEMPE, ARIZONA 85281                                   A    70
 15    C                                                                              A    75
 16    C*****************************************************************************  A    80
 17    C*****************************************************************************  A    85
 18    C*****************************************************************************  A    90
 19    C                                                                              A    95
 20    C          BABALB IS DESIGNED TO ALLOW OPTIMAL LINE BALANCING FOR             A   100
 21    C          MULTIPLE-PRODUCTS - DETERMINISTIC OR STOCHASTIC CASES.             A   105
 22    C          OPTIMAL REFERS TO BOTH STATIONS AND WORKLOAD ASSIGNMENT            A   110
 23    C          IN BABALB. THE PROGRAM FIRST DETERMINES THE MINIMUM                A   115
 24    C          NUMBER OF STATIONS GIVEN A USER CYCLE TIME.  NEXT,                 A   120
 25    C          BABALB DETERMINES THE OPERATION BALANCE FOR THIS                   A   125
 26    C          MINIMUM NUMBER OF STATIONS THAT MINIMIZES THE CYCLE               A   130
 27    C          TIME. THIS ACHIEVES THE OPTIMUM BALANCE WORKLOAD FOR              A   135
 28    C          THE GIVEN CYCLE TIME. THE USER HAS TO DEVELOP A                    A   140
 29    C          COMPOSITE PRECEDENCE DIAGRAM FOR MULTIPLE PRODUCTS,               A   145
 30    C          SPECIFYING OPERATIONS, IMMEDIATE PREDECESSORS,                     A   150
 31    C          OPERATION TIMES, AND OPERATION TIME VARIANCES IF                   A   155
 32    C          STOCHASTIC ANALYSIS IS REQUIRED, AND CYCLE TIME                    A   160
 33    C          DESIRED.  FURTHER, IF STOCHASTIC ANALYSIS IS REQUIRED              A   165
 34    C          THEN THE USER HAS TO STIPULATE THE PERCENTAGE OF                   A   170
 35    C          TIMES THAT A STATION MUST BE EQUAL-TO-OR-LESS THAN                 A   175
 36    C          THE CYCLE TIME. THIS IS INPUT AS THE CORRESPONDING                A   180
 37    C          NORMAL DISTRIBUTION STANDARDIZED VARIABLE Z. SEE                   A   185
 38    C          PRODUCTION CONTROL SYSTEMS BY BEDWORTH AND BAILEY                  A   190
 39    C          - JOHN WILEY AND SONS - NEW YORK.                                  A   195
 40    C                                                                              A   200
 41    C          THE FOLLOWING CONVENTIONS ARE OBSERVED IN IDENTIFYING              A   205
 42    C          OPERATIONS:                                                        A   210
 43    C             1. IF THERE ARE A TOTAL OF N OPERATIONS TO BE                   A   215
 44    C                CONSIDERED IN THE COMPOSITE PRECEDENCE DIAGRAM,              A   220
 45    C                THE LARGEST NUMBER WHICH CAN BE USED TO IDENTIFY             A   225
 46    C                AN OPERATION IS N.                                           A   230
 47    C             2. EACH OPERATION MUST HAVE A UNIQUE IDENTIFICATION            A   235
```

415

```
48    C          NUMBER.                                              A  240
49    C               3. ZERO IS NOT A LEGAL IDENTIFIER.              A  245
50    C               4. AN OPERATION MUST HAVE HAVE AN IDENTIFICATION NUMBER  A  250
51    C                  LARGER THAN THE IDENTIFIER OF ANY OF ITS IMMEDIATE     A  255
52    C                  PREDECESSOR OPERATIONS.                      A  260
53    C                                                               A  265
54    C*************************************************************************  A  270
55    C*************************************************************************  A  275
56    C*************************************************************************  A  280
57    C                                                               A  285
58    C                                                               A  290
59    C          INPUT REQUIREMENTS, USING CARD FORMATS, ARE AS FOLLOWS.  A  295
60    C          CARD J REPRESENTS TYPE J. THERE SHOULD BE MORE THAN 1 CARD  A  300
61    C          OF TYPE 3.                                           A  305
62    C          (ALL INTEGER-FORMAT DATA IS RIGHT-JUSTIFIED IN THE FIELD)  A  310
63    C          CARD 1, COLS 1 - 80: 40A2 FORMAT - USER TITLE INFORMATION.  A  315
64    C          CARD 2, COLS 1 -  5: TOTAL NUMBER OF DIFFERENT OPERATIONS  A  320
65    C                               IN COMBINED PRECEDENCE DIAGRAM - I5.  A  325
66    C                  COLS 6 - 10: NUMBER OF PRODUCTS, I5.          A  330
67    C                  COLS 11- 15: MAXIMUM NUMBER OF IMMEDIATE PREDECESSOR  A  335
68    C                               OPERATIONS FOR ANY SINGLE OPERATION, I5.  A  340
69    C                  COLS 16- 20: LINE CYCLE TIME, F5.0.          A  345
70    C                  COLS 21- 25: STANDARDIZED NORMAL DISTRIBUTION VALUE  A  350
71    C                               REPRESENTING STATION COMPLETION-WITHIN-  A  355
72    C                               CYCLE-TIME PROBABILITY DESIRED.  A  360
73    C          CARD 3+, OPERATION CARDS:                            A  365
74    C                  TWO CARDS ARE REQUIRED FOR EACH OPERATION.   A  370
75    C                  THE FIRST, CARD A, CONTAINS PRECEDENCE INFORMATION.  A  375
76    C                  THE SECOND, CARD B, CONTAINS TIME AND VARIANCE  A  380
77    C                  INFORMATION. THE FIRST TWO CARDS (A,B) ARE FOR  A  385
78    C                  OPERATION 1. THE NEXT TWO ARE FOR OPERATION 2, ETC.  A  390
79    C          CARD 3A, COLS 1 -  5: OPERATION NUMBER FOR THIS A,B. (I5)  A  395
80    C                   COLS 6 - 50: FORMAT 15I5, IMMEDIATE PREDECESSOR  A  400
81    C                               OPERATION NUMBERS IN ASCENDING  A  405
82    C                               ORDER. LEAVE UNUSED RIGHT-JUSTIFIED  A  410
83    C                               COLUMNS BLANK.                  A  415
84    C          CARD 3B, TIMES FOR OPERATION GIVEN ON CARD A FOR EACH  A  420
85    C                  PRODUCT FOLLOWED BY THE ASSOCIATED VARIANCES.  A  425
86    C                  FOR 4 PRODUCTS,THIS WOULD BE T1,T2,T3,T4,V1,V2,  A  430
87    C                  V3 AND V4. FORMAT IS F10.0,14F5.0.           A  435
88    C                                                               A  440
89    C     SEVERAL SETS OF DATA MAY BE STACKED - INCLUDE ALL PREVIOUS CARDS.  A  445
90    C     TWO BLANK CARDS SIGNIFIES END OF DATA SETS.               A  450
91    C                                                               A  455
92    C                                                               A  460
93    C     EXAMPLE FOLLOWS FOR SETUP:                                A  465
94    C                                                               A  470
95    C                                                               A  475
96    C     TWO-PRODUCT, STOCHASTIC, CYCLE IS 10.0  WITH 11 OPERATIONS.  A  480
97    C  11   2   3  10.   2.                                         A  485
98    C   1                                                           A  490
99    C       1.  1.  1.  1.                                          A  495
100   C   2   1                                                       A  500
101   C       5.  0.  1.  0.                                          A  505
102   C   3   1                                                       A  510
103   C       4.  4.  1.  1.                                          A  515
104   C   4   1                                                       A  520
105   C       0.  1.  0.  1.                                          A  525
106   C   5   4                                                       A  530
107   C       0.  5.  0.  1.                                          A  535
108   C   6   5                                                       A  540
109   C       0.  6.  0.  1.                                          A  545
110   C   7   2   3   6                                               A  550
111   C       2.  2.  1.  1.                                          A  555
112   C   8   1                                                       A  560
113   C       4.  0.  1.  0.                                          A  565
```

```
114   C   9   3                                                      A  570
115   C       3.   3.   1.   1.                                      A  575
116   C  10   9                                                      A  580
117   C       0.   5.   0.   1.                                      A  585
118   C  11   7  10                                                  A  590
119   C       3.   3.   1.   1.                                      A  595
120   C                                                              A  600
121   C                                                              A  605
122   C***********************************************************   A  610
123   C***********************************************************   A  615
124   C***********************************************************   A  620
125   C                                                              A  625
126   C        BABALB WAS COMPILED IN ASCII-FORTRAN ON A UNIVAC-1110. A  630
127   C                                                              A  635
128   C***********************************************************   A  640
129   C***********************************************************   A  645
130   C***********************************************************   A  650
131   C        BABALB WAS DEVELOPED BY DR. DONALD DEUTSCH IN:        A  655
132   C            A BRANCH AND BOUND TECHNIQUE FOR MIXED-PRODUCT     A  660
133   C            ASSEMBLY-LINE BALANCING, PHD DISSERTATION IN       A  665
134   C            INDUSTRIAL ENGINEERING, ARIZONA STATE UNIVERSITY,  A  670
135   C            TEMPE, ARIZONA, 85281: 1971                        A  675
136   C***********************************************************   A  680
137   C***********************************************************   A  685
138   C***********************************************************   A  690
139         COMMON BOUND(61,60), NOPN(63,60), XSUM(12), VSUM(12), NA(40) A 695
140         COMMON MP(60,10), TIME(60,6), VTIME(60,6), MPA(61)       A  700
141         COMMON NCCNT(61), NDCNT(61), NRCNT(5,61)                 A  705
142         COMMON NNOP, NPROD, CYC, M, MM, Z, MXP, LLIM, XLIM, XBND A  710
143         COMMON BND1, BND2, BND3, MMM, NT(60), NST(60)            A  715
144         DOUBLE PRECISION XSUM, VSUM                              A  720
145         PRINT 5                                                  A  725
146       5 FORMAT (1H1,/)                                           A  730
147      10 READ 15,NA                                               A  735
148      15 FORMAT (40A2)                                            A  740
149         READ 20,NNOP,NPROD,MXP,CYC,Z                             A  745
150      20 FORMAT (3I5,2F5.0)                                       A  750
151         IF (NNOP) 25,25,30                                       A  755
152      25 CALL EXIT                                                A  760
153      30 DO 40 I=1,NNOP                                           A  765
154         READ 35,NOP,(MP(NOP,J),J=1,MXP)                          A  770
155      35 FORMAT (16I5)                                            A  775
156      40 READ 45,(TIME(NOP,J),J=1,NPROD),(VTIME(NOP,J),J=1,NPROD) A  780
157      45 FORMAT (F10.0,14F5.0)                                    A  785
158         PRINT 50,NA,CYC,Z                                        A  790
159      50 FORMAT (1H1,/,1X,40A2//13H CYCLE TIME =,F8.3,8H    Z = ,F7.3//) A 795
160         N1=NNOP/50                                               A  800
161         N2=NNOP-N1*50                                            A  805
162         NOP=0                                                    A  810
163         IF (N1) 85,85,55                                         A  815
164      55 DO 80 I=1,N1                                             A  820
165         PRINT 60,(II,II=1,NPROD)                                 A  825
166      60 FORMAT (36H OPERATION    PRODUCT    TIME/VARIANCE,//5X,9I14) A 830
167         PRINT 65                                                 A  835
168      65 FORMAT (1H )                                             A  840
169         DO 70 J=1,50                                             A  845
170         NOP=NOP+1                                                A  850
171      70 PRINT 75,NOP,(TIME(NOP,K),VTIME(NOP,K),K=1,NPROD)        A  855
172      75 FORMAT (I6,4X,9(F7.1,2H /,F5.1))                         A  860
173      80 PRINT 5                                                  A  865
174      85 PRINT 60,(II,II=1,NPROD)                                 A  870
175         PRINT 65                                                 A  875
176         DO 90 I=1,N2                                             A  880
177         NOP=NOP+1                                                A  885
178      90 PRINT 75,NOP,(TIME(NOP,K),VTIME(NOP,K),K=1,NPROD)        A  890
179         PRINT 5                                                  A  895
```

```
180          NOP=0                                                      A  900
181          IF (N1) 120,120,95                                         A  905
182       95 DO 115 I=1,N1                                              A  910
183          PRINT 100                                                  A  915
184      100 FORMAT (35H OPERATION    IMMEDIATE PREDECESSORS,/)         A  920
185          DO 105 J=1,50                                              A  925
186          NOP=NOP+1                                                  A  930
187      105 PRINT 110,NOP,(MP(NOP,K),K=1,MXP)                          A  935
188      110 FORMAT (I6,I10,20I5)                                       A  940
189      115 PRINT 5                                                    A  945
190      120 PRINT 100                                                  A  950
191          DO 125 I=1,N2                                              A  955
192          NOP=NOP+1                                                  A  960
193      125 PRINT 110,NOP,(MP(NOP,K),K=1,MXP)                          A  965
194          PRINT 5                                                    A  970
195          XKNT=40000.0                                               A  975
196          PER=.005                                                   A  980
197          XLIM=99999.0                                               A  985
198          LLIM=9999                                                  A  990
199          MMMM=NNOP-1                                                A  995
200          MMM=NNOP+1                                                 A 1000
201          MM=MMM+1                                                   A 1005
202          M=MM+1                                                     A 1010
203          INDEX=1                                                    A 1015
204          XLARG=0.0                                                  A 1020
205          DO 130 I=1,NNOP                                            A 1025
206          DO 130 J=1,NPROD                                           A 1030
207          XVAL=TIME(I,J)+Z*VTIME(I,J)**.5                            A 1035
208      130 XLARG=XMAX(XLARG,XVAL)                                     A 1040
209      135 CONTINUE                                                   A 1045
210    C     CALL FOR A STARTING BOUND HERE; INITIALIZE XBND.           A 1050
211          XBND=99999.0                                               A 1055
212          CALL FEAS                                                  A 1060
213          NNSTA=XBND                                                 A 1065
214          DO 145 I=1,MMM                                             A 1070
215          NDCNT(I)=0                                                 A 1075
216          NCCNT(I)=0                                                 A 1080
217          DO 140 J=1,5                                               A 1085
218      140 NRCNT(J,I)=0                                               A 1090
219      145 NPA(I)=0                                                   A 1095
220          LEVEL=1                                                    A 1100
221          CALL SUMS (LEVEL,+1.)                                      A 1105
222      150 N1=LEVEL-1                                                 A 1110
223          DO 185 I=1,NNOP                                            A 1115
224          IF (NPA(I)) 155,155,185                                    A 1120
225      155 DO 165 J=1,MXP                                             A 1125
226          IF (MP(I,J)) 170,170,160                                   A 1130
227      160 N2=MP(I,J)                                                 A   35
228          IF (NPA(N2)) 185,185,165                                   A 1140
229      165 CONTINUE                                                   A 1145
230      170 CALL BONDS (LEVEL,I,BND,NSTA)                              A 1150
231          IF (NCCNT(MMM)-XKNT) 175,175,260                           A 1155
232      175 IF (BND-XLIM) 180,185,185                                  A 1160
233      180 N1=N1+1                                                    A 1165
234          BOUND(LEVEL,N1)=BND                                        A 1170
235          NOPN(LEVEL,N1)=I                                           A 1175
236          K=N1+1                                                     A 1180
237          NOPN(K,LEVEL)=NSTA                                         A 1185
238      185 CONTINUE                                                   A 1190
239          IF (LEVEL-1) 195,195,190                                   A 1195
240    C     APPLY RULE 5 HERE.                                         A 1200
241      190 CALL RULES (5,LEVEL,N1,BDUM)                               A 1205
242      195 CALL MINOR (LEVEL,N1,BND)                                  A 1210
243          IF (BND-XLIM) 205,235,235                                  A 1215
244      200 N1=NOPN(LEVEL,LEVEL)                                       A 1220
245      205 NOPN(MM,LEVEL)=N1                                          A 1225
```

```
246                K=LEVEL+1                                            A 1230
247                NOPN(M,LEVEL)=NOPN(K,LEVEL)                          A 1235
248                MPA(N1)=LLIM                                         A 1240
249                LEVEL=LEVEL+1                                        A 1245
250                CALL SUMS (LEVEL,+1.)                                A 1250
251                IF (LEVEL-NNOP) 150,210,210                          A 1255
252        C       APPLY RULE 1 HERE.                                   A 1260
253          210 DO 215 I=1,NNOP                                        A 1265
254                IF (MPA(I)) 220,220,215                              A 1270
255          215 CONTINUE                                               A 1275
256          220 CALL BONDS (LEVEL,I,BND,NSTA)                          A 1280
257                IF (BND-XLIM) 225,235,235                            A 1285
258          225 NOPN(MM,LEVEL)=I                                       A 1290
259                NOPN(M,LEVEL)=NSTA                                   A 1295
260                NRCNT(1,LEVEL)=NRCNT(1,LEVEL)+1                      A 1300
261                NRCNT(1,MMM)=NRCNT(1,MMM)+1                          A 1305
262                XBND=BND                                             A 1310
263        C       APPLY RULE 2 HERE.                                   A 1315
264                CALL RULES (2,LDUM,NDUM,BND)                         A 1320
265                DO 230 I=1,NNOP                                      A 1325
266                NT(I)=NOPN(MM,I)                                     A 1330
267          230 NST(I)=NOPN(M,I)                                       A 1335
268                MNSTA=NOPN(M,NNOP)                                   A 1340
269          235 LEVEL=LEVEL-1                                          A 1345
270                IF (LEVEL) 260,260,240                               A 1350
271          240 NDCNT(LEVEL)=NDCNT(LEVEL)+1                            A 1355
272                NDCNT(MMM)=NDCNT(MMM)+1                              A 1360
273                N3=NOPN(MM,LEVEL)                                    A 1365
274                MPA(N3)=0                                            A 1370
275                CALL SUMS (LEVEL,-1.)                                A 1375
276                DO 250 I=LEVEL,MMMM                                  A 1380
277                IF (BOUND(LEVEL,I)-XLIM) 245,255,255                 A 1385
278          245 NI=I+1                                                 A 1390
279                BOUND(LEVEL,I)=BOUND(LEVEL,NI)                       A 1395
280                NOPN(LEVEL,I)=NOPN(LEVEL,NI)                         A 1400
281                NJ=NI+1                                              A 1405
282          250 NOPN(NI,LEVEL)=NOPN(NJ,LEVEL)                          A 1410
283                BOUND(LEVEL,NNOP)=XLIM                               A 1415
284          255 IF (BOUND(LEVEL,LEVEL)-XLIM) 200,235,235              A 1420
285          260 CALL PRNT                                             A 1425
286                GO TO (265,275), INDEX                              A 1430
287          265 ISTA=MNSTA                                            A 1435
288                INDEX=2                                              A 1440
289          270 XCYC=XBND                                             A 1445
290                CYC=XBND-PER                                        A 1450
291                IF (CYC-XLARG) 280,135,135                          A 1455
292          275 IF (ISTA-MNSTA) 280,270,25                           A 1460
293          280 PRINT 285,NA,ISTA,XCYC                                A 1465
294          285 FORMAT (////,1X,40A2////34H THE MINIMUM NUMBER OF STATIONS IS,I2]// A 1470
295                146H THE BEST LOADING IS GIVEN FOR A CYCLE TIME OF,F9.3) A 1475
296                GO TO 10                                            A 1480
297                END                                                A 1485
298                SUBROUTINE FEAS                                        5
299                COMMON BOUND(61,60), NOPN(63,60), XSUM(12), VSUM(12), NA(40) 10
300                COMMON MP(60,10), TIME(60,6), VTIME(60,6), MPA(61)      15
301                COMMON NCCNT(61), NDCNT(61), NRCNT(5,61)               20
302                COMMON NNOP, NPROD, CYC, M, MM, Z, MXP, LLIM, XLIM, XBND 25
303                COMMON BND1, BND2, BND3, MMM, NT(60), NST(60)          30
304                DOUBLE PRECISION XSUM, VSUM                            35
305                DO 5 I=1,NNOP                                          40
306            5 NT(I)=I                                                  45
307                XSTA=0.0                                               50
308                NOP=0                                                  55
309           10 XSTA=XSTA+1.0                                            60
310                DO 15 J=1,NPROD                                        65
311                XSUM(J)=0.0                                            70
```

```
312        15 VSUM(J)=0.0                                              75
313           XSM=0.0                                                  80
314        20 NOP=NOP+1                                                85
315           IF (NOP-NNOP) 25,25,40                                   90
316        25 XSM=0.0                                                  95
317           DO 30 J=1,NPROD                                         100
318           XSUM(J)=XSUM(J)+TIME(NOP,J)                             105
319           VSUM(J)=VSUM(J)+VTIME(NOP,J)                            110
320           T=XSUM(J)+Z*VSUM(J)**.5                                 115
321        30 XSM=XMAX(XSM,T)                                         120
322           NST(NOP)=XSTA                                           125
323           IF (XSM-CYC) 20,10,35                                   130
324        35 NOP=NOP-1                                               135
325           GO TO 10                                                140
326        40 IF (XSM) 45,45,50                                       145
327        45 XSTA=XSTA-1.0                                           150
328        50 XBND=XSTA                                               155
329           RETURN                                                  160
330           END                                                     165
331           SUBROUTINE RULES (NRULE,LEVEL,NOP,BND)                    5
332           COMMON BOUND(61,60), NOPN(63,60), XSUM(12), VSUM(12), NA(40)  10
333           COMMON MP(60,10), TIME(60,6), VTIME(60,6), MPA(61)       15
334           COMMON NCCNT(61), NDCNT(61), NRCNT(5,61)                 20
335           COMMON NNOP, NPROD, CYC, N, MM, Z, MXP, LLIM, XLIM, XBND  25
336           COMMON BND1, BND2, BND3, MMM, NT(60), NST(60)            30
337           DOUBLE PRECISION XSUM, VSUM                              35
338           GO TO (40,5,45,65,70), NRULE                            40
339         5 N1=NNOP-1                                                45
340           DO 35 I=1,N1                                             50
341           NDX=0                                                    55
342           NI=I+I                                                   60
343           DO 20 J=NI,NNOP                                          65
344           IF (BOUND(I,J)-BND) 20,10,10                             70
345        10 IF (BOUND(I,J)-XLIM) 15,25,25                            75
346        15 BOUND(I,J)=XLIM                                          80
347           NRCNT(2,I)=NRCNT(2,I)+1                                  85
348           NRCNT(2,MMM)=NRCNT(2,MMM)+1                              90
349           NDX=1                                                    95
350        20 N2=J                                                    100
351        25 IF (NDX) 35,35,30                                       105
352        30 CALL MINOR (I,N2,DUM)                                   110
353        35 CONTINUE                                                115
354        40 RETURN                                                  120
355        45 IF (BND-XBND) 60,50,50                                  125
356        50 IF (BND-XLIM) 55,60,60                                  130
357        55 BND=XLIM                                                135
358           NRCNT(NRULE,LEVEL)=NRCNT(NRULE,LEVEL)+1                  140
359           NRCNT(NRULE,MMM)=NRCNT(NRULE,MMM)+1                      145
360        60 RETURN                                                  150
361        65 N1=LEVEL-1                                              155
362           N2=NOPN(MM,N1)                                          160
363           IF (NOP-N2) 55,55,60                                    165
364        70 N1=LEVEL-1                                              170
365           N2=NOP-LEVEL+1                                          175
366           N3=0                                                    180
367           IF (N2-1) 105,105,75                                    185
368        75 DO 85 J=LEVEL,NOP                                       190
369           K=J+1                                                   195
370           IF (NOPN(K,LEVEL)-NOPN(M,N1)) 85,85,80                  200
371        80 N3=N3+1                                                 205
372           BOUND(MMM,N3)=J                                         210
373        85 CONTINUE                                                215
374           IF (N2-N3) 105,105,90                                   220
375        90 IF (N3) 105,105,95                                      225
376        95 DO 100 J=I,N3                                           230
377           N2=BOUND(MMM,J)                                         235
```

```
378          BOUND(LEVEL,N2)=XLIM                                  240
379          NRCNT(5,LEVEL)=NRCNT(5,LEVEL)+1                       245
380      100 NRCNT(5,MMM)=NRCNT(5,MMM)+1                           250
381      105 RETURN                                                255
382          END                                                  260
383          SUBROUTINE SUMS (LEVEL,PN)                              5
384          COMMON BOUND(61,60), NOPN(63,60), XSUM(12), VSUM(12), NA(40)   10
385          COMMON MP(60,10), TIME(60,6), VTIME(60,6), MPA(61)    15
386          COMMON NCCNT(61), NDCNT(61), NRCNT(5,61)              20
387          COMMON NNOP, NPROD, CYC, M, MM, Z, MXP, LLIM, XLIM, XBND   25
388          COMMON BND1, BND2, BND3, MMM, NT(60), NST(60)         30
389          DOUBLE PRECISION XSUM, VSUM                           35
390          N1=LEVEL-1                                            40
391          IF (PN) 30,30,5                                       45
392        5 IF (N1) 10,10,25                                      50
393       10 BND1=0.0                                              55
394          DO 20 J=1,NPROD                                       60
395          K=J+NPROD                                             65
396          XSUM(J)=0.0                                           70
397          VSUM(J)=0.0                                           75
398          XSUM(K)=0.0                                           80
399          VSUM(K)=0.0                                           85
400          DO 15 I=1,NNOP                                        90
401          XSUM(K)=XSUM(K)+TIME(I,J)                             95
402       15 VSUM(K)=VSUM(K)+VTIME(I,J)                           100
403          XSM=XSUM(K)+Z*VSUM(K)**.5                            105
404       20 BND1=XMAX(BND1,XSM)                                  110
405          RETURN                                               115
406       25 N2=N1-1                                              120
407          NOP=NOPN(MM,N1)                                      125
408          IF (N2) 35,35,45                                     130
409       30 NOP=NOPN(MM,LEVEL)                                   135
410       35 DO 40 J=1,NPROD                                      140
411          K=J+NPROD                                            145
412          XSUM(J)=XSUM(J)+TIME(NOP,J)*PN                       150
413          VSUM(J)=VSUM(J)+VTIME(NOP,J)*PN                      155
414          XSUM(K)=XSUM(K)-TIME(NOP,J)*PN                       160
415       40 VSUM(K)=VSUM(K)-VTIME(NOP,J)*PN                      165
416          IF (PN) 60,60,90                                     170
417       45 IF (NOPN(M,N2)-NOPN(M,N1)) 50,35,35                  175
418       50 DO 55 J=1,NPROD                                      180
419          XSUM(J)=0.0                                          185
420       55 VSUM(J)=0.0                                          190
421          GO TO 35                                             195
422       60 IF (N1) 100,100,65                                   200
423       65 IF (NOPN(M,LEVEL)-NOPN(M,N1)) 85,85,70               205
424       70 N2=NOPN(M,N1)                                        210
425          DO 80 I=1,N1                                         215
426          N3=LEVEL-I                                           220
427          IF (NOPN(M,N3)-N2) 85,75,75                          225
428       75 NOP=NOPN(MM,N3)                                      230
429          DO 80 J=1,NPROD                                      235
430          XSUM(J)=XSUM(J)+TIME(NOP,J)                          240
431       80 VSUM(J)=VSUM(J)+VTIME(NOP,J)                         245
432       85 N2=LEVEL+1                                           250
433          BND2=BOUND(LEVEL,N1)                                 255
434          BND3=BOUND(N2,N1)                                    260
435          RETURN                                               265
436       90 BND2=0.0                                             270
437          BND3=0.0                                             275
438          DO 95 J=1,NPROD                                      280
439          K=J+NPROD                                            285
440          XSM=XSUM(K)+Z*VSUM(K)**.5                            290
441          BND2=XMAX(XSM,BND2)                                  295
442          T1=XSUM(J)+XSUM(K)                                   300
443          V1=VSUM(J)+VSUM(K)                                   305
```

```
444             XSM=T1+Z*V1**.5                                           310
445          95 BND3=XMAX(XSM,BND3)                                       315
446             N2=LEVEL+1                                                320
447             BOUND(LEVEL,N1)=BND2                                      325
448             BOUND(N2,N1)=BND3                                         330
449         100 RETURN                                                    335
450             END                                                       340
451             SUBROUTINE BONDS (LEVEL,NOP,BND,NSTA)                       5
452             COMMON BOUND(61,60), NOPN(63,60), XSUM(12), VSUM(12), NA(40)  10
453             COMMON MP(60,10), TIME(60,6), VTIME(60,6), MPA(61)         15
454             COMMON NCCNT(61), NDCNT(61), NRCNT(5,61)                   20
455             COMMON NNOP, NPROD, CYC, M, MM, Z, MXP, LLIM, XLIM, XBND   25
456             COMMON BND1, BND2, BND3, MMM, NT(60), NST(60)              30
457             DOUBLE PRECISION XSUM, VSUM                                35
458             N1=LEVEL-1                                                 40
459             IF (N1) 5,5,30                                            45
460           5 BND=BND1                                                  50
461             NSTA=1                                                    55
462          10 IBND=BND/CYC                                              60
463             IF (BND-IBND*CYC) 15,15,20                                65
464          15 IBND=IBND-1                                               70
465          20 IBND=IBND+1                                               75
466             BND=IBND                                                  80
467     C       APPLY RULE 3 HERE.                                        85
468             CALL RULES (3,LEVEL,NDUM,BND)                             90
469          25 NCCNT(LEVEL)=NCCNT(LEVEL)+1                               95
470             NCCNT(MMM)=NCCNT(MMM)+1                                  100
471             RETURN                                                   105
472          30 BND=0.0                                                  110
473             DO 35 J=1,NPROD                                          115
474             T1=XSUM(J)+TIME(NOP,J)                                   120
475             V1=VSUM(J)+VTIME(NOP,J)                                  125
476             XSM=T1+Z*V1**.5                                          130
477          35 BND=XMAX(BND,XSM)                                        135
478             NSTA=NOPN(M,N1)                                          140
479             XSTA=NSTA                                                145
480             IF (BND-CYC) 40,45,75                                    150
481          40 NDX=1                                                    155
482             GO TO 50                                                 160
483          45 NDX=2                                                    165
484     C       APPLY RULE 4 HERE.                                       170
485          50 CALL RULES (4,LEVEL,NOP,BND)                             175
486             IF (BND-XLIM) 55,25,25                                   180
487          55 IF (NDX-1) 60,60,65                                      185
488          60 BND=(XSTA-1.0)*CYC+BND3                                  190
489             GO TO 10                                                 195
490          65 SUM=0.0                                                  200
491             DO 70 J=1,NPROD                                          205
492             K=J+NPROD                                                210
493             T1=XSUM(K)-TIME(NOP,J)                                   215
494             V1=VSUM(K)-VTIME(NOP,J)                                  220
495             XSM=T1+Z*V1**.5                                          225
496          70 SUM=XMAX(SUM,XSM)                                        230
497             BND=XSTA*CYC+SUM                                         235
498             GO TO 10                                                 240
499          75 BND=XSTA*CYC+BND2                                        245
500             NSTA=NSTA+1                                              250
501             GO TO 10                                                 255
502             END                                                      260
503             SUBROUTINE MINOR (LEVEL,NOP,BND)                           5
504             COMMON BOUND(61,60), NOPN(63,60), XSUM(12), VSUM(12), NA(40)  10
505             COMMON MP(60,10), TIME(60,6), VTIME(60,6), MPA(61)         15
506             COMMON NCCNT(61), NDCNT(61), NRCNT(5,61)                   20
507             COMMON NNOP, NPROD, CYC, M, MM, Z, MXP, LLIM, XLIM, XBND   25
508             COMMON BND1, BND2, BND3, MMM, NT(60), NST(60)              30
509             DOUBLE PRECISION XSUM, VSUM                                35
510             IF (NOP-LEVEL) 20,20,5                                    40
```

```
511      5 N1=NOP-1                                                   45
512        DO 15 I=LEVEL,N1                                           50
513        N2=I+1                                                     55
514        DO 15 J=N2,NOP                                             60
515        IF (BOUND(LEVEL,I)-BOUND(LEVEL,J)) 15,15,10                65
516     10 K=I+1                                                      70
517        L=J+1                                                      75
518        XTEM=BOUND(LEVEL,I)                                        80
519        ITEM=NOPN(LEVEL,I)                                         85
520        JTEM=NOPN(K,LEVEL)                                         90
521        BOUND(LEVEL,I)=BOUND(LEVEL,J)                              95
522        NOPN(LEVEL,I)=NOPN(LEVEL,J)                               100
523        NOPN(K,LEVEL)=NOPN(L,LEVEL)                               105
524        BOUND(LEVEL,J)=XTEM                                       110
525        NOPN(LEVEL,J)=ITEM                                        115
526        NOPN(L,LEVEL)=JTEM                                        120
527     15 CONTINUE                                                  125
528        IF (NOP-NNOP) 20,25,25                                    130
529     20 N2=NOP+1                                                  135
530        BOUND(LEVEL,N2)=XLIM                                      140
531     25 NOP=NOPN(LEVEL,LEVEL)                                     145
532        BND=BOUND(LEVEL,LEVEL)                                    150
533        RETURN                                                    155
534        END                                                       160
535        FUNCTION XMAX (ARG1,ARG2)                                   5
536        IF (ARG1-ARG2) 5,5,10                                      10
537      5 XMAX=ARG2                                                  15
538        RETURN                                                     20
539     10 XMAX=ARG1                                                  25
540        RETURN                                                     30
541        END                                                       35
542        SUBROUTINE PRNT                                             5
543        DIMENSION SUM(6), SUMV(6)                                  10
544        COMMON BOUND(61,60), NOPN(63,60), XSUM(12), VSUM(12), NA(40) 15
545        COMMON MP(60,10), TIME(60,6), VTIME(60,6), MPA(61)         20
546        COMMON NCCNT(61), NDCNT(61), NRCNT(5,61)                   25
547        COMMON NNOP, NPROD, CYC, M, MM, Z, MXP, LLIM, XLIM, XBND    30
548        COMMON BND1, BND2, BND3, MMM, NT(60), NST(60)              35
549        DOUBLE PRECISION XSUM, VSUM                                40
550        N1=NNOP/50                                                 45
551        N2=NNOP-N1*50                                              50
552        TOTAL=NDCNT(MMM)+NRCNT(1,MMM)+NRCNT(2,MMM)+NRCNT(3,MMM)+NRCNT(4,MM 55
553       1M)+NRCNT(5,MMM)                                            60
554        IF (NCCNT(MMM)-TOTAL) 15,15,5                              65
555      5 PRINT 10,NA,CYC                                            70
556     10 FORMAT (1X,40A2//46H LAST FEASIBLE SOLUTION AND NODE COUNT SUMMARY 75
557       1,20H       CYCLE TIME =,F8.3//)                            80
558        GO TO 25                                                   85
559     15 PRINT 20,NA,CYC                                            90
560     20 FORMAT (1X,40A2//50H TOTAL NODE COUNT SUMMARY FOR THE OPTIMAL SOLU 95
561       1TION,20H       CYCLE TIME =,F8.3//)                       100
562     25 N3=0                                                      105
563        IF (N1) 60,60,30                                          110
564     30 DO 50 I=1,N1                                              115
565        PRINT 35,(K,K=1,5)                                        120
566     35 FORMAT (83H STATION   OPERATION     LEVEL   NODES CREATED   NODES 125
567       1EXAMINED   NODES ELIMINATED,//49X,6HNORMAL,5(7H   RULE,I2)/) 130
568        DO 40 J=1,50                                              135
569        N3=N3+1                                                   140
570     40 PRINT 45,NST(N3),NT(N3),N3,NCCNT(N3),NDCNT(N3),(NRCNT(K,N3),K=1,5) 145
571     45 FORMAT (I5,I11,I12,I14,3X,6I9)                            150
572     50 PRINT 55                                                  155
573     55 FORMAT (1H1,/)                                            160
574     60 PRINT 35,(K,K=1,5)                                        165
575        DO 65 I=1,N2                                              170
576        N3=N3+1                                                   175
577     65 PRINT 45,NST(N3),NT(N3),N3,NCCNT(N3),NDCNT(N3),(NRCNT(K,N3),K=1,5) 180
```

```
578              PRINT 70,NCCNT(MMM),NDCNT(MMM),(NRCNT(K,MMM),K=1,5)        185
579           70 FORMAT (/24X,6HTOTALS,I12,3X,6I9)                          190
580              PRINT 55                                                   195
581              PRINT 75,NA,CYC                                            200
582           75 FORMAT (1X,40A2//13H LOAD SUMMARY,20H       CYCLE TIME =,F8.3//)  205
583              PRINT 80,(K,K=1,NPROD)                                     210
584           80 FORMAT (20H STATION      PRODUCT,//8X,10I9)                215
585              PRINT 85                                                   220
586           85 FORMAT (1H )                                              225
587              DO 90 I=1,NPROD                                           230
588              SUM(I)=0.0                                                235
589           90 SUMV(I)=0.0                                               240
590              XBND=0.0                                                  245
591              NSTA=1                                                    250
592              DO 125 I=1,NNOP                                           255
593              L=NT(I)                                                   260
594              IF (NST(I)-NSTA) 105,95,105                               265
595           95 DO 100 J=1,NPROD                                          270
596              SUM(J)=SUM(J)+TIME(L,J)                                   275
597          100 SUMV(J)=SUMV(J)+VTIME(L,J)                                280
598              GO TO 125                                                 285
599          105 DO 110 J=1,NPROD                                          290
600              SUM(J)=SUM(J)+Z*SUMV(J)**.5                               295
601          110 XBND=XMAX(XBND,SUM(J))                                    300
602              PRINT 115,NSTA,(SUM(J),J=1,NPROD)                         305
603          115 FORMAT (I5,5X,10F9.2)                                     310
604              DO 120 J=1,NPROD                                          315
605              SUM(J)=TIME(L,J)                                          320
606          120 SUMV(J)=VTIME(L,J)                                        325
607              NSTA=NSTA+1                                               330
608          125 CONTINUE                                                  335
609              DO 130 J=1,NPROD                                          340
610              SUM(J)=SUM(J)+Z*SUMV(J)**.5                               345
611          130 XBND=XMAX(XBND,SUM(J))                                    350
612              PRINT 115,NSTA,(SUM(J),J=1,NPROD)                         355
613              PRINT 55                                                  360
614              RETURN                                                    365
615              END                                                       370
```

INDEX